RACE, ETHNICITY

AND

THE COVID-19 PANDEMIC

# Race, Ethnicity and the COVID-19 Pandemic

*Edited by*

MELVIN E. THOMAS
LOREN M. HENDERSON
HAYWARD DERRICK HORTON

University of
CINCINNATI | PRESS

*About the University of Cincinnati Press*

The University of Cincinnati Press is committed to publishing rigorous, peer-reviewed, leading scholarship accessibly to stimulate dialog among the academy, public intellectuals, and lay practitioners. The Press endeavors to erase disciplinary boundaries in order to cast fresh light on common problems in our global community. Building on the university's long-standing tradition of social responsibility to the citizens of Cincinnati, state of Ohio, and the world, the Press publishes books on topics that expose and resolve disparities at every level of society and have local, national, and global impact.

University of Cincinnati Press Copyright © 2023

All rights reserved. No part of this book may be reproduced or utilized in any form or by any means, electronic or mechanical, or by any information storage and retrieval system, without written permission from the publisher. Requests for permission to reproduce material from this work should be sent to:

*University of Cincinnati Press*
*Langsam Library, 2911 Woodside Drive*
*Cincinnati, Ohio 45221 ucincinnatipress.uc.edu*

ISBN 978-1-947602-87-8 (hardback)

ISBN 978-1-947602-89-2 (e-book, PDF)

ISBN 978-1-947602-88-5 (e-book, EPUB)

Library of Congress Cataloging-in-Publication Data

Names: Thomas, Melvin (Sociologist), editor. | University of Cincinnati. Press.
Title: Race, ethnicity, and the COVID-19 pandemic / Melvin Thomas, Loren Henderson, Hayward Derrick Horton.
Description: Cincinnati, Ohio : University of Cincinnati Press, [2023] | Includes bibliographical references and index. | Summary: "Race, Ethnicity, and the COVID-19 Pandemic is an extensive examination of the causes and consequences of the global pandemic on racial and ethnic minorities, offering analysis of the causes of the unique experiences of Black, Indigenous and Latin communities in the US and the world from multiple social sciences perspectives" — Provided by publisher.
Identifiers: LCCN 2022047683 (print) | LCCN 2022047684 (ebook) | ISBN 9781947602878 (cloth) | ISBN 9781947602892 (ebook) | ISBN 9781947602885 (ebook)
Subjects: LCSH: Race. | Minorities—United States—Social conditions. | Ethnic groups —United States. | COVID-19 Pandemic, 2020—Social aspects.
Classification: LCC HT1521 .R23532 2023 (print) | LCC HT1521 (ebook) | DDC 305.8—dc23/eng/20221201
LC record available at https://lccn.loc.gov/2022047683

LC ebook record available at https://lccn.loc.gov/2022047684

Designed and produced for UC Press by Sam Sheng

Typeset in Baskerville

Printed in the United States of America

First Printing

# Table of Contents

Preface
    Systemic Racism: The Common Thread ....................... ix

## Part I
## COVID-19, Racism, and the Legacy of Colonialism

Chapter 1
Racial Inequality and the Covid-19 Global Pandemic ................. 3
    *Melvin E. Thomas*

Chapter 2
COVID-19 as White Space:
The Collective Perils of Whiteness During the Pandemic ............. 17
    *David L. Brunsma, Letisha Engracia Cardoso Brown,*
    *Inaash Islam, Joong Won Kim, and Steve McGlamery*

Chapter 3
Color-Blind Racial Discourse in Pandemic Times ................... 45
    *Eduardo Bonilla-Silva*

Chapter 4
Actual Racial/Ethnic Disparities in COVID-19
Mortality for the Non-Hispanic Black Population
Compared to Non-Hispanic White Population in
35 US States and Their Association with Structural Racism ........... 71
    *Michael Siegel, Isabella Critchfield-Jain,*
    *Matthew Boykin, and Alicia Owens*

Chapter 5
COVID-19 Exposes Deep Racial Inequities and
Vulnerability in the United States............................109
   *Alana Dass*

Chapter 6
The COVID-19 Crisis Among Native Americans
in the United States..........................................125
   *Loren Henderson*

Chapter 7
Global Racial Capitalism and COVID-19........................137
   *Johnny Eric Williams and David G. Embrick*

## Part II
### COVID-19 and Selected U.S. Institutions

Chapter 8
Essential Yet Expendable:
The Paradoxical Racialization of COVID-19......................165
   *Jan-Martijn Meij and Diane L. Odeh*

Chapter 9
Introducing the Strategic Health and Economic
Emergency Management Plan for Vulnerable Populations:
How to Protect Black Health and Black Wealth in the U.S.
Amid the COVID-19 Pandemic and Beyond......................193
   *Lori Latrice Martin*

Chapter 10
The Value of Incarcerated Black Lives during
the COVID-19 Pandemic: An Exploration of
Healthcare Disparities of Incarcerated and Formerly
Incarcerated Populations......................................215
   *Britany J. Gatewood, Ebony Russ, Yanesia Norris, and A. Cayce*

TABLE OF CONTENTS

Chapter 11
The Impact of COVID-19 on Black Americans Employed
in the Service Sector . . . . . . . . . . . . . . . . . . . . . . . . . . . . . . . . . . . . . . . . . 239
   *Anita Fernander and Lovoria Williams*

Part III
**Personal Experiences with COVID-19**

Chapter 12
Risks, Relationships, and 'Rona:
How Five Black Mothers Navigate the COVID-19 Pandemic . . . . . . . . . 255
   *Sandra Barnes*

Chapter 13
"Sister Space":
Clinical Insights From a Black Women's Support
Group During COVID-19 . . . . . . . . . . . . . . . . . . . . . . . . . . . . . . . . . . . . 295
   *Haley Sparks*

Chapter 14
Black Lives Matter #saytheirnames . . . . . . . . . . . . . . . . . . . . . . . . . . . . . 315
   *Tiffany J. Grant*

Chapter 15
Conclusion: The Path Forward . . . . . . . . . . . . . . . . . . . . . . . . . . . . . . . . 333
   *Loren Henderson, Melvin Thomas,*
   *and Hayward Derrick Horton*

Epilogue: The Pandemic Continues . . . . . . . . . . . . . . . . . . . . . . . . . . . . 339

Contributor Biographies . . . . . . . . . . . . . . . . . . . . . . . . . . . . . . . . . . . . . 347

About the Editors . . . . . . . . . . . . . . . . . . . . . . . . . . . . . . . . . . . . . . . . . . 351

Index . . . . . . . . . . . . . . . . . . . . . . . . . . . . . . . . . . . . . . . . . . . . . . . . . . . . 353

# PREFACE

## SYSTEMIC RACISM: THE COMMON THREAD

THIS BOOK PRESENTS AUTHORITATIVE AND up-to-date theories on the causes and consequences of the COVID-19 pandemic on racial and ethnic minorities in the United States and the world. COVID-19 is the most significant virus to touch people of all ethnic backgrounds in the United States since the 1918 influenza pandemic. The chapters in this edited volume, *Race, Ethnicity, and the COVID-19 Pandemic*, provide a critical examination of the progress and direction of debates on the racial disparities of COVID-19 as well as a foundation for future research. A thread that ties together all the chapters in this volume is a connection between systemic racism and the COVID-19 pandemic. Joe Feagin (2006) states:

> Systemic racism includes the complex array of antiblack practices, the unjustly gained political-economic power of whites, the continuing economic and other resource inequalities along racial lines, and the white racist ideologies and attitudes created to maintain and rationalize white privilege and power.

Ongoing medical and epidemiological research on the nature of the COVID-19 virus is vitally important. However, it is equally important to understand the disparate impact of this pandemic on different social groups and communities.

## PREFACE

Of particular importance is its disparate impact on racial and ethnic groups in the United States. The United States is stratified by race. On nearly all measures of economic and social well-being (e.g., income, education, poverty, housing, etc.), Black Americans, Latinos, and Native Americans are disadvantaged relative to White communities. This racial inequality can be clearly seen in the impact of the COVID-19 pandemic. Specifically, Black Americans, Latinos, and Native Americans are much more likely than White individuals to contract and die from the COVID-19 virus. Because of these disparities, the impact of this pandemic on the lives of Black, Latino, and Indigenous people will the focus of this book.

Systemic racism permeates throughout all the institutions of society and produces the inequalities described above. Racism cannot be understood as simply prejudice or the isolated actions of bigoted individuals (Wellman 1993). Nor can it be understood as just a by-product of individual psychology. It has been an integral part of US history from chattel slavery to the present. Systemic racism has systematically provided material benefits to those people socially defined as White while transferring material benefits away from those socially defined as non-White. There was—and continues to be—"a structure of unjust enrichment and unjust impoverishment" that maintains itself as a structure of inequality and privilege (Feagin 2019). As discussed earlier, this inequality is rationalized by a racist ideology. This may take the form of traditional notions of the innate inferiority of African Americans and other racialized groups. It may also take the form of "new" White supremacist views that focuses on minorities' alleged cultural deficiencies or "color-blind of racism" which completely denies racism's impact on society (Wellman 1993; Bonilla-Silva 2017; Thomas, Herring, and Horton 2010).

The chapters in this volume apply social science perspectives and theories to help shed light on the social factors that have produced the greater vulnerability of certain racial and ethnic groups to the disease. This volume addresses important questions such as: How has the healthcare system contributed to this situation? How have the factors associated with minority status, such as concentrated poverty, low-wage jobs, poorer quality schools, residential segregation, etc., affected racial disparities in COVID-19 infections and deaths? How have minorities responded to the pandemic? How has the pandemic affected racial and ethnic communities more generally?

## Organization of the Book

Because COVID-19 case numbers have rapidly changed, there will be some differences in the statistics between chapters. However, all reported statistics were accurate at the time the chapters were completed.

**Part I: COVID-19, Racism, and the Legacy of Colonialism** highlights the theoretical and empirical connections between the COVID-19 pandemic and systemic racism. Chapter 1 presents the COVID-19 timeline and presents the latest statistical data available on the pandemic as of the completion of this chapter.

The chapters in **Part II: COVID-19 and Selected US Institutions** focus on the connections between institutional and systemic racism, the COVID-19 pandemic, and US economic, criminal, justice, and governmental institutions.

**Part III: Personal Experiences with COVID-19** includes chapters that reflect how the COVID-19 pandemic has affected millions of lives, causing great pain, grief, and loss. For Black Americans, this pain has been particularly acute. The chapters in this section present several personal stories illustrating the impact of the pandemic on people's lives.

Finally, the conclusion provides an overview of the linkages between system racism and the COVID-19 pandemic. It attempts to answer the question, "Where do we go from here?" Policy solutions are presented that may ameliorate some of the deep and serious problems identified in the chapters in this book. It is by no means comprehensive, but it provides a starting point for people interested in positive social change. It concludes with encouragement for all of us to be anti-racist and diligent in the promotion of social justice and accurate, race-based data collection to prevent widespread misinformation and confusion about future pandemics.

## References

Bonilla-Silva, Eduardo. *Racism Without Racists: Color-Blind Racism and the Persistence of Racial Inequality in America*. Lanham, MD: Rowman and Littlefield, 2017.

Feagin, Joe. *Systemic Racism: A Theory of Oppression*. New York: Routledge, 2006.

Feagin, Joe. *Racist America: Roots, Current Realities, and Future Reparations*. New York: Routledge, 2019.

Thomas, Melvin, Cedric Herring, and Hayward D. Horton. "Racial Differences in the Perception of Racial Equality in the Obama Era." In *Race and the Age of Obama*, edited by Donald Cunnigen and Marino Bruce, 177–192. Bingley, UK: Emerald Publishing, 2010.

Wellman, David T. *Portraits of White Racism*. 2nd ed. Cambridge: Cambridge University Press, 1993.

PART ONE

# COVID-19, Racism,
## and the
# Legacy of Colonialism

# CHAPTER 1

# RACIAL INEQUALITY AND THE COVID-19 GLOBAL PANDEMIC

*Melvin E. Thomas*

### The COVID-19 Pandemic Timeline

IN DECEMBER 2019 IN WUHAN, in the Hubei Province of China, a new coronavirus outbreak erupted, initiating what the World Health Organization (WHO) declared a global health emergency. This new coronavirus quickly spread around the globe, continues to infect millions, and has killed hundreds of thousands of people. Below is a timeline of significant events in the spread of this disease:

- Dec. 31, 2019: Cases of an unknown form of pneumonia detected in Wuhan, China, reported to the World Health Organization.
- Jan. 1, 2020: The Chinese government closed the Huanan Seafood Wholesale Market because they suspected it was the source of the virus.
- Jan. 7, 2020: The Chinese authorities identified the virus as a novel coronavirus (2019).
- Jan. 11, 2020: The first death from the coronavirus was reported—a sixty-one-year-old man who had visited the Huanan market in Wuhan, China.
- Jan. 21, 2020: The United States recorded its first confirmed coronavirus case in a man who had visited Wuhan, China.
- Jan. 23, 2020: The Chinese government imposed a strict lockdown in Wuhan.

- Jan. 30, 2020: The first case of person-to-person transmission of the coronavirus was reported in the United States. WHO declares the novel coronavirus as constituting a public health emergency of international concern.
- Feb. 6, 2020: The first "official" death from the coronavirus in the United States was recorded. It was determined to be the first death after the release of the autopsy report on April 23, 2020.
- Feb. 11, 2020: The World Health Organization named the disease caused by the novel coronavirus "COVID-19."
- February 14, 2020: A Chinese tourist died in France from the virus, becoming the first person to die from COVID-19 in Europe. The first case of coronavirus was identified in Africa (Egypt).
- Feb. 26, 2020: The first confirmed case of community transmission of COVID-19 was reported in the United States by the CDC—a patient in California with no travel history and no contact with another known patient. However, it is likely that community transmission was occurring earlier in February.
- Feb. 29, 2020: The first death from COVID-19 in the United States was reported in Washington State, until an autopsy on April 23, 2020, revealed two earlier deaths related to COVID-19 in California.
- March 11, 2020: The World Health Organization declared the COVID-19 to be a pandemic.
- March 17, 2020: COVID-19 cases were confirmed in all fifty states in the United States.
- March 20, 2020: New York City became the epicenter of the coronavirus outbreak and accounted for about half of the infections in the United States at that time.
- March 26, 2020: The United States had the most COVID-19 cases and deaths in the world with eighty-two thousand cases and one thousand deaths.
- March 28, 2020: A record 6.6 million US workers filed for unemployment benefits.
- April 2, 2020: One million COVID-19 cases were reported worldwide.

- April 28, 2020: The United States surpassed one million confirmed cases of COVID-19.
- May 27, 2020: The United States exceeded 100,000 deaths due to COVID, and 355,000 deaths due to COVID-19 were recorded worldwide. This was an average of nine hundred deaths per day since the pandemic began.
- June 11, 2020: The United States recorded two million confirmed cases of COVID-19.
- July 26, 2020: Florida surpassed New York in total COVID-19 cases (425,000 versus 416,000, respectively).
- September 22, 2020: The United States reached 200,000 deaths due to COVID-19.
- September 2020: One million deaths due to COVID-19 were recorded worldwide.
- October 16, 2020: The United States exceeded eight million cases and 218,000 deaths due to COVID-19.
- December 10, 2020: FDA emergency-use authorization was granted for the Pfizer and BioNTech COVID-19 vaccines.
- December 14, 2020: Pfizer vaccine was delivered to all fifty states.
- December 18, 2020: Moderna vaccine received FDA emergency-use authorization.
- February 22, 2021: US death toll due to COVID-19 reached 500,000.
- February 27, 2021. The single-dose Johnson and Johnson vaccine received FDA emergency-use authorization.
- February–May 2021: COVID-19 cases, deaths, and hospitalizations dropped dramatically due to the use and effectiveness of the COVID-19 vaccines.
- April 17, 2021: Deaths from COVID-19 exceeded three million worldwide.
- May 2021: Total US fatalities from COVID-19 reached 600,000, with over thirty-three million reported cases.

As illustrated in Figure 1.1, the number of COVID-19 cases worldwide increased dramatically from April 2020 to early 2021. The disease rapidly became an international health crisis, causing hospitalizations and deaths in nearly every country. However, some countries fared far worse than others. The United States led the world in COVID-19 cases and deaths, followed by Brazil and India. As of May 2021, the United States led the world in the number of COVID-19 cases (33,274,769) and deaths (595,101). As will be discussed in detail below, within the United States, the rates of COVID-19 cases, hospitalizations, and deaths vary significantly by race and ethnicity.

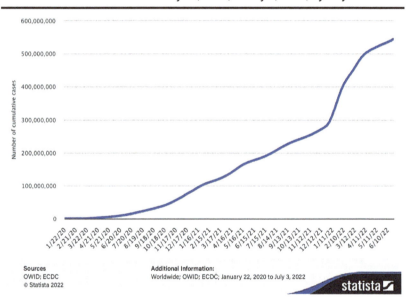

**Figure 1.1** Number of Cumulative Cases of Coronavirus (COVID-19) Worldwide from January 22, 2020, to July 3, 2022, by Day

## Racial Inequality and the COVID-19 Pandemic

Racial inequality has been an intractable characteristic of the United States. From the founding of this country until now, Black, Latino/a, Asian, and Indigenous peoples have not been given the same opportunities and rewards given to those of European descent. On every measure of material well-being, there are large disparities between White Americans and people of color. White Americans have higher median incomes, higher education, lower unemployment, higher status occupations, lower poverty rates, better housing, greater wealth, longer life expectancies, and lower mortality rates than Black, Latino/a, Asian, and Indigenous populations.

To understand the racial disparities in COVID-19 infections and deaths, we must understand the extent to which they are linked to racial inequalities more broadly. Persisting racial inequality in terms of income, occupational attainment, employment, and most other measures of socioeconomic well-being reveal the continuing impact of ongoing discrimination on Black, Latino/a, Asian, and Indigenous communities. Thus, racial and ethnic groups in the United States vary in vulnerability to COVID-19. The work people do not only provides resources for them and their families but it can also determine a person and their family's risk of exposure to COVID-19.

Black, Native American, Latino/a, and Asian individuals are more likely to be unemployed, underemployed, and/or have jobs as essential workers—especially low-paid essential workers. The underemployed include the unemployed, people working part-time for economic reasons, and the marginally attached. The marginally attached are defined by the Bureau of Labor Statistics as those who are neither working or looking for work but indicate that they want and are available to work and have looked for a job within the last twelve months. Although unemployment has been falling since the Great Recession for all groups, Black, Latino/a, Asian, and Native Americans are still more likely to be unemployed than White Americans. As can be seen in Figure 1.2, Black people had the second-highest level of unemployment when the COVID-19 pandemic began in the United States in 2020. For a large portion of the Black community, especially young males, securing steady employment is a highly problematic endeavor. This situation can contribute to them being less likely to survive COVID-19 because they are less likely to have employer-based health insurance or be able to afford quality health care.

Relatedly, Black people and Latino/as are more likely to experience poverty, which means that they lack the financial resources to maintain a minimum standard of living. Their incomes are so low that their basic human needs can't be met. Those in poverty are less likely to have adequate health care,

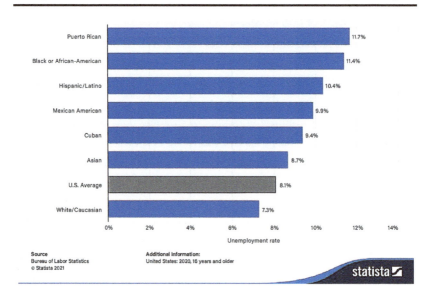

**Figure 1.2** Unemployment Rate in the United States in 2020 by Ethnicity

diets, clothing, transportation, and housing, and to be subject to other factors that increase the risk of contracting and dying from the disease. Figure 1.3 illustrates how Black and Hispanic people are more likely to live in poverty in every age group (Census 2020). Not only do Black Americans experience higher poverty rates than their White counterparts but Black Americans are also more likely than any other racial or ethnic group to live in segregated, impoverished communities. According to the CDC, those living in racially segregated, resource-deprived areas have a greater risk of contracting COVID-19.

Black and Latino/a workers are overrepresented among low-wage frontline essential workers. Black workers comprise only 13 percent of the US workforce, but they make up 19 percent of all low-wage, essential frontline workers (Kinder and Ford 2020). Black workers are 23.2 percent of personal care aides, 17 percent of cashiers, 16.9 percent of janitors and cleaners, 21 percent of laborers, and 35.3 percent of nursing assistants (Figure 1.4).

Black and Latino/a household incomes are much lower than those of White households and show no evidence of catching up. The racial gaps are just as large in the 2010s as they were in the 1960s and 1970s (Kuhn, Schularick

**Figure 1.3** Number of Cumulative Cases of Coronavirus (COVID-19) Worldwide from January 22, 2020, to July 3, 2022, by Day

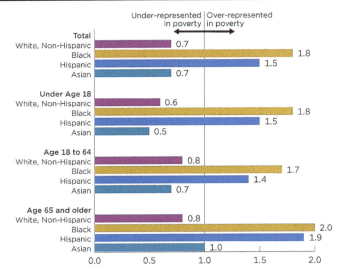

Source: U.S. Census Bureau, Current Population Survey, Annual Social and Economic Supplement, 2020 (CPS ASEC).

**Figure 1.4** Five largest low-wage frontline essential occupations, United States, 2018

| Occupation | Total number of workers | % of workers who are Black | Mean hourly wage |
|---|---|---|---|
| Personal Care Aides | 2,152,540 | 23.2% | $12.06 |
| Cashiers | 1,959,950 | 17.0% | $11.17 |
| Janitors and Cleaners, except Maids and Housekeeping Cleaners | 1,774,500 | 16.9% | $13.92 |
| Laborers and Freight, Stock, and Material Movers | 1,471,370 | 21.7% | $14.85 |
| Nursing Assistants | 1,389,520 | 35.3% | $14.22 |
| All U.S. workers | 144,731,220 | 13.0% | $24.98 |

Source: Brookings analysis of Department of Homeland Security, Bureau of Labor Statistics, and Emsi data.

and Steins 2020; Thomas and Moye 2015). Although the racial gaps in income are large in the United States, they pale in comparison to those of wealth. Wealth is the sum of what people own. It is often measured as "net worth"—total assets (such as stocks, bonds, checking and savings accounts, the value of the family home, vacation homes, and other real estate) minus total liabilities (such as mortgage debt, the balance on credit cards, student loans, and car loans). Unlike income, wealth can provide a safety net for a family when sources of income disappear. Without wealth, a middle-class family could be one layoff or sickness away from poverty. Black American and Latino/a families are much more likely than White families to be in that situation. This means that Black and Latino/a families were more vulnerable to the economic crisis caused by the COVID-19 pandemic. As can be seen in Figure 1.5, the racial wealth gap is massive and is projected to keep widening in the future.

## Race; Ethnicity; and Covid-19 Cases, Hospitalizations, and Deaths

As of May 23, 2021, Black Americans, Native Americans, and Latino/a people are more likely to get COVID-19, become sick enough to require hospitalization (Figure 1.6), and die from it (Figure 1.7). Unfortunately, these health outcomes were both predictable and preventable. Race and ethnicity are risk markers for other underlying conditions that affect health, including socioeconomic status, access to health care, and exposure to the virus related to occupation (e.g., frontline, essential, and critical infrastructure jobs). In the United States, the parallel between racial inequality and COVID-19 infections, hospitalization, and deaths is striking. The social determinants of racial disparities in socioeconomic status and the racial disparities in COVID-19 infections and deaths are the same—the impact of contemporary and historical racism. That is the focus of the next section.

## Racism, Racial Inequality, and the COVID-19 Pandemic

Health disparities are intertwined with the social and economic factors that produce and maintain racial hierarchies in the United States and other places around the world that have a history of colonialism. In the United States, most

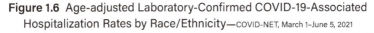

**Figure 1.5** Racial Wealth Inequality Is Rampant in the U.S.
Median household wealth by race/ethnicity in the United States (1983–2024)

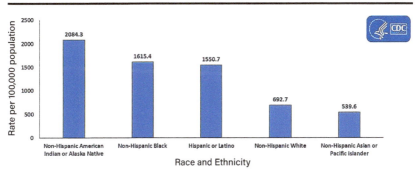

**Figure 1.6** Age-adjusted Laboratory-Confirmed COVID-19-Associated Hospitalization Rates by Race/Ethnicity—COVID-NET, March 1–June 5, 2021

scholars and social commentators link racial inequality to America's long history of racism in the past as well as contemporary expressions of the same. However, some question the role racism plays in producing the racial inequality that

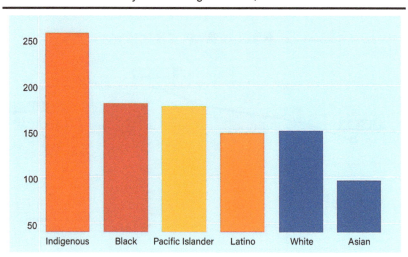

**Figure 1.7** U.S. COVID-19 Death Rates Per 100,000 People by Race through March 2, 2021

we see today. To understand the role racism plays in producing and reproducing racial inequality, and health disparities in particular, we must understand what racism is.

Racism is more than just individual attitudes and actions; racism is both an ideology and a social structure that has shaped the culture and institutions of the United States. Systemic racism exists when power and resources are routinely unequally distributed to the benefit of one racial group and to the detriment of other racial groups, resulting in a racially stratified society. White people experience material advantages and Black, Asian, Latino/a, and Native Americans experience material disadvantages because of their position in the hierarchy. The institutional actions and practices that reinforce the racial hierarchy become embedded in the social structure of society.

Ideological racism is a defense of White privilege and power that cannot be reduced to psychological prejudice. David Wellman (1993, 4) has provided a more sociologically grounded definition of racism: "culturally sanctioned beliefs, which, regardless of intentions involved, defend the advantages Whites have because of the subordinated position of racial minorities." Racism is not rooted in irrational feelings and emotions, although such feelings may be expressed or felt. As Wellman (1993, 4) states:

> The essential feature of racism is not hostility or misperception, but rather the defense of a system from which advantage is derived on the basis of race. The manner in which the defense is articulated—either with hostility or subtlety—is not nearly as important as the fact that it insures the continuation of a privileged relationship. Thus, it is necessary to broaden the definition of racism beyond prejudice to include sentiments that in their consequence, if not in their intent, support the racial status quo.

Rather than being grounded in psychology, racism is grounded in "real and material conditions" (Wellman 1993, 4).

## Traditional versus New White Supremacy

Commonly held beliefs about racism as well as many definitions of racism found in sociological texts characterize it as a belief system that declares the innate superiority of certain groups over others. For example:

> "Racism, the belief that one race is supreme and all others are innately inferior." (Schaefer 2016, 230)
>
> "Prejudice, discrimination, or antagonism directed against someone of a different race based on the belief that one's own race is superior." (Oxford Dictionary)
>
> "1. The belief that race accounts for differences in human character or ability and that a particular race is superior to others. 2. Discrimination or prejudice based on race." (American Heritage Dictionary of the English Language, 5th ed. 2016).
>
> "1. Racism: the prejudice that members of one race are intrinsically superior to members of other races. 2. Racism: discriminatory or abusive behavior toward members of another race." (Merriam-Webster.com).

These definitions apply to traditional forms of racism that justify racial inequality by claiming that there are innate differences between the so-called races. These differences, for example, may be believed to be genetic or God-ordained. Unfortunately, some of these definitions falsely equate racism to prejudice or prejudice-motivated actions of individuals.

None of the above definitions capture new forms of White supremacist views. These views have been referred to as "symbolic racism," "laissez-faire racism," or "cultural racism." These more recently popular views identify cultural and character flaws within the minority community as the cause of its disadvantaged position. For example, these views include the idea that Black Americans would rather receive welfare than work and young women would rather have babies before they get married. Thus, the disadvantaged position of Black Americans is a result of a misguided liberal government that creates lazy Black folk, rather than a result of discrimination.

The new (and old) White supremacist beliefs provide an ideological justification for the position of White people at the top of the racial hierarchy. They provide a defense of White privilege. White supremacist views all share the idea that the position of White people at the top of the racial hierarchy is deserved and the position of other subordinate racial/ethnic groups is also deserved.

To understand the relationship between race, ethnicity, and the COVID-19 global pandemic, we must understand the nature of racial inequality in society and the racism that justifies and reproduces it. It appears that the racial disparities in COVID-19 infections and deaths clearly map along with other racial disparities. Being White, in addition to material advantages, means lower rates of infections and deaths from COVID-19 than for Black Americans, Latino/a people, and Native Americans. Understanding the mechanisms through which this material advantage for White Americans translates into COVID-19 and other health disparities for people of color is important if we are going to arrive at solutions to this vexing problem.

## References

Centers for Disease Control and Prevention. "COVID-19." https://www.cdc.gov/coronavirus/2019-ncov/covid-data/covidview/index.html.

Kinder, Molly, and Tiffany Ford. "Black Essential Workers' Lives Matter. They Deserve Real Change, Not Just Lip Service." *Brookings Institute Report* (2020).

Kuhn, Moritz, Moritz Schularick and Ulrike I. Steins. "Income and Wealth Inequality in America, 1949–2016." *Journal of Political Economy* 128, no. 9 (2020): 3469–3519.

Schaefer, Richard T. *Sociology: A Brief Introduction*. New York: McGraw-Hill, 2016.

Thomas, Melvin, Cedric Herring, Moshe Semyonov, Hayward Derrick Horton, Loren Henderson, and Patrick L. Mason. "Race and the Accumulation of Wealth: Racial Differences in Net Worth over the Life Course, 1989–2009." *Social Problems* 67 (2020): 20–39.

Thomas, Melvin, and Richard Moye. "Race, Class and Gender and the Impact of Social Class and Racial Segregation on Black-White Income Inequality." *Sociology of Race and Ethnicity* 1 (October 2015): 490–502.

Wellman, David. *Portraits of White Racism*. Berkeley: University of California Press, 1993.

CHAPTER 2

# COVID-19 AS WHITE SPACE
## *The Collective Perils of Whiteness During the Pandemic*

*David L. Brunsma*

*Letisha Engracia Cardoso Brown*

*Inaash Islam*

*Joong Won Kim*

*Steve McGlamery*

**THERE ARE MANY KINDS OF HUMAN** coronaviruses in the human population, like that which causes the common cold. Now a pandemic of global proportions, COVID-19 was named so by the World Health Organization (WHO) in February of 2020 though it originally emerged sometime in 2019. Public health crises, including pandemics, as well as the epidemiological distribution of health disparities, such as diabetes (Walker et al. 2016), cardiovascular disease (Forouhi and Wareham 2019), asthma, and cancer (Hardeman et al. 2020), tend to fall hardest on the most structurally vulnerable of society, namely the poor, the elderly, women, and racialized minorities. As such, the intersection of all of these social categories is crucial to consider (Evans et al. 2018; Sewell 2016). While this phenomenon is true globally, there is a fundamental political economy of classism, sexism, regionalism, and indeed, racism, at the core of the distribution of health disparities in the United States, the richest, most technologically and medically advanced society on the planet. It is into this context that COVID-19 entered a hyper-segregated, White supremacist capitalist patriarchy.

## RACE, ETHNICITY, AND THE COVID-19 PANDEMIC

As the virus was spreading across the United States in March and April 2020—from early "hot spots" in Washington State and California, and later New York City—these communities saw the deaths tolls continue to rise. The Johns Hopkins Coronavirus Research Center (JHCRC 2020) estimated there were 8.7 million confirmed COVID-19 cases from January 22, 2020, to the time of writing, September 2020, with 221,000 deaths (although, some estimates are currently higher than 300,000). Some nine months into the pandemic, the ten areas with the highest death counts were Los Angeles, Queens, Kings County, Cook County, the Bronx, Miami-Dade, Maricopa County, Wayne County, Harris County, and New York. These areas are more likely to be communities of color—with two to three times the national average of Latino/a populations; 1.5 to three times the national average of Black populations; a much lower percentage White population than the national average; immigrant populations two to three times the national average; and much higher general, elderly, and childhood poverty rates. This represents a significantly disproportionate impact on the most vulnerable, particularly Black, Indigenous, and people of color (BIPOC) communities, while seemingly preserving the White collective body (Census Reporter 2020).

Significant federal efforts in collecting data on racial disparities related to COVID-19 were not heavily pursued until late spring/early summer 2020. It is now clear what was glimpsed in those early requests and disjointed attempts to gather the data: the COVID-19 pandemic fundamentally uncovered the racialized distribution in contraction and death due to COVID-19. The history of medical apartheid (Washington 2006), reproductive injustices (Roberts 1997), using the Black person and Black body as a laboratory (Skloot 2017), and the construction of racialized diabetes (Montoya 2011) continue to significantly affect the operation of our health care system and other dominant institutions in the United States. The racialized distribution of suffering, economic disruption, hunger, sickness, and death shows not only the structure of White supremacy but also its cultural and ideological counterpart—Whiteness—that creates the path forward through a pandemic: one by, of, and for White people. The response thus far has certainly made visible who makes COVID-19 decisions, for whom these decisions are made, whose individual bodies are ontologically central, and by extension, whose collective bodies are worth saving.

Though the structure of White supremacy is at work in the racialized impact of COVID-19, the *meanings* of that structure are equally important in understanding how we got here, who belongs, and who survives in a pandemic. Racial capitalism is a "fundamental cause" of public health issues and the racial disparities that exist in the United States. Whiteness, White discourse, White ownership of the media, White frames, and White symbols are the glue that holds that connection together—making some visible and others invisible.

The preparation for, framing of, response to, and the political economy of the COVID-19 global pandemic laid bare the fundamentals of a racialized social structure as well as the racialized production of meaning, particularly in the United States. Recent theorizing into the cultural logics of Whiteness and the social, institutional, and discursive spaces where it is continuously reproduced offers insight into the racialized discourse surrounding the pandemic and, ultimately, its racialized outcomes. Using the five cultural logics of White spaces developed by Brunsma and colleagues (2020)—establishing the White space, the ideology of the White space, the aesthetics of White space, the interaction order of the White space, and the protection of the White space—this chapter will illuminate the cultural logics of Whiteness that undergird and motivate the discursive White space of COVID-19. This White space has served to protect its central beneficiaries (White people) and its central organizing principle (White supremacy) through its racialized production of meaning and meaningful actions within the pandemic (Whiteness). In this chapter, we will wrestle with the cultural manifestations of White supremacy when documenting its material realities.

## The Cultures of White Space and The Racialized Production of Meaning

The scholarship on Whiteness (Twine and Gallagher 2008), and particularly White spaces, has grown in the past decade. The geography of White supremacy—its reach, its emplacement, its space-(re)making—is investigated at the global (Christian 2019), national (Harris 1993), and important regional, local, and interactional (Rosino 2017) levels across a wide variety of disciplines. Much of the work is at its core interdisciplinary. While sociologists and geographers look at distributions, variations, and structures, some scholars hone in on the cultural meanings associated with these social architectures because they are finding that meanings matter for the (re)production of such spaces. White spaces can certainly be physical, but they are also historical, institutional, and discursive, perhaps usefully seen as storied structures and structured stories that animate how we can experience the social world as well as whose experience matters. COVID-19 is perhaps, as DiFranco (2002) has poetically expressed, "10 percent literal, 90 percent metaphor." The all-important, socially-constructed "metaphors" matter, leading to significant racialized parameters, realities, and outcomes—who is *seen*, who is *heard*, and whose body is *assumed*. Who makes sense to White supremacy and Whiteness? While White spaces are not only recognizable by the racial identities of those who populate the space, they are clearly governed by several cultural logics that produce and maintain them *as* White spaces, while deflecting and containing challenges in important cultural ways.

In a recent piece, Brunsma and colleagues surveyed the scholarship on White spaces as seemingly disparate as academia, the craft beer industry, segregated neighborhoods, online social media platforms, and subcultural scenes in order to see how these spaces work, how they are challenged, and how they are reconstituted. They found that these White spaces shared similar cultural glue that held them together under White supremacy. The authors theoretically develop five cultural processes, concluding that further research would likely heighten some of these processes while diminishing others, as White spaces are not monolithic despite their interactional and institutional buttressing of White identities, ideas, lives, and futures. In this chapter, we certainly find this to be the case. Before embarking on a look at the cultural workings of COVID-19 as a White space, we provide an overview of the five basic cultural processes.

### *Establishing the White Space*

In order to understand White spaces and the ways they culturally operate, scholars should pay close attention to the historical establishment of such spaces and the associated origin stories. Paying attention to the initial impetus and the symbolic and cultural underpinnings has the potential to illuminate contemporary functions as well as their likely White, settler-colonial cognitive mappings. Looking at the early structures of power, positions, and socially constructed rules and norms allows White people and their space-supported sense-making activities to hoard opportunities, create order, and signify to others the kind of space it has been, is, and will likely continue to be. Thus, understanding the establishment of the White space under analysis will inform all other elements of its cultural functioning.

*The Ideological Terrain of White Space*

Given our various research experiences and understanding of these White spaces, it is crucial for scholars to interrogate the ideologies that animate them. This involves grappling with the collective and possessive investment in Whiteness and White identities that underwrite and buttress the economy of meaning in White spaces. The ideological terrain of the White space serves to normalize the frames (i.e., Whiteness-as-normality) through which the space is culturally maintained. Significant analytic payoff should be found for those who dig deep into the cultural repertoires and logics of the spaces that develop cultures of anti-Blackness (which is pro-Whiteness by dialectical definition) and White epistemologies and logics. There is a colonization of the mind at work here that often operates through actively producing and supporting White ignorance, as well as color-blind racial ideology.

*The Aesthetics of White Space*

One of the important ways that culture works to maintain White spaces is through the development, expectation, and underwriting of the White habitus. These spaces thrive, insidiously and collectively unconsciously, from the racist fertilizer that permeates their grounds. White spaces mobilize Whiteness through a variety of mechanisms of creating effective flows that keep the wheels of White sociability greased and turning. The aesthetic/affective fuels are derived from a cultural assemblage of White tastes, preferences, and experiences that create an emotional economy of Whiteness, a

"White vibe" that "makes sense" and "feels right" to those who have been socialized in the White habitus. These spaces socially and culturally craft "comfort" and safety for Whites where the talk, the ideas, the current events discussed, and the heroes worshiped are of White people, by White people, and for White people. An affective and epistemological apartheid is evidenced while all others are minimized, sequestered, delegitimized, or laughed at—"Dude, we're just having fun. Chill out."

*The White Space as Interaction Order*

White spaces, therefore, are *established* to *make sense* and *feel right* for their primary constituents—White people. The cultural order is the nameless, unspoken, ethereal glue that holds the cultural space together; however, there are material and social realities at play here too that work to ensure the culture is invoked in real-time, in real sociability, in the social connection to embodied White cultural capital. Those who spend time examining the ways White spaces function are often able to point clearly to White interaction orders and exchange orders. These are where White cultural capital that is derived from the White habitus and is culturally bolstered in these spaces is constantly traded—both when the White space is online (where anonymity is often a variable) or off-line (where visible symbols are often variables). These social orders of the White space are fundamentally dialectical belongings and alienation of BIPOC, and those without White habiti must do the "dance," codeswitch, and show their "fitness" for the White space. Those who cannot are bodies out of place (Combs 2016), reminded of their place, and *still* will not be welcomed. Meanwhile, the White space and its beneficiaries consume such diversity, appropriate non-White cultures, and often send the message, disingenuously, that "We want your culture, not you."

*The Protection of White Space*

Often the glue that is the culture of White spaces cannot keep it all together through its lullaby that is comfortable for Whites and "softly kills" others in such spaces. Thus, we see histories and contemporary practices of *active* efforts on the parts of those within White spaces to ensure they remain of, by, and for White people and Whiteness. From protective strategies that are put in place before the arrival of BIPOC, whether culturally (see all of the above) or through laws, regulations (e.g., "dress codes"), ordinances, conventions, and a wide variety of other strategies, the bodies within White spaces often collectively work to protect their space. Sometimes these strategies are overt, like interpersonal violence, active policing, discrimination, gatekeeping, harassment, and displacement. Other times they are more covert, like surveillance, stigmatization, assaults on worth/dignity (Lamont et al. 2016), invisibilization, and interpersonal ostracization.

In this chapter, we think through each of the five theoretical processes whereby White spaces culturally function to solidify White spaces, and therefore, Whiteness and White supremacy. We analyze the myriad ways that the particular theoretical element/process: a) is evident in the pandemic response; b) helps us understand the pandemic; and c) illuminates the disparate impact of the virus on communities of color. We also examine how the element makes certain aspects visible and invisible along with the (il)logics of such from a policy perspective (What to do? For whom? By whom? With what goal?). We take each in turn and come back around to conclude.

## The Pandemic Comes to (White) America: The Establishment of the White Space

The entrance of a pandemic like COVID-19 into a social, economic, political, and discursive space that has long been established under a White supremacist capitalist patriarchy brought about policies that supported, spoke to, resonated with, and ultimately, protected White people. Indeed, sociologists and race scholars across a wide swath of disciplines have shown the role of institutions in shaping the racialized social structure of the United States. Such work reveals how White supremacist institutions develop White supremacist structures and identities to maintain a system that privileges White people, who are, therefore, collectively and individually complicit in that privilege. This institutionalization of White norms and practices buttresses White power by positioning White norms and practices as normal and objective

(Doane and Bonilla-Silva 2003). In this way, the White structuring of institutional life becomes hegemonic and mostly invisible (Jackman 1994), meaning few people question or challenge the institutional policies and practices that benefit White and disadvantage BIPOC. This includes the preparation for, framing of, and response to COVID-19. The military and civilian strategists had been planning pandemic scenarios since the 1950s (Saad-Fihlo 2020). Such planning was rooted in White supremacy and implicates other institutions—education, healthcare, the legal system, etc.—that have been built to support White life, White liberty, and White pursuit of happiness.

Critical social sciences have documented for decades the realities for individuals that have been disenfranchised, disinvested in, and dehumanized—namely Black, Brown, Indigenous, immigrant, disabled, poor, elderly, and LGBTQ communities. This structure that perpetrates these realities wreaks havoc on the lives, livelihoods, bodies, opportunities, and health of these groups. The US government is fully aware of the extent to which such inequalities have exacerbated the everyday lives of generations of racialized minorities and other marginalized communities. At the start of the pandemic, the rich ran to their multiple havens and the middle class "sheltered in place" to "telework" in their homes. BIPOC, overrepresented in lower-paid, "essential (to White people's economy) worker" positions such as construction workers, poultry plant packers, care workers, and delivery workers were and remain fundamentally expendable. Instead, when we finally saw data come out about the racial disparities, a color-blind racial ideology that was fundamentally dismissive of the role of racism in the pandemic was front and center (Bonilla-Silva 2020).

Thus, "our" representatives in government could have easily stood up, once it was clear that we were about to face a global pandemic, and said something like, "So, we know that minority communities are likely to be highest at risk for contracting and complications from COVID-19 because of the institutionalized history of racism in our nation. As such, we will need to focus on those communities first and foremost to ensure their health. Such will ensure the health of all of us." However, this is *not* what happened, and with a good reason for a White supremacist society. The Trump administration actively encouraged its (White) fan base to disregard public health mandates and requirements, including mask-wearing and social distancing, which further exacerbated the effects of the virus on BIPOC, the most vulnerable, and their intersections. In such a White discursive space, called a "White frame" (Feagin 2020), the Whiteness of such actions is rendered invisible to White people, yet was consistently circumnavigated by communities of color. In a pandemic or otherwise, communities of color face the most significant consequences of such "value-neutral" policies.

Regardless of the administration, the history of the racial state and its politics of Whiteness in the neoliberal era has been one of a Republican Party as the party of White grievance and of a Democratic Party as the party of White guilt. Both have done increasingly less to ameliorate the structural inequalities that have been so clearly exposed by COVID-19.

American exceptionalism has been on full, grotesque display throughout this entire global pandemic. Initially, and still to this day, the response in the United States has been framed as anti-Chinese. However, the reality is quite different from the rhetoric. China gave the world plenty of time to prepare for the virus and, along with East Asian countries like South Korea and Taiwan, showed the world (including the isolationist United States) many options that have worked in combating the spread of the virus. Whiteness is always about rhetoric; Blackness is always about action and the real work. This kind of social order breeds social inequality such that "catastrophic events brought on by natural and unnatural disasters have exposed the racial asymmetries of this neoliberal social order and its intrinsic racism and anti-Black logic" (Viola 2020). As the pandemic came to America, we saw profits favored over people and the destruction of collectivity. In such a cultural frame of sense-making, despite consistent protests of the most vulnerable, the disenfranchised, and the excluded, #Black and #Blacklives do not seem to matter to the White polity. The long-established White space of America helps to partially explain the preparation for, framing of, and continued response to COVID-19. But there is more.

## The Ideological Terrain of the White Space: Herrenvolk Ideology and COVID-19

In the current context of COVID-19, White spaces have become ideologically hypervigilant, further accentuating the Herrenvolk ideology (the Nazi's concept of "master race") at the center of Whiteness (Mills 1997). This is apparent in the sharp increase in racial discrimination toward BIPOC, particularly Black and Asian Americans (Ruiz, Horowitz, and Tamir 2020). The White space amid the COVID-19 pandemic ideologically frames White people as inherently "belonging" in space—the counterpoint to the "iconic ghetto"—(Anderson 2015; Harrison 2013) and BIPOC as the racial "other," described as "bodies out of place" (Combs 2016). Even more than in pre-pandemic years, White spaces have openly operated on an ideological agenda of racial domination with open intolerance, racial ignorance, and contradictory logic.

White people continue to practice the ideology of racial color-blindness (Bonilla-Silva 2020). Particularly with "Trumpism" in the United States, it is important to see racial ideology as enacted through a form of racial ignorance (Bonilla-Silva 2019; Mueller 2020). Racial ignorance becomes evident in the ways that White people frame the COVID-19 lockdown as the state's infringement of their bodily sovereignty (Hoskin 2020) while having a hostile attitude toward the protests for #BlackLivesMatter. The contradiction presented here is a form of racial ignorance, a purposeful act of White agency (Mueller 2020). Protesting for their (White) liberty against state control while calling for "law and order" over Black and Brown bodies demonstrates a logical inconsistency of racial ignorance. This also makes salient White people's practice of Herrenvolk ideology that is foundational to the cultural logic of White space (Brunsma et al. 2020).

In the wake of the tragic death of George Floyd and the subsequent #BlackLivesMatter protests at a global level, some White people supported the protests, but many White individuals framed the demonstration against racial injustice as incivility—all without reconciling their previous demonstrations against state-ordered lockdown a couple of months prior. The ideological terrain of White space amid COVID-19 constructs normality toward and for Whiteness (i.e., White bodies perceived as belonging). To a large extent, the White discursive spaces ideologically frame White people as under attack from "foreign" bodies that "do not" belong. White people's contradiction when invoking state legitimacy, based on White logic, therefore frames White bodies as "belonging" in the "space" with "rights to exist." In other words, it is an open practice of Herrenvolk republicanism. This ideological notion is not just limited to Trump and his supporters, who are easily visible as "the racists" (Bonilla-Silva 2019). On the contrary, racial ideology is deeply pervasive among White people occupying all socioeconomic statuses (Lipsitz 1998; Mills 1997). White people occupying the upper echelon of the US socioeconomic ladder have expressed anti-Black sentiments ranging from the technology sector (see Canales 2020 for an example of racialized face recognition systems) to the infamous "Central Park Karen," Amy Cooper (Closson 2020). This increasing ubiquity of racially charged incidents demonstrates the increasing racial tensions and the hyper-vigilance of Whiteness amid the COVID-19 pandemic; it is the galvanization of the Herrenvolk ideology.

The hyper-vigilance of White space has only further exacerbated deeply structured, preexisting racial inequalities. The detrimental material consequences of the COVID-19 pandemic for BIPOC (Kim 2020; Ruiz et al. 2020) illustrate this point. For example, a recent report shows Black American small business owners have been more financially affected than their White counterparts (da Costa 2020). Furthermore, racial barriers exist in unequal access to COVID-19 testing, contact tracing, medical care, and later, vaccine access, for BIPOC (Kim 2020). White supremacy maintains and structures materiality and corporeality, determining who belongs and who does not belong in White spaces, which include, not coincidentally, health treatment centers. Such spaces are meant to be for all people, but are typically mostly run by White people who demand more than their share of the community. Erasing and revolting against racial matters through a process of unknowing, vis-à-vis ignorance (Mills 1997; Mueller 2017, 2020), is characteristic of the Herrenvolk ideology in US politics amid the COVID-19 pandemic. Consistent with the ways that Donald Trump, as well as the Republican Party at large, ideologically weaponize racial tensions, Pew Research reports that "Democrats and those who lean Democratic (52 percent) are more likely than Republicans and Republican leaners (25 percent) to say that it is more common for people to express racist views about Asian Americans since the coronavirus outbreak" (Ruiz et al. 2020). In sum, the process by which Whiteness is ideologically weaponized goes as follows: (1) White people insist that racial inequalities do not exist (Bonilla-Silva 2020); (2) White people believe that they themselves are never racist (Mueller 2017); and (3) White people construe racial accounts that are oftentimes fictional (e.g., reverse racism) (Cabrera 2018; Vera, Feagin, and Gordon 1995). Overall, the ideological "cultural war" over racial matters was further inflamed and promulgated by Trump's continuous use of racial hate as a political strategy (Lopez 2016). His insistence on referring to COVID-19 during press briefings and public speeches as "the China virus" (Budryk 2020) was further evidence of this.

## The Aesthetics of White Space: Crafting White Comfort During the Pandemic

A central element of the cultural logics of White space is the aesthetics that create, maintain, and reinforce an emotional economy of Whiteness. During the pandemic, the emotional economy of Whiteness has been crafted by prioritizing White comfort. The federal response to the pandemic, news representations of COVID-19 victims, and the public response to Black Lives Matter (BLM) protests and state mask mandates contribute to creating an emotional economy of White comfort and invulnerability at the cost of BIPOC lives.

Early reports of COVID-19 cases in China and Europe received little acknowledgment by the US federal government in January 2020. Despite the WHO and CDC's acknowledgment of the possible severity of the outbreak, the Trump administration publicly treated the virus as a minor threat to the American public and took few steps to prepare for the spread of the virus. Even while the number of cases in the United States increased during February and March 2020, in his press briefings to address the pandemic, Trump touted narratives of American exceptionalism through misleading claims that the outbreak was effectively under control in the United States and that the number of confirmed cases was decreasing. Meanwhile, conservative media outlets such as Fox News began to claim that the pandemic was a hoax created by the Democratic Party to undermine Donald Trump's reelection (Sullivan 2020). According to a national poll from Survey 160 and Gradient metrics, the role of conservative media in spreading misinformation led to the increased practice of risky behaviors, with Republicans who watched Fox News more likely to state that the pandemic was exaggerated and least likely to stay home during the pandemic (Beauchamp and Animashaun 2020). Ultimately, the federal government's inadequate response to the pandemic, Trump's exaggerated narratives of American exceptionalism, and the dissemination of misleading information through conservative media created an emotional economy of Whiteness, which maintained White comfort by portraying perceived American invulnerability to the virus. Early efforts to maintain White comfort came at the cost of undermining the WHO and CDC's recommended preemptive measures that would have critically mitigated the devastating effects of the virus on the US population.

At the time of writing in fall of 2020, as the number of COVID-19 cases in the United States continued to surge, analyses of mortality rates continued to indicate that BIPOC and lower socioeconomic groups were the most vulnerable populations to be affected by the virus. In June 2020, during a hearing on racism as a public health crisis in Ohio, State Senator Stephen A. Huffman questioned the head of the Ohio Commission on Minority Health, asking her whether the "colored population" is more susceptible to COVID-19 because they "do not wash their hands as well as other groups" (Gabriel 2020). On August 14, the CDC released a report indicating that there is a disproportionate incidence of COVID-19 among communities of color, with Hispanic, Black, and American Indian/Alaskan Native populations especially vulnerable (CDC 2020). Through skewed reporting, news coverage of these data ignored the social factors responsible for the disproportionate impact of the virus on communities of color, spinning a color-blind racist narrative that BIPOC bodies are biologically more vulnerable than White bodies, ultimately reinforcing White comfort. The cultural racism and minimization of structural racism evident in such rhetoric place the blame for the rise of cases on minority groups and their cultures. Such reporting has also dangerously portrayed the pandemic as a fortunate event in White supremacist eyes, with White supremacist visions of America reinforced through mass deaths among BIPOC populations.

Despite the constant affirmation of White comfort by the federal government and news outlets, one can look more closely at two incidents during the pandemic when White comfort was threatened: state mandates on lockdowns and face masks, and the BLM movement. In the former, there were several anti-lockdown and anti-mask protests in April 2020 across several states that had instituted stay-at-home orders and mask mandates. These protests were comprised mainly of White protesters and far-right extremists, some of whom were armed, and others who carried Confederate flags or signs with Nazi symbols (Perrett 2020). Each protest was against perceived state tyranny and infringement of people's liberty and freedom. However, underlying the narrative of unconstitutional state actions was the threat to White comfort through the restriction of behavior. White anger over limits on behavior was clearly evident in the sheer number of viral videos that showed White men and women becoming angry at being denied service at various establishments for not adhering to mask mandates. The belief in the right to White comfort continues to place all Americans at risk, with BIPOC bodies most vulnerable.

The second case—the BLM movement demonstrations in summer 2020—inherently threatened White comfort because it threatened the racial hierarchy. With BLM protests taking place in every state, state governments and the Trump administration were quick to draw connections between the movement and rising cases of COVID-19 (Smith 2020). Clearly, this was an attempt to redirect blame of the administration's failure to contain the outbreak—including the mismanagement of state governments, the premature reopening of the economy, police brutality in response to the protests, and risky behaviors of anti-maskers, anti-lockdown protesters, and partygoers in places like Florida and Texas—to the protesters in the BLM movement. Contradicting this, data actually suggests that BLM protests have caused no uptick in the number of cases, and in fact, after these protests, stay-at-home tendencies increased (Dave et al. 2020). The redirection of blame reinforces color-blind racist frameworks, making minority populations responsible for protecting White health, crafting White comfort, and for maintaining the racial hierarchy at the cost of their own oppression.

Should the state seek to redress the disastrous outcomes of the pandemic, and prevent case resurgences in the near future, health and safety mandates must be reframed as being patriotic—pandering to the White American habitus—and risky populations must be targeted through centralizing social identity in policy and dissemination of information.

## "Dance for Your Lives": COVID-19, White Space, and the Interaction Order

In addition to establishment, ideological terrain, and aesthetics of the White space during COVID-19, one can also take a closer look at how the White interaction order has affected "bodies in space" in a pandemic. Particularly, we look at public spaces, workspaces, and incarceration spaces.

Asian Americans have encountered fear and animosity from people who blame them for the virus or see them as carriers. Hate crimes against Asian Americans have risen exponentially during the pandemic. Thirty-nine percent of Asians report people acting uncomfortable around them since the pandemic, 31 percent have been subjected to slurs or jokes, and 26 percent feared being physically attacked (the corresponding percentages for White people, respectively: 13 percent, 5 percent, and 5 percent). Documented actions toward Asian Americans include verbal harassment ("They should be banned"), shunning, and physical assault (Ruiz et al. 2020). A starker illustration of the "alienation" of POC versus the "belonging" of White people is hard to imagine.

Meanwhile, African Americans and other BIPOC find it problematic to wear masks in public spaces. Because public spaces such as stores and banks are generally considered White spaces, White people can wear masks (or not) freely, without incident. But the stereotype of BIPOC as criminals means they must weigh the risk of being shot or arrested against the risk of contracting a potentially deadly virus. If they choose to mask, they must "do the dance" (Anderson 2015), a performance to mitigate the danger and gain conditional acceptance in space where they are "bodies out of place" (Harrison 2013). Take, for example, Kam Buckner, an African American attorney and Illinois state senator. He wore a mask while shopping at a hardware store in the Chicago Loop (read: "White space"). He bought only flowers, but a security man picked him out of numerous White shoppers to check his receipt and ID. "When I asked why, he said, 'I can't see your face. You look like you might have been up to something'" (McFarling 2020). Though he danced around threatening items like chainsaws or hammers, his dark, masked face broke step.

Another example was Armen Henderson, a Black, University of Miami physician working with a team who was testing people experiencing homelessness for COVID-19. In a viral video (Cetoute 2020), Henderson, masked, sorted supplies from his curbside van when a White cop pulls up to question him. Though Henderson made no threatening gestures, the cop got out and soon handcuffed Henderson. A lighter-skinned Black woman appeared and spoke to the cop, after which he uncuffed Henderson while she retrieved identification proving, presumably, that Henderson was a doctor on his own property. The cop's "reason" for detaining Henderson was supposed reports of "illegal dumping" in the area. Again, professionals are regarded as suspects when the professional dance outfit and dance floor are missing.

And it is not just masks. Of forty people arrested for "social distancing violations" in Brooklyn from March 17 to May 5, 2020, thirty-five were Black (Joseph et al. 2020). Of course, what was really being enforced was physical distancing; social distancing was a way to preserve Whiteness in interactions long before COVID-19. Arresting BIPOC was a means to enforce White people's interests and privileges.

"Essential" work settings are another site where the imposition of White space social ordering during the pandemic has disproportionately hurt BIPOC. Though minority workers are common in these settings, the primarily White ownership, management, and government oversight make these White spaces that secure White racial interests and subordinate non-White individuals (Anderson 2015). Meat-processing plant workers were considered "critical infrastructure workers" that were thereby "permitted to continue work following potential exposure to COVID-19" (CWEA 2020). A presidential order forced meat-processing plants to remain open during lockdown; thus, the emotional economy of "White comfort" and the fiscal economy of White profits overrule the health of laborers. These workers were at higher risk because processing lines required prolonged close contact with coworkers. Although the CDC recommends six feet spacing, this was disregarded to maintain higher production (Paschal 2020). One CEO called social distancing "a nicety that makes sense only for people with laptops" (Grabell et al. 2020). Thus, outbreaks among meat packers were numerous, and 87 percent of infected meatpackers were minorities (Perez 2020). Such stark statistics bring to mind old Westerns where the gunslinger demands "dance!" of a hapless soul trying to dodge bullets flying around his feet. Some of those bullets are going to find their mark and wound—some will even kill.

Minorities are overrepresented in positions as direct care workers such as nurse aides. In 2010, 30 percent of direct care workers were Black and sixteen percent were Hispanic (PHI 2011, 5). These are high-risk positions that are often in close physical contact with a population devastated by COVID-19. Distancing is impossible when bathing, feeding, dressing, toileting, and lifting residents. Yet, workers have been fired for demanding protective equipment and hazard pay.

Management and the White superstructure they undergird expect to control the workers like slaves that dance for the plantation owners' amusement.

Perhaps no population is more susceptible to infection due to an interaction order than the incarcerated. Prisons are vastly overrepresented by minorities and notoriously overcrowded. People in prison often have twenty-five square feet or less of unencumbered space, beds are often only three feet apart, and eating, bathroom, and recreation facilities offer no distancing and are unsanitary (Kajstura and Landon 2020). Saloner et al. (2020) found that, as of June 6, 2020, the case rate among prisoners was 5.5 times higher than the US population case rate. The death rate, adjusted for age and sex, was three times higher. The process for releasing those more vulnerable to the virus has been underused, inconsistent, and biased. The Prison Policy Initiative says, "Jails and prisons have reduced their populations" in response, "but not enough to save lives" because "the drops have been too small and too slow" (Kajstura and Landon 2020).

Maintaining safe "White spaces" on the outside prevents the mass release of the mass incarcerated, although criminology data suggest that release of the older adults, the medically vulnerable, the nonviolent, and short-timers "would pose little risk to public safety" (Hawks et al. 2020). The music as written would accommodate a mass release dance, but the dance stage, where Whiteness's culture is enacted in real-time, moves to the perceived need to protect privileges; thus, the tune changes.

## "To Protect and Serve":
## Protecting White Spaces in the Age of COVID-19

The protection of White spaces is fundamental to the creation, expansion, and maintenance of a White supremacist state. As mentioned throughout this chapter, White spaces are the uncontested arenas in which Whiteness operates unmolested. From sidewalks to university classrooms, to boardrooms and public parks, Whiteness operates within these spaces as a matter of *fact*, making all others who enter these spaces immediately suspect. Over time, the protection of White spaces has evolved as technologies have changed. The foundation, however, has remained the same—the sanctity of White space is maintained by the exclusion of undesirable "others" who too often become marked as expendable. This exclusion is maintained by practices of surveillance, over-policing, stigmatization, and the criminalization of the "other." In the era of COVID-19, protecting White spaces has manifested in numerous ways including staunch anti-Blackness, racist police violence, hyper-surveillance, and an overall disregard for Black life.

For instance, in May 2020, a bird watcher named Christian Cooper, an African American man, was in Central Park when he requested that a White woman, Amy Cooper, put her dog on a leash. Rather than comply, Amy Cooper weaponized her Whiteness and proceeded to call the police and tell them that she was being threatened by an "African American man" in Central Park. Fortunately, Mr. Cooper recorded her while she attempted to have the police set upon him—a tactic that reeks of an era that has never truly disappeared. Throughout history, the word of a White woman against a Black man was justification enough to have civil citizens as well as law enforcement rain down violence upon Black men—innocent until proven guilty is only for those perceived as human (i.e., White). Protecting (and serving) White spaces comes at a cost, and often that cost is the loss of Black life via the weaponization of Whiteness in general, and White women's tears, in particular.

The devaluation of Blackness and Black life is made even more central when living through a pandemic that keeps many within the confines of their homes. One example is the recent verdict regarding the officers who shot and killed Breonna Taylor, a twenty-six-year-old EMT, in her home. The only charge laid against an officer was that of "wanton endangerment," for the shots that missed Taylor and entered a neighbor's home damaging their walls. Now the offending officer is suing Taylor's boyfriend for "emotional distress and assault and battery." These actions highlight the ways that infringement upon White spaces, including property damage that results as a side effect of Black death, means more than actual Black lives. For instance, on Monday, September 28, 2020, a Christin Evans, Black female college student in Texas, said that university police stormed into her room on September 14th with their guns drawn after a group of girls (mostly White) falsely accused her of a crime (Burke 2020). Evans was asleep in her bed when the police entered, armed, their flashlights in her eyes. She was occupying a White space in the age of

COVID (a university dorm room) and was rendered suspicious on the word of White women. Unlike Breonna Taylor and Fred Hampton (former chairman of the Illinois chapter of the Black Panther Party), however, her bed did not become her final resting place. However, it just as easily could have been. So far, there have been no formal charges made against those who falsely accused her of wielding a weapon (scissors). In the time in which we live, calling the police on a Black person has the potential to lead to their death—whether those responsible are charged or not.

It is within such a climate that the images of people in the streets "rioting," and "looting," some with facial coverings due to the pandemic, were now constantly on repeat via social and mainstream media outlets. Protecting White spaces in this climate (one of a global pandemic and state unrest) often means more police intervention, which often leads to the further endangerment of BIPOC who take to the streets to protest injustice. Protecting White spaces has always come at the expense of others, those who are marked as "bodies out of place," (Puwar 2004) as they exist in and occupy spaces not designed for them. Anderson (2018) notes that many White people are still uncomfortable with the idea that Black people are now more regular fixtures in places of power and privilege where they were once (and to a certain extent remain) unwelcomed—consider the backlash to US Vice President Kamala Harris or the confirmation process of Justice Brown Jackson. As a result, the desire to protect (and serve) such spaces has been made more acute by the stress of the pandemic as well as the current political climate. Protecting White spaces has been central to the American project since the "birth" of this nation; COVID-19 has served to amplify that fact.

## Conclusion

On nearly the fifteenth anniversary of Hurricane Katrina's landfall, Dr. Michael Viola, associate professor of justice, community, and leadership at Saint Mary's College of California, reminded us of the racist federal response to that disaster in Truthout (Viola 2020). His comparison of that federal response to Katrina and its aftermath with the current federal response to COVID-19 was indeed striking. Because he knows the historical and contemporary context of racial capitalism, Viola discusses the "before" and "after" of both Katrina and COVID-19 and argues that a vaccine will not save us from COVID-19 apartheid in the aftermath. Ultimately, he calls for radical, as opposed to reactionary, imaginations. Indeed. However, looking at the ways that White spaces function culturally to protect their primary constituents illuminates that such a call would also require a cultural reality outside the culture of White space. This society does not show much evidence that this will be possible from inside the White cultural imaginary and its discursive White space. Those assumptions, those frames, those narratives, those starting points, those views of who is worthy and not, who is human and not, whose lives matter and not, are always the starting point. These exist in order to shore up White supremacy from attacks on it—including a global pandemic like COVID-19. Herein lie the collective perils of Whiteness.

In a powerful piece published in the *New England Journal of Medicine* in mid-July 2020, called "Stolen Breaths," Rachel Hardeman and her colleagues remind us:

> We got here because we live in a country established by indigenous dispossession and genocide. Because slavery and the racial ordering of humans and goods it established constructed a political economy predicated on devaluing Black labor, demeaning Black bodies, and denying Black humanity. We got here because stolen lives and stolen breaths are profitable and we work in systems that continue to reap the gains. (Hardeman, Medina, and Boyd 2000)

They offer some solutions that require health care systems to engage in the dismantling of structural racism that improves the health and well-being of the Black community and country as a whole: (1) divesting from racial health inequities; (2) desegregating the healthcare workforce; (3) make mastering the health effects of structural racism a professional medical competency; (4) mandate and measure equitable outcomes; and (5) protect and serve/advocate for all patients. Of course, we have shown that there are powerful cultural elements at play animating all of these, making structures harder to change, harder to reimagine, and harder to remake meaning. It is important to wrestle with the cultural manifestations of White supremacy when documenting its material realities.

## References

Anderson, Elijah. "The White Space." *Sociology of Race and Ethnicity* 1, no. 1 (January 2015):10–21.

Anderson, Elijah. "Black Americans Are Asserting Their Right in 'White Spaces.' That's When Whites Call 911." *Vox*, August 10, 2018. https://www.vox.com/the-big-idea/2018/8/10/17672412/911-police-Black-white-racism-sociology.

Beauchamp, Zack, and Chritstina Animashaun. "New Poll Finds Fox News Viewers Think the Coronavirus Threat Is Exaggerated." *Vox*, March 27, 2020, https://www.vox.com/policy-and-politics/2020/3/27/21195940/coronavirus-fox-news-poll-republicans-trump.

Bonilla-Silva, Eduardo. (2020). "Color-blind Racism in Pandemic Times." *Sociology of Race and Ethnicity*, https://doi.org/10.1177/2332649220941024.

Bonilla-Silva, Eduardo (2019). "Toward a New Political Praxis for Trumpamerica: New Directions in Critical Race Theory." *American Behavioral Scientist* 63, no. 13, 1776–1788.

Bourdieu, Pierre. "The Forms of Capital." In *Handbook of Theory and Research for the Sociology of Education*, edited by John Richardson, 241–258. Westport, CT: Greenwood, 1986.

Brunsma, D. L., Chapman, N. G., Kim, J. W. (2019). "The Culture of White Space, the Racialized Production of Meaning, and the Jamband Scene." *Sociological Inquiry*. https://doi.org/10.1111/soin.12313.

Brunsma, D. L., Chapman, N. G., Kim, J. W., Lellock, J. S., Underhill, M., Withers, E. T., and Wyse, J. P. 2020. "The Culture of White Space: On the Racialized Production of Meaning" *American Behavioral Scientist* 64, no. 14: 2001–2015.

Brunsma, D. L., and Wyse, J. P. (2019). "The Possessive Investment in White Sociology." *Sociology of Race and Ethnicity*, 5, no. 1: 1–10.

Budryk, Zack. "Trump: 'Fake News' Not Reporting 'Big China Virus Breakouts All Over the World.'" *The Hill*, August 2, 2020, https://thehill.com/policy/healthcare/510162-trump-fake-news-not-reporting-big-china- virus-breakouts-all-over-the-world.

Burke, Minyvonne. "Black College Student Says Campus Police Stormed into Dorm After False Report." *NBC News*, September 29, 2020, https://www.nbcnews.com/news/us-news/Black-college-student-says-campus-police-stormed-dorm-after-false-n1241346.

Cabrera, Nolan. *White Guys on Campus: Racism, White Immunity, and the Myth of Post-Racial Higher Education*. New Brunswick, NJ: Rutgers University Press.

Canales, Katie. "A 'Handful' of Cisco Employees Were Fired After Posting Offensive Comments Objecting to The Company's Support of The Black Lives Matter Movement." *Business Insider*, July 17, 2020, https://www.businessinsider.com/cisco-employees-fired-racist-comments-Black-lives-matter-2020-7.

Census Reporter. "Profiles." https://censusreporter.org/.

Centers for Disease Control and Prevention. "Workplaces and Businesses." https://public4.pagefreezer.com/browse/CDC%20Covid%20Pages/11-05-2022T12:30/https://www.cdc.gov/coronavirus/2019-ncov/community/guidance-business-response.html.

Centers for Disease Control and Prevention. "Workplaces and Businesses." https://public4.pagefreezer.com/browse/CDC%20Covid%20Pages/11-05-2022T12:30/https://www.cdc.gov/coronavirus/2019-ncov/community/workplaces-businesses/index.html?CDC_AA_refVal=https:/www.cdc.gov/coronavirus/2019-ncov/community/organizations/meat-poultry-processing-workers-employers.html.

Centers for Disease Control and Prevention. "Disparities in Incidence of COVID-19 Among Underrepresented Racial/Ethnic Groups in Counties Identified as Hotspots During June 5–18, 2020–22 States, February–June 2020." *Morbidity and Weekly Report*, Volume 69, Retrieved August 27, 2020, http://www.cdc.gov/mmwr/volumes/69/wr/mm6933e1.htm.

Cetoute, Devoun. "Miami Police Investigating Detainment of Doctor Who Gives Homeless Virus Tests, Chief Says." *Miami Herald*, April 11, 2020, https://www.miamiherald.com/news/article241943371.html.

Christian, Michelle. "A Global Critical Race and Racism Framework: Racial Entanglements and Deep and Malleable Whiteness." *Sociology of Race and Ethnicity* 5, no. 2:169–185.

Closson, Troy. "Amy Cooper's 911 Call, and What's Happened Since." *New York Times*, July 8, 2020, https://www.nytimes.com/2020/07/08/nyregion/amy-cooper-false-report-charge.html.

Coleman, Justin. "Trump Again Refers to Coronavirus as 'Kung Flu.'" *The Hill*, June 23, 2020, https://thehill.com/homenews/administration/504224-trump-again-refers-to-coronavirus-as-kung-flu.

Combs, Barbara Harris. "Black (and Black) Bodies Out of Place: Towards a Theoretical Understanding of Systematic Voter Suppression in the United States." *Critical Sociology* 42, no. 4–5: 535–549.

The Conversation. "Donald Trump's 'Chinese Virus': The Politics of Naming." *The Conversation*, April 21, 2020, https://theconversation.com/donald-trumps-chinese-virus-the-politics-of-naming-136796.

The Conversation. "What Are the 'Reopen' Protesters Really Saying?" *The Conversation*, May 1, 2020, https://theconversation.com/what-are-the-reopen-protesters-really-saying-137558.

CWEA. 2020. "New CDC Interim Guidance for Essential Workers Exposed to Suspected or Confirmed COVID 19 Patient." *CWEA* https://www.cwea.org/news/new-cdc-interim-guidance-for-essential-workers-exposed-to-suspected-or-confirmed-covid-19-patient/.

da Costa, Pedro Nicolaci. "The COVID-19 Crisis Has Wiped Out Nearly Half of Black Small Businesses." *Forbes*, August 10, 2020, https://www.forbes.com/sites/pedrodacosta/2020/08/10/the-covid-19-crisis-has-wiped-out-nearly-half-of-black-small-businesses/?sh=4fd7b9b84310.

Dave, Dhaval, Andrew Friedson, Kyutaro Matsuzawa, Joseph Sabia, and Samuel Safford. "Black Lives Matter Protests, Social Distancing and COVID-19." National Bureau of Economic Research Working Paper Series, January 2021. https://www.nber.org/papers/w27408.pdf.

DiFranco, Ani. "Self Evident" from *So Much Shouting, So Much Laughter*. Righteous Babe Records.

Doane, Ashley W. and Bonilla-Silva, Eduardo eds., 2003. *White out: The continuing significance of racism*. Psychology Press.

Evans, Clare, David Williams, Onnela Jukka-Pekka, and S.V. Subramanian; "A Multilevel Approach to Modeling Health Inequalities at the intersection of Multiple Social Identities." *Social Science & Medicine* 203 (2018): 64–73.

Feagin, Joe, and José Cobas. "Latinos/as and White Racial Frame: The Procrustean Bed of Assimilation." *Sociological Inquiry* 78, no. 1(2008): 39–53.

Feagin, Joe. *The White Racial Frame: Centuries Old Framing and Counter-Framing*. New York: Routledge, 2020.

Forouhi, Nita, and Nicholas Wareham. "Epidemiology of Diabetes." *Medicine* 47, no. 1 (2019): 22–27.

Gabriel, Trip. "Ohio Lawmaker Asks Racist Question About Black People and Hand-Washing." *New York Times*, June 11, 2020, https://www.nytimes.com/2020/06/11/us/politics/steve-huffman-african-americans-coronavirus.html.

Grabell, Michael, Claire Perlman, and Bernice Yeung. "Coronavirus: Emails Reveal Chaos as Meatpacking Companies Fought Health Agencies Over COVID-19 Outbreaks in Their Plants." *ProPublica*, June 12, 2020, https://www.propublica.org/article/emails-reveal-chaos-as-meatpacking-companies-fought-health-agencies-over-covid-19-outbreaks-in-their-plants.

Hardeman, Rachel, Eduardo Medina, and Rhea Boyd. "Perspective: Stolen Breaths" *New England Journal of Medicine* 383 (2020):197–199.

Harris, Cheryl. "Whiteness as Property." *Harvard Law Review* 106, no. 8 (June 1993):1707–1791.

Harrison, Anthony Kwame. "Black Skiing, Everyday Racism, and the Racial Spatiality of Whiteness." *Journal of Sport and Social Issues* 37, no. 4 (2013): 315–339.

Hawks, Laura, Steffie Woolhandler, and Danny McCormick. "COVID-19 in Prisons and Jails in the United States." *JAMA Intern Med* 180, no. 8 (April 28, 2020):1041–1042. https://doi.org/10.1001/jamainternmed.2020.1856.

Henderson, Loren, Hayward Derrick Horton, and Melvin Thomas. Linking Higher Black Mortality Rates from COVID-19 to Racism and Racial Inequality" *Footnotes*: *SPECIAL ISSUE, Sociologists and Sociology During COVID-19* 48, no.3 (May/June 2020). https://www. asanet. org/news-events/footnotes/may-jun-2020/research-policy/linking-higher-black-mortality-rates-COVID-19-racism-and-racial-inequality-racial-and-ethnic.

Hoskin, Maia Niguel. "The Whiteness of Anti-Lockdown Protests." *Vox*, April 25, 2020, https://www.vox.com/first-person/2020/4/25/21234774/coronavirus-covid-19-protest-anti-lockdown).

Jackman, Mary R. "The Velvet Glove." In *The Velvet Glove: Paternalism and Conflict in Gender, Class, and Race Relations*. Davis, CA: University of California Press, 1994.

Jackson, Ronald. "White Space, White Privilege: Mapping Discursive Inquiry into the Self." *Quarterly Journal of Speech* 85 (1999):38–54.

Johns Hopkins Coronavirus Research Center. "COVID-19 United States Cases by County," Retrieved October 27, 2020. https://coronavirus.jhu.edu/us-map.

Joseph, Elizabeth, Mallika Kallingal, and Elizabeth Hartfield. "35 of the 40 People Arrested for Social Distancing Violations in Brooklyn Were Black." *CNN*, May 8, 2020, https://www.cnn.com/2020/05/08/us/nypd-social-distancing-35-of-40-people-arrested-black-trnd/index.html.

Kajstura, Aleks, and Jenny Landon. "Since You Asked: Is Social Distancing Possible Behind Bars?" *Prison Policy Initiative*, April 3, 2020. https://www.prisonpolicy.org/blog/2020/04/03/density/.

Kim, Soo Rin, Matthew Vann, Laura Bronner, and Grace Manthey. "Which Cities Have the Biggest Racial Gaps In COVID-19 Testing Access?" *FiveThirtyEight*, July 22, 2020. https://fivethirtyeight.com/features/white-neighborhoods-have-more-access-to-covid-19-testing-sites/.

Lamont, Michèle, Graziella Moraes Silva, Jessica Welburn, Joshua Guetzkow, Nissim Mizrachi, Hanna Herzog, and Elisa Reis. *Getting Respect: Responding to Stigma and Discrimination in the United States, Brazil, and Israel*. Princeton, NJ: Princeton University Press, 2016.

Lipsitz, George. *The Possessive Investment in Whiteness: How White People Profit from Identity Politics*. Philadelphia: Temple University Press, 1998.

Lopez, German. (2016). "Donald Trump's Long History of Racism, from the 1970s to 2020." *Vox*, August 13, 2020, https://www.vox.com/2016/7/25/12270880/donald-trump-racist-racism-history.

McFarling, Usha Lee. "'Which Death Do They Choose?': Many Black Men Fear Wearing a Mask More Than the Coronavirus." *Stat*, June 3, 2020, https://www.statnews.com/2020/06/03/which-deamany-Black-men-fear-wearing-mask-more-than-coronavirus/.

Montoya, Michael. *Making the Mexican Diabetic: Race, Science, and the Genetics of Inequality*. Oakland: University of California Press, 2011.

Mueller, Jennifer C. "Producing Colorblindness: Everyday Mechanisms of White Ignorance." *Social Problems* 64, no. 2 (May 2017): 219–238.

Mueller, Jennifer C. "Racial Ideology or Racial Ignorance? An Alternative Theory of Racial Cognition." *Sociological Theory* 38, no. 2 (2020):142–169.

Paschal, Olivia. "Poultry Work Groups Sue Tyson and JBS over COVID-19 Response, Alleging Civil Rights Violations." *The Counter*, July 17, 2020, https://thecounter.org/poultry-worker-groups-tyson-jbs-covid-19-civil-rights/.

Perez, Matt. "87% of Meatpacking Workers Infected with Coronavirus Have Been Racial and Ethnic Minorities, CDC Says." *Forbes*, July 7, 2020, https://www.forbes.com/sites/mattperez/2020/07/07/87-of-meatpacking-workers-infected-with-coronavirus-have-been-racial-and-ethnic-minorities-cdc-says/#14e672a2634f.

Perrett, Connor. "Why Anti-Lockdown Protests Are a 'Magnet' For White Supremacists and Far-Right Extremists." *Business Insider*, May 20, 2020, https://www.businessinsider.com/why-white-supremacists-have-protested-lockdown-orders-2020-5.

PHI. "Who Are Direct-Care Workers?" *PhiFacts: Quality Care Through Quality Jobs*. February 2011 Update. Number 3. https://phinational.org/wp-content/uploads/legacy/clearinghouse/NCDCW%20Fact%20Sheet-1.pdf.

Puwar, Nirmal. *Space Invaders: Race, Gender and Bodies Out of Place*. New York: Berg, 2004.

Roberts, Dorothy. *Killing the Black Body: Race, Reproduction and the Meaning of Liberty*. New York: Vintage Books, 1997.

Rosino, Michael. "Dramaturgical Domination: The Genesis and Evolution of the Racialized Interaction Order." *Humanity & Society* 41, no. 2 (2017), 158–181.

Ruiz, Neal G., Juliana Menasche Horowitz, and Christine Tamir. "Many Black, Asian Americans Say They Have Experienced Discrimination Amid Coronavirus." Pew Research Center, July 1, 2020, https://www.pewsocialtrends.org/2020/07/01/many-Black-and-asian-americans-say-they-have-experienced-discrimination-amid-the-covid-19-outbreak/.

Saad-Fihlo, Alfredo. "From COVID-19 to the End of Neoliberalism" *Critical Sociology* 46, no. 4–5 (2020): 477–485.

Saloner, Brendan, Kalind Parish, Julie A. Ward, Grace DiLaura, and Sharon Dolovich, "COVID-19 Cases and Deaths in Federal and State Prisons. *Journal of American Medical Association* 324, no. 6 (2020): 602–603.

Sewell, Abigail. "The Racism-Race Reification Process: A Mesolevel Political Economic Framework for Understanding Racial Health Disparities." *Sociology of Race and Ethnicity* 2, no. 4 (2016): 402–432.

Skloot, Rebecca. *The Immortal Life of Henrietta Lacks*. Portland, OR: Broadway Paperbacks, 2017.

Smith, David. "Trump Falsely Ties Climbing COVID-19 Cases to Black Lives Matter Protests." *The Guardian*, July 22, 2020, https://www.theguardian.com/us-news/2020/jul/22/trump-coronavirus-briefing-black-lives-matter-protests.

Southall, Ashley. "Scrutiny of Social-Distance Policing as 35 of 40 Arrested Are Black." *New York Times*, May 7, 2020, https://www.nytimes.com/2020/05/07/nyregion/nypd-social-distancing-race-coronavirus.html.

Sullivan, Margaret. "The Data Is In: Fox News May Have Kept Millions from Taking the Coronavirus Threat Seriously." *Washington Post*, June 28, 2020, https://www.washingtonpost.com/lifestyle/media/the-data-is-in-fox-news-may-have-kept-millions-from-taking-the-coronavirus-threat-seriously/2020/06/26/60d88aa2-b7c3-11ea-a8da-693df3d7674a_story.html.

Twine, France, and Charles Gallagher. (2008). "The Future of Whiteness: A Map of the 'Third Wave'." *Ethnic and Racial Studies* 31, no. 1: 4–24.

Vera, Amir, and Laura Ly. "White Woman Who Called Police on Black Man Bird Watching in Central Park Has Been Fired." CNN, May 26, 2020, https://www.cnn.com/2020/05/26/us/central-park-video-dog-video-african-american-trnd/index.html.

Vera, Hernán, Joe R. Feagin, and Andrew Gordon. "Superior Intellect?: Sincere Fictions of the White Self." *Journal of Negro Education* 64, no. 3 (1995): 295–306.

Viola, Michael J. "Racist Neoliberal Response to Hurricane Katrina Foreshadowed Response to COVID." *Truthout*, August 17, 2020, https://truthout.org/articles/racist-neoliberal-response-to-hurricane-katrina-foreshadowed-response-to-covid/.

Walker, Rebekah, Joni Strom Williams, and Leonard Egede. "Influence of Race, Ethnicity and Social Determinants of Health on Diabetes Outcomes." *American Journal of the Medical Sciences* 351, no. 4 (2016): 366–373.

Washington, Harriet. *Medical Apartheid: The Dark History of Medical Experimentation on Black Americans from Colonial Times to the Present.* New York: Harlem Moon, 2006.

Zagury Orly, Ivry. "Unmasking Reasons for Face Mask Resistance." *Global Biosecurity* 2, no.1 (2020).

CHAPTER 3

# COLOR-BLIND RACIAL DISCOURSE IN PANDEMIC TIMES

*Eduardo Bonilla-Silva*

IDEOLOGIES ARE ALWAYS ON THE move as they must be capable of expanding their influence and adapting to new situations. This is the case of color-blind racism (Bonilla-Silva 2017; Doane 2017) during the COVID-19 pandemic. Its major frameworks have significantly shaped how Americans think about race since the 1970s, including racialized discussions surrounding COVID. The core of color-blind racism, unlike Jim Crow racism, is explaining race matters as the outcome of non-racial dynamics (for similar arguments, see Bobo and Smith 1997). The four central frameworks of color-blind ideology are *abstract liberalism* (explaining racial matters in an abstract, decontextualized manner), *naturalization* (naturalizing racialized outcomes such as neighborhood segregation), *cultural racism* (attributing racial differences to cultural practices), and *minimization of racism*. These frameworks mold how we understand, among other things, (1) the work and role of essential workers, (2) the differential mortality rate due to COVID-19, and (3) hunger in the pandemic.

These color-blindness-infused discussions are dangerous as they transpire in a mostly innocuous manner. For instance, who would object to the idea that "we are all in this together"? Why might such a statement of unity in the middle of a pandemic be regarded as having racial implications? The former New York governor Andrew Cuomo, who after learning that his younger brother had contracted the virus in April, tweeted that COVID-19 is "the great equalizer."[1] Many people have similar thoughts about the virus. The

---

[1] Andrew Cuomo, March 31, 2020, https://twitter.com/nygovcuomo/status/1245021319646904320?lang=en.

power of ideology in general, and of racial ideology in particular: it works best when it is not direct and seems to represent ubiquitous opinions (Bonilla-Silva 2001).

In this chapter, we discuss how color-blind racism has affected our understanding of the three aforementioned subjects. We concentrate on analyzing the messages they convey as well as what they fail to make explicit. This project is based on a momentous, still-unfolding event in which researchers are home-bound. Thus, there is little to gain in trying to be "methodologically correct"—waiting for systematic, representative data would likely make the analysis less relevant as such information will only be available long *after* the pandemic ends. However, this is not a call for sloppiness; I will be as clear about the relevance of the material selected for discussion and, when possible, provide evidence of a source's level of influence.[2]

My main argument is that the color-blind racial framing of these three issues limits recognizing their structural nature (e.g., class and racial inequalities, the lack of a proper safety net, and the need for universal health care). More significantly for my analysis, structural racism is mostly dislodged (or minimized) as a central factor shaping the nation. Consequently, color-blind racism-inflected discussions obscure how the problems at hand are *worse* for communities of color and may require race-based social policies to address them. Official discourse during disasters tends to ignore marginalized communities' viewpoints and reflects dominant narratives (Tierney, Bevc, and Kuligowski 2006). My claim is not that these issues are being framed anew (White people's idea that Black and Brown people are sick because of their culture, behavior, or because they are biologically different is not new), but that color-blind racism has made these ideas more palatable to the general public and thus more salient.

I proceed by first defining "racial ideology." Second, I discuss the three subjects shaped by color-blind discourse, indicate their connection to racial stratification, and clarify their connections to systemic racism obscured by color-blind framing. In the discussion section, I summarize how the discussion of these three issues reifies color-blind ideologies. Finally, I mention two other

---

2 For a similar methodological strategy, see Bonilla-Silva (2012).

emerging subjects influenced by color-blind racism. As ideologies are not without contradictions and cracks, I briefly highlight how the fluid conjuncture in which we are living—the confluence of a pandemic, a recession, and a race-based protest movement—has allowed for counternarratives to emerge and for alternative policies to be contemplated.

## Racial Ideology

My goal in this section is modest. I outline the central features of the racial ideology paradigm to orient my analysis (for a full discussion, see Bonilla-Silva 2003). For good reasons, most theorizations on ideology begin with Marx's classic *The German Ideology* (McLellan 2000). Marx's premise is that the fundamental division of any society is based on class, hence the dominant class attempts to present its views as universal. Second, the privileged position of the dominant class facilitates representing their views as universal. Third, the dominant class's ideas are fundamentally the "ideal expression of the dominant material relationships" (McLellan 2000, 92). Many Marxists assume that class explains all divisions in any society, but racially progressive and feminist scholars have long contended that race and gender are central axes of division in modernity that cannot be relegated to "secondary contradictions" (Omi and Winant 2014; Hill Collins 1990). Marx's general insights about class ideology are still useful and can be extended to the analysis of racism. Thus, *racial ideology* is:

> The racially-based frameworks used by actors to explain and justify (dominant race) or challenge (subordinate race or races) the racial status quo. Although modern societies articulate various forms of hierarchy and, thus, societal ideology encompasses frames from gender, racial, class, and other forms of hierarchical structurations, I focus here on how aspects of the larger "ideological ensemble" play out in the field of race relations. I label these frameworks "racial" albeit I recognize that many (e.g., the frame of abstract liberalism) are used to justify gender and class inequality. (Bonilla-Silva 2003, 65)

Of all the functions of racial ideology, a central one is providing arguments to "account for racial inequality" (Bonilla-Silva 2003, 74). This is a key part of my argument: pandemic-related issues that are framed by color-blind ideologies discount racism or minimize its role.

Several points of clarification are necessary before I proceed. First, ideologies are embedded not only in newspaper articles and speeches by politicians but also in social texts (e.g., films, pictures, etc.). Thus, although I include comments from politicians, I rely heavily on material from popular media as "ideologies are acquired, expressed, enacted and reproduced by discourse" (van Dijk 2006, 124). Second, students of ideology have pointed out that ideological fields are always partial and never "pure" (Irvine 2019). Rarely do ideological expressions exclusively represent the dominant group's views—they usually incorporate some ideas from subordinated groups (Poulantzas 1978). Second, as racial ideology is often articulated within ideological items expressive of other social divisions or wedged in generic arguments (Hall 1986), most of the material analyzed here does not reflect specific discussions on race. Yet, I will show that race looms large in these seemingly non-racial discussions. Last, in any ideological formation, various gender, class, or racial ideological iterations coexist. In contemporary America, most White people espouse color-blindness. However, a segment clearly does not, including President Trump, who has a long history of overtly racist statements and practices (Bonilla-Silva 2019a) that he continued dispensing during and after his term (from labeling COVID-19 as the "Chinese virus" to advocating a Nixon-like "law and order" approach to deal with Black Lives Matter protesters).

### Praise for "Our Heroes"

Stories about heroes during this pandemic are ubiquitous. Companies like Kraft-Heinz, Budweiser, Amazon, and Walmart have all produced commercials or symbols heralding "essential workers" as heroes. These advertisements are broadcasted on a variety of mainstream networks. Cable news anchors salute "our heroes" and the print media bears headlines such as, "Heroes of the Front Lines: Stories of the courageous workers risking their own lives to save ours" (*Time* 2020). A writer of a piece about cartoonists celebrating "the heroes amid the pandemic" stated the core elements of this framing:

> Companies and community members at all levels are celebrating and elevating these unsung heroes in countless ways: Some are donating personal protective equipment, giving them free products or offering free meals. Others are simply saying thank you to those continuing to work. Residents, streamers and students around the Bay Area have united to collect hand sanitizer for local shelters, hospices and jails, create masks for hospital workers or donate money to international groups aiding other countries fighting the pandemic. (Bouscher 2020)

One of the cartoons accompanying the story depicts a "Supernurse" (a White woman dressed as Superman) flying a frail man away from the virus while another echoes the iconic image of Iwo Jima, featuring a White-looking scientist, nurse, doctor, and first responder symbolically planting an American flag (Bouscher 2020). While there is no question that "essential workers" deserve praise, labeling them as "heroes" clouds our vision. *Our economy and our health care system cannot depend on "heroes," particularly when so many of them are workers of color.* Instead of hailing their heroic efforts, state and corporations must provide workers with the necessary protection to safely fulfill their jobs, as well as adequate pay for their sacrifices. Framing these workers as "heroes" makes us less likely to empathize with and support those who choose to strike, protest, or remain absent from work during the pandemic. Nurses, for example, are organizing and filing complaints to OSHA, and delivery workers at Amazon and Instacart threatened to strike unless they receive adequate protection, sick leave, and hazard pay (DeSantis 2020).

Protests from these essential workers are already happening and will likely increase.[3] As recent cases have shown, when "heroes" do not behave according to our archetypal notion of heroism, they become villains. For example, ten nurses at Providence Saint John's Health Center in Santa Monica, California, were suspended after refusing to enter coronavirus patient rooms before being supplied with N95 masks (Murphy 2020). Hospital management justified

---

**3** According to recent reports, approximately 39% of healthcare workers are making plans to leave the profession (Clinician of the Future Report 2022).

the suspension by citing, "[Nurses'] refusal to treat the patients," which "constituted abandonment and negligence" (Murphy 2020). The hospital management's statement exemplifies how the hero framework deflects responsibility and blames workers:

> We are so grateful for the heroic work our nurses perform each day and will not let the actions of a few diminish the appreciation we have for all our nurses and their commitment to our community. . . . Saint John's cherishes its nurses and is taking precautions sanctioned by leading world, national, state and local health agencies to ensure their safety. (Baker 2020)

How is color-blind racism shaping the discussion of "our heroes"? Heroes, particularly those more exposed to the virus, are *disproportionally* workers of color, even though this fact is rarely discussed in the media. Our racialized class structure places Black and Brown workers in higher-risk jobs for COVID-19 exposure than White workers. Black and Brown workers are 50 percent of the janitors, the bulk of the nurses in supportive positions (who are more exposed to hazardous conditions and receive less protection), 44 percent of construction workers, 50 percent of correctional officers, 52 percent of bus drivers, and a whopping 70 percent of the graders and sorters of agricultural products (i.e., these are the workers at Tyson, Smithfield, JBS, and other meatpacking companies) (Bureau of Labor Statistics 2020b). The abstract liberal way we discuss "our heroes" blinds us to how people of color are overwhelmingly in these positions, preventing the deeper question to surface: why are workers of color overrepresented in dangerous, low-paying jobs in the first place? This praise from corporations, politicians, and celebrities *naturalizes* the racial status quo.

One occupation that clearly shows the high exposure of workers of color to the virus is phlebotomy, as 50 percent of phlebotomists are Black and Latino. Their job is to draw blood from patients, and during the pandemic, many have been asked to "volunteer" to do coronavirus testing (Velasquez-Caldera 2020). Due to their high rates of exposure to fluids and people, phlebotomists have a higher-than-average rate of exposure to the virus.

Adding testing for COVID-19 to their duties, which required quick training because "prior to the pandemic, only nurses and doctors were allowed to do the swabbing" (Velasquez-Caldera 2020), has made their job even more dangerous without adequate compensation (median pay is $35,000) (Bureau of Labor Statistics 2020a).

The level of exposure to the virus is even higher for bus drivers, janitors, and workers in the meatpacking industry—all occupations with very high representations of workers of color. Hence, rather than admiration, salutes from our porches and windows, or a "Good Job" song by Alicia Keys, what all essential workers need, but particularly workers of color, are masks, hazard pay, sick leave, and higher wages. The virus has exposed the detrimental impacts of our limited, highly racialized welfare state, which has left large segments of society vulnerable to health and economic disasters (Ward 2005). Further, the burden of long-COVID will also fall disproportionately upon those with the least resources. This erosion was catapulted by the highly racialized politics of the 1980s and 1990s when the image of the "welfare queen" and the notion of "welfare dependency" were pushed by Republicans and Democrats (Quadagno 1994). Accordingly, the kryptonite debilitating our *true* superheroes—essential workers of color—is not the virus, but years of anti-government, neoliberal, racialized rhetoric, and structural racism.

## "Donate to Feeding America's Coronavirus Fund"

The title for this section comes from the website of Feeding America, the nation's "largest domestic hunger-relief organization" (2020). Almost two weeks after the United States initiated social distancing measures to mitigate the spread of the virus, non-essential workers began to lose their jobs. In April 2020, the US unemployment rate reached a staggering 14.8%, the highest rate observed since 1948 (Congressional Research Service 2021). Adding underemployed workers to the mix, early in the pandemic saw that the number of food-insecure Americans skyrocketed to about 30 percent of the working class and, for workers of color, an even higher proportion![4]

---

4 Estimates of the rate of underemployment place it at about 100 percent of the general unemployment rate since 1994. But that rate is racially stratified as Latinos have experienced a rate that has been about 80 percent higher than

In response, the media, churches, and other organizations have blanketed the airwaves with stories about food banks serving two to six times more clients than usual. These stories are heart-wrenching and invariably end with reporters or organizations asking viewers for donations. The precarious condition of workers in America is such that many of those deemed "non-essential" are now food insecure and rely on food banks. Food insecurity, however, is not due to the virus. Between 12 to 15 percent of households have been food insecure for a long time and the rate has been much higher for households of color. According to Odoms-Young (2018), the rate of food insecurity for White people fluctuated between 7 percent to 10 percent in the 2001–2016 period, but 17 percent to 27 percent for Black and Latino/a Americans. This is why hunger is a racial equity issue (Nitschke 2017).

Framing hunger as a charity matter derails us from thinking about why workers were out of food after just a few weeks of unemployment, why there were such high levels of food insecurity *before* the pandemic, and more significantly for my discussion, the fact that hunger is also a racialized affair. COVID-19 discussions of hunger universalize this issue through abstract liberalism, but this issue is directly related to structural racism. A quarter of households of color were food insecure before the pandemic hit, and this rate has likely increased since the pandemic began. The racialized facts around food insecurity will require in the short-term race-targeted, creative approaches to help those most affected by the pandemic.[5]

The United States is food insecure despite being one of the most powerful, developed nations in the world because wealth and income inequality have returned to Gilded Age levels. In 1929, the Gini Coefficient

---

Whites and Blacks at 100 percent. If the unemployment rate today is 16 percent to 18 percent, then it is safe to extrapolate that more than 30 percent of workers of color are food insecure (Nunn, Parsons, and Shambaugh 2019).

**5** Latinos are twice as likely as Whites to live in households without vehicles (12.0 percent compared to 6.5 percent) and Blacks are three times as likely (19.7 percent) (National Equity Access 2020). Thus, depending on food banks to distribute food may not help equally all households in need of food. On this, as with many other policies, what is needed are "targeted universal" polices so that all in need benefit from the policy. To be equitable, the policy should be calibrated by need (those who need more should get more) (Powell, Menendian, and Ake 2019).

was 49.91, and by 2018, after decades of staying in the thirties, it increased to 48.22 (Atkinson et al. 2017; DePrieto 2020). Data on inequality is telling: Whereas "S&P 500 firm CEOs were paid 278 times as much as average US workers in 2018," (Income Inequality 2020) restaurant servers, to use one relevant example, hardly improved their earnings since the early 1990s and their federal minimum wage has remained stagnant at $2.13 (Income Inequality 2020).

A 2019 study revealed that about 40 percent of Americans do not have enough savings (a minimum of $400) to deal with an emergency (Board of Governors of the Federal Reserve System 2020). This figure does not show racial disparities in liquid savings, and it is estimated that whereas "the typical household had . . . 31 days of income in such savings, the typical Black household had just five days' worth" (Currier and Elmi 2018). The billionaire class that Bernie Sanders talked about during his presidential campaign run is real and cannibalizing everyone. Three members of this class—Jeff Bezos, Bill Gates, and Warren Buffett—own more assets than the bottom half, and the top 1 percent owns more than half of the entire stock market (Income Inequality 2020). Shamefully, the wealth of the billionaire class has increased by at least 10 percent (close to three hundred billion dollars) between January 1, 2020, and April 10, 2020 (Collins, Ocampo, and Paslaski 2020). As is the case with almost all data on inequality, the gaps are larger for families of color. For example, in 2016, 37 percent of Black and 33 percent of Latino/a families had zero wealth, compared to 15.5 percent of White families (Collins, Ocampo, and Paslaski 2020).

Racial disparities in food insecurity are a direct reflection of the general trends in racial inequality: higher rates of unemployment and underemployment, less wealth, poor access to retirement plans (older folks of color are poorer than their White counterparts), and access to grocery stores (Nitschke 2017). The charity framing leads people to pity the less fortunate, which may be a good thing, but it also absolves the government and businesses from responsibility. After all, if the state enforced a "living wage" across the nation, had programs to deal with unemployment and a decent safety net, adequately taxed the rich, and implemented race-targeted programs on a variety of areas (e.g., employment, education, wealth, etc.), we would not have hunger in

America.[6] Hunger is the outcome of the lack of democracy and the concentration of power in the hands of the few (Moore Lappé and Collins 2015). Therefore, *charity is not the fundamental way of addressing hunger or of closing the racial gap in food insecurity.*

## "It's Very Sad. It's Nothing We Can Do About It Right Now..."

The heading for this section comes from a statement made by Dr. Anthony Fauci at a press conference where Donald Trump and his Coronavirus Task Force acknowledged racial mortality disparities (Hellmann 2020). The subject of racial health disparities extending beyond the pandemic has garnered media attention and was heightened by statements by Trump and his officers. In a press conference, Trump pondered the huge differences in mortality between Black (and Latino/a and Native Americans)[7] and "other citizens." He said:

> We're seeing tremendous evidence that African Americans are affected at a far greater percentage number than other citizens of our country. But why is it that the African American community is so much, numerous times more than everybody else? We want to find the reason to it. (Trump quoted in Collins 2020)

---

**6** USDA gives out about half a billion dollars of the food distributed by food banks (USDA 2020). However, this amount is less than 10 percent of the total amount of food distributed and needed by banks (Bouek 2010), the food USDA purchases benefits large companies and are done at the expense of programs such as SNAP (Charles 2020), and the investment pales in comparison to government's corporate welfare, which usually supersedes social welfare by about 50 percent (Reich 2019).

**7** States and the CDC are not reporting Native American mortality due to COVID-19 and reports suggest their mortality rate is among the highest in the nation (Nagle 2020). The "health preconditions" of Native Americans living on reservations (about a quarter of Native Americans) are worse than those of any other group in America. This situation, combined with overcrowding, lack of sanitation, and extreme poverty, will likely lead to a repeat of the 1918 influenza in which nations such as the Navajo experienced a 12 percent mortality rate (Brady and Bahr 2014).

Although it is very important for the media to cover racial disparities in morbidity and mortality due to COVID-19, by not offering an adequate explanation for these disparities, we were left with the quasi-explanations from members of Trump's Task Force such as Dr. Fauci, Ben Carson, Surgeon General Jerome Adams, and other media personalities.[8] Their comments converge on one point: Black and Brown people are viewed as unhealthy, which naturalizes their health preconditions. To be clear, these (non)explanations are thrown into fertile soil as White people already believe that people of color's (I have labeled this perspective the "biologization of culture" as it presents culture as immutable) culture and biology were different from theirs (Graves 2001). Color-blindness is a curious standpoint as White people can claim that race is largely irrelevant while at the same time believe that race is biology ("All Black people are . . .") or reified in culture ("They don't have jobs because they are lazy").

An example of these (non)explanations comes from Dr. Fauci:

> As Dr. [Deborah] Birx said correctly, it's not that they are getting infected more often, it's that when they do get infected, their underlying medical conditions—the diabetes, hypertension, the obesity, the asthma—those are the kind of things that wind them up in the ICU and ultimately give him a higher death rate. (Nelson 2020)

This statement reifies the deficiency narrative and opens the door for racist "culture of poverty" discourses (Cunningham and Scarlatto 2018). Similarly, in a very telling moment, Surgeon General Adams said:

> Avoid alcohol, tobacco, and drugs. And call your friends and family. Check in on your mother; she wants to hear from you right now . . . . And speaking of mothers, we need you to do this, if

---

**8** I wrote this article early into the transition from the Trump-to-Biden administration. While one may argue that Biden's administration has done a somewhat better job of communicating these rates to the public, the real numbers are still being tabulated.

> not for yourself, then for your *abuela*. Do it for your granddaddy. Do it for your Big Mama. Do it for your Pop-Pop. We need you to understand—especially in communities of color, we need you to step up and help stop the spread so that we can protect those who are most vulnerable. (Aleem 2020)

This statement was uttered after he had hinted at the social determinants of people of color's preconditions:

> We do not think people of color are biologically or genetically predisposed to get COVID-19. There is nothing inherently wrong with you. But they are socially predisposed to coronavirus . . . and to have a higher incidence of the very diseases that put you at risk for severe complications of coronavirus. (Aleem 2020)

Although Adams, who is Black, began his comments by acknowledging that the disproportionate mortality rates were due to communities of color experiencing the "burden of social ills," by not elaborating on this point, his statement on culture strengthened preexisting racialized interpretations given that this part of his commentary got the most playback in the news.[9] Adams defended his remarks when PBS's Yamiche Alcindor pushed back during the press conference. Dr. Fauci came to Adams's defense after Alcindor's question: "Jerome, you did it beautifully. You can't do it any better than that. I know Jerome personally. I can just testify that he made no—not even a hint of being offensive at all with that comment" (Concha 2020).

Fauci has been heralded for his straight talk during the pandemic, but on this matter, his views are as problematic as those of most White people.

---

**9** A Google search on the media follow-up to Adams's comment revealed that neither critics such as CNN's Bakari Sellers, *Essence*, Congresswoman Maxine Waters, nor supporters such as *The Wall Street Journal*, *The New York Post*, and John McWhorter stressed Adams's comment on the "burden of social ills."

He has not advocated for a *single* policy to address health disparities before, during, or after the pandemic. In contrast, experts on health disparities have urged immediate interventions such as providing hazard pay to workers, reopening the Obamacare exchange, dropping Medicaid work requirements, and reversing plans to allow Medicaid spending caps to reduce the mortality gap (Collins 2020).

Social scientists have addressed how the effects of structural racism affect racial health disparities. They have shown that segregated communities of color endure high levels of pollution, joblessness, poverty, and crime, and that their inhabitants experience higher levels of stress. This "American apartheid" is not natural or by choice, but the product of the racialized practices of banks, realtors, White individuals, and the government (Massey and Denton 1993). At the individual level, the pivotal work of David R. Williams has amply shown that people of color self-report higher levels of exposure to discrimination and this affects their poor health outcomes (Williams and Collins 1995). Yet, as important as it is to assess the health effects of discrimination at the individual level, the most significant effects of racism are structural and do not require intent.

In a more recent review, Yearby (2018) shows how residents of segregated communities of color have less access to healthy food, good hospitals, and playgrounds, and are more exposed to pollution, noise, overcrowded housing, and high rates of crime. The combined effects of these factors in addition to interpersonal discrimination generate chronic racialized stress among people of color, which correlates with poor health outcomes (Goosby, Cheadle, and Mitchell 2018). To be clear, racial segregation and the concentration of poverty and joblessness in communities (the improperly labeled "neighborhood effects") are the product of "ghettoization and racism" (Marable 1983).

It is important to explain how structural racism affects the health of minority populations—especially in disasters such as the current one—because the naturalization of health disparities appears in many guises. For example, Louisiana Senator Bill Cassidy, who is also a doctor, claimed that (emphasis added):

> I think if you control for diabetes and hypertension, a lot of racial difference would go away. And I say that not to dismiss the problem of health disparities. We have to focus on health disparities, *but we can't get distracted by that which is true, perhaps, but unrelated to the problem at hand.* (Doubek 2020)

The "distraction" Senator Cassidy does not want to address is how structural racism creates these disparities. His call for "controlling for" is an important statistical practice, but one often used in race research to obscure huge absolute disparities (Bonilla-Silva and Baiocchi 2001). I must add that in the case of health outcomes, class, whether measured by income, education, or occupation, does not inoculate middle-class people of color from racial health inequalities (Simons et al. 2018). By not addressing the elephant in the room—why do Black, Latino/a, and Native Americans have high rates of obesity, asthma, and hypertension?—statements such as Cassidy's open the door for cultural explanations of racial health disparities (i.e., "They eat the wrong kinds of food, smoke too much, and drink liquor all the time!").

For instance, in CNN's "The Color of COVID," the behavioral explanation raised its ugly head when the former NBA player Charles Barkley said:

> We as Black people, we have to accept the fact there is systematic racism. But that does not give you a reason to go out and be overweight, have diabetes . . . . We got to eat better, we need better access to health care, we need better access to being able to work out, and things like that. But unless we get better health care, which is part of the system, unless we learn to work out better and take better care of our bodies, we are always going to be at a disadvantage. (Regan et al. 2020)

Although Barkley mentioned systemic racism in connection to COVID-19 and claimed he was not blaming poor Black individuals, his narrative reinforced the cultural framework to explain differential mortality. Similar to Barkley, Van Jones (2020), who cohosted the show, stated a week before this program aired that he used his "social justice activism as an excuse to neglect (his) health" and asked Black people "to take more responsibility for (their) individual health choices." People of color are dying disproportionally from COVID-19, not because they are Black, Brown, or Native American or because they use drugs, smoke, eat bad food, and drink more than White Americans (Mack, Jones, and Ballesteros 2017). Rather, their deaths are at the hands of our racialized social system (Bonilla-Silva 1997).

## Discussion

In this chapter, I discussed how several subjects related to the effects of the pandemic are shaped by the major framework of color-blind racism. This framing prevents understanding how structural racism affects people of color, both before and during the COVID-19 pandemic. I showed how these discussions center our attention on individual-level action, culture, or biology and away from the structural causes behind inequality as well as from the need for collective action. We focus our attention on believing that workers should work at all costs,[10] that hunger can be solved by the actions of good Samaritans, and that Black and Brown people are dying at a higher rate than White people because of underlying health conditions and problematic behaviors. Instead of addressing the poor work conditions of essential workers (particularly of workers of color), America's limited welfare state, and systemic racism, we use flowery, feel-good rhetoric. A "feeling good" story works precisely because

---

**10** One of the most egregious cases is meatpacking plants where workers have been for a long time dealing with line speed, high illness rates and injuries, inadequate health units in factories as a 2017 GAO report found (cited in Bagenstose, Chadde, and Wynn 2020). And facing high rates of infection and deaths in these plants, the government's response has been inadequate. Factory workers, unions, and even managers say the federal government—including the US Centers for Disease Control and Prevention and the Occupational Safety and Health Administration—has done little more than issue non-enforceable guidance. On its website, for example, the CDC has released safety guidelines for critical workers and businesses, which primarily promote common-sense measures of sanitization and personal distancing (Bagenstose, Chadde, and Wynn 2020).

we are in the middle of a horrid pandemic that has taken the lives of over 100,000[11] people; it works because Americans, perhaps more than most people in the world, have been conditioned to both "a rugged individualism" foundational myth and, lately, to a self-help cultural logic (McLean and Dixit 2018). As the color-blind–shaped issues I highlighted operate obliquely, they fit the slippery nature of most post–civil rights racial affairs (Bonilla-Silva 2015b).

I limited my examination to three subject areas, but the frameworks of color-blind racism are extending their tentacles in all directions. Thus, I will briefly offer two other examples of color-blindness during the pandemic. First, as I mentioned earlier, the refrain "We are all in this together" has become a normative response to the pandemic. *USA Today*, for instance, has had a running column titled "Coronavirus: We're in This Together" (French 2020) accompanied by a unity graphic. Many media outlets have an equivalent. For example, Fox News uses the more Trumpesque label, "America Together" (Fox News 2020).

Although "community resilience and unity, strengthening of social ties, self-help, heightened initiative, altruism, and prosocial behavior more often prevail" during disasters (der Heide 2004, 341), it is pure fantasy that pain and suffering are equally distributed across all segments of the population. Vulnerable populations—old, rural, poor, undocumented, or people of color—*always* fare worse during disasters and in their aftermaths. The unity framing irons out the tremendous levels of inequality in our nation and screens out concerns about how class, race, gender, and other social divisions exacerbate the pandemic's impacts. How can we believe the pandemic is the "great equalizer" given the huge mortality rates experienced by people of color? If "we are in this together" was not an empty nationalist (Bratta 2009), color-blind slogan, our future, as *Forbes*'s Lisa Fitzpatrick admonished, would "include, plan for and protect our most vulnerable too" (Fitzpatrick 2020).

My second example is how science is being presented as a neutral practice. Pfizer, for instance, has a commercial ("Science will win") where the narrator straightforwardly states this: "Science can overcome diseases, create

---

[11] The number of deaths from COVID-19 has now surpassed one million people in the U.S. The CDC has a tracker with daily updates to give the latest on these numbers: https://covid.cdc.gov/covid-data-tracker/#datatracker-home.

cures and yes, beat pandemics. It has before; it will again" (Snyder Bulik 2020). This framing is pervasive as the media and politicians of all stripes have placed their faith in science as the ticket out of this pandemic. The problem here is that the rationality project of modernity is highly racialized (Barnor 2007). The fact that science and scientists are socially situated cannot be ignored even in the middle of a pandemic. The history of science, particularly in the medical area, was and is plagued with racism (Washington 2008; Duster 2015; Roberts 2011). I already mentioned problems with Drs. Fauci's and Adams's stand on health disparities, and Dr. Birx has shown her political partisanship as she did not rebuke Trump's statements on hydroxychloroquine or injecting disinfectant as potential cures for the virus. Instead, she blamed the media for focusing on these matters rather than moving on (O'Brien 2020).

To be clear, I am not anti-science. Rather, I advocate for a critical engagement of science to address "how power relations of race, class, gender, and imperialism have already shaped the sciences and technologies we have" (Harding 2008, 92). Such a stance might produce a more democratic and inclusive science field (Berg and Lidskog 2018) and limit the likelihood of repeating racialized medicine during this epidemic. However, we already have had two French doctors suggesting testing a potential vaccine in Africa because "there are no masks, no treatment or intensive care, a little bit like it's been done for certain AIDS studies, where among prostitutes, we try things, because we know that they are highly exposed and don't protect themselves" (Rosman 2020).

Nevertheless, as toxic as the color-blind framing of all these issues is, the present multidimensional crisis has opened the largest space in recent history to make demands and frame matters differently.[12] The murder of George Floyd by the Minneapolis police on May 25, 2020, has propelled massive, multiracial mobilizations across the nation and the world. The notion of systemic racism, which surveys consistently showed was alien to White people, has gained currency and is propelling discussions and analyses that were not possible before. Although the "public square" is still controlled by corporations

---

**12** I began work on this paper before the race rebellion began.

(Lutz 2012), the movement has cracked everything giving voice to the ideas, aspirations, and hopes of the racial subaltern. Social protest is advancing alternative perspectives (not just on policing) as their actions are deemed "newsworthy" (Tierney, Bevc, and Kuligowski 2006). In fact, the same media that has been pushing the color-blind framing of the topics discussed here is now frantically producing critical stories on racism in America. These stories have increased exponentially, allowing the public to seriously consider the viability of universal health care, expanded welfare benefits, higher wages, better working conditions, prison reform, defunding the police, and many other policy options that were not in play just a few months ago (Baradaran 2020).

The structural interpretations of race-class issues in the nation seem to be getting a hold of the masses, but at this point, it is unclear if White people realize the *implications* of the arguments. Do the White masses truly understand the concept of "systemic racism"? Do White people appreciate that if people of color experience systemic disadvantages, they experience systemic advantages? And what are White people doing, particularly those who proclaim to be "liberal," to uproot their "deep whiteness" (Bonilla-Silva 2015a)? Are White protesters changing their White network of friends and pondering about their White neighborhoods and churches or are they returning to their segregated lives every night? We had a race rebellion in the 1960s, and once the protest moment ended, the idealistic White people who participated in it quickly morphed into the color-blind racists of today (Caditz 1976). For White people to change their mental and emotional racial map, they must adopt a "feeling of equality" stand (Bonilla-Silva 2019b), and social protest will be key in this process (Piven and Cloward 1977). But the fire this time must be accompanied by a relentless, thorough effort to reimagine *every* aspect of our racialized world. If we seize the moment, then we will no longer have to proclaim something as simple as "Black Lives Matter." Will we become Martin Luther King Jr.'s beloved community or will the raisin need to continue exploding? Stay tuned, as this time, the revolution will definitely be televised.

*A version of this chapter appeared in Bonilla-Silva, Eduardo. "Color-Blind Racism in Pandemic Times."* Sociology of Race and Ethnicity, *(July 2020)*. https://doi.org/10.1177/2332649220941024. © *American Sociological Association 2020. Reprinted with permission of SAGE Publishing.*

## References

Aleem, Zeeshan. "The Problem with the Surgeon General's Controversial Coronavirus Advice to Americans of Color." *Vox*, April 11, 2020, https://www.vox.com/2020/4/11/21217428/surgeon-general-jerome-adams-big-mama-coronavirus.

Atkinson, Tony, Joe Hasell, Salvatore Morelli, and Max Roser. "The Chartbook of Economic Inequality." https://www.chartbookofeconomicinequality.com/about/.

Bagenstose, Kyle, Sky Chadde, and Matt Wynn. "Coronavirus at Meatpacking Plants Worse Than First Thought, *USA Today* Investigation Finds." *USA Today*, April 22, 2020, https://www.usatoday.com/in-depth/news/investigations/2020/04/22/meat-packing-plants-covid-may-force-choice-worker-health-food/2995232001/.

Baker, Sinéad. "10 Nurses Were Suspended from a California Hospital for Refusing to Treat Coronavirus Patients Without N95 masks." *Business Insider*, April 17, 2020, https://www.businessinsider.com/10-california-nurses-suspended-refusing-to-work-without-n95-masks-2020-4.

Baradaran, Mehrsa. 2020. "Unsanitized: A Crisis to End All Crises: How Our Response to the Coronavirus Can Inform Our Ongoing Challenges." March 29. The American Prospect. https://prospect.org/coronavirus/unsanitized-a-crisis-to-end-all-crises/.

Barnor, Hesse. "Racialized Modernity: An Analytics of White Mythologies." *Ethnic and Racial Studies* 30, no. 4 (2007): 643–663.

Berg, Monika, and Rolf Lidskog. "Deliberative Democracy Meets Democratised Science: A Deliberative Systems Approach to Global Environmental Governance." *Environmental Politics* 27, no. 1 (2018): 1–20.

Board of Governors of the Federal Reserve System. "Report on the Economic Well-Being of US Households in 2018–May 2019." https://www.federalreserve.gov/publications/files/2018-report-economic-well-being-us-households-201905.pdf.

Bobo, Lawrence, and Ryan Smith. "From Jim Crow Racism to Laissez-faire Racism: An Essay on the Transformation of Racial Attitudes in America." In *Beyond Pluralism*, edited by Wendy Katchin, Ned Landsman, and Andrea Tyree, 15–42. Urbana: University of Illinois Press, 1997.

Bonilla-Silva, Eduardo. "Rethinking Racism: Toward a Structural Interpretation." *American Sociological Review* 62, no. 3 (1997): 465–480.

Bonilla-Silva, Eduardo. *White Supremacy and Racism in the Post-Civil Rights Era*. Boulder, CO: Lynne Rienner Publishers, 2001.

Bonilla-Silva, Eduardo. "Racial Attitudes or Racial Ideology? An Alternative Paradigm for Examining Actors' Racial Views." *Journal of Political Ideologies* 8, no. 1 (2003): 63–82.

Bonilla-Silva, Eduardo. "The Invisible Weight of Whiteness: The Racial Grammar of Everyday Life in Contemporary America." *Ethnic and Racial Studies* 35, no. 2 (2012):173–194.

Bonilla-Silva, Eduardo. "More than Prejudice: Restatement, Reflections, and New Directions in Critical Race Theory." *Sociology of Race and Ethnicity* 1, no. 1 (2015a): 73–87.

Bonilla-Silva, Eduardo. "The Structure of Racism in Color-Blind, 'Post-Racial' America." *American Behavioral Scientist* 59, no. 11 (2015b): 1358–1376.

Bonilla-Silva, Eduardo. *Racism Without Racists: Color-Blind Racism and the Persistence of Racial Inequality in America*. Lanham, MD: Rowman and Littlefield, 2017.

Bonilla-Silva, Eduardo. "Feeling Race: Theorizing the Racial Economy of Emotions." *American Sociological Review* 84, no. 1 (2019a): 1–25.

Bonilla-Silva, Eduardo. "'Racists,' 'Class Anxieties,' Hegemonic Racism, and Democracy in Trump's America." *Social Currents* 6, no. 1 (2019b): 14–31.

Bonilla-Silva, Eduardo, and Gianpaolo Baiocchi. "Anything but Racism: How Sociologists Limit the Significance of Racism." *Race and Society* 4 (2001): 117–131.

Bouek, Jennifer W. "Navigating Networks: How Nonprofit Network Membership Shapes Response to Resource Scarcity." *Social Problems* 6, no. 1 (2018): 11–32.

Bouscher, Dylan. 2020. "Coronavirus Cartoons: Honoring Healthcare Workers, the Heroes amid the Pandemic." *The Mercury News*, April 1, 2020, https://www.mercurynews.com/2020/04/01/coronavirus-cartoons-honoring-healthcare-workers-the-heroes-amid-the-pandemic/.

Brady, Benjamin R., and Howard M. Bahr. "The Influenza Epidemic of 1918–1920 Among the Navajos: Marginality, Mortality, and the Implications of Some Neglected Eyewitness Accounts." *American Indian Quarterly* 38, no. 4 (2014): 459–491.

Bratta, Phillip M. "Flag Display Post-9/11: A Discourse on American Nationalism." *The Journal of American Culture* 32, no. 3 (2009): 232–243.

Bureau of Labor Statistics. "Phlebotomists." Accessed April 25, 2020. (2020a) https://www.bls.gov/ooh/healthcare/phlebotomists.htm.

Bureau of Labor Statistics. "Labor Statistics from the Current Population Survey." Accessed April 15, 2020. (2020b) https://www.bls.gov/cps/cpsaat11.htm.

Caditz, Judith. *White Liberals in Transition: Current Dilemmas of Ethnic Integration*. New York: Spectrum Publications, 1976.

Charles, Don. "Food Banks Get the Love, But SNAP Does More to Fight Hunger." *NPR*, May 22, 2020, https://www.npr.org/sections/thesalt/2020/05/22/859853877/food-banks-get-the-love-but-snap-does-more-to-fight-hunger.

Clinician of the Future Report. "Clinician of the Future Report 2022." *Elsevier Health*. Accessed May 19, 2022. https://www.elsevier.com/__data/assets/pdf_file/0004/1242490/Clinician-of-the-future-report-online.pdf.

Collins, Charles, Omar Ocampo, and Sophia Paslaski. *Billionaire Bonanza 2020: Wealth Windfalls, Tumbling Taxes, and Pandemic Profiteers*. Jamaica Plain, MA: Institute for Policy Studies, 2020. https://ips-dc.org/wp-content/uploads/2020/04/Billionaire-Bonanza-2020.pdf.

Collins, Sean. "The Trump Administration Blames COVID-19 Black Mortality Rates on Poor Health. It Should Blame Its Policies." *Vox*, April 8, 2020, https://www.vox.com/policy-and-politics/2020/4/8/21213383/coronavirus-black-americans-trump-administration-high-covid-19-death-rate.

Concha, Joe. "Fauci Defends Jerome Adams's remarks on African American Alcohol, Tobacco Usage Amid Pandemic." *The Hill*, April 10, 2020, https://thehill.com/social-tags/white-house-press-briefing.

Cunningham, Brooke A., and Andre S. M. Scarlatto. "Ensnared by Colorblindness: Discourse on Health Care Disparities." *Ethnicity & Disease* 28, no. 1(2018): 235–240.

Currier, Eric, and Sheida Elmi. "The Racial Wealth Gap and Today's American Dream: Data Suggest Dramatic Differences in Financial Well-being by Race." *Pew Research Center*, February 16, 2018, https://www.pewtrusts.org/en/research-and-analysis/articles/2018/02/16/the-racial-wealth-gap-and-todays-american-dream.

DePrieto, Anthony. "Income Inequality in America Continues Its Inexorable Rise." *Forbes*, July 1, 2020, https://www.forbes.com/sites/andrewdepietro/2020/01/07/income-inequality-rise/#434a90be22a8.

der Heide, Eric Auf. "Common Misconceptions About Disasters: Panic, the 'Disaster Syndrome,' and Looting." In *The First 72 Hours: A Community Approach to Disaster Preparedness*, edited by Margaret O'Leary, 340–381. Lincoln, NE: iUniverse Publishing, 2004.

DeSantis, Rachel. "Amazon and Instacart Workers Are Threatening to Strike—How Are They Avoiding Disaster?" *People*, March 30, 2020, https://people.com/food/amazon-instacart-workers-threatening-strike/.

Doane, Ashley "Woody." "Beyond Color-blindness: (Re) Theorizing Racial Ideology" *Sociological Perspectives* 60, no. 5 (2017): 975–991.

Doubek, James. "The Coronavirus Crisis: Louisiana Sen. Cassidy Addresses Racial Disparities in Coronavirus Deaths." *NPR*, April 7, 2020, https://www.npr.org/sections/coronavirus-live-updates/2020/04/07/828827346/louisiana-sen-cassidy-addresses-racial-disparities-in-coronavirus-deaths.

Duster, Troy. "A Post-genomic Surprise. The Molecular Reinscription of Race in Science, Law and Medicine." *British Journal of Sociology* 66, no. 1 (2015): 1–27.

Feeding America. "Why should you support Feeding America?" Accessed April 1, 2020. https://www.feedingamerica.org/about-us/why-feeding-america.

Fitzpatrick, Lisa. "Coronavirus and the Underserved: We Are Not All in This Together." *Forbes*, April 2, 2020, https://www.forbes.com/sites/lisafitzpatrick/2020/04/02/covid-and-the-underserved-we-are-not-all-in-this-together/#c6de4995a71e.

Fox News. "America Together: Send us your Photos and We'll tell your Story as the Nation Battles Coronavirus." *Fox News*, April 1, 2020, https://www.foxnews.com/us/america-together-send-us-your-photos-and-well-tell-your-story-as-the-nation-battles-coronavirus.

French, Kelley Benham. "Stories Connect Us and Heal Us. These Powerful, Human Stories Offer Some Good News: Our Families, Friends and Neighbors are Moving Forward Amid Coronavirus." *USA Today*, April 9, 2020, https://www.usatoday.com/in-depth/news/2020/04/09/good-news-coronavirus-in-this-together/2955620001/.

Goosby, Bridget S., Jacob E. Cheadle, and Colter Mitchell. "Stress-Related Biosocial Mechanisms of Discrimination and African American Health Inequities." *Annual Review of Sociology* 44 (2018): 319–340.

Graves, Joseph L. *The Emperor's New Clothes: Biological Theories of Race at the Millennium.* New Brunswick, NJ: Rutgers University Press, 2001.

Harding, Sandra. *Sciences from Below: Feminisms, Postcolonialities, and Modernities.* Durham, NC: Duke University Press, 2008.

Hall, Stuart. "Gramsci's Relevance for the Study of Race and Ethnicity." *Journal of Communication Inquiry* 10, no. 2 (1986): 5–27.

Hellmann, Jessie. "White House Acknowledges Coronavirus Disproportionately Taking African American Lives." *The Hill*, April 7, 2020, https://thehill.com/policy/healthcare/491666-white-house-acknowledges-coronavirus-disproportionately-taking-african.

Hill Collins, Patricia. *Black Feminist Thought: Knowledge, Consciousness, and the Politics of Empowerment.* Boston: Unwin Hyman, 1990.

Inequality.org. "Income Inequality." Accessed May 11, 2020. https://inequality.org/facts/income-inequality/.

Irvine, Judith T. "Regimenting Ideologies." *Language and Communication* 6 (2019): 67–71.

Jones, Van. "Van Jones: 'I'm Someone COVID-19 Could Easily Kill. Here Is What I'm Doing About It.'" *CNN*, April 24, 2020, https://www.cnn.com/2020/04/24/opinions/creating-a-pandemic-resistant-black-community-jones/index.html.

Lutz, Ashley. "These 6 Corporations Control 90% of the Media in America." *Business Insider* June 14, 2020, https://www.businessinsider.com/these-6-corporations-control-90-of-the-media-in-america-2012-6.

Mack, Karin, Christopher M. Jones, and Michael F. Ballesteros. "Illicit Drug Use, Illicit Drug Use Disorders, and Drug Overdose Deaths in Metropolitan and Nonmetropolitan Areas—United States." *American Journal of Transplantation* 66, no. 19 (October 20, 2017): 1–12.

Marable, Manning. *How Capitalism Underdeveloped Black America.* Boston: South End Press, 1983.

Massey, Douglas, and Nancy Denton. *American Apartheid: Segregation and the Making of the Underclass.* Cambridge: Harvard University Press, 1993.

McLean, Scott, and Jaya Dixit. "The Power of Positive Thinking: A Hidden Curriculum for Precarious Times." *Adult Education Quarterly* 68, no. 4 (2018): 280–296.

McLellan, David, ed. *Karl Marx: Selected Writings*. Oxford: Oxford University Press, 2000.

Moore Lappé, Frances, and Joseph Collins. *World Hunger: 10 Myths*. New York: Grove Press, 2015.

Murphy, Paul P. "10 Coronavirus-unit Nurses Are Suspended, Potentially for Weeks, for Refusing to Work Without N95 masks." *CNN*, April 17, 2020, https://www.cnn.com/2020/04/17/us/california-coronavirus-nurses-suspended-trnd/index.html.

Nagle, Rebecca. "Native Americans Being Left Out of US Coronavirus Data and Labelled as 'Other.'" *The Guardian*, April 24, 2020, https://www.theguardian.com/us-news/2020/apr/24/us-native-americans-left-out-coronavirus-data.

National Equity Atlas. "Car Access." Accessed April 15, 2020. https://nationalequityatlas.org/indicators/Car_access.

Nelson, Steven. "Anthony Fauci Compares Race Disparities of Coronavirus to AIDS Epidemic." *The New York Post*, April 7, 2020, https://nypost.com/2020/04/07/anthony-fauci-compares-race-disparities-of-coronavirus-to-aids-epidemic/.

Nitschke, Margot. "Factsheet: Hunger If a Racial Equity Issue." Alliance to End Hunger. Accessed May 7, 2020. https://alliancetoendhunger.org/wp-content/uploads/2017/07/Hill-advocacy-factsheet_HUNGER-IS-A-RACIAL-EQUITY-ISSUE_Alliance-to-End-Hunger.pdf.

Nunn, Ryan, Jana Parsons, and Jay Shambaugh. "Race and Underemployment in the US Labor Market." Brookings Institute, 2019.

O'Brien, Connor. "'It Bothers Me That This Is Still in the News Cycle,' Birx Says of Trump's Disinfectant and Light Comments." *Politico*, April 26, 2020, https://www.politico.com/news/2020/04/26/birx-trump-disinfectant-coronavirus-209063.

Odoms-Young, Angela. "Examining the Impact of Structural Racism on Food Insecurity: Implications for Addressing Racial/Ethnic Disparities." *Family & Community Health* 41 (Apr–Jun 2018): S3–S6.

Omi, Michael, and Howard Winant. *Racial Formation in the United States*. New York: Routledge, 2014.

Piven, Frances, and Richard A. Cloward. *Poor People's Movements: Why They Succeed, How They Fail.* New York: Vintage Books, 1977.

Powell, John, Stephen Menendian, and Wendy Ake. "Targeted Universalism: Policy & Practice." *Haas Institute for a Fair and Inclusive Society.* https://www.haasinstitute.berkeley.edu/targeteduniversalism.

Poulantzas, Nicos. *Political Power and Social Classes.* London: Verso, 1978.

Quadagno, Jill S. *The Color of Welfare: How Racism Undermined the War on Poverty.* Oxford: Oxford University Press, 1994.

Regan, Helen, Jenni Marsh, Laura Smith-Spark, Fernando Alfonso III, and Amir Vera. "April 19 Coronavirus News." *CNN* Accessed April 19, 2020. https://www.cnn.com/world/live-news/coronavirus-pandemic-04-19-20-intl/h_13609268cd74568529be87d071584f60.

Reich, Robert. "How Corporate Welfare Hurts You." *American Prospect,* July 23, 2019, https://prospect.org/economy/corporate-welfare-hurts/.

Roberts, Dorothy. *Fatal Invention: How Science, Politics, and Big Business Re-create Race in the Twenty-first Century.* New York: New Press, 2011.

Rosman, Rebecca. "Racism Row as French Doctors Suggest Virus Vaccine Test in Africa," *Al Jazeera,* April 4, 2020, https://www.aljazeera.com/news/2020/04/racism-row-french-doctors-suggest-virus-vaccine-test-africa-200404054304466.html.

Simons, Ronald, Man-Kit Lei, Steven Beach, Ashley Barr, Leslie Simons, Frederick Gibbons, and Robert A Philibert. "Discrimination, Segregation, and Chronic Inflammation: Testing the Weathering Explanation for the Poor Health of Black Americans." *Developmental Psychology* 54, no. 10 (2018): 1993–2006.

Snyder Bulik, Beth, "Pfizer Promotes Prescription Drug Help and the Power of Science in New TV Ads Aimed at COVID-19 Concerns." *Fierce Pharma,* April 21, 2020, https://www.fiercepharma.com/marketing/pfizer-promotes-prescription-drug-help-and-science-power-messages-new-tv-ads-aimed-at.

Tierney, Kathleen, Christine Bevc, and Erica Kuligowski. "Metaphors Matter: Disaster Myths, Media Frames, and Their Consequences in Hurricane Katrina." *Annals of the American Academy of Political and Social Science* 604, no. 1 (2006): 57–81.

*Time.* "Heroes of the Front Lines: Stories of the Courageous Workers Risking Their Own Lives to Save Ours." *Time.* Accessed May 10, 2020. https://time.com/collection/coronavirus-heroes/.

USDA. "The Emergency Food Assistance Program." Accessed April 1, 2020. https://www.fns.usda.gov/tefap/emergency-food-assistance-program.

van Dijk, Teun. "Ideology and Discourse Analysis." *Journal of Political Ideologies* 11, no. 2 (2006): 115–140.

Velasquez-Caldera, Vivian. "I Work at a Coronavirus Drive-thru Testing Site in New York. Here's What a 12-hour Shift Looks Like." *CNBC Make it*, March 26, 2020, https://www.cnbc.com/2020/03/26/working-at-coronavirus-drive-thru-testing-site-new-york.html.

Ward, Deborah E. *The White Welfare State: The Racialization of US Welfare Policy*. Ann Arbor: University of Michigan Press, 2005.

Washington, Harriet. *Medical Apartheid: The Dark History of Medical Experimentation on Black Americans from Colonial Times to the Present*. New York: Harlem Moon, 2008.

Williams, David, and Collins, Chiquita. "US Socioeconomic and Racial Differences in Health: Patterns and Explanations." *Annual Review of Sociology* 21 (1995): 349–386.

Yearby, Ruqaiijah. "Racial Disparities in Health Status and Access to Healthcare: The Continuation of Inequality in the United States Due to Structural Racism." *American Journal of Economics and Sociology* 77, no. 3–4 (2018): 1113–1152.

CHAPTER 4

# ACTUAL RACIAL/ETHNIC DISPARITIES IN COVID-19 MORTALITY FOR THE NON-HISPANIC BLACK POPULATION COMPARED TO NON-HISPANIC WHITE POPULATION IN 35 US STATES AND THEIR ASSOCIATION WITH STRUCTURAL RACISM

*Michael Siegel*

*Isabella Critchfield-Jain*

*Matthew Boykin*

*Alicia Owens*

NO COUNTRY IN THE WORLD HAS suffered a greater burden from COVID-19 mortality than the United States of America, which had experienced 534,000 deaths as of mid-March 2021, accounting for 19.6 percent of the worldwide total (Johns Hopkins University and Medicine 2021). Within the United States, the burden of COVID-19 death has not been experienced equally by all racial/ethnic groups. People who are Black are dying from COVID-19 at 3.6 times the rate of people who are White, and people who are Hispanic, non-Hispanic American Indian/ Alaska Native, and non-Hispanic Asian/Pacific Islander are also experiencing disproportionately high COVID-19 mortality rates (with death rate ratios compared to the White population of 2.8, 2.2, and 1.6, respectively) (Bassett, Chen, and Krieger 2020). While racial disparities in health outcomes have always existed, COVID-19 has brought the starkness of these disparities to the public eye in a uniquely visible way (Lee and Ahmed 2021). In turn, the pandemic has focused attention on the potential role of structural racism in creating and exacerbating racial disparities in health. Although many studies have investigated the overall national racial disparity in COVID-19 mortality, few have explicitly compared race-specific mortality rates within states. Similarly, although many studies have suggested a role for structural racism in explaining these disparities, few have empirically demonstrated such a connection by attempting to actually quantify structural racism as a specific measure.

Most existing studies that have demonstrated racial disparities in COVID-19 mortality have done so in one of three ways: (1) showing that the number of people in specific racial/ethnic groups dying from COVID-19 exceeds their representation in the overall population (Tirupathi et al. 2020; Raine, Liu, Mintz, Wahood, Huntley, and Haffizulla 2020); (2) demonstrating that the percentage of a non-White racial/ethnic group in a county, city, or neighborhood significantly predicts the overall COVID-19 death rate in that county, city, or neighborhood (Figueroa et al. 2021; Cyrus et al. 2020; Adhikari et al. 2020; Khanijahani 2020; Mahajan and Larkins-Pettigrew 2020; Kim and Bostwick 2020; Millett et al. 2020; Figueroa Wadhera, Lee, Yeh, and Sommers 2020; Hamman et al. 2021; Akanbi, Rivera, Akanbi, and Shoyinka 2020; Strully, Yang, and Liu 2020; Do and Frank 2020; Cheng, Sun, and Monnat 2020; Feinhandler, Cilento, Beauvais, Harrop, and Fulton 2020; Richmond et al. 2020; DiMaggio, Klein, Berry, and Frangos 2020; Liao and DeMaio 2021; Karmakar, Lantz, and Tipirneni 2021; Anaele, Doran, and McIntire 2021); and (3) quantifying death rates among individual patients of different racial/ethnic groups in clinical settings such as hospitals, health systems, or regional or national registries (Igedegbe et al. 2020; Muñoz-Orice et al. 2020; Vahidy et al. 2020; Poulson et al. 2020; Cromer et al. 2020). Surprisingly, only a limited number of studies have explored racial disparities in COVID-19 mortality by explicitly calculating and comparing death rates across racial/ethnic groups. Of these, only a few considered the age distribution of the population by generating age-specific mortality rates.

Age is perhaps the single most important predictor of COVID-19 mortality (Wrigley-Field, Garcia, Leider, Robertson, and Wurtz 2020). Because different racial/ethnic groups have different population age distributions, comparing crude COVID-19 death rates can be dangerously misleading. For example, in Minnesota, people who are White account for 80 percent of the population and 82 percent of COVID-19 deaths, suggesting that there is no racial disparity (Wrigley-Field et al. 2020). However, after adjusting for age, the Black population was found to have COVID-19 death rates that were 5.3 times higher than the White population (Wrigley-Field et al. 2020). The misleading impression from the crude death rate comparison could be dangerous because it may lead to the conclusion that there is no need to address racial disparities and therefore no need to examine deeply underlying structural conditions that have made one racial group more than five times more likely to die from this virus. Similarly, another study found that among four academic hospitals in Atlanta, the odds of Black patients dying from COVID-19 were actually lower than those of non-Black patients (the death rate ratio was 0.9) (Wiley et al. 2021). However, after adjusting for age, Black patients were 1.5 times more likely to die. Because the Black population tends to be younger than the White population, unadjusted COVID-19 death rate disparities are underestimates of the true disparities (Ford, Reber, and Reeves 2020; APM Research Lab 2021). The American Public Media (APM) Research Lab has demonstrated that while the ratio of crude national COVID-19 death rates among Black people compared to White people is just 1.4, the ratio is 2.3 after indirect age standardization (APM Research Lab 2021).

Perhaps the most widely used tool to understand racial disparities in COVID-19 mortality is the COVID-19 Racial Data Tracker (COVID Tracking Project and the Boston University Center for Antiracist Research, 2021). While this is an immensely useful tool, it is limited because it does not present age-adjusted death rates. Thus, the racial disparities presented by the tracker are greatly underestimated. For example, the Racial Data Tracker reports that Black people in Minnesota make up 6 percent of the population, but account for only 5 percent of COVID-19 deaths, making it appear that there is no racial disparity (COVID Tracking Project and the Boston University Center for Antiracist Research 2021). However, as shown earlier, after accounting for age, the Black population in Minnesota is dying at a rate that is more than five times higher than that of the White population (Wrigley-Field et al. 2020). This demonstrates the critical need for studies that compute and compare age-adjusted COVID-19 death rates across racial groups.

Several previous studies have examined racial disparities in COVID-19 mortality using crude death rates (Abedi et al. 2020; Anyane-Yeboa, Sato, and Sakuraba 2020; Parcha et al. 2020; Boserup, McKenney, and Elkbuli 2020). Two studies reported national, race-specific COVID-19 mortality rates without age adjustment (Abedi et al. 2020; Anyane-Yeboa et al. 2020). Two presented state-specific estimates of the crude COVID-19 mortality rate by racial/ethnic group (Parcha et al. 2020; Boserup et al. 2020). We are aware of only three papers that have calculated age-adjusted, race/ethnicity-specific COVID-19 death rates (Bassett et al. 2020; Goldstein and Atherwood 2020; Gross et al. 2020). Bassett et al. (2020) reported that nationally, the age-adjusted COVID-19 death rate for the non-Hispanic Black population was 3.6 times higher than for the non-Hispanic White population. This study is limited, however, because it only presents national data. Goldstein and Atherwood (2020) reported that on a national level, the Black population had an 80 percent higher age-adjusted COVID19 mortality rate than the White population. Their estimate of the racial disparity is much lower than that of Bassett et al. because they used indirect rather than direct age standardization. This study also presents state-specific estimates of the racial disparity in COVID-19 mortality based on indirectly age-standardized death rates. Gross et al. (2020) also present state-specific estimates of racial disparities in COVID-19 mortality rates using indirect age standardization. The APM Research Lab also provides state-specific estimates of racial disparities in COVID-19 death rates using indirectly standardized rates (APM Research Lab 2021). A summary of the previous studies that have presented state-specific estimates of the Black-White racial disparity in COVID-19 mortality rates is shown in Figure 4.1.

**Figure 4.1** Summary of previous studies that presented state-specific estimates of COVID-19 mortality rates among the non-Hispanic Black and non-Hispanic White or Black and White populations

| Study | Description | Age standardization |
|---|---|---|
| Parcha et al., 2020[36] | Analyzes ratio of crude COVID-19 mortality rates for the Black compared to White population (regardless of ethnicity) for 40 states using data from state websites as of August 16, 2020 | None |
| Baserup et al., 2020[37] | Presents crude COVID-19 death rates by state for non-Hispanic Black and non-Hispanic White population in 44 states using COVID-19 Tracking Project data as of July 15, 2020 | None |
| Gross et al., 2020[39] | Presents ratio of crude COVID-19 mortality rates for non-Latinx Black vs. non-Latinx White population in 27 states using data from state websites as of April 21, 2020 | Indirect |
| Goldstein and Atherwood, 2020[38] | Presents ratio of age- and place-adjusted COVID-19 mortality rates for non-Hispanic Black compared to non-Hispanic White population in 32 states using CDC provisional COVID-19 death counts as of May 13, 2020 | Indirect |
| APM Research Lab[32] | Website presents periodically updated age-adjusted COVID-19 death rates for non-Hispanic Black and non-Hispanic White populations in 39 states using both state websites and CDC provisional COVID-19 death counts | Indirect |

The validity of indirect age standardization has been questioned because this method produces only an approximation of the age-specific mortality rates in a state and because it generates rate estimates that cannot necessarily be compared across different locations, such as states (APM Research Lab 2021; Curtin and Klein 2021). The APM Research Lab points out that, "Indirect standardization may deviate more from directly age-adjusted rates when comparing two populations that differ significantly in their age distribution, as race groups may. For this reason, data from individual states that are directly age-adjusted should be considered superior" (APM Research Lab 2021). Therefore, there is an urgent need for a state-level analysis of racial disparities in COVID-19 mortality based on directly age-adjusted death rates. The reason indirect standardization has been used in previous COVID-19 studies is that there has been a lack of state-level data on the age distribution of COVID-19 deaths by race/ethnicity. Recent improvements in reporting, however, make it possible to generate directly standardized rates for most states. This paper helps to fill this critical gap by reporting, for the first time, the magnitude of the Black-White racial disparity in COVID-19 mortality at the state level based on an analysis of age-adjusted death rates using direct age standardization.

With national age-adjusted death rates revealing an even more profound racial disparity in COVID-19 mortality, it is even more crucial to determine the reasons for these disparities. Although many papers have suggested that structural racism is a critical factor in explaining racial disparities in COVID-19 mortality, we are aware of only six that have demonstrated this relationship empirically by explicitly measuring structural racism (Tan, deSouza, and Raifman 2021; Khanijahani and Tomassoni 2021; Cunningham and Wigfall 2020; Li et al. 2020; Yang, Choi, and Sun 2020; Yu et al. 2021). Tan et al. (2021) examined the relationship between four measures of structural racism (residential segregation and differences in incarceration rates, economic status, and employment status) and county-level COVID-19 death rates, finding that the degree of residential segregation was significantly related to higher overall death rates.

However, a limitation of this study was that it did not actually calculate or model race-specific mortality rates. Five other studies examined the relationship between measures of structural racism and overall county-level COVID-19 mortality (Khanijahani and Tomassoni 2021; Cunningham and Wigfall 2020; Li et al. 2020; Yang et al. 2020; Yu et al. 2021). The measures used in these studies were the proportion of individuals living in "Black-concentrated" census tracts (Khanijahani and Tomassoni 2021), implicit and explicit racial attitudes (Cunningham and Wigfall 2020), and racial residential segregation (Li et al. 2020; Yang et al. 2020; Yu et al. 2021). Like Tan et al. (2021), none of these studies modeled race-specific mortality rates.

This study helps to fill this critical gap by explicitly modeling the relationship between measures of structural racism and the Black-White racial disparity in COVID-19 mortality rates. The previous studies examined overall county- or tract-level COVID-19 mortality rates and estimated the effect of various population compositional characteristics, such as the percentage of racial/ethnic subpopulations. Directly modeling disparities in race-specific mortality rates is a preferred approach because the proportion of a certain racial/ethnic group living in a county could be related to any number of factors that might increase the overall risk for COVID-19, including among White people. Thus, finding a relationship between, for example, the percentage of Black people in a county and the overall COVID-19 mortality rate does not necessarily demonstrate that there is a racial disparity. Here, we do not infer such a relationship but measure it directly.

This paper advances the previous literature in a third way: calculating the Black–White disparity in age-standardized death rates among states—in this paper, thirty-five—provides a standard unit of comparison across states, enabling a more pointed exploration of the reasons for these racial disparities. Understanding racial disparities at the state level is imperative because states have the primary responsibility for implementing policies related to the prevention, control, and response to COVID-19 and therefore are directly responsible for the emergence, and amelioration, of racial disparities related to COVID-19 (American Bar Association 2020). In addition, identifying differences in the degree of the racial disparities across states may be enlightening because states have a very different history of their implementation of racist policies (Mesic et al. 2018) that may help explain the cause of the observed racial disparities in COVID-19 mortality today. As Goldstein and Atherwood state: "State-level variation in disparities may help us to understand the causes of disparities in COVID-19 death rates. We find that the highest excess mortality for Blacks is the Deep South and the Upper Midwest, while disparities are smallest in the Northeast and West. Understanding the reasons for this pattern are an important topic for future research" (Goldstein and Atherwood 2020, 9). This paper advances the literature by being the first to explicitly model and investigate the difference in the Black–White disparity in COVID-19 mortality across states, allowing us to investigate whether differences in the level of structural racism across these states help to explain the level of the disparity in health outcomes.

## Methods

*Design Overview*

Using data from the Centers for Disease Control and Prevention's (CDC) National Center for Health Statistics, we calculated both crude and age-adjusted COVID-19 mortality rates for the non-Hispanic White and non-Hispanic Black populations in each state. We defined the Black-White disparity in COVID-19 mortality as the ratio of the age-adjusted death rate among the Black population to the age-adjusted death rate among the White population. Using a previously developed state-level index of structural racism (Mesic et al. 2018), we explored the relationship between this state racism index and the observed differences in the racial disparities in COVID-19 mortality across thirty-five states by conducting linear regression analyses. Also, using linear regression analysis, we explored the potential mediating effects of three variables identified in the literature as possible explanations for observed racial disparities in COVID-19 mortality: disparities in exposure based on occupation; disparities in weathering effects based on the presence of underlying medical conditions that could increase COVID-19 severity; and disparities in healthcare access.

## Measures and Data Sources

*Outcome Variable*

The outcome variable was the Black-White racial disparity in age-adjusted COVID-19 death rates in each state, defined as the ratio of the non-Hispanic Black age-adjusted death rate to the non-Hispanic White age-adjusted death rate. In epidemiology terminology, this is known as the standardized rate ratio (SRR).

Data on confirmed COVID-19 deaths by age, race, and state were obtained from the National Center for Health Statistics' COVID-19 Death Data and Resources (Centers for Disease Control and Prevention 2021). We used the following data sets: (1) Provisional COVID-19 Deaths by Week (State); (2) Provisional COVID-19 Deaths by Sex, Age, and State; (3) Provisional COVID-19 Deaths by Race and Hispanic Origin (State); and (4) Provisional COVID-19 Deaths by Race and Hispanic Origin and Age (State). These data sets, updated weekly, represent provisional counts of COVID-19 deaths from the National Vital Statistics System maintained by the CDC National Center for Health Statistics. These data sets are derived from death certificate information reported directly to the National Center for Health Statistics, which processes, codes, and tabulates the data. At the time we downloaded the data sets, they included a cumulative count of confirmed COVID-19 deaths from February 2, 2020, through November 28, 2020, for each state: total, stratified by age, stratified by race, and stratified by age and race.

We calculated crude COVID-19 death rates for the non-Hispanic White and non-Hispanic Black population by dividing the total number of deaths among that racial group by the population of the racial group. We calculated age-standardized rates using direct standardization with the standard population being the age/race distribution of the United States in 2019. We standardized death rates using six age groups: 0–29, 30–49, 50–64, 65–74, 75–84, and 85+. We chose these age categories to optimize the balance between having enough age strata to generate age-adjusted estimates and having too narrow age strata such that there were missing data and therefore precluding us from generating age-adjusted estimates for certain states. Using these categories, we were able to generate age-adjusted COVID-19 death rates for both the non-Hispanic White and non-Hispanic Black populations in thirty-five of the fifty states (Table 1). There were missing data for deaths of non-Hispanic Black people in some age strata because the CDC suppresses any cell counts less than ten. The fifteen excluded states were all less populated states with small Black populations. Thus, their exclusion should not substantially alter conclusions regarding the relationship between structural racism on the vast majority of Black communities in the United States. In fact, the thirty-five states included in the study account for 97.8 percent of the national non-Hispanic Black American population. Population data by age, race, and state were obtained from the *2019 American Community Survey*.

## Main Predictor Variable

The main predictor variable was the state racism index, which we developed and validated in previous research exploring the relationship between structural racism and racial disparities in fatal police shootings (Mesic et al. 2018; Siegel

2020). The state racism index was adapted from previous scales developed by Wallet Hub (McCann 2017) and by Lukachko et al. (Lukachko, Hatzenbuehler, and Keyes 2014) and was shown to significantly predict differences between states in the Black-White disparity in fatal police shooting rates of unarmed victims (Mesic et al. 2018). The state racism index was listed in the Ford et al. book entitled "Racism: Science and Tools for the Public Health Professional" (see Appendix B: Selected Measures of Racism) (Ford, Griffith, Bruce, and Gilbert 2019). The dimensions in the state racism index are identical to those used by Tan et al. (2021) in their study of structural racism and county-level COVID-19 death rates (residential segregation, incarceration, economic status, and employment status), except that we additionally consider racial disparities in education. Our methods are also similar to those of Chambers et al. (2018), who examined the relationship between structural racism at the county level and birth outcomes, and to those of Liu et al. (2019), who measured structural racism at the county level and related it to maternal morbidity. We consulted the Groos et al. review of methods used to quantify structural racism (Groos, Wallace, Hardeman, and Theall 2018) and confirmed that our approach is consistent with that used in multiple other studies.

Details of the state racism index have been presented elsewhere (Mesic et al. 2018). Briefly, the index measures structural racism at the state level across five dimensions: (1) residential segregation; (2) incarceration; (3) educational attainment; (4) economic indicators; and (5) employment status. The residential segregation dimension consists of two components: (a) the index of dissimilarity, a measure of the differential distribution of two population groups; and (b) the isolation index, a measure of the spatial isolation of one racial group from another. The incarceration dimension has one component: the ratio of the incarceration rate of Black people to the incarceration rate of White people. The educational attainment dimension has one component: the ratio of the proportion of Black people without a college education to the proportion of White people without a college education. The economic dimension consists of three components: (a) the ratio of the proportion of Black people in rental housing to that of White people in rental housing; (b) the ratio of the Black poverty rate to the White poverty rate; and (c) the ratio of median household income for the White population to median household income for the Black population. The employment dimension has two components: (a) the ratio of the Black unemployment rate to the White unemployment rate and (b) the ratio of the Black labor nonparticipation rate to the White labor nonparticipation rate. For each measure, the values across the fifty states are converted into a scale from zero to one hundred. The components are then averaged to obtain a dimension score for each state. Finally, the scores for the five dimensions are averaged to yield the final state racism index. We constructed the state racism index using data from the *2019 American Community Survey* (education, economics, and employment), 2018 national prisoner data from the Bureau of Justice Statistics (incarceration rates) (Bureau of Justice Statistics 2020), and the *2010 Decennial Census* (segregation measures). The index of dissimilarity and the isolation index were calculated for the non-Hispanic White and non-Hispanic Black populations using the census block as the lower-level geographic unit. Details are shown in Figure 4.2.

## Potential Mediating Variables

Although our primary objective was to explore the relationship between structural racism and Black-White disparities in COVID-19 mortality, a secondary aim was to examine potential mediating factors and to investigate whether these factors completely explained any observed association. Therefore, we collected data on racial disparities in several areas that could potentially explain racial differences in COVID-19 effects. We were guided by the work of Garcia et al. (2020), who—in an article on structural racism and the disproportionate impact of the pandemic on Black and Latinx adults—identified three mechanisms through which structural racism may operate to increase the burden of COVID-19 among these racial/ethnic groups: (1) increased risk of exposure (e.g., disproportionate proportion of the population in high-contact essential jobs); (2) weathering processes (disproportionate presence of preexisting health conditions that may exacerbate the impact of COVID-19); and (3) disparities in health care access and quality. We selected variables in each of these three categories that are available at the state level and by race/ethnicity.

**Figure 4.2** Definitions and methods for calculation of the state racism index

| Dimension | Measure | Description |
|---|---|---|
| Exposure risk* | Dissimilarity Index | D = 1/2 SUM [blackpct - Whitepct] * 100, where blackpct is the proportion of the state's Black population living in each block and Whitepct is the proportion of the state's White population living in that block. Values are on a scale from 0-100 with 100 being the most spatially segregated by race. It represents the percentage of Black people who would have to move in order to achieve an equal distribution of White and Black people across all blocks within a state. |
| | Isolation Index | I = 100 - (SUM((blackpct)*(proportionblack)) * 100), where blackpct is the proportion of the state's Black population living in each block and proportionblack is the proportion of people in that block who are Black. Values are on a scale from 0-100 with higher values representing higher levels of segregation. It can be interpreted as the probability a Black person does not share a block area with a White person or as the extent to which Black members of a block are exposed only to one another. |
| | Segregation Index | Average of Dissimilarity Index and Segregation Index |
| Incarceration** | Incarceration Index | Ratio of Black incarceration rate to White incarceration rate for each state. Converted to 0-100 scale. |
| Education | Education Index | Ratio of proportion of Black adults ages 25+ without a college degree to the proportion of White adults ages 25+ without a college degree for each state. Converted to 0-100 scale. |

**Figure 4.2** Definitions and methods for calculation of the state racism index *(continued)*

| Dimension | Measure | Description |
|---|---|---|
| Economic | Poverty Index | Ratio of proportion of Black people living Ratio of proportion of Black people living under the poverty level to the proportion of White people living under the poverty level for each state. Converted to 0-100 scale. |
| | Income Index | Ratio of White median annual household income to Black median annual household income for each state. Converted to 0-100 scale. |
| | Rental Index | Ratio of proportion of Black people in rental housing to proportion of White people in rental housing for each state. Converted to to 0-100 scale. |
| | Economic Index | Average of Poverty Index, Income Index, and Rental Index |
| Employment | Labor Force Participation Index | Ratio of proportion of Black people not participating in the labor force to proportion of White people not participating in the labor force for each state. Converted to 0-100 scale. |
| | Unemployment Index | Ratio of proportion of unemployment rate among Black people to the unemployment Community Survey rate among White people for each state. Converted to 0-100 scale. |
| | Employment Index | Average of Labor Force Participation Index and Unemployment Index |
| Overall State Structural Racism Index | Racism Index | Average of Segregation Index, Incarceration Index, Education Index, Economic Index, and Employment Index |

*Sources:* U.S. Census Bureau - American Community Survey (2019), *U.S. Census Bureau - US Decennial Census (2010), **US Bureau of Justice Statistics - National Prisoner Statistics

## Differential Exposure Due to Occupation

We used race- and state-specific occupational data from the *2019 American Community Survey* (American Community Survey 2019) to derive two estimates of Black-White disparities in occupations that may disproportionately expose workers to COVID-19. First, we calculated the proportion of workers for each racial/ethnic group in "exposed" jobs. Following the classification suggested by Baker et al. (Baker, Peckham, and Seixas 2020), exposed workers included those in health care occupations and those in protective service occupations. Second, we calculated the proportion of workers in "essential" jobs. The categories included here were health care occupations, protective service occupations, food preparation and serving, cleaning and maintenance, personal care and services, construction, repair, production, transportation, and material moving. For each measure, we operationalized the racial disparity as the ratio of the proportion of Black workers in those occupations to the proportion of White workers in those occupations. Details are shown in Figure 4.3.

## Differential Severity of Disease Due to Comorbidities

Using the *2019 Behavioral Risk Factor Surveillance System* (BRFSS) surveys (Centers for Disease Control and Prevention 2019), we calculated the proportion of adults in each state who self-reported the presence of each of the following conditions: hypertension, asthma, heart attack, angina, diabetes, obesity, kidney disease, cancer, stroke, and chronic obstructive lung disease (COPD). We also calculated the proportion of adults who reported any one or more of these conditions and the proportion who reported two or more of these conditions. These calculations were performed separately for the non-Hispanic White population and the non-Hispanic Black population. We estimated the Black-White racial disparity in these comorbidities by dividing the proportion of Black adults with the condition by the proportion of White adults with the condition.

## Differences in Medical Care Due to Insurance Coverage Disparities

Using the 2019 BRFSS surveys (Centers for Disease Control and Prevention 2019), we calculated the race-specific proportion of adults in each state who reported not having health insurance and the proportion who reported not being able to afford medical care at some point in the past year. The Black-White disparity in health care access was defined as the ratio of non-Hispanic Black adults who were not insured or could not afford medical care divided by the proportion of non-Hispanic White adults who were uninsured or could not afford medical care.

## Data Analysis

We began by calculating crude COVID-19 death rates for the non-Hispanic White and non-Hispanic Black population in each state. We then calculated race-specific, age-adjusted COVID-19 death rates and compared these to the unadjusted rates. Next, we conducted linear regression analyses to examine the relationship between the state racism index and differences in the magnitude of the Black-White disparity in age-adjusted COVID-19 death rates across states. We then examined the relationship between each of the three mediating variables and the racial disparity in death rates. Finally, we explored whether including the mediating variables in the same linear regression would nullify the relationship between the state racism index and any observed racial disparities in COVID-19 mortality. Because of the multicollinearity between many of these predictor variables (Figure 4.4), we examined variance inflation factors for these multiple linear regressions and did not draw any inferences from analyses unless all variance inflation factors were below three.

## Sensitivity Analysis

Because the racial disparity in incarceration rates is one component of the state racism index and differences in incarceration rates have been shown to have a direct effect on the likelihood of COVID-19 exposure (Nowotny, Bailey, and Brinkley-Rubinstein 2021), we repeated the analyses with a recalculated state racism index that did not include the incarceration dimension. The finding of an association between this revised racism index and racial disparities in COVID-19 mortality would suggest that any observed relationship between structural racism and differences in the racial disparity in COVID-19 across states was not being driven completely by racial differences in incarceration rates.

**Figure 4.3** Definitions and methods for calculation of the potential mediating variables

| Dimension | Measure | Description |
|---|---|---|
| Disparities in potential exposure (operationalized as the ratio of the proportion of Black workers in each category to the proportion of White workers in each category) | Proportion of workers in jobs with likely exposure | Proportion of workers in the following job categories:<br>Healthcare practitioners and technical occupations (29-0000);<br>Healthcare support occupations (31-0000);<br>and Protective service occupations (33-0000). |
| | Proportion of workers in essential jobs | Proportion of workers in the following job categories:<br>Healthcare practitioners and technical occupations (29-0000);<br>Healthcare support occupations (31-0000);<br>Protective service occupations (33-0000);<br>Food preparation and serving related occupations (35-0000);<br>Building and grounds cleaning and maintenance occupations (37-0000);<br>Personal care and service occupations (39-0000);<br>Construction and extraction occupations (47-0000);<br>Installation, maintenance and repair (49-0000);<br>Production occupations (51-0000);<br>and Transportation and material moving (53-0000). |

**Figure 4.3** Definitions and methods for calculation of the potential mediating variables *(continued)*

| Dimension | Measure | Description |
|---|---|---|
| Disparities in weathering (operationalized as the ratio of proportion of the Black adults with co-morbidities affecting COVID-19 mortality risk to the proportion of White self-reported COPD adults with that co-morbidity)* | Hypertension | Proportion of adults with self-reported hypertension |
| | Asthma | Proportion of adults with self-reported asthma |
| | COPD | Proportion of adults with self-reported chronic bstructive pulmonary diseas |
| | Obesity | Proportion of adults with self-reported obesity |
| | Kidney disease | Proportion of adults with self-reported kidney disease |
| | Cancer | Proportion of adults with self-reported cancer |
| | Heart attack | Proportion of adults with self-reported heart attack |
| | Angina | Proportion of adults with self-reported angina |
| | Stroke | Proportion of adults with self-reported stroke |
| | Any condition | Proportion of adults with 1+ of the above conditions |
| | Two or more conditions | Proportion of adults with 2+ of the above conditions |
| Disparities in health care access (operationalized as the ratio of the proportion of the Black population without access/affordability to the proportion of the White population without access/affordability* | Health insurance | Proportion of the population without health insurance |
| | Health care affordability | Proportion of the population who reported not being able to afford medical care at some point in the past year |

*Sources:* U.S. Census Bureau - American Community Survey (2019), *Centers for Disease Control and Prevention - Behavioral Risk Factor Surveillance System Surveys (2019)

**Figure 4.4** Correlation matrix for main predictor variables

| | State racism index | Black-White disparity in exposed jobs | Black-White disparity in essential jobs | Black-White disparity in any comorbidity | Black-White disparity in health insurance coverage | Black-White disparity in inability to afford healt care |
|---|---|---|---|---|---|---|
| State racism index | 1.00 | | | | | |
| Black-White disparity in exposed jobs | 0.57 | 1.00 | | | | |
| Black-White disparity in essential jobs | 0.45 | 0.56 | 1.00 | | | |
| Black-White disparity in any comorbidity | 0.25 | -0.11 | -0.22 | 1.00 | | |
| Black-White disparity in health insurance coverage | 0.73 | 0.64 | 0.58 | -0.19 | 1.00 | |
| Black-White disparity in inability to afford health care | 0.34 | 0.39 | 0.32 | -0.05 | 0.52 | 1.00 |

## Results

*Descriptive Results*

For all thirty-five states, the Black-White disparity in COVID-19 mortality rates was substantially greater when examining age-adjusted rates compared to crude rates (Figure 4.1). This shows that relying on the crude death rates results in a marked underestimation of the magnitude of the racial disparity in

COVID-19 mortality between the Black and White populations. For example, in eight states, the crude death rates suggested that there was either no disparity or that the Black population was dying from COVID-19 at a lower rate than the White population. After direct age standardization, it became apparent that the COVID-19 death rate for the Black population was higher than that for the White population in all eight states, with the rate ratio ranging from 1.4 to 3.2. Perhaps the most dramatic difference was in Minnesota, where the crude death rates were essentially the same for the Black and White populations, but the age-adjusted rates revealed a marked disparity, with Black Minnesotans dying at a rate 3.2 times greater than White Minnesotans. For the United States overall, the ratio of Black to White crude COVID-19 death rates was 1.6, while the ratio of age-adjusted death rates was 2.7.

The age-adjusted death rate disparity ratios ranged from a low of 1.4 in Oklahoma to a high of 4.5 in Michigan (Figure 4.1). The five states with the highest disparity ratios were Michigan (4.5), New York (3.3), Minnesota (3.2), Florida (3.0), and Pennsylvania (3.0). The five states with the lowest disparity ratios were Oklahoma (1.4), Washington (1.6), Arkansas (1.6), Rhode Island (1.8), and Ohio (1.9).

Among the thirty-five states, the state structural racism index ranged from a low of 25.6 in Kentucky to a high of 72.3 in Wisconsin (Figure 4.5). The five states with the highest racism index were all located in the Midwest or Northeast: Wisconsin (72.3), New Jersey (66.3), Minnesota (62.6), Illinois (61.0), and Connecticut (60.3). The five states with the lowest racism index were all located in the Southeast or West: Kentucky (25.6), Arizona (27.4), Nevada (31.1), Washington (33.0), and Tennessee (33.7). The overall racism index for each state along with the component indices are displayed in Figure 4.5.

## Analytic Results

The five states with the highest Black-White disparity in COVID-19 mortality rates had an average state structural racism index of 52.3, compared to 40.8 for the five states with the lowest disparity (Figure 4.1). The five states with the highest structural racism indices had an average disparity ratio of 2.7, compared to 2.1 for the five states with the lowest racism indices. A scatterplot

**Figure 4.5** Overall state structural racism index and component indices

| State | Racism index | Segregation index | Incarceration index | Education index | Employment index | Economic index | Black/White death rate ratio |
|---|---|---|---|---|---|---|---|
| Alabama | 35.0 | 72.8 | 1.4 | 33.5 | 36.6 | 30.8 | 1.9 |
| Arizona | 27.4 | 44.5 | 21.9 | 36.3 | 16.6 | 17.9 | 2.2 |
| Arkansas | 34.3 | 72.6 | 10.0 | 26.7 | 37.8 | 24.4 | 1.6 |
| California | 53.1 | 60.6 | 67.4 | 79.5 | 44.1 | 13.7 | 2.4 |
| Colorado | 52.7 | 53.0 | 42.3 | 99.7 | 43.7 | 24.8 | 2.7 |
| Connecticut | 60.3 | 63.5 | 69.7 | 100.0 | 30.8 | 37.8 | 2.7 |
| Florida | 35.2 | 66.4 | 16.2 | 56.1 | 19.1 | 18.0 | 3.0 |
| Georgia | 34.9 | 70.3 | 2.1 | 45.0 | 32.2 | 25.1 | 2.1 |
| Illinois | 61.0 | 77.9 | 50.7 | 69.1 | 60.0 | 47.1 | 2.5 |
| Indiana | 41.9 | 68.3 | 19.1 | 29.2 | 50.5 | 42.6 | 2.4 |
| Iowa | 52.4 | 52.7 | 59.5 | 53.1 | 38.6 | 58.1 | 2.5 |
| Kansas | 48.5 | 56.1 | 39.9 | 61.1 | 49.2 | 36.3 | 2.7 |
| Kentucky | 25.6 | 58.9 | 4.2 | 20.6 | 23.3 | 21.2 | 2.1 |
| Louisiana | 41.1 | 74.2 | 11.8 | 40.8 | 42.3 | 36.4 | 2.4 |
| Maryland | 46.7 | 73.2 | 26.9 | 70.4 | 38.5 | 24.4 | 2.6 |
| Massachusetts | 51.5 | 59.6 | 41.9 | 92.8 | 33.0 | 30.2 | 2.1 |
| Michigan | 51.9 | 75.1 | 40.2 | 46.4 | 50.7 | 47.3 | 4.5 |
| Minnesota | 62.6 | 57.5 | 70.8 | 67.1 | 35.9 | 81.4 | 3.2 |
| Mississippi | 39.4 | 74.8 | 0.0 | 34.0 | 45.2 | 42.8 | 2.1 |
| Missouri | 39.3 | 71.9 | 13.8 | 41.7 | 39.3 | 29.6 | 2.1 |
| Nebraska | 58.2 | 61.3 | 63.7 | 52.8 | 69.4 | 43.7 | 2.1 |
| Nevada | 31.1 | 45.8 | 12.4 | 44.1 | 31.8 | 21.6 | 2.6 |
| New Jersey | 66.3 | 70.8 | 100.0 | 90.1 | 38.8 | 31.8 | 2.3 |
| New York | 58.5 | 79.1 | 54.8 | 85.9 | 48.0 | 24.8 | 3.3 |
| North Carolina | 38.6 | 64.3 | 13.5 | 51.6 | 36.1 | 27.7 | 2.4 |
| Ohio | 48.6 | 68.6 | 30.6 | 45.3 | 53.3 | 45.0 | 1.9 |
| Oklahoma | 37.3 | 59.0 | 21.8 | 32.3 | 42.0 | 31.4 | 1.4 |
| Pennsylvania | 53.2 | 72.6 | 49.2 | 50.4 | 52.3 | 41.3 | 3.0 |
| Rhode Island | 50.6 | 54.3 | 60.3 | 59.2 | 43.9 | 35.1 | 1.8 |
| South Carolina | 43.4 | 66.9 | 13.4 | 62.1 | 36.1 | 38.4 | 2.3 |
| Tennessee | 33.7 | 71.1 | 8.4 | 30.1 | 33.0 | 25.7 | 2.1 |
| Texas | 34.7 | 65.0 | 8.5 | 54.7 | 31.0 | 14.2 | 2.0 |
| Virginia | 42.8 | 60.5 | 17.7 | 74.7 | 35.6 | 25.6 | 2.1 |
| Washington | 33.0 | 46.1 | 26.0 | 51.5 | 17.4 | 24.0 | 1.6 |
| Wisconsin | 72.3 | 74.2 | 96.0 | 63.9 | 67.0 | 60.3 | 2.9 |

**Figure 4.6** Crude and Age-Adjusted Racial/Ethnic Disparities in COVID-19 Mortality Rates between the Non-Hispanic Black and Non-Hispanic White Populations (N=35 states)

| State | Crude | | | Age-Adjusted | | | Racism Index |
|---|---|---|---|---|---|---|---|
| | Black death rate | White death rate | Disparity ratio rate | Black death rate | White death rate | Disparity ratio | |
| Alabama | 114.0 | 88.2 | 1.3 | 142.7 | 73.3 | 1.9 | 35.0 |
| Arizona | 62.4 | 66.5 | 0.9 | 95.9 | 44.1 | 2.2 | 27.4 |
| Arkansas | 80.6 | 86.0 | 0.9 | 110.2 | 69.9 | 1.6 | 34.3 |
| California | 60.9 | 39.5 | 1.5 | 66.7 | 27.6 | 2.4 | 53.1 |
| Colorado | 71.6 | 43.0 | 1.7 | 112.8 | 42.3 | 2.7 | 52.7 |
| Connecticut | 194.8 | 144.0 | 1.4 | 258.0 | 94.4 | 2.7 | 60.3 |
| Florida | 105.3 | 79.6 | 1.3 | 139.2 | 46.0 | 3.0 | 35.2 |
| Georgia | 90.8 | 73.3 | 1.2 | 137.5 | 66.1 | 2.1 | 34.9 |
| Illinois | 129.3 | 79.8 | 1.6 | 151.5 | 61.7 | 2.5 | 61.0 |
| Indiana | 119.1 | 81.9 | 1.5 | 176.3 | 72.8 | 2.4 | 41.9 |
| Iowa | 70.7 | 88.4 | 0.8 | 174.1 | 70.1 | 2.5 | 52.4 |
| Kansas | 88.6 | 58.2 | 1.5 | 125.1 | 47.1 | 2.7 | 48.5 |
| Kentucky | 67.1 | 48.5 | 1.4 | 93.7 | 45.3 | 2.1 | 25.6 |
| Louisiana | 167.0 | 105.5 | 1.6 | 219.3 | 92.2 | 2.4 | 41.1 |
| Maryland | 108.9 | 71.1 | 1.5 | 136.8 | 53.9 | 2.5 | 46.7 |
| Massachusetts | 149.3 | 141.5 | 1.1 | 215.9 | 104.7 | 2.1 | 51.5 |
| Michigan | 193.9 | 62.9 | 3.1 | 230.0 | 51.4 | 4.5 | 51.9 |
| Minnesota | 61.7 | 63.3 | 1.0 | 163.5 | 51.5 | 3.2 | 62.6 |
| Mississippi | 142.8 | 111.2 | 1.3 | 194.1 | 92.3 | 2.1 | 39.4 |
| Missouri | 95.8 | 71.1 | 1.3 | 126.6 | 59.6 | 2.1 | 39.3 |
| Nebraska | 59.7 | 62.5 | 1.0 | 106.4 | 51.9 | 2.1 | 58.2 |
| Nevada | 83.4 | 58.1 | 1.4 | 113.8 | 44.6 | 2.6 | 31.1 |
| New Jersey | 238.8 | 170.5 | 1.4 | 277.1 | 118.7 | 2.3 | 66.3 |
| New York | 288.4 | 145.3 | 2.0 | 308.8 | 94.4 | 3.3 | 58.5 |
| North Carolina | 43.7 | 27.0 | 1.6 | 54.7 | 22.5 | 2.4 | 38.6 |
| Ohio | 70.5 | 56.3 | 1.3 | 87.4 | 46.6 | 1.9 | 48.6 |
| Oklahoma | 47.3 | 60.9 | 0.8 | 66.6 | 48.5 | 1.4 | 37.3 |
| Pennsylvania | 135.3 | 80.4 | 1.7 | 168.2 | 57.0 | 3.0 | 53.2 |
| Rhode Island | 122.5 | 137.2 | 0.9 | 168.2 | 93.2 | 1.8 | 50.6 |
| South Carolina | 116.9 | 75.2 | 1.6 | 141.3 | 62.7 | 2.3 | 43.4 |
| Tennessee | 82.7 | 62.9 | 1.3 | 114.6 | 55.0 | 2.1 | 33.7 |
| Texas | 68.7 | 62.3 | 1.1 | 105.5 | 53.9 | 2.0 | 34.7 |
| Virginia | 68.5 | 47.0 | 1.5 | 84.5 | 40.0 | 2.1 | 42.8 |
| Washington | 25.7 | 32.1 | 0.8 | 44.1 | 27.6 | 1.6 | 33.0 |
| Wisconsin | 78.3 | 61.9 | 1.3 | 143.9 | 49.8 | 2.9 | 72.3 |
| **United States** | **108.9** | **69.0** | **1.6** | **149.3** | **55.1** | **2.7** | — |

The age-adjusted mortality rates were calculated using direct standardization to the 2019 U.S. population.

of this relationship for all thirty-five states showed a pattern of increasing racial disparities as the state structural racism index increased (Figure 4.7). A heat map also showed a pattern of higher racism indices being associated with greater Black-White disparities in age-adjusted COVID-19 death rates (Figure 4.3). The linear regression indicated that for each standard deviation increase in the state racism index, the COVID-19 death rate disparity ratio increased by 0.26 (95% CI, 0.08 to 0.44, P = 0.006) (Figure 4.4). Each of the five separate components of the state racism index was positively associated with the magnitude of the Black-White disparity in COVID-19 death rates, although this relationship was statistically significant only for the incarceration index and the economic index.

In the multivariate analyses, the addition of racial disparities in occupational exposure, comorbidities, and health care insurance or affordability did not substantially alter the relationship between the state racism index and the Black-White racial disparity in COVID-19 mortality (Figure 4.10). In the final model, which controlled for all three of the potential mediating factors, the regression coefficient for the state racism index was 0.29 (95% CI, 0.04–0.54; P = 0.022).

**Figure 4.7** Ratio of Black Age-Adjusted COVID-19 Death Rate to White Age-Adjusted COVID-19 Death Rate as a Function of the State Racism Index. The Racism Index is on a Scale of 0 to 100 with Higher Numbers Indicating a Greater Level of Structural Racism. Mortality Rates Are per 100,000 Population

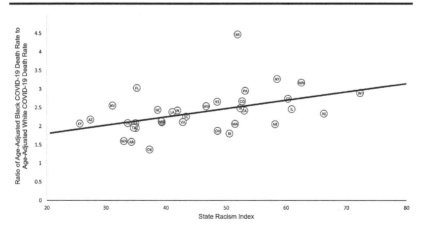

Supplementary material available at https://doi.org/10.1007/s40615-021-01028-1.

## ACTUAL RACIAL/ETHNIC DISPARITIES IN COVID-19 MORTALITY

**Figure 4.8** Heat map showing the state structural racism index in gradations of color with the ratio of the age-adjusted Black COVID-19 mortality rate to the age-adjusted White COVID-19 mortality rate shown in text in the middle of each state.

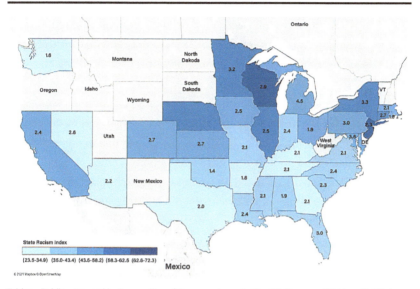

Tableau Public was used in the creation of the map shown in Fig. 4.3. The use of Tableau Public is governed by the terms of service outlined at https://www.tableau.com/tos.

### Sensitivity Analysis

We reran the regressions using a state racism index that did not include the incarceration component. In the bivariate analysis, the regression coefficient associated with a one standard deviation increase in the state racism index was 0.31 instead of 0.26 and remained statistically significant. In the multivariate analysis, the regression coefficient associated with a one standard deviation increase in the state racism index was 0.37 instead of 0.29 and remained statistically significant.

### Discussion

To the best of our knowledge, this is the first paper to quantify the Black-White disparity in COVID-19 mortality at the state level using directly standardized age-adjusted death rates. It is also the first paper to explicitly model the Black-White disparity in COVID-19 mortality at the state level as a function of an empirical measure of structural racism. We found that relying upon crude death rate ratios resulted in a substantial underestimation of the true magnitude of the disparity between Black and White COVID-19 mortality rates. We also found that there is a robust relationship between the state structural racism index and the magnitude of the Black-White disparity in COVID-19 mortality rates. Each standard deviation increase in the racism index was associated with an increase of 0.26 in the ratio of directly age-adjusted COVID-19 mortality rates among the non-Hispanic Black compared to the non-Hispanic White population.

The importance of direct age standardization in examining racial/ethnic disparities in COVID-19 mortality is illustrated by a comparison of our estimate of the Black-White death rate ratio in Minnesota (3.2) to that in previous studies. Two studies that relied upon crude death rates reported ratios of 1.45 (Gross et al. 2020) and 1.7 (Boserup et al. 2020), and one study that relied upon indirectly age-adjusted death rates reported a ratio of 1.4 (Goldstein and Atherwood 2020). The COVID Racial Data Tracker (as of February 2021), which relies upon crude death rate estimates, reported no racial/ ethnic disparity between non-Hispanic Black and non-Hispanic White COVID-19 mortality rates in Minnesota (COVID Tracking Project and the Boston University Center for Antiracist Research 2021). Finally, the APM Research Lab, which uses indirect age standardization, reported a Black-White death rate ratio of 2.1 for Minnesota as of February 2021 (APM Research Lab 2021). We found a similar pattern of underestimation of the Black-White racial disparity in COVID-19 mortality rates for the other states in our study as well.

The most likely explanation for the discrepancy between the crude and age-adjusted estimates of the Black-White disparity in COVID-19 mortality is that life expectancy is lower for Black people compared to White people (Bharmal, Tseng, Kaplan, and Wong 2012); therefore, the age distribution for the Black population is skewed toward lower ages. Since lower age correlates with lower COVID-19 mortality risk, the crude death rate ratios provide an underestimate of the true racial disparities. The lower life expectancy for Black people is itself associated with structural racism; thus, ironically, it is structural racism that explains why the age-adjusted COVID-19 death rate ratios are much higher than the crude ones. In fact, in our data set, the absolute magnitude of the difference between the crude and adjusted death rate ratios is strongly correlated with the state racism index ($r = 0.45$).

**Figure 4.9** Results of Linear Regression Showing Coefficients Representing the Change in the Ratio of Black to White Age-Adjusted COVID-19 Death Rates for Each One Standard Deviation Increase in the State Racism Index and Its Components, 95% Confidence Intervals (CI), and P Values in Bivariate Models (N=35 states)

| Racism index | Regression coefficient | 95% CI | P value |
|---|---|---|---|
| Overall racism index | 0.26 | (.08, .44) | 0.006 |
| Segregation index | 0.19 | (-0.07, 0.45) | 0.140 |
| Incarceration index | 0.18 | (0.02, 0.35) | 0.034 |
| Education index | 0.19 | (-0.01, 0.40) | 0.067 |
| Economic index | 0.25 | (0.01, 0.50) | 0.041 |
| Employment index | 0.15 | (-0.07, 0.37) | 0.178 |

The regression coefficient shows the change in the ratio of Black to White COVID-19 death rates for each one standard deviation increase in the relevant index

While many previous studies have documented the Black-White racial disparity in COVID-19 mortality, this is the first to explicitly model the differences in the level of this racial disparity between states as an outcome variable in an attempt to find factors that explain what one might call the "disparity in the racial disparity" across states. This "disparity in disparities" is quite striking. For example, in Michigan, a Black person is 4.5 times more likely to die of COVID-19 than a White person, while in Oklahoma, a Black person is just 1.4 times more likely to die of COVID-19 than a White person. We have shown that one factor associated with the magnitude of this racial disparity in a state is the level of structural racism in that state. The highest Black-White disparities in COVID-19 mortality rates were observed in the Upper Midwest and the Northeast, precisely those regions that have the highest structural racism indices.

Although six other studies (Tan et al. 2021; Khanijahani and Tomassoni 2021; Cunningham and Wigfall 2020; Li et al. 2020; Yang et al. 2020; Yu et al. 2021) found a relationship between measures of structural racism and racial disparities in COVID-19 mortality at the county level, this paper documents such a relationship at the state level. This finding is important because it is at the state level that most power resides to enact or refine laws related to public health and safety that could directly impact these observed disparities (American Bar Association 2020).

Notably, the robust relationship between the state structural racism index and the state-level Black-White disparity in COVID-19 mortality persisted even after controlling for racial differences in the proportion of the population with various comorbidities, the proportion of workers in essential jobs, or those with high levels of exposure, and the proportion of the population without health insurance or without the ability to pay for health care. This finding is significant because it suggests that the explanation for the observed disparities goes beyond differences in health care access, preexisting health conditions, and the likelihood of exposure. This implies that intervening at the level of the individual (i.e., medical treatment or reducing exposure) or at the level of the health care system (i.e., improving health care access) is not adequate to eliminate racial disparities in COVID-19-related mortality. As structural racism in the United States has been a four hundred–year process of deeply rooted racist practices and sustained inequity, it is important to recognize that changes in underlying economic and political power structures are necessary in order to genuinely abridge racial disparities. It is still important to address downstream consequences of structural racism, such as inequities in health conditions, access, and exposure; however, interventions must dismantle structural racism directly since it is the upstream process, embedded within the culture of the United States, which has created and sustained those inequities. This research suggests that structural racism itself should be considered an underlying cause of COVID-19 racial/ethnic disparities. Thus, it provides empirical data to support the view that structural or institutionalized racism must be viewed as the fundamental or root cause of COVID-19-related racial health disparities (Garcia, Homan, Garcia, and Brown 2020; Churchwell et al. 2020; Yaya, Yeboah, Charles, Out, and Labonte 2020; Gaynor and Wilson 2020; Ford 2020; Maness et al. 2021; Egede and Walker 2020; Milner, Franz, and Braddock 2020; Kullar et al. 2020; Poteat, Millett, Nelson, and Beyrer 2020; Gee 2002).

**Figure 4.10** Results of Linear Regression Showing Coefficients Representing the Change in the Ratio of Black to White Age-Adjusted COVID-19 Death Rates for Each One Standard Deviation Increase in the State Racism Index, 95% Confidence Intervals (CI), P Values, and Variance Inflation Factors (VIF) in Multivariate Models (N=35 states)

| Variables in model | Regression coefficient | 95% CI | P value | VIF |
|---|---|---|---|---|
| **Model 1** | | | | |
| State racism index | 0.26 | (0.04, 0.49) | 0.023 | 1.49 |
| Black-White disparity in exposed jobs | 0.00 | (-0.24, 0.23) | 0.967 | 1.49 |
| **Model 2** | | | | |
| State racism index | 0.30 | (0.09, 0.50) | 0.006 | 1.26 |
| Black-White disparity in essential jobs | -0.25 | (-0.87, 0.37) | 0.416 | 1.26 |
| **Model 3** | | | | |
| State racism index | 0.26 | (0.07, 0.45) | 0.008 | 1.07 |
| Black-White disparity in any comorbidity | -0.02 | (-0.48, 0.44) | 0.925 | 1.07 |
| **Model 4** | | | | |
| State racism index | 0.42 | (0.16, 0.68) | 0.002 | 2.13 |
| Black-White disparity in health insurance coverage | -0.28 | (-0.61, 0.06) | 0.099 | 2.13 |
| **Model 5** | | | | |
| State racism index | 0.30 | (0.11, 0.49) | 0.003 | 1.13 |
| Black-White disparity in inability to afford health care | -0.18 | (-0.49, 0.13) | 0.241 | 1.13 |
| **Model 6** | | | | |
| State racism index | 0.29 | (0.04, 0.54) | 0.022 | 1.79 |
| Black-White disparity in exposed jobs | 0.02 | (-0.24, 0.28) | 0.854 | 1.74 |
| Black-White disparity in any comorbidity | -0.05 | (-0.55, 0.45) | 0.839 | 1.21 |
| Black-White disparity in inability to afford health care | -0.19 | (-0.53, 0.14) | 0.240 | 1.20 |

The regression coefficient shows the change in the ratio of Black to White COVID-19 death rates for each one standard deviation increase in the independent variable

## Limitations

The primary limitation of this study is the limited availability of age-specific and race/ethnicity-specific COVID-19 mortality data in several states. This forced us to limit our analysis to thirty-five states for which sufficient data were provided to generate directly age-standardized death rates. Therefore, our results cannot necessarily be generalized to all fifty states. Similarly, there were data limitations in calculating the racism indices for several states. However, since these were the same states for which there were limited mortality data, it did not result in our having to eliminate any further states from the analysis. A second important limitation is that in controlling for factors that are directly related to COVID-19 mortality risk, our analysis was subject to the problem of multicollinearity, as these factors tend to be correlated with structural racism as well. It is reassuring that the variance inflation factors were generally less than two, a level that would indicate a multicollinearity problem. Additionally, since COVID-19 is not well understood, there could be unknown factors that confound the relationship between structural racism and disease mortality rates. Third, our state racism index is just one of many that have been used to quantify structural racism for empirical analyses. Although we have previously used and validated this measure, we acknowledge that there is no singular approach to operationalizing such a complex phenomenon. While the intent of this paper was specifically to examine Black-White differences in COVID-19 mortality, it is important to acknowledge that other racial-ethnic groups, including Latinx, Asian American, and Indigenous populations, are also experiencing a disproportionate burden of disease and death, and the causes of those disparities deserve attention as well. There is evidence that the nature and effects of racial residential segregation and structural racism are different for various racial/ethnic groups (Gee 2002). As Gee emphasizes, "One should not assume a 'one size fits all' conceptualization of contextual effects" (Gee 2002: 621). Future research should explore both common and group-specific mechanisms by which structural racism creates racial disparities in COVID-19 morbidity and mortality.

## Conclusion

Despite these limitations, this paper demonstrates that actual disparities in COVID-19 mortality between the non-Hispanic Black and non-Hispanic White populations are greater than what has previously been reported in studies that failed to consider the race/ethnicity-specific age distribution of the population. Furthermore, this research documents that there are marked differences in the magnitude of the Black-White disparity in COVID-19 mortality across states and that these differences are associated with the level of structural racism in those states. We conclude that structural racism must now be considered a root cause of the observed Black-White disparity in COVID-19 mortality. Our research suggests that the dismantling of long-standing systems of racial oppression is critical to adequately address both the downstream and upstream causes of racial inequities in the disease burden of COVID-19. As vaccination campaigns are now being implemented, there is a danger that inequities in vaccine distribution may further exacerbate racial/ethnic disparities in COVID-19-related morbidity and mortality. Therefore, prioritization of Black communities for vaccine distribution is essential in the nation's COVID-19 recovery plan.

*This article is reproduced under a Creative Commons license from the Journal of Racial and Ethnic Health Disparities 2021; original source: https://doi.org/10.1007/s40615-021-01028-1. To view a copy of this license, visit http://creativecommons.org/licenses/by/4.0/.*

## References

Abedi, Vida, Oluwaseyi Olulana, Venkatesh Avula, Durgesh Chaudhary, Ayesha Khan, Shima Shahjouei, Jiang Li, and Ramin Zand. "Racial, Economic and Health Inequality and COVID-19 Infection in the United States." *MedRxiv*(2020): 1–21. https://doi.org/10.1007/ s40615-020-00833-4.

Adhikari, Samrachana, Nicholas P. Pantaleo, Justin M. Feldman, Olugbenga Ogedegbe, Lorna Thorpe, and Andrea B. Troxel. "Assessment of Community-Level Disparities in Coronavirus Disease 2019 (COVID-19) Infections and Deaths in Large US Metropolitan Areas." *JAMA* 3, no. 7 (2020): e2016938. https://doi.org/10.1001/jamanetworkopen.2020.16938.

Akanbi, Maxwell O., Adovich S. Rivera, Folake O. Akanbi, and Adenike Shoyinka. "An Ecologic Study of Disparities in COVID-19 Incidence and Case Fatality in Oakland County, MI, USA, During a State-Mandated Shutdown." *Racial/Ethnic Health Disparities*. https://doi.org/10.1007/s40615-020-00909-1.

American Bar Association. "Two Centuries of Law Guide Legal Approach to Modern Pandemic. 2020." *ABA*, https://www.americanbar.org/news/abanews/ publications/youraba/2020/youraba-april-2020/law-guides-legalapproach-to-pandemic/.

American Community Survey. "Sex by Occupation for the Civilian Employed Population 16 Years and Over, by Race/Ethnicity (Table B24010)." Washington, DC: United States Census Bureau, 2019.

Anaele, Beverly I., Cierrah Doran, and Russel McIntire. "Visualizing COVID-19 Mortality Rates and African-American Populations in the USA and Pennsylvania." *Racial/Ethnic Health Disparities* 8, no. 6 (2021): 1356–1363. https://doi. org/10.1007/s40615-020-00897-2.

Anyane-Yeboa, Adjoa, Toshiro Sato, and Atsushi Sakuraba. "Racial Disparities in COVID-19 Deaths Reveal Harsh Truths About Structural Inequality in America." *Internal Medicine* 288 (2020): 479–480.

APM Research Lab. "The Color of Coronavirus: COVID-19 Deaths by Race and Ethnicity in the US." *American Public Media*, March 15, 2022, https://www.apmresearchlab.org/ covid/deaths-by-race.

Baker Marissa G., Trevor K Peckham, and Noah S. Seixas. "Estimating the Burden of United States Workers Exposed to Infection or Disease: A Key Factor in Containing Risk of COVID-19 Infection." *PLoS ONE* 15, no. 4 (2020): e0232452. https://doi.org/10.1371/journal.pone.0232452.

Bassett, Mary T., Jarvis T. Chen, and Nancy Krieger. "Variation in Racial/Ethnic Disparities in COVID-19 Mortality by Age in the United States: A Cross-sectional Study." *PLoS Med.* 17, no. 10 (2020): e1003402. https://doi.org/ 10.1371/journal.pmed.1003402.

Bharmal, Nazleen, Chi-Hong Tseng, Robert Kaplan, and Mitchell D. Wong. "State-Level Variations in Racial Disparities in Life Expectancy." *Health Serv Res* 47, no. 1 Pt 2 (2012): 544–555.

Boserup, Brad, Mark McKenney, and Adel Elkbuli. "Disproportionate Impact of COVID-19 Pandemic on Racial and Ethnic Minorities." *Am Surg* 86, no. 12 (2020): 1615–1622.

Bureau of Justice Statistics. "Prisoners In 2019." Accessed November 30, 2020. https://www.bjs.gov/index.cfm?ty=pbdetail&iid=7106.

Centers for Disease Control and Prevention. "BRFSS Survey Data and Documentation." Accessed January 15, 2021. https://www.cdc.gov/brfss/annual_data/annual_2019.html.

Centers for Disease Control and Prevention. "COVID-19 Death Data and Resources." Accessed January 14, 2021. https://www.cdc.gov/nchs/nvss/covid-19.htm.

Chambers, Brittany D., Jennifer Toller Erausquin, Amanda E. Tanner, Tracy R. Nichols, and Shelly Brown-Jeffy. "Testing the Association Between Traditional and Novel Indicators of County-Level Structural Racism and Birth Outcomes Among Black and White Women." *Racial Ethn Disparities* 5 (2018): 966–977.

Cheng, Kent Jason G., Yue Sun, and Shannon M Monnat. "COVID-19 Death Rates Are Higher in Rural Counties with Larger Shares of Blacks and Hispanics." *J Rural Health* 36 (2020) 602–608.

Churchwell, Keith, Mitchell S.V. Elkind, Regina M. Benjamin, April P. Carson, Edward K. Chang, Willie Lawrence, Andrew Mills, Tanya M. Odom, Carlos J. Rodriguez, et al. "Call to Action: Structural Racism As a Fundamental Driver of Health Disparities. A Presidential Advisory from the American Heart Association." *Circulation* 142 (2020): e454–68. https://doi.org/10.1161/CIR.0000000000000936.

COVID Tracking Project and the Boston University Center for Antiracist Research. "The COVID Racial Data Tracker." Accessed January 26, 2021. https://covidtracking.com/race Accessed 26 Jan 2021.

Cromer, Sara J., Chirag M. Lakhani, Deborah J. Wexler, Sherri-Ann M. Burnett-Bowie, Miriam Udler, and Chirag J. Patel. "Geospatial Analysis of Individual and Community-Level Socioeconomic Factors Impacting SARS-Cov-2 Prevalence and Outcomes." *MedRxiv* (2020): 1–21. https://doi.org/10.1101/2020.09.30. 20201830.

Cunningham, George B., and Lisa T. Wigfall. "Race, Explicit Racial Attitudes, Implicit Racial Attitudes, and COVID-19 Cases and Deaths: An Analysis of Counties in the United States." *PLoS ONE* 15, no. 11(2020): e0242044. https://doi.org/10.1371/journal.pone.0242044.

Curtin, Lester R., and Richard J. Klein. "Direct Standardization (Age-Adjusted Death Rates). Healthy People 2000 Statistical Notes." Accessed January 26, 2021. https://www.cdc.gov/ nchs/data/statnt/statnt06rv.pdf.

Cyrus, Elena, Rachel Clarke, Dexter Hadley, Zoran Bursac, Mary Jo Trepka, Jessy G. Devieux, Ulas Bagci, Debra Furr-Holden, Makella Coudray, Yandra Marianao, et al. "The Impact of COVID-19 on African American communities in the United States." *MedRxiv*. (2020): 1–19. https://doi.org/10.1101/ 2f2020.05.15.20096552.

DiMaggio, Charles, Michael Klein, Cherisse Berry, and Spiros Frangos. "Black/African American Communities Are at Highest Risk of COVID-19: Spatial Modeling of New York City Zip Code-Level Testing Results." *Ann Epidemiol* 51(2020): 7–13.

Do, D. Phuong, and Reanne Frank. "Unequal Burdens: Assessing the Determinants of Elevated COVID-19 Case and Death Rates in New York City's Racial/Ethnic Minority Neighbourhoods." *J Epidemiol Community Health* 75, no. 4 (2020): 321–326. https://doi.org/10.1136/jech-2020-215280.

Egede, Leonard E., and Rebekah J. Walker. "Structural Racism, Social Risk Factors, and COVID-19—A Dangerous Convergence for Black Americans." *N Engl J Med* 383, no. 12 (2020): e77. https://doi.org/10.1056/NEJMp2023616.

Feinhandler, Ian, Benjamin Cilento, Brad Beauvais, Jordan Harrop, and Lawrence Fulton. "Predictors of Death Rate During the COVID-19 Pandemic." *Healthcare* 8, no. 3. (2020): 339. https://doi.org/10.3390/healthcare8030339.

Figueroa, Jose F., Rishi K. Wadhera, Dennis Lee, Robert W. Yeh, and Benjamin D. Sommers. "Community-Level Factors Associated with Racial and Ethnic Disparities in COVID-19 Rates in Massachusetts." *Health Affairs* 39, no. 11 (2020): 1984–1992.

Figueroa, Jose F., Rishi K. Wadhera, Winta T. Mehtsun, Kristen Riley, Jessica Phelan, and Ashish K. Jha. "Association of Race, Ethnicity, and Community-Level Factors with COVID-19 Cases and Deaths Across US Counties." *Healthcare* 9 (2021): 100495. https://doi.org/10.1016/j.hjdsi.2020.

Ford, Chandra L., Derek M Griffith, Marino A Bruce, and Keon L Gilbert. *Racism: Science and Tools for the Public Health Professional*. Washington, DC: APHA Press; 2019.

Ford, Chandra L. "Commentary: Addressing Inequities in the Era of COVID19. The Pandemic and the Urgent Need for Critical Race Theory." *Family Community Health* 43, no. 3 (2020): 184–186.

Ford, Tiffany N., Sarah Reber, and Richard V. Reeves. "Race Gaps in COVID-19 Are Even Bigger Than They Appear." *Up Front* (blog), *Brookings*, June 16, 2020, https://www.brookings.edu/blog/up-front/2020/06/16/race-gaps-in-covid-19-deaths-are-even-bigger-than-they-appear/.

Garcia, Marc A., Patricia A Homan, Catherine Garcia, and Tyson H. Brown. "The Color of COVID-19: Structural Racism and the Disproportionate Impact of the Pandemic on Older Black and Latinx Adults." *J Gerontol B Psychol Sci Soc Sci* 76, no. 3 (2021): e75–e80.

Gaynor, Tia Sherèe, and Meghan E Wilson. "Social Vulnerability and Equity: The Disproportionate Impact of COVID-19." *Public Adm Rev* 80, no. 5 (2020): 832–838.

Gee, Gilbert C. "A Multilevel Analysis of the Relationship Between Institutional and Individual Racial Discrimination and Health Status." *Am J Public Health* 92, no. 4 (2002): 615–623.

Goldstein, Joshua R., and Serge Atherwood. "Improved Measurement of Racial/Ethnic Disparities in COVID-19 Mortality in the United States." *MedRxiv* (2020): 1–13. https://doi.org/10.1101/2020.05.21.20109116.

Groos, Maya, Maeve Wallace, Rachel Hardeman, and Katherine Theall. "Measuring Inequity: A Systematic Review of Methods Used to Quantify Structural Racism." *J Health Dispar Res Pract* 11, no.2 (2018): 190–206.

Gross, Cary P., Utibe R. Essien, Saamir Pasha, Jacob R. Gross, Shi-yi Wang, and Marcella Nunez-Smith. "Racial and Ethnic Disparities in Population-Level COVID-19 Mortality." *J Gen Intern Med* 35, no. 10 (2020): 3097–3099.

Hamman, Mary K. "Disparities in COVID-19 Mortality by County Racial Composition and the Role of Spring Social Distancing Measures." *Econ Hum Biol* 41 (2021): 100953. https://doi.org/10.1016/j.ehb.2020. 1009053.

Igedegbe, Gbenga, Joseph Ravenell, Samrachana Adhikari, Mark Butler, Tiffany Cook, Fritz Francois, Eduardo Iturrate, Girardin Jean-Louis, Simon A. Jones, and Deborah Onakomaiya. "Assessment of Racial/Ethnic Disparities in Hospitalization and Mortality in Patients with COVID-19 in New York City." *JAMA Netw Open* 3, no. 12 (2020): e2026881. https://doi.org/10.1001/ Jamanetworkopen.2020.26881.

Johns Hopkins University and Medicine. "Coronavirus Resource Center." Accessed January 25, 2021. https://coronavirus.jhu.edu/.

Karmakar, Monita, Paula M. Lantz, and Renuka Tipirneni. "Association of Social and Demographic Factors with COVID-19 Incidence and Death Rates in the US." *JAMA Netw Open* 4, no.1 (2021): e2036462. https://doi.org/10.1001/jamanetworkopen.2020.36462.

Khanijahani, Ahmad, and Larisa Tomassoni. "Socioeconomic and Racial Segregation and COVID-19: Concentrated Disadvantage and Black Concentration in Association with COVID-19 Deaths in the USA." *J Racial Ethn Health Disparities* 9, no. 1 (2022): 367–375. https://.org/10.1007/s40615-0210965-1.

Khanijahani, Ahmad. "Racial, Ethnic, and Socioeconomic Disparities in Confirmed COVID-19 Cases and Deaths in the United States: A County-Level Analysis as of November 2020." *Ethn Health* 26, no. 1 (2020): 22–35. https://doi.org/10.1080/13557858.2020.1853067.

Kim, Sage J., and Wendy Bostwick. "Social Vulnerability and Racial Inequality in COVID-19 Deaths in Chicago." *Health Educ Behav* 47, no. 4 (2020): 509–513.

Kullar, Ravina, Jasmine R. Marcelin, Talia H. Swartz, Damani A. Piggott, Raul Macias Gil, Trini A. Mathew, and Tina Tan. "Racial Disparity of Coronavirus Disease 2019 in African American Communities." *J Infect Dis* 222 (2020): 890–893.

Laurencin, Cato T., and Aneesah McClinton. "The COVID-19 Pandemic: A Call to Action to Identify and Address Racial and Ethnic Disparities." *J Racial Ethn Health Disparities* 7, no. 3 (2020): 398–402. https://doi.org/10.1007/2Fs40615-020-00756-0.

Lee, Ian J., and Nasar U. Ahmed. "The Devastating Cost of Racial and Ethnic Inequity in the COVID-19 Pandemic." *J Natl Med Assoc* 113, no. 1 (2021): 114–117. https://doi.org/10.1016/j.jnma.2020.11.015.

Li, Daniel, Sheila M. Gaynor, Corbin Quick, Jarvis T. Chen, Briana J.K, Stephenson, Brent A. Coull, and Xihong Lin. "Unraveling US National COVID-19 Racial/Ethnic Disparities Using County Level Data Among 328 Million Americans." *MedRxiv* (2020): 1–45. https://doi.org/10.1101/2020.12.02.20234989.

Liao, Tim F., and Fernando De Maio. "Association of Social and Economic Inequality with Coronavirus Disease 2019 Incidence and Mortality Across

US Counties." *JAMA Netw Open* 4, no. 1 (2021): e2034578. https://doi.org/ 10.1001/jamaanetworkopen.2020.34578.

Liu, Sze Yan, Christina Fiorentini, Zinzi Bailey, Mary Huynh, Katharine McVeigh, and Deborah Kaplan. "Structural Racism and Severe Maternal Morbidity in New York State." *Clin Med Insights Women's Health* 12 (2019): 1–8.

Lukachko, Alicia, Mark L. Hatzenbuehler, and Katherine M. Keyes. "Structural Racism and Myocardial Infarction in the United States." *Soc Sci Med* 103 (2014): 42–50.

Mahajan, Uma V., and Margaret Larkins-Pettigrew. "Racial Demographics and COVID-19 Confirmed Cases and Deaths: A Correlational Analysis of 2886 US Counties." *J Public Health* 2020. 2020;42(3): 445–7.

Maness, Sarah B., Laura Merrell, Erika L. Thompson, Stacey B. Griner, Nolan Kline, and Christopher Wheldon. "Social Determinants of Health and Health Disparities: COVID-19 Exposures and Mortality Among African American People in the United States." *Public Health Rep* 136, no. 1 (2021): 18–22.

McCann, Adam. "2017's States with the Most Racial Progress." *Wallet Hub* (blog). *Evolution Finance, Inc.*, January 11, 2022, https://wallethub.com/edu/states-with-the-most-and-least-racial-progress/18428/#rankings-integration.

Mesic, Aldina, Lydia Franklin, Alev Cansever, Fiona Potter, Anika Sharma, Anita Knopov, and Michael Siegel. "The Relationship Between Structural Racism and Black-White Disparities in Fatal Police Shootings at the State Level." *J Natl Med Assoc* 110, no. 2 (2018): 106–116.

Millett, Gregorio A., Austin T. Jones, David Benkeser, Stephan Baral, Laina Mercer, Chris Beyrer, Brian Honermann, Elise Lankiewicz, Leandro Mena, Jeffrey S Crowley, et al. "Assessing Differential Impacts of COVID-19 on Black Communities." *Ann Epidemiol* 47(2020): 37–44.

Milner, Adrienne, Berkeley Franz, and Jomills Henry Braddock. "We Need to Talk About Racism—In All of Its Forms—to Understand COVID-19 Disparities." *Health Equity* 4, no. 1(2020): 397–402.

Muñoz-Price, L. Silvia, Ann B. Natinger, Frida Rivera, Ryan Hanson, Cameron G. Gmehlin, Adriana Perez, Siddhartha Singh, Blake W. Buchan, Nathan A. Ledeboer, and Liliana E. Pezzin. "Racial Disparities in Incidence and Outcomes Among Patients with COVID-19." *JAMA Netw Open* 3, no. 9 (2020): e2021892. https://doi.org/10.1001/jamanetworkopen.2020.21892.

Nowotny, Kathryn M., Zinzi Bailey, and Lauren Brinkley-Rubinstein. "The Contribution of Prisons and Jails to US Racial Disparities During COVID-19." *Am J Public Health* 111, no. 2 (2021): 197–199.

Parcha, Vibhu, Gargya Malla, Sarabjeet S. Suri, Rajat Kaira, Brittain Heindl, Lorenzo Berra, Mona N Fouad, Garima Arora, and Pankaj Arora. "Geographic Variation of Racial Disparities in Health and COVID-19 Mortality." *Mayo Clin Proc Inn Qual Out* 4, no.6 (2020): 703–716.

Poteat, Tonia, Gregorio A. Millett, LaRon E. Nelson, and Chris Beyrer. "Understanding COVID-19 Risks and Vulnerabilities Among Black Communities in America: The Lethal Force of Syndemics." *Ann Epidemiol* 47 (2020): 1–3. https://doi.org/10.1016/j.annepidem.2020.05.004/.

Poulson, Michael, Alaina Geary, Chandler Annesi, Lisa Allee, Kelly Kenzik, Sabrina Sanchez, Jennifer Tseng, and Tracey Dechert. "National Disparities in COVID-19 Outcomes Between Black and White Americans." *J Natl Med Assoc* 113, no. 2 (2020): 125–132. https://doi.org/10. 1016/j.jnma.2020.07.009.

Raine, Samuel, Amy Liu, Joel Mintz, Waseem Wahood, Kyle Huntley, and Farzanna Haffizulla. "Racial and Ethnic Disparities in COVID-19 Outcomes: Social Determination of Health." *Int J Environ Res Public Health* 17 (2020): 8115. https://doi.org/10.3390/ijerph17218115.

Richmond, Holly L., Joana Tome, Haresh Rochani, Isaac Chun-Hai Fung, Gulzar H. Shah, and Jessica S Schwind. "The Use of Penalized Regression Analysis to Identify County-Level Demographic and Socioeconomic Variables Predictive of Increased COVID-19 Cumulative Case Rates in the State of Georgia." *Int J Environ Res Public Health* 17 (2020): 8036. https://doi.org/10. 3390/ijerph17218036.

Siegel, Michael. "Racial Disparities in Fatal Police Shootings: An Empirical Analysis Informed by Critical Race Theory." *Boston Univ Law Rev* 100 (2020): 1069–1092.

Strully, Kate, Tse-Chuan Yang, and Han Liu. Regional Variation in COVID-19 Disparities: "Connections with Immigrant and Latinx Communities in US Counties." *Ann Epidemiol* 53, no. 1 (2020): 56–62. https://doi.org/10.1016/j.annepidem.2020.08.016.

Tan, Shin Bin, Priyanka deSouza, and Matthew Raifman. "Structural Racism and COVID-19 in the USA: A County-Level Empirical Analysis." *J Racial*

Ethn Health Disparities 9, vol. 1 (2022): 236–246. https://doi.org/10.1007/s40615-020-00948-8.

Tirupathi, Raghavendra, Valeriia Muradova, Raj Shekhar, Sohail Abdul Salim, Jaffar Al-Tawfiq, and Venkataraman Palabindala. COVID-19 Disparity Among Racial and Ethnic Minorities in the US: A Cross Sectional Analysis. *Travel Med Infect Dis*. 2020;38:101904. https://doi.org/10.1016/j.tmaid.2020.101904.

Vahidy, Farhaan S., Juan Carlos Nicolas, Jennifer R. Meeks, Osman Khan, Alan Pan, Stephen L. Jones, Faisal Masud, H. Dirk Sostman, Robert Phillips, Julia D. Andrieni, et al. "Racial and Ethnic Disparities in SARS-Cov2 Pandemic: Analysis of a COVID-19 Observational Registry for a Diverse US Metropolitan Population." *BMJ Open* 10 (2020): e039849. https://doi.org/10.1136/bmjopen-2020-039849.

Wiley, Zanthia, Julianne N Kubes, Jason Cobb, Jesse T Jacob, Nicole Franks, Laura Plantinga, and Janice Lea. "Age, Comorbid Conditions, and Racial Disparities in COVID-19 Outcomes." *J Racial Ethn Health Disparities* 9, vol. 1 (202s): 117–123. https://doi.org/10. 1007/s40615-020-00934-0.

Wrigley-Field, Elizabeth, Sarah Garcia, Jonathon P Leider, Christopher Robertson, and Rebecca Wurtz. "Racial Disparities in COVID-19 and Excess Mortality in Minnesota." *Socius* 6 (2020): 1–4. https://doi.org/10.1177/2378023120980918.

Yang, Tse-Chuan, Seung-won Emily Choi, and Feinuo Sun. "COVID-19 Cases in US Counties: Roles of Racial/Ethnic Density and Residential Segregation." *Ethn Health* 26, no. 1 (2020): 11–21. https://doi.org/10.1080/13557858.2020.1830036.

Yaya, Sanni, Helena Yeboah, Carlo Handy Charles, Akaninyene Otu, and Ronald Labonte. "Ethnic and Racial Disparities in COVID-19-Related Deaths: Counting the Trees, Hiding the Forest." *BMJ Global Health* 5 (2020): e002913. https://doi. org/10.1136/bmjgh-2020-002913.

Yu, Qinggang, Cristina E Salvador, Irene Melani, Martha K Berg, Enrique W Neblett, and Shinobu Kitayama. "Racial Residential Segregation and Economic Disparity Jointly Exacerbate COVID-19 Fatality in Large American Cities." *Ann N Y Acad Sci* 1494, no. 1 (2021): 18–30. https://doi.org/10.1111/nyas.1456

CHAPTER 5

# COVID-19 EXPOSES DEEP RACIAL INEQUITIES AND VULNERABILITY IN THE UNITED STATES

*Alana Dass*

IN LATE 2019, A NEW, MYSTERIOUS, and highly infectious virus, SARS-CoV-2, which causes COVID-19, was being described and watched as it spread throughout China. Soon, it arrived in the United States where, according to Catherine Offord (2020) of *The Scientist*, the first fatality from COVID-19 in the United States is estimated to have occurred in Santa Clara, California, on February 6, 2020. This precedes the original Washington State fatality recorded on February 29, 2020. Within that time, SARS-CoV-2 had countless opportunities to spread beyond the West Coast. By March 17, 2020, the entire United States was consumed by the virus, with West Virginia being the last state to confirm cases (Chappell and Romo 2020). Hospitals around the United States and the world, by that point, were facing supply shortages and massive patient overflow.

In the process of monitoring the spread of the virus and the states' responses to the large quantities of people needing testing and treatment, the racial and socioeconomic fissures of the US health care system surfaced for the public to see. Between late May and early June, societal unrest centralized that racial disparities in healthcare and policing are the outgrowth of centuries of racist, colonial societal and political structures; the racial disparities in higher infection and mortality rates for Black people became exposed to the broader public through data models showing correlations between race and death (Ogbunu 2020). To address the health inequities and advance as a society, the idea of a vulnerability index, proposed by the Barbadian Prime Minister Mia Mottley, and developed by J. Jason Cotton, Alicia Nicholls, and Jan Yves Remy (2019), was conceptually formatted and adapted for the United States by state. This paper examines the issues that created vulnerabilities in the United States and argues for the necessity of a vulnerability index to ameliorate the conditions of disadvantaged communities.

## Historical Exploitation of Black Bodies

The disparities observed in the current political and social climate are historical legacies of colonial structural hegemony through which European powers extracted resources from around the world. Exploitation and abuse of Black bodies predate the formation of the United States primarily through the institution of slavery. Frantz Fanon in *The Wretched of the Earth* (Fanon 2004) states:

> Decolonization is the encounter between two congenitally antagonistic forces that in fact owe their singularity to the kind of reification secreted and nurtured by the colonial situation. Their first confrontation was colored by violence and their cohabitation—or rather the exploitation of the colonized by the colonizer. (2)

Here, Fanon refers to the impetus to decolonize in the presence of a legacy of colonial violence that began at the very first encounter between European colonists and African peoples. The act and practice of enslavement were justified by European colonists through the principle of divine right as well as the emergence of scientific racism, as Angela Davis explains in *Are Prisons Obsolete?*, the very nature of justifying the conquest of other humans in such ways perpetuates the idea of racially stratified extents of humanity. In other words, the justification for slavery would become the same justification for the continuation of oppression directed at Black people through systemic means (Davis 2003). Similarly, the colonial justification of slavery involved the progressive and hegemonic erasure of humanity from Black bodies through a series of stages ranging from the declaration of Black bodies as White property, to the economy based on the trafficking of Black bodies, to the association of Blackness with supposed inherent criminality (Davis 2003).

In this sense, Blackness became the marker for dehumanization, which enabled the entitlement of White colonialists to Black bodies. In C. Riley Snorton's *Black on Both Sides: A Racial History of Trans Identity*, this relationship between Blackness, dehumanization, and medical exploitation is explored in more detail. Snorton confronts the postcolonial prescriptions of sex, gender, and sexuality in relation to the racialized components of colonial hegemony that ultimately influence the perception of individual identities based on racial phenotype. More specifically, Snorton uses a vivid historical account of J. Marion Sims, the inventor of the gynecological speculum, to illustrate the extent of dehumanization directed at Black people. Sims had operated on a multitude of women in his practice; he developed techniques and tools for viewing vaginal walls and performing surgery primarily on three enslaved women: Lucy, Anarcha and Betsey. Anarcha alone had been operated on around thirty times; none of the surgeries were performed with anesthesia (Snorton 2017). Sims's ability to acquire Lucy, Anarcha, and Betsey for experimental purposes essentially indicates that "their flesh functioned as a disarticulation of human form from its anatomical features and their claims to humanity were controverted in favor of the production and perpetuation of cultural institutions" (Snorton 2017, 19). The constant violations of dignity, the exposure to pain and illness, as well as the principles underlying the use of enslaved women as experiments epitomized the colonial perceptions of Black bodies as inhuman, as these women were not afforded the same bashful dignity that their White counterparts had (Snorton 2017). In fact, "their collective status as slaves organized a way of encountering their bodies, as test subjects that were innately analgesic or congenitally impervious to pain, and, by the very condition of slavery, inexhaustibly available through their interchangeability" (Snorton 2017, 24)—the perception of their inhuman status had connotations of both permanent captivity and an inability to suffer.

This inhuman status would persist as time progressed past the supposed eradication of slavery, as in the case of the "Tuskegee Study of Untreated Syphilis in the Negro Male," which began in 1932 and ended in 1972 (Newkirk II 2016). During the study, the progression of syphilis infection (inoculation to death) within six hundred Black men from rural Alabama was observed (Newkirk II 2016). Throughout the forty years of the experiment, however, the observed men were consistently denied treatments, medications, and advice from researchers (Newkirk II 2016). For four uninterrupted decades, the observation of Black men and their families suffering from the disease went unchallenged—no equivalent study has ever been performed on White bodies.

Sylvia Wynter's "Toward the Sociogenic Principle: Fanon, Identity, the Puzzle of Conscious Experience, and What It Is Like to Be 'Black'" (1999) brings to light the comparison between the biological and ontological basis for human experiential differences. Within her essay, Wynter extends the concept of sociogeny introduced by Fanon to include an analytical breakdown of the composition of the human experience. For Wynter, the relative consciousness that dictates the perception of experiences is fundamentally "inseparable from the physical (i.e., neurobiological) processes" (Wynter 1999, 3)—consciousness is thus not solely attributable to emergent biological properties but also includes highly individualized psychological elements. More specifically, consciousness and experience are both functions of an individual, yet are shaped by the socialization one receives about the inescapable definitions or labels applied to the individual's physical identity, one of which is race. Wynter further notes that socialization, being dependent on an individual's perceived position in society (relative to the overarching hierarchy), is affected by the dominant definition of humanity (Wynter 1999, 2). The prolonged suffering of Black Americans could, therefore, be completely attributed to the prevalent hegemonic enforcement of inhuman status toward Blackness as both the result and enabling factor for a reciprocal, self-perpetuating socialization of the White ruling class to deny humanity to Black people.

Predictably, the hegemonic concept of dehumanization was not limited to the institution of Western science alone. The hegemony settled into the basis of all societal structures, regardless of whether the structures were strictly legal, economic, or social. To elaborate, throughout the history of the United States leading up to the present day, the consistent, generationally perpetuated social dehumanization of Black identities developed into insidiously anti-Black legal and economic oppression. Specifically, dehumanization of Black identities enabled the formation of policies that led to redlining, racially discriminative loan lending practices, predatory surveillance, and limits on economic mobility.

The most persistent of these is redlining, which began eighty years ago and was the Home Owners' Loan Corporation's (HOLC) carefully engineered breakdown of major urban centers in regard to the safety of the residents (Mitchell and Franco 2018). To the HOLC, "hazardous" areas would be outlined in red ink; these areas would not be given the "capital investment, which could improve the housing and economic opportunity of residents" (Mitchell and Franco 2018, 4). In contemporary times, 74 percent of the redlined areas deemed "hazardous" are also low-income areas and about 64 percent have a high density of minority residents (Mitchell and Franco 2018, 4). The act of redlining "buttressed the segregated structure of American cities" (Mitchell and Franco 2018, 4). Due to essentially confining racial minorities to specific areas, redlining also stratified regions along class lines, which limits the wealth concentration in predominantly-minority neighborhoods.

The effects of segregation and the paucity of wealth become amplified in situations where survival and success are dictated by access to resources, as in the case with the current COVID-19 pandemic. The effects of redlining have manifested in the form of "Black communities [being] more susceptible to hospital closings" (Perry 2020, para. 5) and "a corresponding decrease in the availability of surgical equipment" (Perry 2020, para. 5) in areas with high densities of Black residents. Additionally, redlining has inevitably led to the overcrowding of demarcated areas, meaning that social distancing measures are incredibly difficult to implement while indoors due to multigenerational living arrangements and tightly packed apartment units (CDC 2020). All the same, staying outside in order to maintain an appropriate distance from others within a residence plays into the increased policing of Black neighborhoods and furthers the racially disparate arrests through contributions from social distancing violations (Gabbatt 2020). On the other hand, many industries that rely on in-person interaction employ Black workers at a disproportionately high rate (Perry 2020). Black workers within the "health care support, personal care, and protective services, as well as in [the] gig-economy" (Perry 2020, para. 8) industries are upholding society through their essential work. To compound the high risk of exposure to Black communities, social determinants of health also factor into the survival rates observed. Due to the inequities in investment allocations as well as perceptions of Black people influenced by the structural and social enforcement of dehumanization, the infrastructure for establishing and maintaining sufficient, generational health is lacking. As such, Black people "have the highest death rate and shorter survival rate for all cancers combined compared with whites in the United States" (Cunningham et. al 2015, para. 5) along with high rates of chronic illness. In the scope of COVID-19, Black communities in the United States consistently observe high rates of infection and low rates of recovery, to the point where Black communities "account for more than half of coronavirus cases and nearly 60 percent of deaths" (Williams 2020, para. 1).

## Indigenous (Indian) Communities in the United States

It is also important to examine the similarity of systemic traumas that Indigenous cultures across the Western Hemisphere have experienced in regard to deterritorialization and ongoing colonial oppression. Within the US context specifically, Indigenous history is marked by a brutal past of several genocides, assimilation tactics, and displacement as well as present-day "[Subjection] to grave human rights abuses" ("Land Rights" n.d., para. 1). Early in the process of colonizing North America, European settlers and Indigenous groups experienced tensions and small-scale warfare over control of local resources and land. Eventually, the European system of bounty rewards for the scalps of any Indigenous people and the living children captured through war "erased any remaining distinction between Indigenous combatants and noncombatants and introduced a market for Indigenous slaves" (Dunbar-Ortiz 2015, para. 4). Given the broad history between European settlers and Indigenous peoples, the same method of dehumanization that African-descended peoples face is applied to Indigenous bodies in order to justify the seizure of their lands, the enactment of gruesome genocides, and the perpetuation of systemic oppression that persists to this day. The logic follows, then, that dehumanized Indigenous people also face medical racism and neglect at-large in addition to compromised terms of sovereignty as exemplified by the COVID-19 pandemic.

While many Indigenous peoples worldwide were considered to be their own entities, the process of displacing Indigenous groups into reservations occurred to all groups of Indigenous North and Central Americans. However, the existence of Indigenous nations within the United States still depended on access to resources and land controlled by the US economic framework; the constraints and limitations on Indigenous migration in adhering to strict borders resulted in the loss and dispossession of crucial resources for many Indigenous nations. Indeed, "Indian land and natural resources are often expropriated or degraded, and sometimes destroyed. When indigenous peoples are deprived of their ways of life and their ties to the earth, they suffer, and many have disappeared completely" (Indian Law Resource Center n.d., para. 1).

More specifically, actions on the part of the US government, such as the move to build the Dakota Access Pipeline through Standing Rock Reservation without testing the pipeline for environmental hazard risks, not only extracted hundreds of gallons of crude oil from sacred sites on reservation land but also leaked over ten times during three years (McKenna 2019). Considering the extreme disregard for environmental safety, the Army Corps of Engineers effectively poisoned the residents of Standing Rock while profiting from their resources. This one instance does not account for the hundreds of other treaty violations by the United States from 1722 onward—the United States consistently oversteps terms of agreements to siphon resources and profits, which signifies a lack of respect for the humanity of Indigenous tribes (Lhaman et. al 2018). Similarly, violating the treaties threatens the sovereignty and ability of Indigenous nations to negotiate with the US government.

Historically, the terms of sovereignty in terms of self-government varied by group, with some cultures recognized by the US federal government as sovereign nations and others still fighting for secured rights after hundreds of years (Indian Law Resource Center n.d.). At the same time, however, "In 2007, [Indigenous peoples] succeeded in winning UN General Assembly adoption of the UN Declaration on Rights of Indigenous Peoples containing a clear right of self-determination for indigenous peoples as distinct peoples within existing countries" (Indian Law Resource Center n.d, para. 1). With this measure in place, the sovereignty of all Indigenous groups and nations would be protected and respected. In the United States, however, the spread of COVID-19 and the national focus on controlling the damage allowed lawmakers to proceed with little public oversight. For example, the Trump administration pushed to pass laws that would threaten the sovereignty of Indigenous groups, as in the case of the attacks on mail-in ballots, which would further silence Indigenous voices in US politics ("Intercepted Podcast" 2020).

In regard to handling the pandemic, the Oglala Sioux tribe established checkpoints throughout the Cheyenne River Sioux Reservation in order to frequently check for symptoms of COVID-19 in people passing through (Goodman and Moynihan 2020). The frequency of symptom tracking for individuals compensated for a lack of test kits and was effective in encouraging symptomatic individuals to return to quarantine; the governor of South Dakota, however, "demanded they remove the checkpoints or face state government intervention" (Goodman and Moynihan 2020, para. 2). Despite the order, at the time of this writing, the checkpoints are still being enforced while the threat to Ogala Sioux sovereignty remains in place (Goodman and Moynihan 2020). The constant attempts to undermine the autonomy of and concessions made to independent, culturally distinct groups highlight the stripped-away basic rights of Indigenous peoples, which would render them as unrepresented, voiceless subjects of the United States.

The disparities in health, wellness, treatment, and death observable among Indigenous groups are informed by a long, continuous history of denying the agency and humanity of Indigenous societies. By the year 2000, the Office of General Counsel in the US Commission on Civil Rights (2004) had found that over a period of thirty-five years, "equal access to health care was not afforded the same federal protection as equal opportunity in housing, education and employment" (1). Currently, according to the journalist Liz Mineo (2020), "As of April 30, the Navajo Nation had the third-highest per capita rate of COVID-19 in the country, after New Jersey and New York," which indicates that the Navajo Nation is seeing incredibly high rates of transmission even with the current social distancing measures and hygienic best practices in place. Due to the structure of the reservations—meaning the sparse, inconvenient access to grocery stores or medical facilities, which require hours-long trips to reach—many members of the Navajo Nation find themselves unable to adhere to quarantine measures as multiple communities share single facilities (Morales 2020a). Additionally, the disproportionately high rates of illnesses—some of which are the result of uranium exposure, according to Laurel Morales (2020a)—such as diabetes, tuberculosis, heart disease, various cancers, and influenza or pneumonia further complicate the survival factors for many members of the Navajo Nation ("Navajo Center Epidemiology Update" 2016).

While the Navajo Nation received $8 billion of aid from the CARES Act as Mineo (2020) reports, the cultural losses incurred cannot be reversed—a number of medicine people and elders with knowledge of traditions have died (Morales 2020b). Moreover, the Navajo Nation has been failed by the United States such that "the Treaty Agreements between the USA and its 573 federal sovereign tribes require the government to provide for the health and well-being of Indigenous peoples" (Burnette, Renner and Figley 2019, para. 3). The US infrastructure for addressing the health needs of the Navajo Nation has proven to be substandard enough that Doctors Without Borders was dispatched to Navajo grounds to provide aid (Peacher 2020). The financial assistance for Indigenous peoples would have worked more effectively as a preventative measure to address the vulnerability of the populations rather than as a restorative measure.

### Concept of a Vulnerability Index

The magnitude of death among Black and Indigenous communities across the United States was ultimately the result of structural racism that allows for the perpetuation of Black suffering and Indigenous invisibility. Likewise, such a scale of loss is preventable: the current structures can be remedied to account for the disparities in health care along intersecting race and class lines. In her interview with CNN's Christiane Amanpour, Prime Minister Mia Mottley from Barbados brought up the concept of a vulnerability index for the nations of the world, stating that the commonwealth secretariat had developed a framework for the index, known as the Commonwealth Vulnerability Index (2020). The most updated framework, which Cotton et. al (2019, 8) provided publicly, estimates various nations' economic and trade needs based on the vulnerability of the respective populations to (a) remoteness from global markets; (b) lack of diversification and adequate market access opportunities for few export products; (c) dependence on external financing;

(d) susceptibility to natural disasters; (f) small internal markets and lack of economies of scale; (e) dependence on non-renewable sources of energy; and (f) openness of their economies. The framework also acknowledges the susceptibility of small nations to "adverse climatic and other natural events" as well as "severe environmental and ecological threats" that affect economic volatility (Cotton et al. 2019, 8).

A model of a vulnerability index adapted for the United States' use would ideally not focus on addressing trade vulnerabilities but rather social vulnerabilities such as the ones discussed in previous sections regarding Black and Indigenous health. However, the United States already has a social vulnerability tool known as the US Climate Resilience Toolkit, which is formatted specifically for monitoring and potentially addressing the needs of different US regions based on the susceptibility of loss or damage due to climate change according to census data (NOAA n.d. a). This tool, although relevant, does not cover the entire scope of healthcare inequity and does not address issues of access to health-promoting services along any sociological lines. The five-step process involved in running the tool consists of determining hazards, assessing the risks of the hazards to the target region, hashing out options, deciding on a plan, then acting (NOAA n.d. b). The ability for the process to proceed, however, depends on "[gathering] a team who wants to protect local assets" and "[engaging] stakeholders" (NOAA n.d. b, para. 1). This setup necessitates that the start of an effective movement depends on collective action by citizens or independent organizations instead of a government branch or program devoted to identifying and solving existential threats to a community—the resources for addressing any risks would then have to be provided by the people of a community rather than the government overseeing the area.

Such a model does not suffice in accounting for class and racial inequities built into the structures of US societal institutions. Instead, a fair basis to begin designing a social vulnerability index for the United States would integrate the social determinants of health into the basis of the metrics. To be specific, a social vulnerability index that could work to address health inequities would be sensitive to historical and ongoing oppression as well as the distribution of wealth and access to resources along demographic lines for any given region. Essentially, the creation of a tool meant to provide a social impact must be informed by all aspects of the social history involved; the basis for the current distributions of wealth as it corresponds to race cannot be ignored or overlooked. One model that is centralized on humanity is the United Nations Development Programme's social vulnerability index, called the Human Development Index (HDI). The HDI was designed to quantitate and compile data for the standard of living in a multitude of nations around the world using records from as far back as 1543 (Roser 2014). The HDI quantities are determined by scoring a nation's average life expectancy, educational attainment, and standard of living (Roser 2014). To be more precise, these metrics can provide an image of the availability of healthcare, resources, knowledge, and assistance available within a given country. The data itself is collected from demographic information provided by countries and processed through mathematical formulas that essentially establish each nation's statistics as a percentage of a chosen standard (Roser 2014). While that data is accessible and public, the models provide a comparative perspective of the advancement of nations but make no mention of the reasons behind the distributions and disparities of human development. In other words, the history of imperialism that has pillaged the Global South is not discussed nor are the reasons behind the successes of the richest countries, not even in Esteban Ortiz-Ospina and Max Roser's article addressing global economic inequality (2013).

Although the premise of a large-scale economic model is useful for identifying regions that are particularly susceptible to economic or social volatility, constructing a model without regard to the social context under which the current trends have emerged does not inform the public about the depth of inequities. The existing US Climate Resilience Toolkit relies too heavily on the will of individuals within communities to inspire change, despite the likelihood that the most afflicted communities also experience a vast lack of resources. Similarly, the premise of the Human Development Index overlooks and avoids confronting the deeply colonial history of globalization that has resulted in the observable inequalities of contemporary times. Ideally, the US state-based vulnerability index would not be the sole responsibility of local nonprofit organizations and stakeholders but rather a social branch of the government. The composition of the index would also account for the same metrics as the Human Development Index except on a local region-by-region basis and would incorporate further measures of inequity, such as the distribution of schools within various districts as well as the quality of supplies within the schools; assessment of soil, air, and water quality; assessment of housing quality (for asbestos, lead, black mold, or other carcinogens as well as readiness for earthquakes, hurricanes, or tornadoes); distribution of grocery stores and quality of items available; standard of public transport; availability of medical services; and rates of homelessness. While these suggestions ultimately do propose a high-maintenance model that requires both census data for demographic information and fieldwork to constantly monitor the status of the environment and living conditions, communications would drastically improve between residents of areas most affected by inequities and the government. In addition, by assessing the quality of life in an area, the government will have a more cohesive idea of the aspects of physical and systemic infrastructure that need improvement.

The concern about this model is that it obviously involves a premise in which racial and economic class information are concentrated in the hands of government institutions that have proven to consistently dodge accountability. Although the inclusion of race- and class-based data is intended to inform the level of assistance needed for a region, it could also be used to further isolate and exploit a region in the event that there exist exploitable resources, as in the case with reservation lands, specifically Standing Rock. To prevent that, the fieldwork statistics gathered for an area (meaning the quality of air, water, soil, housing, resource availability, and transportation for an area) could be peer-reviewed for accuracy and released as public knowledge. Alongside that released data would be a contract signed by the federal government to protect the interests and advancement of the most vulnerable people. This proposed contract would contain an itemized list of agreed-upon resources that would be allocated to the region; the transparency between the identified vulnerable regions and the deliverables promised by the government will create grounds for accountability of the government. In this sense, the public health needs of vulnerable areas could be analyzed, discussed, and addressed through methods that provide special attention to the demographics within areas that experience disproportionate levels of economic disadvantage. While the solutions would vary by region, the communication between communities and the government would work to construct plans oriented around addressing the most pressing issues for a given area. Combining the application of a social vulnerability index in this manner and consistent efforts to ameliorate inequities, the damage of large-scale disasters, such as the COVID-19 pandemic, could be minimized since access to life-saving resources will be improved. Acknowledging the inequities caused and perpetuated by US institutions admits the damage done to historically oppressed peoples. Creating measures to work past those inequities serves to rehumanize the people who have had their humanity worn down through the centuries.

## References

"CNNi's Amanpour (April 29) Featuring Barbados Prime Minister Mia Amor Mottley." *CNNi*, April 29, 2020. https://www.youtube.com/watch?v=lVC9k04TkP4.

Burnette, C. E., L. M Renner, and C. R. Figley. "The Framework of Historical Oppression, Resilience and Transcendence to Understand Disparities in Depression Amongst Indigenous Peoples." The British Journal of Social Work 49, no. 4 (2019): 943–962. https:/doi.org/10.1093/bjsw/bcz041.

Centers for Disease Control and Prevention. "COVID-19 in Racial and Ethnic Minority Groups." *CDC*, April 22, 2020, https://www.cdc.gov/coronavirus/2019-ncov/need-extra-precautions/racial-ethnic-minorities.html.

Chappell, B., and V Romo. "Coronavirus: All 50 States Report Cases; South America Has Nearly 1,000 Cases." NPR.org, March 17, 2020, https://www.npr.org/sections/ health-shots/2020/03/17/817096232/coronavirus-radical-change-to-life-as-covid-19-reaches-152-countries.

Cotton, J. J., A Nicholls, and J.Y. Remy. "Using a Trade Vulnerability Index to Determine Eligibility for Developing-Country Status at the WTO: A Conceptual Response to the Ongoing Debate." *SSRN Electronic Journal* (September 25, 2019).https://doi.org/10.2139/ssrn.3582486.

Cunningham, T. J., J. B. Croft, Y. Liu, H Lu., P. I Eke, and W.H. Giles. (2017, May 5). "Vital Signs: Racial Disparities in Age-Specific Mortality Among Blacks or African Americans—United States, 1999–2015." Morbidity and Mortality Weekly Report 66, no. 17 (May 5, 2017): 444–456.

Davis, A. Y. *Are Prisons Obsolete?* New York: Seven Stories Press, 2003.

Dunbar-Ortiz, R. *An Indigenous Peoples' History of the United States.* Beacon Press, 2015.

Fanon, F., and R. Philcox. *The Wretched of the Earth.* New York: Grove Press, 2004.

Gabbatt, A. "Social Distancing: New York Police Arresting Black People at Far Higher Rate." Guardian, May 8, 2020, https://www.theguardian.com/us-news/2020/may/08/social-distancing-arrests-black-people-new-york-police.

Goodman, A., and Moynihan, D. "On South Dakota's Sioux reservations, Checkpoints Save Lives." *Indianz.com*, May 21, 2020, https://www.indianz.com/News/2020/05/21/on-south-dakotas-sioux-reservations-chec.asp.

Indian Law Resource Center. (n.d.). "Land Rights." https://indianlaw.org/issue/Land-Rights.

Indian Law Resource Center. (n.d.). "Native Sovereignty and Self-Governance." https://indianlaw.org/issue/Native-Sovereignty-and-Self-Governance.

Intercepted. "Trump's Attack on Voting Rights and the Threat to Native Sovereignty," May 27, 2020, https://theintercept.com/2020/05/27/the-disenfranchiser-donald-trumps-attack-on-voting-rights-and-the-threat-to-native-sovereignty/.

Lhaman, C.E., Timmons-Goodson, P., Adegbile, D. P., Heriot, G. L., Kirsanow, P. N., Kladney, D., Narasaki, K., Yaki, M. *Broken Promises: Continuing Federal Funding Shortfall for Native Americans—Briefing Report.* U.S. Commission on Civil Rights, 2018.

McKenna, Phil. "Standing Rock Asks Court to Shut Down Dakota Access Pipeline as Company Plans to Double Capacity." *Inside Climate News*, August 20, 2019, https://insideclimatenews.org/news/20082019/standing-rock-dakota-access-pipeline-impact-assessment-court-double-capacity.

Mineo, Liz. "The Impact of COVID-19 on Native American Communities." *Harvard Gazette*, May 11, 2020, https://news.harvard.edu/gazette/story/2020/05/the-impact-of-covid-19-on-native-american-communities/.

Mitchell, B., and J. Franco. "HOLC 'Redlining' Maps: The Persistent Structure of Segregation and Economic Inequality." Washington, DC: National Community Reinvestment Coalition, February 2018. https://ncrc.org/wp-content/uploads/dlm_uploads/2018/02/NCRC-Research-HOLC-10.pdf.

Morales, L. "Coronavirus Infections Continue to Rise on Navajo Nation." *NPR.org*, May 11, 2020, https://www.npr.org/sections/coronavirus-live-updates/2020/05/11/854157898/coronavirus-infections-continue-to-rise-on-navajo-nation.

Morales, L. (2020). "Navajo Nation Loses Elders and Tradition to COVID-19." *National Public Radio*. https://www.npr.org/2020/05/31/865540308/navajo-nation-loses-elders-and-tradition-to-covid-19.

Navajo Epidemiology Center. *Navajo Epidemiology Center Update* 1 (May 2016): 1–8. https://www.nec.navajo-nsn.gov/Portals/0/Announcements/NavajoEpidemiologyCenterUpdateMay2016.pdf.

Newkirk, Vann. R. "A Generation of Bad Blood." *Atlantic*, June 17, 2020, http://www.theatlantic.com/politics/archive/2016/06/tuskegee-study-medical-distrust-research/487439/.

NOAA. (n.d. a). *US Climate Resilience Toolkit*. https://toolkit.climate.gov/content/about.

NOAA. (n.d. b). "Explore Hazards." https://toolkit.climate.gov/steps-to-resilience/explore-hazards.

Office of the General Counsel—US Commission on Civil Rights. (2004). *Executive Summary. Native American Health Care Disparities Briefing* (2004): 1–51. http://libraries.ucsd.edu/bib/fed/usccr_natam_disparities.pdf.

Offord, C. "First US COVID-19 Deaths Happened Weeks Earlier Than Thought." *Scientist*, April 22, 2020, https://www.the-scientist.com/news-opinion/first-us-covid-19-deaths-happened-weeks-earlier-than-thought-67457.

Ogbunu, C. "The Pandemic and the Protests Are Mirror Images." *Wired*, June 10, 2020, https://www.wired.com/story/opinion-the-pandemic-and-the-protests-are-mirror-images/.

Peacher, A. (2020). "Doctors Without Borders aids Navajo Nation in fighting coronavirus." *KUNC—National Public Radio*.

Perry, A. M. (2020, March 20). "Black Americans Were Forced into 'Social Distancing' Long Before the Coronavirus." *The Avenue* (blog), *Brookings*, https://www.brookings.edu/blog/the-avenue/2020/03/20/black-americans-were-forced-into-social-distancing-long-before-the-coronavirus/.

Roser, Max. "Global Economic Inequality." Our World in Data, November 24, 2013. https://ourworldindata.org/global-economic-inequality.

Roser, Max. "Human Development Index (HDI)." Our World in Data, July 25, 2014, https://ourworldindata.org/human-development-index#country-by-country-perspective-over-the-last-three-decades.

Snorton, C. R. *Black on Both Sides: A Racial History of Trans Identity*. Minneapolis: University of Minnesota Press, 2017.

Williams, V. "Disproportionately Black Counties Account for Over Half of Coronavirus Cases in the US and Nearly 60% of Deaths, Study Finds." *Washington Post*, May 6, 2020, https://www.washingtonpost.com/nation/2020/05/06/study-finds-that-disproportionately-black-counties-account-more-than-half-covid-19-cases-us-nearly-60-percent-deaths/.

Wynter, S. "Towards the Sociogenic Principle: Fanon, The Puzzle of Conscious Experience, of 'Identity' and What it's Like to be 'Black.'" http://www.coribe.org/pdf/wynter_socio.pdf.

CHAPTER 6

# THE COVID-19 CRISIS AMONG NATIVE AMERICANS IN THE UNITED STATES

*Loren Henderson*

### The COVID-19 Crisis

THE SPREAD OF THE SEVERE acute respiratory syndrome coronavirus 2 (SARS-CoV-2) led to a global pandemic that shed light on existing racial health disparities in the United States. Although most cases of coronavirus disease 2019 (COVID-19) are mild or asymptomatic, SARS-CoV-2 is highly infectious, and there is a mortality rate of 3 percent to 4 percent, with an increased rate among the elderly and those with comorbid conditions, which is particularly alarming for the medical community (Pedersen and Ho 2020). The first reported case of coronavirus infectious disease (COVID-19) in the United States was on January 21, 2020 (Holshue et al. 2020). By March 17, 2020, the Navajo Nation had reported its first case of COVID-19, and within less than fifteen months of the first reported case of COVID-19 in the world, we have gone from a novel virus with a few clusters of cases to a global pandemic that at the time this chapter was written has infected 110 million and killed 2.3 million.

Globally, we shifted from a dearth of scientific data on the virus's origin, transmissibility, and mortality rate to evidence-based practices to prevent its spread and the development of effective vaccines. The rate at which this was all taking place felt both like traveling at the speed of light, wading through scientific discoveries about the virus, while simultaneously being stuck in political and social sludge when trying to find "true" answers on how to protect ourselves and our families. New scientific information was emerging by the hour, yet scientific and political consensus was moving at a snail's pace or not at all. Tragically, during the early weeks and months of the COVID-19 pandemic in the United States, the president of the United States was intentionally downplaying the seriousness of the virus (Keith 2020). This was coupled with vast social media disinformation campaigns about the existence of COVID-19 and the use and efficacy of the two most effective means of preventing transmission of COVID-19: masks and social distancing (Starbird 2020). The public was bombarded with conflicting disinformation concerning the spread and effects of COVID-19, along with federal repudiation and censorship of public health officials. It was simply unimaginable how ill-prepared the United States government was to manage this crisis and just how confusing and anxiety-provoking this time was for the average citizen as well as the academic and medical community. Conventional wisdom suggests that a new virus in the human population with little immunity and no vaccine would act as a leveler of opportunity for infection.

However, what became glaringly obvious was that COVID-19 exploited existing inequalities in our racist social system and targeted those most vulnerable to infectious disease: low-income racial minorities such as Black, Latino/a, and Native Americans, essential workers, and those living in residential housing such as nursing homes and prisons. On March 16, 2020, the president referred to SARS-CoV-2 as "the Chinese Virus" on Twitter. This was a clear example of anti-Chinese racism in the initial response by US government leaders that continued throughout his presidency. As the demand for racial data of COVID-19 increased, it became clear that racial minorities, including Native Americans, were facing a disparate impact. As COVID-19 rates rapidly increased and state and local lockdowns went into effect, scholars studying racial inequalities in health expressed that they were gravely concerned for vulnerable Black, Latino/a, and Native American communities. Prior to the COVID-19 pandemic, many of these communities were already plagued by poverty, a lack of sufficient health care access, high rates of obesity, heart disease, and diabetes, all of which were identified early on as risk factors for transmission and mortality from (SARS-CoV-2). This chapter draws on Critical Race Theory (CRT) as a framework to understand the emerging disparities of COVID-19 among Native Americans and those living on the Navajo Nation tribal lands.

## Theory

"CRT has three primary objectives: (1) to present stories about discrimination from the viewpoint of people of color; (2) to argue for the eradication of racial subjugation while simultaneously acknowledging that race is a social construct; and (3) to deal with other matters of dissimilarity, such as sexuality and class, and any injustices experienced by communities" (Graham et al. 2011). By centering the experiences of Native Americans under COVID-19 and demanding concerted efforts on behalf of the federal government to reduce inequality for Native Americans, we examine the resulting racial disparities in COVID-19 among Native Americans through the lens of Critical Race Theory. Scholars argue that institutionalized systemic racism is a fundamental cause of racial health disparities (Williams et al. 2019; Phelan and Link 2015). "Structural racism has been defined as policies, laws, and regulations that systematically result in differential access to services and opportunities in society based on race" (Wakeel and Njoku 2021, 195). Systemic racism is both a historical and current system that operates by affording societal privileges to some racial groups while cultivating cumulative disadvantage for others through residential segregation that shapes neighborhood access to good schools, foods, jobs, health care, transportation, and appropriate policing to those in White neighborhoods compared with Native American reservations. Among racial scholars and grassroots organizations such as the Black Lives Matter movement, structural racism became a leading explanation of the rapidly evolving health disparities in COVID-19 cases and mortality between Black, Latino/a, White, and Native Americans. They argue that institutionalized colonialist policies created marginalized communities prior to COVID-19, and coupled with the reality that those who were most likely get COVID-19 were also more likely to be essential workers, lose their jobs because of COVID-19, and live in multigenerational homes were Native American, Black, or Latino.

The widespread disinformation about biological/racial immunity against COVID-19 on social media, combined with dismal testing rates, limited collection of racial data by the medical community, and a lack of transparency by the federal government cultivated an environment of "loony lies"[1] about the effectiveness of hydroxychloroquine and chlorine bleach to cure coronavirus. Medical conspiracy theories, anti-Chinese racism, and the seemingly relentless default to explaining racial outcomes in COVID-19 spread as a result of biological and individual behavior. Even the surgeon general Jerome Adams, in his "Focus on the Family" address, initially spoke of discrimination as a factor in the racial disparities in COVID-19, but ultimately placed the responsibility on individuals to protect themselves and their loved ones.

While wearing masks and social distancing are inherently individual-level behaviors, they must be understood to occur in a specific historical context in the United States, a nation rooted in systemic racism and internal colonialist policies that reduce the likelihood that whole groups of marginalized and vulnerable populations are able to follow these recommendations. Researchers suggest that adherence to CDC recommendations is related to socioeconomic factors such as higher education and income, which makes it possible to sift through complex CDC websites and the ability to safely work from home and follow other social distancing measures (Weiss and Paasche-Orlow 2020). Much of the mainstream discussion around COVID-19 adherence continues to distort the reality that following CDC recommendations is more of a privilege than a choice. For example, prisoners in Maryland correctional facilities were used to produce personal protective equipment (PPE) for the prison guards and politicians. Yet, prisoners made less than a dollar a day and were often unable to access masks or hand sanitizer for themselves and were exposed to infected individuals (Broadwater 2020). Essential workers such as grocery clerks, meat packers, farm workers, and hospital staff were called "heroes" while simultaneously they were threatened with termination if they failed to show up for work, even when PPE or social distancing was not possible. While the rich flew off to COVID-19-free havens, the poor remained stuck in place.

---

**1** As stated by Mitch McConnell, minority leader at the time, about Marjorie Taylor Greene's rhetoric, reported by NBC News (https://www.nbcnews.com/now/video/mcconnell-looney-lies-are-a-cancer-on-the-gop-100421701630 )

The lack of PPE in the community, the limited ability for most essential workers to work from home, reduced geographic mobility for the increased amount of multigenerational households within poor and minority communities, and the overwhelming representation of Black and Brown people among the incarcerated highlight the structural constraints that limit the ability for whole groups of people to systematically engage in protective individual behaviors. Prior to the COVID-19 pandemic, scholars called for a shift in the traditional explanations of racial disparities in health among Black, Latino/a, and Native Americans that focus on personal responsibility and individual behaviors to those that highlight systemic racism and internal colonialist policies (Oré et al. 2016). However, given the rapidly emerging racial disparities in COVID-19, it became glaringly obvious that biological and individual behaviors were not adequate explanations for the disparities among Native Americans.

## Historical Context for the Present-Day Racial Disparities in COVID-19 among Native Americans and the Navajo Nation

The United States has maintained a unique relationship with Native American tribal nations based on Article I, Section 8 of the Constitution, which maintains treaties that set the stage for the creation of a federally funded health agency, the Indian Health Service, which serves about 2.6 million Native Americans on tribal lands and throughout the United States (Indian Health Service 2021). Currently, all individuals who are federally recognized as Native American have access to health care services under the treaty obligations of the United States (Hatcher et al. 2020, 1169). Despite the federal policy to provide healthcare access to Native Americans, Native Americans still face some of the worst racial inequalities in health due to limited federal funding and geographic barriers that Native Americans experience when attempting to travel to remote medical centers (Korenbrot et al. 2003).

Researchers have noted the devastating and disproportionate impact that viruses such as smallpox (which killed millions of Aztecs), the 1918 flu (that resulted in a 2 percent population loss of American Indians and Alaska Natives), and the hantavirus (found in the Four Corners Area that resulted in a 75 percent mortality rate) have had on Native Americans (Jones 2006;

Kakol 2021). Not surprisingly, at the outset of the COVID-19 pandemic, those who care deeply about the health and well-being of Native Americans were concerned that this newly emerging SARS-CoV-2 virus could potentially "wipe out" these vulnerable, yet resilient groups of tribal nations (Kakol 2021). Native Americans prior to the COVID-19 pandemic suffered disproportionately from coronary heart disease and diabetes mellitus (Poudel et al. 2018), both underlying risk factors for severe illness and death from SARS-COV-2 (CDC 2021). Native Americans are 50 percent more likely than White Americans to have coronary heart disease (CDC 2017) and 2.5 times more likely to die from diabetes than White Americans (CDC 2016).

Traditional explanations concerning racial disparities in health put forth by the medical community and the federal government focus primarily on individual behavioral choices such as lack of exercise, smoking, obesity, and high blood pressure as the leading causes of heart disease and diabetes (NIDDK 2020; Benjamin et al. 2017). As of February 18, 2021, the Indian Health Service reported 184,585 cases of COVID-19 in their areas. Although Native Americans are 0.7 percent of the US population, they are overrepresented in their rates of COVID-19 (1.3 percent) (Hatcher et al. 2020).

"The Navajo, or Diné, are speakers of an Athabaskan language, and their contemporary homeland is located geographically in the 'Four Corners' region where New Mexico, Arizona, Utah, and Colorado meet." (Csordas 2000, 463). They refer to COVID-19 as *Dikos Ntsaaígíí-19*. They are the second-largest Native American tribe in the United States with the largest reservation held by tribal members. As a result of internal colonialist policies enforced upon the Navajos since the treaty of 1868, what we see today among the Navajo people is a tribal nation with seventeen million acres of land that is land-rich but economically dirt-poor (Robles et al. 2006). In addition, the Navajos are disproportionately burdened with health inequities. As COVID-19 made its way across the ocean, and into Native lands, Navajos were unjustly positioned to suffer some of the most devastating consequences. The Navajo Nation, along with all tribal nations, have historically faced striking health inequalities as a result of systemic racism.

In addition, quality data collection about healthcare outcomes among Navajos continues to be dismal due to the inaccurate reporting of racial categories and the institutionalized policies of disenfranchisement and oppression that situate them to remain invisible in the scientific literature (LaVeist 1995; Horse et al. 2021). Data collection of COVID-19 cases and mortality among Navajos is only collected and reported for those living on tribal lands, and with more than half of Navajos living off the Navajo Nation, this has contributed to the pervasive systematic erasure of Navajos concerning COVID-19 (Horse et al. 2021). Data from the Navajo Nation Health Department and the Centers for Disease Control shows that those living on the Navajo Nation tribal lands and across the United States suffer disproportionately from COVID-19 in both cases and deaths. As of December 2, 2020, there were 2,689 COVID-19–associated deaths among non-Hispanic Native American persons in the United States (Arrazola et al. 2020). The Navajo homeland has a population of approximately 173,637, and as of February 18, 2021, reported 29,386 COVID-19 cases and 1,127 deaths (Navajo Department of Health 2021). In addition, Horse et al. (2020, 1), using geographically weighted regression, found a positive relationship between structural inequality indicators and increased cases of COVID-19 on the Navajo tribal lands. These disparities are accelerating, and public health officials continue to sound the alarm to not reduce social distancing practices or mask-wearing because of the new variant strains of the coronavirus in the United States, which are more virulent.

## Conclusion

Early in the crisis, racial data on COVID-19 cases and mortality were significantly incomplete or omitted by state and local officials. Due to the limited racial data on COVID-19, on March 12, 2020, I began to collaborate with scholars who were interested in the role of systemic racism in maintaining health inequalities related to COVID-19. It quickly became evident that the racial data for Black, Latino/a, and Native Americans on COVID-19 cases and mortality were scattered or not reported at all at the federal, state, or local levels. My coauthors Hayward Horton and Melvin Thomas and I began following the data on the CDC website, the Johns Hopkins Resource Center website, local State Health Departments, and in the news.

It was a rapidly changing and extremely inefficient way to collect, analyze, and compare racial disparities on COVID-19. It was at this point that social justice activists, public health officials, journalists, researchers, and congresspersons began demanding race-based data collection on cases and mortality related to COVID-19. As stratification researchers, we understood the role of systemic racism in maintaining inequality for Native Americans and we were skeptical that the absence of racial data was an innocent omission. We were fully aware that there has been a call to examine and reduce health disparities in the United States since January 2000, when the Department of Health and Human Services launched Healthy People 2010, a comprehensive, nationwide health promotion and disease prevention agenda. This agenda set the stage for examining the social determinants of health—"the conditions in the environments in which people are born, live, learn, work, play, worship, and age that affect a wide range of health, functioning, and quality-of-life outcomes and risks" (CDC 2021) that create and maintain health inequality. According to the CDC, the social determinants of health absolutely include examining the role of residential segregation, one specific form of systemic racism leading to racial disparities, so how was is it possible that public health departments and the federal government were collecting COVID-19 data on other demographic characteristics such as age and gender, but not race? It made no sense at all.

That is of course unless you use a Critical Race Theory framework—a framework that examines racism as both a group and individual phenomenon that functions on many levels and offers a means by which to identify the functions of racism as an institutional and systemic phenomenon (Stovall 2005). Using this framework, we were able to situate our findings and fully digest the reality of the intentional systemic omission of race-based COVID-19 data not as a result of poor coding or innocent oversight but as a result of institutionalized racism in operation. And if it were not for the growing demand of those social justice activists putting pressure on their congresspersons to collect the data, these disparities would have continued to be logged as nothing more than anecdotal reports, situated in the narrative of the "unjustified" mistrust of the medical community among Black and American Natives. During our data collection process, it was almost dizzying how quickly the data was changing (that is how rapidly cases were increasing), but more importantly, it became glaringly obvious that racial disparities were emerging even though the data were incomplete and poorly collected. As researchers, we became deeply concerned about what we were finding, and as social justice advocates, we became rife with anger and frustration at the growing inequality in COVID-19 cases and mortality. The CDC report "COVID-19 Among American Indian and Alaska Native Persons (AI/AN)—23 States, January 31–July 3, 2020" noted that the high rate of missing racial data on Native Americans reported to the CDC made it impossible to conduct critical analyses that would "identify overall prevalence, possible risk factors for COVID-19, and patient outcome" (Hatcher et al. 2020). Such omissions were viewed at minimum as public health failures, and at worst intentional negligence to obscure the realities of structural racism and its impact on the perpetuation of the erasure of Native Americans during the emerging health crisis (Horse et al. 2021; Henderson et al. 2020).

This chapter has attempted to answer the call to center the conversation about COVID-19 racial disparities on Native Americans (Horse et al. 2021). It highlighted data reported by the CDC and Indian Health Services that continues to show that, even with methodological limitations, Native Americans faced some of the largest health disparities in diabetes and heart disease prior to the pandemic and are currently grappling with the devastating disparities in COVID-19 cases and mortality. It remains critical to create a historical record for future generations who will seek answers to manage a pandemic and prevent the vast inequalities in health that viruses create when exploiting the existing structural inequalities. Notwithstanding the limited racial data on COVID-19 among Native Americans, the pervasive nature of structural racism and internal colonialism continues to materialize as a health disparity among Native Americans in COVID-19 cases and mortality. Since systemic racism is a dynamic process of interlocking systems, public health officials and sociologists studying racial disparities in COVID-19 continue to demand the increased and accurate reporting of self-identified racial classification of potential cases, triangulation of multiple forms of health reports such as death certificates, medical documents, and laboratory tests to ascertain an accurate accounting of cases and mortality (Arrazola et al. 2020). In addition, there is an ever-present need to provide culturally sensitive policies targeted to reduce poverty, unemployment, and the lack of adequate health care that results from systemic racism against Native Americans. As the COVID-19 pandemic continues to ravage Native American communities, a glimmer of hope has emerged. With the advent of FDA-approved vaccines, time will tell whether systemic racism will once again result in vaccine hesitancy and the disproportionate access to vaccines among Native Americans.

## References

Arrazola, Jessica, Matthew M. Masiello, Sujata Joshi, Adrian E. Dominguez, Amy Poel, Crisandra M. Wilkie, Jonathan M. Bressler et al. "COVID-19 Mortality Among American Indian and Alaska Native Persons—14 States, January–June 2020." *Morbidity and Mortality Weekly Report* 69, no. 49 (2020): 1853.

Benjamin EJ, MJ Blaha, SE Chiuve, Mary Cushman, Sandeep R. Das, Rajat Deo, and Sarah D. de Ferranti American Heart Association Statistics Committee and Stroke Statistics Subcommittee. "Heart Disease and Stroke Statistics—2017 Update: A Report from the American Heart Association." https://doi.org/10.1161/CIR.0000000000000485.

Broadwater, Luke. "As Coronavirus Spreads in Maryland Prisons, a Small Team of Inmates Makes 24,000 Masks, Other Protective Gear." *Baltimore Sun* April 27, 2020, https://www.baltimoresun.com/coronavirus/bs-md-pol-prison-masks-20200427-fewq4quw6bd63n7fbdcx66rkj4-story.html.

CDC. "Quitting Smoking Among Adults—United States, 2000–2015. Table 2." MMWR 65 (2017): https://www.cdc.gov/mmwr/volumes/65/wr/pdfs/mm6552a1.pdf.

CDC. "Healthy People 2020 Database. Table D-10." http://www.healthypeople.gov/2020/Data/default.aspx.

CDC. "Social Determinants of Health: Know What Affects Health." https://www.cdc.gov/socialdeterminants/index.htm.

Csordas, Thomas J. "The Navajo Healing Project." *Medical Anthropology Quarterly* 14, no. 4 (2000): 463-475.

Graham, Louis, Shelly Brown-Jeffy, Robert Aronson, and Charles Stephens. "Critical Race Theory as Theoretical Framework and Analysis Tool for Population Health Research." *Critical Public Health* 21, no. 1 (2011): 81–93.

Hatcher, Sarah M., Christine Agnew-Brune, Mark Anderson, Laura D. Zambrano, Charles E. Rose, Melissa A. Jim, Amy Baugher et al. "COVID-19 Among

American Indian and Alaska Native Persons—23 States, January 31–July 3, 2020." *Morbidity and Mortality Weekly Report* 69, no. 34 (2020): 1166. https://doi.org/10.15585/mmwr.mm6934e1.

Holshue, Michelle L., Chas DeBolt, Scott Lindquist, Kathy H. Lofy, John Wiesman, Hollianne Bruce, Christopher Spitters et al. "First Case of 2019 Novel Coronavirus in the United States." *New England Journal of Medicine* no. 382 (2020): 929–936. https://doi.org/10.1056/NEJMoa2001191.

Horse, Aggie J. Yellow, Tse-Chuan Yang, and Kimberly R. Huyser. "Structural Inequalities Established the Architecture for COVID-19 Pandemic Among Native Americans in Arizona: A Geographically Weighted Regression Perspective." *Journal of Racial and Ethnic Health Disparities* 9, no.1 (2022): 165–175.

Kakol Monika, Dona Upson, and Akshay Sood. "Susceptibility of Southwestern American Indian Tribes to Coronavirus Disease 2019 (COVID-19)." *Rural Health* 37, no. 1(January 2021): 197–199. https://doi.org/10.1111/jrh.12451.

Keith, Tamara. "Trump Says He Downplayed Coronavirus Threat in US to Avert Panic." *NPR.org*, September 11, 2020, https://www.npr.org/2020/09/11/911828384/trump-says-he-downplayed-coronavirus-threat-in-u-s-to-avert-panic.

Korenbrot, Carol C., Sara Ehlers, and James A. Crouch. "Disparities in Hospitalizations of Rural American Indians." *Medical Care* 41, no. 5 (2003): 626–636.https://doi.org/ 10.1097/01.MLR.0000062549.27661.91.

National Center for Immunization and Respiratory Diseases (NCIRD), Division of Viral Diseases. "Medical Conditions," February 3, 2021. https://www.cdc.gov/coronavirus/2019-ncov/need-extra-precautions/people-with-medical-conditions.html.

National Institute of Diabetes and Digestive and Kidney Diseases "Diabetes, Heart Disease, and Stroke." 2020, https://www.niddk.nih.gov/health-information/diabetes/overview/preventing-problems/heart-disease-stroke.

Navajo Department of Health. "COVID-19." 2021. https://www.ndoh.navajo-nsn.gov/COVID-19.

Navajo Department of Health. "COVID-19," February 18, 2021. https://www.ndoh.navajo-nsn.gov/covid-19.

Oré, Christina E., Nicolette I. Teufel-Shone, and Tara M. Chico-Jarillo. "American Indian and Alaska Native Resilience Along the Life Course and Across Generations: A Literature Review." *American Indian & Alaska Native Mental Health Research: The Journal of the National Center* 23, no.3 (2016): 134–157.

Pedersen, Savannah F., and Ya-Chi Ho. "SARS-CoV-2: A Storm is Raging." *The Journal of Clinical Investigation* 130, no. 5 (2020): 2202–2205. https://doi.org/10.1172/JCI137647.

Phelan, Jo C., and Bruce G. Link. "Is Racism a Fundamental Cause of Inequalities in Health?." *Annual Review of Sociology* 41 (2015): 311–330.

Poudel Anil, Joseph Yi Zhou, Darren Story, and Lixin Li. "Diabetes and Associated Cardiovascular Complications in American Indians/Alaskan Natives: A Review of Risks and Prevention Strategies." *Journal of Diabetes Research* (September 13, 2018): 2742565.https://doi.org/10.1155/2018/2742565.

Robles, Barbara J., Bárbara Yuste, Betsy Leondar-Wright, Rose M. Brewer, and Rebecca Adamson. *The Color of Wealth: The Story Behind the US Racial Wealth Divide*. New York: The New Press, 2006.

Starbird, Kate. Disinformation Campaigns Are Murky Blends of Truth, Lies and Sincere Beliefs—Lessons from the Pandemic. *The Conversation*, July 23, 2020, https://theconversation.com/disinformation-campaigns-are-murky-blends-of-truth-lies-and-sincere-beliefs-lessons-from-the-pandemic-140677.

Stovall, David. "A Challenge to Traditional Theory: CRT, African-American Community Organizers, and Education." *Discourse: Studies in the Cultural Politics of Education* 26, no. 1 (2010), 95–108.

Weiss, Barry D., and Michael K. Paasche-Orlow. "Disparities in Adherence to COVID-19 Public Health Recommendations." *HLRP: Health Literacy Research and Practice* 4, no. 3 (2020): e171–e173.

Williams, David R., Jourdyn A. Lawrence, and Brigette A. Davis. "Racism and Health: Evidence and Needed Research." *Annual Review of Public Health* 40 (2019): 105–125.

CHAPTER 7

# GLOBAL RACIAL CAPITALISM AND COVID-19

*Johnny Eric Williams*
*David G. Embrick*

AS OF MAY 19, 2022, there have been 6.284 million reported deaths across the globe because of the coronavirus (COVID-19) pandemic.[1] In the United States alone, there are over 1 million deaths, close to 16 percent of the total reported global deaths, making the United States the top country with the most recorded deaths, followed by Brazil at slightly over 665,000 deaths, with India in third place with over 524,000 deaths.[2] For a first-world nation,[3] the sheer number of deaths seems astonishing, especially considering the United States outspends other wealthy nations when it comes to health care (Tikkanen and Abrams 2020).[4] However, although the number of deaths across the world resulting from the COVID-19 is mind-boggling, it does not paint a complete picture of who is bearing the brunt of this pandemic.

---

[1] We took this number from the Johns Hopkins University of Medicine Coronavirus Resource Center found at: https://coronavirus.jhu.edu/map.html; retrieved May 19, 2022.

[2] The United States also leads the world in the number of reported COVID-19 cases at 82,971,049 (as of May 19, 2022), followed by India at 43,129,563 and Brazil at 30,701,900; the number of global cases at this time sit at 525,609,269.

[3] We note that while we do find the term "First-world nation" problematic, especially when used in paternalistic and oppressive ways that set them opposite and superior to other nations, our intent is to highlight the irony in how the United States is often portrayed in comparison to its realities.

[4] It is also true that while the United States has access to some of the most expensive and advanced medical technologies, it has the lowest life expectancy and some of the highest suicide rates in comparison to other high-income countries such as Australia, Canada, France, Germany, United Kingdom, and more.

For example, according to Lisa Cooper of Johns Hopkins Bloomberg School of Public Health and School of Medicine, COVID-19 has been disastrous for Black Americans. In states that report racial and ethnic breakdown on reported deaths as a result of COVID-19, Black Americans, representing roughly 13 percent of the US population, account for 34 percent of the total deaths in those states.[5] Asian Americans and Latinx groups only fare slightly better. According to the Centers for Disease Control and Prevention (2020), American Indians, Black Americans, and Latinx are over 2.5 times more likely than their White, Non-Hispanic counterparts to have COVID-19; over 4.5 times more likely to be hospitalized; and for Black Americans, over two times more likely to die from COVID-19 (see also Scott and Animashaun 2020).[6]

Such inequitable outcomes are not just emblematic of the United States alone; these inequalities are also evident in regions of the world that also have high degrees of inequality and marginalization. More than 160,000 Palestinians in the occupied territories tested positive for the coronavirus since March 2020, with more than 1,756 deaths related to COVID-19 and counting. More than 1,800 new cases of COVID-19 are registered a day in 2021. The rate of infection in the occupied territories is 30 percent, compared to 7.4 percent in Israel.[7] Many feared that COVID-19 would especially devastate Gaza—which has been under siege by Israel for decades—with its bare-bones health care system. However, the impact has been mitigated in part by the international community's effort to shore up Gaza's health system (Hincks 2021). Notably, South Africa has the highest number of coronavirus infections on the African continent with more than 1.3 million cases and 37,000 deaths as of January 2021.[8] However, these are only the confirmed figures. Government statistics at the beginning of January 2021 showed a spike

---

[5] For more information see: https://coronavirus.jhu.edu/data/racial-data-transparency; see also the COVID Tracking Project at *The Atlantic*: https://covidtracking.com/race.

[6] For more information see: https://www.cdc.gov/coronavirus/2019-ncov/covid-data/investigations-discovery/hospitalization-death-by-race-ethnicity.html.

[7] For more information, see: World Meters Coronavirus Update https://www.worldometers.info/coronavirus.

[8] See World Meters Coronavirus Update https://www.worldometers.info/coronavirus and South African National Department of Health https://sacoronavirus.co.za/2021/01/18/update-on-covid-19-18th-january-2021.

of almost twenty thousand fatalities in December 2020, with 55,676 deaths compared with 38,620 a year earlier. People from oppressed South African racial groups (Black, Coloured, and Indian) are enduring the most COVID-19 infections and death because they have less access to economic resources. Their economic vulnerability translates into poorer health outcomes that are linked directly to food insecurity, defined as a household not having sufficient resources to consistently access enough food. Pre-pandemic, 91.1 percent of South African households headed by a Black person, compared to 1.3 percent for households headed by a White person (though White people make up 7.9 percent of the population) were vulnerable to hunger (Ro 2020). There are several consequences of lacking access to consistent nutrition, including a higher risk of underlying health conditions that put Black South Africans at a higher risk for developing severe COVID-19 symptoms.

What accounts for these racial inequalities? How do we make sense of these disparate numbers? And how might we best sociologically and critically explain what is going on? Part of the answer lies in the fact that the United States, Israel, and South Africa are racialized social systems (Bonilla-Silva 1997), and as such, the roots of White supremacy run deep (Feagin 2005). In such systems, according to Bonilla-Silva (2020: 2), White racism not only shapes our national discussion about the pandemic, but it also limits our recognition of the problems made apparent during the COVID-19 pandemic as structural in nature. Such framing initially exacerbated myths of Black immunity to COVID-19 that severely limited the seriousness of not only the disease itself toward Black populations but also their reaction to treatments and preventative measures (see Laurencin and McClinton 2020 for one of the earliest empirical publications to tackle this issue).

As oppressed racialized people around the world continue to be infected by coronavirus and die at disproportionate rates, we are reminded how global White supremacist capitalism deprives racially oppressed people of care. As Cedric Robinson (1983) noted, the modern world system of racial capitalism is dependent on imperialism, violence, and consistent racial and class forms of oppression to sort and subjugate people in ideological, mental, and physical ways. For example, the United States has a long and storied history with deep roots in capitalism and White supremacy that continues to drive oppressive economic, social, political, and psychological inequities advantaging so-called White people over racialized Others. Andrew Hacker notes, in his book *Two Nations: Black and White, Separate, Hostile, Unequal* (2003) that this deadly tradition continues despite the increased incorporation of Black people into US capitalism.

In this chapter, we argue that racial capitalism as a global phenomenon best explains racial inequalities in coronavirus infection and death around the world. Specifically, we contend that the COVID-19 crisis reveals how racial capitalism's structures of violence operate through anti-Black governments' policies and practices implemented to address the pandemic. We aim to expand upon recent research on this subject (Pirtle 2020; McClure et al. 2020; Freshour and Williams 2020). Using racial capitalism as our theoretical interpretive frame, we demonstrate how racist and classist measures further intensify existing oppressive structural conditions of Black people and other racially oppressed groups in the United States, Palestine, and South Africa, who are dying and suffering at higher rates from COVID-19. We conclude with implications and suggestions for rethinking systemic White racism, health inequalities, and anti-Black racism.

## Racial Capitalism

The phrase "racial capitalism" first emerged in the context of the anti-Apartheid and South African liberation struggles in the 1970s. Racial capitalism was used by people aligned with the Black Consciousness Movement in South Africa to counter liberal analyses suggesting Apartheid is reformable through a reorganization of capitalism that was insufficiently attentive to questions of "race" (Hudson 2018). Their use of racial capitalism enabled them to introduce a stronger structural and class analysis into the interpretive discourse of Black Consciousness. Burden-Stelly, Hudson, and Pierre (2020) argue that despite racial capitalism's South African origins, neither Robinson nor his contemporary interlocutors engaged with African scholarship on racial capitalism. As Hudson (2018) poignantly notes, engaging African racial capitalism forces its proponents to center in their work what Du Bois called the "dark proletariat": racialized toilers whose historical presence dislodges the pretension of a universal working-class subject, who is invariably

White. Robinson popularized the term "racial capitalism" in his book *Black Marxism* (1983), in which he specifies that racial capitalism relies upon and reinforces commodification of racial identity, reducing racially oppressed people to a thing to be bought and sold. Because racialized Black folx are commodified in ways that ensure they die prematurely from the violent and exploitive conditions that racial capitalism generates, they resist its thingification of their person.

## On Racial Capitalism

The elementary thesis of the racial capitalism concept is as follows: capitalism as an economic system subsists on the perpetual accumulation of capital and an increasing rate of said accumulation, and capital "can only accumulate by producing and moving through relations of severe inequality among human groups" (Melamed 2015, 77). To survive, capitalism exploits and depends upon differentiating human value (Melamed 2015, 77). As Robinson (1983, 2) put it, "The development, organization, and expansion of capitalist society pursued essentially [material] racial directions [that] inevitably permeate the social structures emergent from capitalism." Thus, the term racial capitalism requires its proponents to recognize that "capitalism is never *not* racial,"[9] and "race" is constitutive of capitalism.

Robinson challenged the Marxist notion of capitalism's negation of the basic discriminatory tenets of European feudalism, namely its rigid caste system and reliance upon multigenerational serfdom. Rather than considering capitalism as revolutionary and radically liberating, as, say, Michael Novak (1982) does, Robinson (1983, 27) argued for the inverse: capitalism did not liberate the racially oppressed nor did it reject feudal principles of order. That is to say, capitalism bred a new world order that extended rather than deconstructed feudalism's ethical faults; it intertwined with various forms of racial oppression: slavery, colonialism, imperialism, and genocide.

Robinson asserted that although racial capitalism is not limited to European territories or those previously under Europe's colonial or imperial rule, it was in the context of seventeenth-century Western Europe

---

**9** Emphasis is ours.

that capitalism and racialism were first conflated to facilitate economic exploitation. Thus, racial capitalism, according to Robinson (1983, 27), emanated from the "tendency of European civilization . . . not to homogenize [groups of peoples] but to differentiate"—differentiation that led to racial hierarchization and resulting exploitation and expropriation. Through racialism, capitalism facilitates the accumulation of wealth through the unequal differentiation of human value using race as an ideology and White racism as a practice to exploit and dominate human beings. It accomplishes this by displacing the uneven life chances that are a characteristic part of capitalist social relations onto raced fictions of differing human capacities (Malemed 2015, 17). A fiction grounded in anti-Blackness that cast African people as non-humans. This distinction between lives that matter and lives that matter less is evident during the COVID-19 pandemic. The lives of White people, especially wealthy White people, are protected over precarious and otherized people whose lives do not matter.

## COVID-19, Racial Capitalism, and Global Racial Oppression

Though racial capitalism is usually associated with the White supremacist capitalism development, including slavery, colonialism, genocide, incarceration regimes, and migrant exploitation, the social conditions it generates are also the fundamental cause of health inequalities (Pirtle 2020). Because the violent accumulation processes of racial capitalism operate at all layers of society's socioeconomic stratification, it contributes to health inequalities. Public health and social science research (Link and Phelan 1995; Roberts 1997; Williams and Collins 2001; Washington 2006; Hatch 2016) have long documented the devastating health consequences of conjoined systemic racial and class oppression.

Although the virus does not discriminate, racial capitalist policies and institutions do. This chapter highlights racial capitalism's institutional processes rather than the habits of racially oppressed people. Our analysis lies with the former rather than the latter given individual responsibility does not ensure societal health but scapegoats racially and class-oppressed people for spreading disease. This was very much evident when the Trump administration's surgeon general, Jerome Adams, suggested that Black people's overconsumption of "alcohol, tobacco, and drugs" was the fundamental reason they are more likely to succumb to COVID-19. His claim contradicted evidence demonstrating Black people have lower user rates for alcohol, tobacco, and drugs than White people. Their susceptibility to COVID-19 is therefore an institutional rather than individual issue (Christian 2020). Rather than connect Black folx's disproportionate susceptibility to COVID-19 to the social forces of racial capitalism's effect on their living conditions, working circumstances, and lower access to health care, Trump administration officials found it easier to blame comorbidity conditions on their behavior rather than structural design making them more susceptible to contracting and dying from the virus.

The racialized use of individual-level risk factors is prominent in medical literature as well. According to Roberts, such individualism leads researchers, physicians, and politicians to focus irrationally on disease etiology as an outcome of "underlying" health conditions and behavioral risk factors that cause them "to ignore how disease is caused by political inequality [that] justif[ies] an unequal system by pointing to the inherent racial difference [in] disease [susceptibility]" (2011, 402). Under racial capitalism, attention is drawn away from the inequalities it produces by creating narratives insinuating that the racially oppressed are inherently at risk of contracting and dying of coronavirus due to their own racial and behavioral susceptibility. In short, the attribution of increased coronavirus susceptibility to individual-level etiologies—including higher rates of comorbidities and sociocultural differences such as health-seeking behavior and intergenerational cohabitation—overshadow differential transmission related to structural factors, in particular, racial capitalism (Pareek et al. 2020; Bailey and Moon 2020).

Capitalism is a violent exploitive system of domination intertwined with various forms of oppression—slavery, imperialism, and genocide. As such, people residing in racial capitalist societies are inclined to use anti-Black logic to contend that the higher contraction and death rates of coronavirus among Black folx and other racially oppressed people are related to underlying medical conditions (e.g., hypertension, cardiovascular disease, diabetes, lung disease, obesity, or asthma) common within the group. One would expect that the comorbidities problem would move people to ask and investigate the fundamental cause of these underlying health conditions making Black folx susceptible to die from coronavirus rather than blaming them for contracting and dying from the coronavirus. However, in racial capitalist societies that devalue and treat racially oppressed people as expendable, the latter happens even though it is widely recognized in the medical literature that disease burden and mortality are greatest for the poor and racially oppressed (Adler and Ostrove 1999; Adler and Stewart 2010).

Though people share a common humanity, racial capitalism, through scientific racism, racializes different populations and acts as if they are biologically different. Nevertheless, all humans are at risk for coronavirus infection, but most people who contract the disease do not die. This differentiation in susceptibility to death from COVID-19 is not simply a biological difference given humans are not just biology. We are social beings as well—with social divisions in our society and histories of structural oppression, particularly around White racism and economic exploitation. Therefore, we must grapple with the histories of racial capitalism and settler colonialism to better ascertain why some human groups are more at risk for adverse exposure to the coronavirus and susceptible to death after infection. To this end, we examine the unequal and devastating effects of COVID-19 among oppressed racialized people, particularly Black folx, through a focus on racial capitalism as a mode of ordering vulnerability and exposure to harm. To this end, we compare how the settler-colonial racial capitalism contexts of the United States, Israel, and South Africa drive uneven susceptibility to coronavirus.

## US Context

Racial capitalism consistently imposes a brutal, rolling triage on Black people in the United States that started with the kidnapping and enslavement of African people that cost them their lives and health while racial capitalists accrued benefits from their suffering. This continues to the present in the form of a privatized health care system that positions the well-being of prosperous White people over Black people. Though the coronavirus does not differentiate whom it infects based on race or class, it is more of a problem for Black people because of racial capitalism. For instance, though people are encouraged to telework, this is not an option for most Black people since racial capitalism ensures they are chronically underemployed or employed in low paying "essential" service industries (see Saenz et al. 2007; Douglas et al. 2018). Given this, less than 20 percent of Black workers are able to work from home, increasing the possibility of their exposure and infection (Doumas et al. 2020). Moreover, although physical distancing is an effective measure for preventing the spread of coronavirus, racial capitalism mechanisms such as chronic unemployment and underemployment, redlining, and loan discrimination deem it necessary for Black folx to reside in multigenerational households, resulting in close contact among both the elderly and youth (Omer et al. 2020). Because youth are less likely to conform to social distancing, they are more likely to spread the virus throughout their household.

Additionally, many Black workers are low-paid essential employees (e.g., sanitation, customer service, store clerks and stockers, custodians, and social care) who have little control over their workplace, are not given adequate protective personal equipment, go without paid sick leave, and lack adequate health insurance coverage. These factors coalesce to help create the conditions for high COVID-19 infection and mortality (Bonilla-Silva 2020). Moreover, because Black workers are compensated poorly, they cannot afford to stay at home nor do many have the budget for two weeks of groceries, or, as we alluded to earlier, homes with extras rooms for self-isolating. The coronavirus pandemic has also exacerbated Black folx's financial despair, with many experiencing a disproportionate high-income loss and housing insecurity. Opinion polls show that 60 percent of Black households report serious financial problems like using up all their savings, food insecurity, and an inability to pay for housing. The economic insecurity matches the inordinate health toll the pandemic is having on Black folx. To try to scrape by with the basics needed to subsist, Black workers have to work for precarious wages and with no benefits.

On the other hand, the beneficiaries of neoliberal racial capitalism can protect themselves by virtue of their Whiteness and class power in the form of gated communities, exclusive luxurious beaches, and high-rise apartments. That is, physical distance works for them because their Whiteness and class position separate them from the majority of the population susceptible to infection because of their lack of status and resources. This is also applicable to middle and upper-middle class White folx who are able to adhere to state guidelines to stay indoors and practice physical distancing. They too have the necessary capital reserve, spacious housing, and various modes of private transportation to work from home and stay isolated for an extended period. This inequality necessitates that we account for the structural causes of Black susceptibility to COVID-19 before placing blame on them for contracting the virus.

According to Ford, Reber, and Reeves (2020), not only are COVID-19 death rates among Black Americans (and Latinx) much higher than White people in all age categories but also Black Americans "are dying from COVID at roughly the same rate as White people more than a decade older." Black health and welfare are always incompatible with racial capitalism. During a pandemic in a racial capitalist society, Black people's death follows the same pattern as the historical excessive mortality visited upon them due to their subordinate, despised, and expendable status. During the last great pandemic to ravage the United States, the 1918 flu, over a half a million Americans perished, but the mortality level for White people was lower than that of Black people in any given non-pandemic year (Wrigley-Field 2020). The infectious mortality experienced by urban White people in 1918 was lower than that of urban Black people in every documented year through 1920 (Feigenbaum et al. 2019). By all major mortality measures—infectious mortality, total mortality, and life expectancy—in the early decades of the twentieth century, Black people experienced a scale of death comparable to White people's experience of the 1918 flu every year (Wrigley-Field 2020). These inequalities persisted even when both Black and White people resided in densely populated urban areas. This suggests the system of racial capitalism preceding the current pandemic structurally concentrates exposures and exacerbates COVID-19 risk for Black folk through its historically bred inequities and state-sanctioned subjection of them to premature death (Pirtle 2020).

Racial capitalism usually restricts Black people to residing in densely populated urban areas that are environmentally unsound and devoid of grocery stores and medical facilities, making it difficult for them to lead healthy lives. Typically, Black folx dying of coronavirus are limited to residing in highly polluted and under-resourced areas like those in Louisiana who are concentrated in a corridor of parishes along the Mississippi River between Baton Rouge and New Orleans. These parishes rely on a petrochemical industry built on the lands of former plantations. The "double curse of oil dependency layered on top of a foundation of plantation dependency" environmentally and socially heightens Black people's susceptibility to COVID-19 (Woods 2017, 222). The pernicious effects of racial capitalism's logic are evident in political decisions about how to combat the coronavirus. On the national level, there was no coordinated plan, until Joseph Biden assumed the presidency, to address the disproportionate death of Black people from COVID-19. Though some states have been proactive, most are not. Instead, state politicians took a business-as-usual approach that put people, particularly Black folx, in harm's way. States also resisted demands for decarceration, even though prisons and immigrant detention centers are ideal sites for the spread of the coronavirus. Racial capitalism enables a racially marked and uneven spread of COVID-19 among low-wage, nonunionized, and undervalued workers (Wilson 2000). It constructs avoidable, yet woefully permissible premature death for Black people through disinvestment from their communities and expansion of the carceral state. This amplification and intensification of deprivation and suffering during the pandemic crisis highlighted people exposed to toxic environments, anti-worker and anti-union organizing, denial of social service and access to healthcare, food deserts, over-policing, and individualism. These conditions and practices produce coronavirus mortality rates for Black people that mirrors their excessive rates of unemployment, infant mortality, and premature death by violence. This is evident in the higher COVID-19 mortality rates for Black people. Though White, Latino/a, and Black people comprise 60.1 percent, 18.5 percent, and 12.5 percent of the United States' population, Black individuals die of COVID-19 at disproportionately higher rates. According to the 2020 Centers for Disease Control and Prevention (CDC) weekly COVID-19 data release, White people account for 59.6 percent, Latino/a/s for 18.6 percent, and Black people for 16.1 percent of COVID-19 deaths in the United States.[10] The higher mortality rate for Black people, as we demonstrate, is highly correlated with underlying mechanisms of racial capitalism.

---

**10** Truman BI, Chang M, Moonesinghe R. Provisional COVID-19 Age-Adjusted Death Rates, by Race and Ethnicity—United States, 2020–2021. MMWR Morb Mortal Wkly Rep 2022; 71: 601–605. DOI: http://dx.doi.org/10.15585/mmwr.mm7117e2

*Israel/Palestine Context*

Though separated by geography and different political contexts, Black Americans and Palestinians have a shared experience with racial capitalism. Consider how they both use the term "occupied" to describe their economically devastated cities/nation controlled by racist paramilitary police and military force. In addition, both United States and Israeli officials and media criminalize Black and Palestinian existence, portraying violence against them as "isolated incidents," and claiming their resistance to state repression is "illegitimate" or "terrorism."[11] Israel and the United States also use detention and mass incarceration, including political imprisonment of social change agents who challenge their settler-colonial racial capitalist hegemony. This shared experience with racial capitalism means that Black Americans and Palestinians are keenly aware that their struggle against racial capitalism is global, and that people with completely different historical and political trajectories are affected by its formidable hegemony. Because the struggle against racial capitalism is worldwide and intersectional, it is possible to see clearly how it fuels the spread of COVID-19.

As of January 1, 2021, more than 160,000 Palestinians in the occupied Palestinian territory had tested positive and over 1,700 had succumbed to COVID-19. And as the coronavirus continues to ravage the 4.5 million Palestinians of the East Jerusalem, West Bank, and Gaza—fracturing an already badly under-resourced Palestinian health care system—particularly in Gaza, which is enduring an ongoing blockade, serious water and electricity shortages, and endemic poverty and unemployment. Similar to Black Americans, Palestinians in Gaza live in an area with little space for physical distancing. Jabalia, for example, the largest of Gaza's eight refugee camps houses 110,000 people in the area that is only 1.4 square kilometers (345 acres) (Deutsch 2020). Like their counterparts in the US settler-colonial state, Palestinians are resource-deprived and cordoned off in ways that increase the probability of their contracting and dying from coronavirus as compared to resource-rich Israeli occupiers. Exports from Gaza are almost completely blocked, imports and cash transfer are severely restricted, and the flow of all

---

11 2015 Black Solidarity Statement with Palestine. http://www.blackforpalestine.com/read-the-statement.html.

but the most basic goods are suspended. Israel has destroyed Gaza's water and sewage system, making it difficult to maintain the required standard of hygiene required to help fend off COVID-19 infection (Deutsch 2020). This all does not bode well for racialized Palestinians' health.

The source of coronavirus infection for Palestinians in the West Bank and Gaza, similar to Black Americans who labor predominantly in the service sector, thus designated "essential" workers, is among their laborers who prop up Israel's construction and agricultural economies who commute back and forth to Israel and Israeli settlements in the West Bank. According to Garbett (2020), the COVID-19 crisis in occupied Palestine highlights the multiple ways Israeli racial capitalism exploits Palestinian labor to bolster Israel's settler-colonial racial capitalist project, while cutting costs and displacing responsibility for the protection of workers on the weak, besieged infrastructure of the Palestinian health system and economy. Israel is using the pandemic to assist its racial capitalist settler-colonial project by accelerating infrastructural projects restricting Palestinian access to land in both Israel and the West Bank (Garbett 2020). For example, in Jerusalem, Israel is fast-tracking work on the Begin highway, with the expansion of light train and settlement projects in Romot, Pizagat Ze'ev, and French Hill. In addition, West Bank settlements are speeding up infrastructure and construction work. The continuation of these projects is of deep importance to Israel because they ensure the movement of goods, people, and capital. Thus, the Palestinians building this infrastructure are expendable and necessarily so to cleanse the land of their presence and to ensure the Israeli economic sector, which is dependent on construction, does not halt during the pandemic. Garbett (2020) contends that if construction work were to stop, it would cause considerable damage to the Israeli economy by triggering a cascade of delayed payments to banks and insurance companies—with major consequences for the banking sector. For this reason, Israeli authorities are reluctant to test workers before they return home after a day's labor.

The disregard for Palestinian health is not new but a feature of the racial capitalist settler-colonial state of Israel. Occupied Palestine is entirely dependent on Israeli occupiers. Palestinians are routinely denied access to basic health care by Israeli land confiscations and checkpoints. In the West Bank town of Negev, for example, over eighty thousand Palestinians have no access to emergency health care. As the coronavirus rapidly spreads in the West Bank, Palestinians' public health infrastructure is being undermined by Israel's withholding of revenues to the Palestinian Authority (PA) and austerity measures imposed on the PA by the World Bank and International Monetary Fund (Nithya 2020). Even when Palestinians are able to scrape together funding to secure equipment needed to fend off the COVID-19 among them, Israel decides whether to let these medical tools into the occupied territories. At this moment, the coronavirus pandemic is deliberately being used by Israel to further intensify military actions, and electronic and other mechanisms of surveillance to escalate the annexation of Palestinian land. This all deepens Palestinian food insecurity and susceptibility to contracting the virus, given many Palestinian families have no money to buy food because Israel has starved Gaza and the West Bank by holding on to taxes and duties it collects on their behalf.

For five decades, the racial capitalist settler-colonial Israeli project has pursued a policy of treating Palestinians as less than human. Israel controls Palestinian lives while denying any meaningful responsibility for their welfare. For example, Israel selectively rolled out its COVID-19 vaccine campaign in December 2020. It secured eight million doses of the Pfizer vaccine, which did not include dosages for Palestinians residing in the West Bank and Gaza. This was the case even though Israel transported batches of the Pfizer/BioNTech vaccine deep inside the West Bank to distribute to Jewish settlers, and not Palestinians living around them, who waited for weeks or months.[12] Furthermore, the Israeli public security minister directed health officials not to administer the vaccine to so-called security prisoners—all of whom are Palestinians (Breiner 2020). Because racial capitalism exploits and preys upon the "unequal differentiation of human value," it runs counterintuitively to scientific insights for containing the spread of COVID-19. Offering vaccines to just two-thirds of the people under Israeli control is not effective in combating the spread of the coronavirus (Karmi 2020). In contrast to racial capitalism's differentiation of human groups, the coronavirus makes it plain that we are a single species whose differing susceptibility to virus infection and death is

---

**12** See the Guardian at: https://www.theguardian.com/world/2021/jan/03/palestinians-excluded-from-israeli-covid-vaccine-rollout-as-jabs-go-to-settlers.

the result of the structural regimes of settler-colonial racial capitalism. This requires us to recognize that though people have differences in phenotype, these apparent differences are not understandable using racial capitalism's narratives of COVID-19 to understand differentiation rates of infection and death because they do not allow us to see racial capitalism's essentialist differentiating structures as the source of the problem.

## South African Context

South Africa presents an interesting case concerning the pandemic and its history underwritten by settler-colonial racial capitalism. As we noted earlier, while we freely acknowledge Robinson's contributions to racial capitalism and find it useful for our comparative analysis here, Robinson did not coin the term "racial capitalism," although he was instrumental in popularizing it. The term "racial capitalism" emerged prior to Robinson's framework in South Africa to explain how anti-Black racism and capitalism work in tandem. While Apartheid as a formal national policy is outdated, racial capitalism continues to devastate Black individuals, the majority of whom live in the poorest households in South Africa. On average, these households consist of five members with a total monthly household income of R2,600 ($173 US), or R567 per person ($37.64). These households typically have only one person employed. During the ongoing COVID-19 pandemic, this person has lost 45 percent of their household income. In contrast, more affluent and White households, with approximately two people per household have a monthly income of R38,000 ($2,422.50), or R21,000 per person ($1,394). Almost 80 percent of these households have at least one employed member who is working far more hours at a higher wage than those in the poorest household (Francis et al. 2020).

South Africans in the richest households are able to telework from home while those in poor households work for lower pay in the service sector and must continue to work or lose their jobs. The South African unemployment insurance fund provides some temporary relief to workers who lose their job, but it, like state unemployment insurance in the United States, is beset with administrative failures. People who work in the gig economy or temp work do not even have this protection. Labor Force Survey data reveals that

2.6 million people working in the informal labor sector are self-employed; another million or so are domestic workers who have no employment benefits (Francis et al. 2020). These folx have no wealth to sustain them during the protracted COVID-19 and economic crisis in wake of settler-colonial racial capitalism. In the ever-important, life-sustaining, undervalued service sector, Black people are exposed to increased pauperization due to rising unemployment rates, adequate benefits, and racial capitalism-driven environmental racism, poor living conditions, food and housing insecurities, regressive taxation, and inadequate education (Alexander 2002), all factors increasing Black folx's susceptibility to coronavirus infection and resulting in death.

Although not as large in sheer case numbers, as of January 15, 2021, South Africa reported 1,259,748 cases and 34,334 deaths related to COVID-19 and Israel has just over 500,000 cases (517,271) and 3,803 deaths. It is appropriate to note that the West Bank and Gaza are counted separately by the Coronavirus Resource Center at Johns Hopkins and are listed at 149,769 cases and a reported 1,658 deaths. South Africa has been tagged by the United States[13] and other countries as a Level 4[14] (Very High) danger with a warning to restrict all travel to that country as a result of new variants of SARS-CoV-2 (known as 501Y.V2) that are deemed to be a greater threat than the variant detected in the United Kingdom. The new mutation allows the virus to better attach to cells and enter them making them highly transmittable, and while not deemed a deadlier strain in comparison to its predecessor, faster spread of the virus would further stress already strained health care resources.[15] The majority of COVID-19 cases in South Africa are in the Eastern (14.2 percent) and Western Cape (19.4 percent) and in KwaZulu-Natal (20.8 percent), where the three provinces have a combined 705,350 cases as of January 14, 2021.[16]

---

**13** See US Centers for Disease Control and Prevention data at: https://wwwnc.cdc.gov/travel/notices/covid-4/coronavirus-south-africa.
**14** As of January 15, 2021.
**15** See Schumaker (2021) for more information on the COVID-19 variant spreading in South Africa.
**16** According to the National Institute of Communicable Diseases: https://www.nicd.ac.za/latest-confirmed-cases-of-covid-19-in-south-africa-14-jan-2021/.

Racial inequalities are high in these provinces, and in South Africa, in general, as many poor Black people are unable to social distance as a result of living in crowded townships that are remnants of the Apartheid era and ongoing racial capitalism (Steinhauser and Patel 2020). In a racialized social system undergirded by racial capitalism, most White people live in spacious homes and have the resources necessary to avoid public transport and other generally overcrowded areas in their day-to-day lives. The reality of the situation is that in a settler-colonial racial capitalist context, the South African Black majority has taken the brunt of the additional inequalities brought on by the COVID-19 pandemic because of the legacies of Apartheid and continued racial capitalism that panders to wealthier White people. For example, one report in South Africa suggests that Black and mixed-race patients are at higher risk of dying of COVID-19 than their White counterparts.[17] In a more comprehensive picture of the realities faced by Black and mixed-race South Africans, Machaka (2020) argues that COVID-19 has intensified already existing racial inequalities brought on by racial capitalism. Because White people have more resources due to their control of the land and economic system, they are less likely to be affected economically by COVID-19. In comparison, Black and mixed-raced folx, particularly poor Black people, who were forcefully removed to infertile lands and crowded inhumane spaces, face additional challenges brought on by the pandemic that keep them locked in a never-ending battle for survival. The spread of COVID-19, as we mentioned earlier, makes it nearly impossible for most Black people to keep their heads above water.

The realities of how racial capitalism affects Black people in South Africa are made more apparent regarding their lack of health care access, in general, which is even more profound during the COVID-19 pandemic. The latter is fueled, in part, by a South African health system that has systematically neglected Black and mixed-race people. Despite a number of commendable goals set by the government to improve the quality-of-service delivery in healthcare settings, reports by media and communities in 2009

---

17   See "Mixed Race COVID-19 Patients Dying More than White Patients in South Africa, Says Report." *DeccanHerald*, August 15, 2020. Retrieved January 15, 2021, from: https://www.deccanherald.com/international/mixed-race-covid-19-patients-dying-more-than-white-patients-in-south-africa-says-report-873801.html.

revealed that services in public health institutions were nonetheless failing to meet basic standards of care and patient expectation for Black patients (National Department of Health 2012, 4). Thus, they have little confidence the healthcare system works to ensure they lead healthy lives.

Many of the problems in the South African healthcare system can be traced back to the Apartheid period (1948–1993) during which the healthcare system was highly fragmented, with discriminatory effects, between four different racial groups (Black, mixed-race, Indian, and White) (Baker 2010, 79). This worsened when the capitalist Apartheid government established ten Bantustans (the so-called ethnic homelands) into which Black people were forcefully segregated to include segregated departments of health with their professional bodies (Baker 2010, 80). This segregation created separate vastly under-resourced and equipped health systems (Chassin and Loeb 2013; Digby 2013). Though the South African government has taken up efforts to improve the quality of healthcare delivery in South Africa since 1994, several issues remain, among them, the following: prolonged waiting time because of shortage of human resources, adverse events, poor hygiene, and poor infection control measures, increased litigation because of avoidable errors, shortage of resources in medicine and equipment, and poor record-keeping. (Maphumulo and Bhengu 2019). Lack of access to health care is only the tip of the iceberg of an overall racial capitalist system in which Black individuals face institutionalized racial discrimination and professional marginalization in health care professions (Digby 2013; see also Mkize 2020) such as mental health care (Swartz 1991) and medical mistrust (Moll 2021). People living in informal settlements (overwhelmingly Black and mixed-race people), similar to conditions faced in Palestine as well as the United States, are particularly vulnerable in that it is not just access to health care but basic human rights necessities that would enable preventative measures such as access to clear water for handwashing and adequate housing (see Karim 2020).

Global racial capitalism solidifies and strengthens existing forms of oppression in ways that tie countries such as South Africa, Palestine, and the United States together, even as their historical, political, and social contexts differ. The settler-colonial racial capitalist systems exacerbate and embrace anti-Blackness to fuel the unequal distribution of resources, exploitation of human labor, and devaluing of Black lives. Racial capitalism as a system of oppression requires us to see that liberating ourselves from its various global tentacles of harm necessitates oppressed people around the world to coordinate their resistance.

## Conclusion

To summarize, we argue that racial capitalism as a global phenomenon best explains racial inequalities in coronavirus infections and deaths around the globe. Racial capitalism is inextricably linked to settler colonialism, apartheid, imperialism, and anti-Blackness. We evidence this in three case examples of South Africa, Palestine, and the United States to illustrate how racial capitalism as a global system of oppression operates similarly, regardless of these countries varied individual histories. We demonstrated, using racial capitalism as our theoretical interpretive frame, how racist and classist state measures exacerbate existing oppressive structural conditions of Black people, specifically, but also other racialized people, who are disproportionately affected by COVID-19.

So, why does this matter? The racial capitalism healthcare system's disparate treatment and neglect of Black and other racialized people's health concerns is centuries long. Racial capitalism governments, particularly those intertwined with settler-colonial histories, which are central sites for coordinating a response to something as relational and far-reaching as a pandemic, have neither the political will nor an effective plan for ameliorating Black suffering and death. Instead, their responses simply asked individuals to engage in preventative behaviors: washing hands, avoiding large gatherings, and staying at home if sick. Even these requests at the individual level ignore who has access to resources (e.g., water, clean air) and who does not. While individual decisions matter in terms of disease spread, an effective response to something as social and general as a pandemic requires state action rather than individualized remediation and blame (Freshour and Williams 2020). Consequently, the virus spreads with alarming speed among Black people because racial capitalism deems them expendable in its relentless quest for capital accumulation. Hence, though the coronavirus does not discriminate, there are so many ways that racial capitalism acts upon, intensifies, and produces COVID-19 inequalities.

As we mentioned, many health experts attribute Black people's disproportionate coronavirus mortality rate to the existence of multiple preexisting conditions that make them more susceptible to COVID-19 (Gupta et al. 2021). These compounding risk factors are inseparable from racial capitalism–induced environmental racism and healthcare inequalities as well as other inequities affecting Black people's lives. For example, exposure to toxins and particulate matter through pollution contributes to diabetes, respiratory issues, and a whole host of other health complications and chronic illnesses is a consequence of racial capitalism processes confining Black people to low-wage service labor and poor housing in segregated, polluted communities (Freshour and Williams 2020). These factors, in turn, increase the likelihood that Black people and authorized people will develop severe or even fatal complications from COVID-19. Alongside this (unnatural) vulnerability, access to healthcare and testing remains highly uneven. White racism as state-sanctioned vulnerability to premature death is the fatal infrastructure for COVID-19's spread and constitutes a central dynamic in the racial capitalist state's responses to the pandemic (Gilmore 2007).

In order to get at the root of these global systems of oppression, we must, as the noted historian Robin D. G. Kelly has suggested, think and be more than just anti-racist: we should think intersectionally and engage inter/transdisciplinary so we can be more pro-emancipation and pro-liberation. Rethinking the COVID-19 pandemic along racial capitalism lines allows us to think about the bigger picture of how countries with settler-colonial, racialized histories have been similarly affected by global White supremacy and anti-Blackness.

## References

Adler, Nancy and Judith Stewart. "Health Disparities across the Lifespan: Meaning, Methods, and Mechanisms." *Annals of the New York Academy of Science* 1186 (2010) 5–23.

Adler, Nancy and Joan Ostrove. "Socioeconomic Status and Health: What we know and What we don't." *Annals of the New York Academy of Science* 896, (1999): 3–15.

Alexander, N. *An Ordinary Country: Issues in the Transition from Apartheid to Democracy in South Africa*. Scottsville, South Africa: University of Natal Press, 2002.

Bailey, Z. D. and J. R. Moon. Racism and the Political Economy of COVID-19: Will we continue to resurrect the past? *The Journal of Health Politics, Policy and Law* (2020) 45 (6): 937–950.

Baker, P. 2010. "From Apartheid to Neoliberalism: Health Equity in Post-Apartheid South Africa." *International Journal of Health Services*, 40, 79–95.

Bonilla-Silva, E. (2020). "Color-Blind Racism in Pandemic Times." *Sociology of Race and Ethnicity*. https://doi.org/10.1177/2332649220941024.

Bonilla-Silva, E. "Rethinking Racism: Toward A Structural Interpretation." *American Sociological Review* 62, no. 3 (1997): 465–480.

Breiner, J. "Israeli Minister Orders Not to Vaccinate Palestinian Security Prisoners, Despite COVID Directives." *Haaretz*, December 27, 2020, https://www.haaretz.com/israel-news/.premium.highlight-against-covid-directives-israeli-minister-orders-not-to-vaccinate-prisoners-1.9402652.

Burden-Stelly, C, P. J. Hudson, and J. Pierre. "Racial Capitalism, Black Liberation, and South Africa." *Black Agenda Report*, December 16, 2020, https://www.blackagendareport.com/racial-capitalism-black-liberation-and-south-africa.

Centers for Disease Control and Prevention. "COVID-19 Hospitalization and Death by Race/Ethnicity." Accessed November 8, 2020. https://www.cdc.gov/coronavirus/2019-ncov/covid-data/investigations-discovery/hospitalization-death-by-race-ethnicity.html.

Chassin, M.R., and J. M. Loeb. "High-Reliability Health Care: Getting There from Here." *The Milbank Quarterly* (2013): 459–490.

Christian, T. A. "Twitter Rips into Surgeon General for Telling Blacks to 'Step Up' Amid COVID-19 Pandemic." *Essence*, November 4. Accessed November 8, 2020. https://www.essence.com/news/jerome-adams-step-up-remarks-twitter-reaction/.

COVID Tracking Project. (2020). "The COVID Racial Data Tracker." Accessed November 9, 2020. https://covidtracking.com/race.

Deutsch, J. "Guilt and Impunity: Gaza and COVID-19." *Counterpunch*, April 14, 2020, https://www.counterpunch.org/2020/04/14/guilt-and-impunity-gaza-and-covid-19.

Digby, A. (2013). "Black Doctors and Discrimination Under South Africa's Apartheid Regime." *Medical History*, 57(2), 269–290.

Douglas, K.M., Sjoberg, G., Sáenz, R., Embrick, D.G. (2018). Bureaucratic Capitalism, Mass Incarceration and Race and Ethnicity in America. In: Batur, P., Feagin, J. (eds) Handbook of the Sociology of Racial and Ethnic Relations. Handbooks of Sociology and Social Research. Springer, Cham. https://doi.org/10.1007/978-3-319-76757-4_20.

Doumas, Michael, Dimitrios Patoulias, Alexandra Katsimardou, Konstantinos Stavropoulos, Konstantinos Imprialos, and Asterios Karagiannis. "COVID19 and increased mortality in African Americans: socioeconomic differences or does the renin angiotensin system also contribute?" *Journal of Human Hypertension* 34, (2010): 764–767.

Feagin. J. R. *Systemic Racism: A Theory of Oppression*. New York: Routledge, 2005.

Feigenbaum, James J., C. Muller, E. Wrigley-Field. "Regional and racial inequality in infectious disease mortality in U.S. cities, 1900–1948." *Demography* 56, (2019): 1371–1388.

Ford, T. N., S. Reber, and R. V. Reeves. "Race Gaps in COVID-19 Deaths Are Even Bigger Than They Appear." *Brookings*, June 16, 2020, https://www.brookings.edu/blog/up-front/2020/06/16/race-gaps-in-covid-19-deaths-are-even-bigger-than-they-appear/.

Francis, D., K. Ramburth-Hurt, and I. Valodia. "Estimates of Employment in South Africa Under the Five-Level Lockdown Framework." *Southern Centre of Inequality Studies*, May 1, 2020, https://www.wits.ac.za/media/wits-university/faculties-and-schools/commerce-law-and-management/research-entities/scis/documents/scis%20working%20paper%204.pdf.

Freshour, C., and B. Williams. "Abolition in the Time of COVID-19." *Antipode Online*, April 9, 2020, https://antipodeonline.org/2020/04/09/abolition-in-the-time-of-covid-19.

Garbett, L. "Palestinian Workers in Israel Caught Between Indispensable and Disposal." Accessed May 15, 2020. https://merip.org/2020/05/palestinian-workers-in-israel-caught-between-indispensable-and-disposable.

Gilmore, Ruth Wilson. *Golden Gulag: Prisons, Surplus, Crisis, and Opposition in Globalizing California*. Berkeley, CA: University of California Press, 2007.

Gupta, Raavi, Raag Agrawal, Zaheer Bukhari, Absia Jabbar, Donghai Wang, John Diks, Mohamed Alshal, Dokpe Yvonne Emechebe, F. Charles Brunicardi, Jason M. Lazar, Robert Chamberlain, Aaliya Burza, and M. A. Haseeb. "Higher comorbidities and early death in hospitalized African-American patients with Covid-19." BMC Infectious Diseases 78 (2021): 1–11.

Hacker, Andrew. *Two Nations: Black and White, Separate, Hostile, Unequal*. New York: Scribner, 2003.

Hatch, Anthony J. *Blood Sugar: Racial Pharmacology and Food Justice in America*. Minneapolis, MN: University of Minnesota Press, 2016.

Hincks, J. "Israel Is Leading the World in COVID-19 Vaccination. But Palestinians Aren't on the List." *Time*, January 15, 2021, from: https://time.com/5930060/israel-covid-vaccine-palestinians.

Hudson, P. J. "To Remake the World: Slavery, Racial Capitalism, and Justice." *Boston Review*, February 20, 2018, https://www.bostonreview.net/forum/walter-johnson-to-remake-the-world/.

Karim, S. S. A. "The South African Response to the Pandemic." *New England Journal of Medicine* 382 (May 29, 2020): E95.https://doi.org/10.1056/Nejmc2014960.

Karmi, O. "Israel's Vaccine Rollout Excludes Palestinians." *The Electronic Intifada*, December 29, 2020, https://electronicintifada.net/blogs/omar-karmi/israels-vaccine-rollout-excludes-palestinians.

Kon, Z. R., and N. Lackan. "Ethnic Disparities in Access to Care in Post-Apartheid South Africa." *American Journal of Public Health* 98, no. 12 (2008): 2272–2277.

Laurencin, C. T., and A. McClinton. "The COVID-19 Pandemic: A Call to Action to Identify and Address Racial and Ethnic Disparities." *Journal of Racial and Ethnic Disparities* 18 (2020): 1–5.

Link, Bruce G. and Jo Phelan. "Social Conditions as Fundamental Causes of Disease." *Journal of Health and Social Behavior* (Extras Issue) (1995): 80–94

Machaka, L. L. "Linking Racism and Climate Justice during COVID-19 Era." *CIDSE: Together for Social Justice*, August 4, 2020, https://www.cidse.org/2020/08/04/linking-racism-and-climate-justice-during-covid-19-era.

McClure, E. S., P. Vasudevan, Z. Bailey, S. Patel, and W. R. Robinson. "Racial Capitalism Within Public Health—How Occupational Settings Drive COVID-19 Disparities." *American Journal of Epidemiology* 189, no. 11 (2020): 1244–1253.

Manish Pareek, Manish, Mansoor N Bangash, Nilesh Pareek, Daniel Pan, Shirley Sze, Jatinder S Minhas, Wasim Hanif, and Kamlesh Khunti. "Ethnicity and COVID-19: An Urgent Public Health Research Priority." *The Lancet* 395, 2020: 1421–1422.

Maphumulo, W. T. and B. R. Bhengu. "Challenges of Quality Improvement in the Healthcare of South Africa Post-Apartheid. A Critical Review." *Curationis* 42, no. 1 (2019): 1901.

Melamed, J. "Racial Capitalism." *Critical Ethnic Studies* 1, no. 1 (2015): 76–85.

Mkize, V. "Racism Still Alive: Healthcare Industry in SA Hasn't Been Spared." *News24.com*, September 13, 2020, https://www.news24.com/citypress/news/racism-still-alive-healthcare-industry-in-sa-hasnt-been-spared-20200913.

Moll, T. (2021). "Medical Mistrust and Enduring Racism in South Africa." *Journal of Bioethical Inquiry*. 18 (2021) 117–120. https://doi.org/10.1007/s11673-020-10072-1.

National Department of Health. *The National Health Care Facilities Baseline Audit. National Summary Report*. Pretoria, South Africa: Health E-News, 2012.

Nithya, G. N. "'Between the Rock of the Occupation, and the Hammer of Coronavirus.'" *Socialist Project*, April 19, 2020, https://socialistproject.ca/2020/04/between-rock-of-occupation-and-hammer-of-coronavirus.

Novak, M. *The Spirit of Democratic Capitalism*. New York: Simon & Schuster, 1982.

Omer SB, Malani P, Del Rio C. 2020. "The COVID-19 Pandemic in the US: A Clinical Update." *JAMA*, Vol. 323(18): 1767–1768. doi: 10.1001/jama.2020.5788. PMID: 32250388.

Pirtle, W. N. L. "Racial Capitalism: A Fundamental Cause of Novel Coronavirus (COVID-19) Pandemic Inequities in the United States." *Health Education & Behavior* 47, no. 40 2020: 504–508.

Ro, C. "Coronavirus: Why Some Racial Groups Are More Vulnerable." *BBC*, April 20, 2020, https://www.bbc.com/future/article/20200420-coronavirus-why-some-racial-groups-are-more-vulnerable.

Roberts, Dorothy. *Killing the Black Body: Race, Reproduction, and the Meaning of Liberty*. New York: Pantheon Books, 1997.

Robinson, Cedric. *Black Marxism: The Making of the Black Radical Tradition*. London: Zed Press, 1983.

Saenz, R., K. M. Douglas, D. G. Embrick, and G. Sjoberg. "Pathways to Downward Mobility: The Impact of Schools, Welfare, and Prisons on People of Color." In *Racial and Ethnic Relations Handbook*, edited by H. Vera and J. R. Feagin, 373–409. New York: Kluwer/Springer, 2007.

Schumaker, E. "What We Know About the COVID-19 Variant Spreading in South Africa." *ABC News*, January 9, 2021, https://abcnews.go.com/health/covid-19-variant-spreading-south-africa/story?id=75062211.

Scott, D., and C. Animashaun. "COVID-19's Stunningly Unequal Death Toll in America, in One Chart." *Vox*, October 2, 2020, https://www.vox.com/coronavirus-covid19/2020/10/2/21496884/us-covid-19-deaths-by-race-black-white-americans.

Steinhauser, G., and A. D. Patel. "South Africa's Promise of Racial Equality Falters Under Pandemic." *The Wall Street Journal*, September 25, 2020, from: https://www.wsj.com/articles/south-africas-promise-of-racial-equality-falters-under-pandemic-11601031600.

Swartz, L. "The Reproduction of Racism in South African Mental Health Care." *South African Journal of Psychology* 21, no. 4 (1991): 240–246.

Tikkanen, R., and M. K. Abrams. "US Health Care from a Global Perspective, 2019: Higher Spending, Worse Outcomes?" *The Commonwealth Fund*, January 30, 2020, https://www.commonwealthfund.org/publications/issue-briefs/2020/jan/us-health-care-global-perspective-2019.

Washington, Harriet. *Medical Apartheid: The Dark History of Medical Experimentation on Black Americans from Colonial Times to the Present*. New York: Doubleday, 2006.

Williams, D. R., and C Collins. "Racial Residential Segregation: A Fundamental Cause of Racial Disparities in Health." Public Health Reports, 116 (September/October) 2001: 404–416.

Wrigley-Field, Elizabeth. "US racial inequality may be as deadly as COVID-19." *Proceedings of the National Academy of Sciences* 117 (36) (2020): 21854–21856.

# PART TWO

# COVID-19
## and
# Selected U.S. Institutions

CHAPTER 8

# ESSENTIAL YET EXPENDABLE
## The Paradoxical Racialization of COVID-19

*Jan-Martijn Meij*

*Diane L. Odeh*

THE COVID-19 PANDEMIC IS KNOWN for being a harbinger of unprecedented times. However, for people of color, the way this emergency has been managed is more of the same. In particular, hegemonic governance practices combined with income and work disparity have resulted in the disproportionate hospitalizations and deaths of people of color with COVID-19 in the United States.

Sociologists have long grappled with discussions of racialization in all facets of society; environmental inequality, resource access, and barriers to participation have long been topics worthy of consideration and critique. This chapter intends to further the discussion of racialization as it pertains to work, capitalism, and emergencies. It is our contention that occupational segregation exists and is exacerbated during times of crisis. We argue that this partially describes why people of color have experienced more negative health outcomes than White individuals during the COVID-19 pandemic.

In addition to the class disparity caused by occupational segregation, we argue that governmental methods that squarely place economic health as a top priority further subjugate Black people and Hispanic people while placing them in high-risk situations with unequal access to the same resources White people have had.

We draw on three bodies of research that help us offer insight into the disparate racialized context of COVID-19. First, we demonstrate how neoliberalism articulates racial capitalism through precarious work and is helpful in understanding the racialized context of COVID-19. Second, through explaining path dependency, we argue that further understanding of racialized impacts can be explored. Finally, the governmentality of capitalism is an effective way to make obvious that what the US government prioritizes is the economy first.

Using the approach of sociological institutionalism offers a powerful methodological tool to examine how the theoretical ideas from the literature review have articulated during the handling of the COVID-19 pandemic. Because our goal is to offer a research agenda for future scholars and policy makers, we draw upon secondary data, prior studies, and news articles. In fact, given that the pandemic is still ongoing when this chapter was written, few clear answers exist.

In the substantive discussion, we go in depth for all three dimensions: the reification of path dependence, the governance during COVID-19, and the racialization of work in COVID. Through this, we learn that historical antecedents are relevant to the current pandemic. Furthermore, the implications of a work-from-home culture need to be dissected as to the racialized impacts. As was the case in the past, during the current crisis we see a governmentality that prioritizes economics over safety. Finally, we learn that racialized occupational segregation in conjunction with the lack of unionization (and as such likely the lack of access to quality benefits) leads to income segregation. In other words, precarity and risk during COVID-19 are salient elements.

We end the chapter with a conclusion of our work and offer a research agenda for future scholars and policy makers.

## Context, State of the Art, Concepts and Methods

### Racial Disparities of COVID-19

The Centers for Disease Control (CDC 2020a) has been tracing the racialized impacts of the SARS-CoV-2 (herein referred to as COVID-19) pandemic. Based on data from mid-August 2020, we now have an understanding of the disproportionate impacts on non-White people compared to White people. On the "COVID-19 Hospitalization and Death by Race/Ethnicity" page on their website, the CDC clearly illustrates that the pandemic hits harder on, in particular, American Indian, Black, and Hispanic communities, but that Asians also experience a greater impact compared to White people. This information is shown in Figure 8.1.

**Figure 8.1** Cases, Hospitalization and Deaths by Race/Ethnicity

| Rate ratios compared to White, Non-Hispanic Persons | American Indian or Alaska Native, Non-Hispanic persons | Asian, Non-Hispanic persons | Black or African American, Non-Hispanic persons | Hispanic or Latino/a People |
|---|---|---|---|---|
| Cases | 2.8x higher | 1.1x higher | 2.6x higher | 2.8x higher |
| Hospitalization | 5.3x higher | 1.3x higher | 4.7x higher | 4.6x higher |
| Deaths | 1.4x higher | No Increase | 2.1 higher | 1.1x higher |

Source: CDC 2020a.

## Racial Capitalism and Its Operation through Precarious Work

In the United States, efforts have been made to "hollow out" the authority and resources available to the formal government system, instead shifting governance and service delivery to private and nonprofit institutions. This shift has largely been attributed to have started in the 1970s, as Margaret Thatcher and Ronald Reagan made efforts to evoke images of an oft-assumed Black "welfare queen" that took advantage of government benefits in grossly lavish ways. As resources shifted away from government organizations toward private businesses, a wave of governance now known as neoliberalism firmly placed itself in the American system (see Harvey 2005 and Brown 2015 for more information regarding neoliberalism). Neoliberalism, to many scholars, marks a change that can explain current inequities in society and racial segregation in the workplace (Reed 2020).

Despite the relevance of neoliberalism in explaining a lot of current government arrangements relevant to this chapter, the temporality of neoliberal practice is a point of departure from how we understand the racialization of outcomes during the COVID-19 pandemic. Instead, we argue that people of color have been exposed to the capitalistic practices inherent in neoliberal thought since the inception of the United States. Focusing on neoliberalism, we argue, eschews the systemic ways racial capitalism has been a primary mode of governing people of color.

One glaring example of racism since the nation's inception has to do with the fact that John Locke, long considered a foundational thinker in our governance systems today, declared that Indigenous land was a "free gift from God" that was exploitable since Indigenous people did not "develop" it (Locke 1689). At the same time, colonizers exposed Indigenous populations to smallpox, causing mass deaths that economically and culturally devastated tribes (Gale Encyclopedia of US Economic History 2015). They never recovered from this pandemic. Viewing Indigenous people as being expendable in favor of economic prosperity for Anglo-Saxon colonizers is one of the first examples of how racial capitalism took hold in the United States.

"Racial capitalism," a term coined by Cedric Robinson, is the argument that in order to grow, capitalism necessarily dehumanizes non-White bodies in order to create profits (Robinson 2000). Racial capitalism is rooted in Marxist conceptions of the world, but with the added assertion that race has been a primary driving factor in how wealth is accumulated.

Racial capitalism has been articulated through what is now coined as "precarious work." Precarious work is characterized by job insecurity, lack of health care, and unsafe work conditions (Kalleberg 2009). It is largely traced to emerging as the result of neoliberalism. Precarious work has numerous consequences related to access and class disparity, but perhaps the most sinister outcome lies in the area of health. When work becomes more precarious such as in the recent version of "the gig economy" or other forms of "flexible employment," it also has health-related consequences due to lack of health care access and the physical labor required to engage in this work (Benach, Vives, Amable, Vanroelen, Tarafa, and Muntaner 2014, 230).

## Path Dependency: A Scapegoat for Reification

One primary way government policy works has to do with the concept of path dependency. Path dependency is the patternistic behavior of relying on past policy decisions to inform new policies and perspectives (Wilson 2014). With each policy passed on that issue, analysts argue that paths are carved that add to the context in which a policy issue is considered. In essence, once a policy has been created, it sets a standard for how that issue is handled. Subsequent policies are often analyzed based on how well they complement previous policy paths.

Although the concept sounds simple enough, the implications of such a lens in government policy have implications for people of color and their continued marginalization in society. That is because, we argue, path dependency supports the reification of racial capitalism. Reification is a process by which outcomes are viewed as being naturalistic to groups in society. In the context of government policy, the failure of Black and Brown people to thrive post-disasters is potentially blamed on naturally occurring circumstances instead of the continued subjugation that is reinforced through path dependencies within structures (Young 2000). Authors have written about the "lock-in" effects path dependency has in promoting neoliberalism and hindering community resilience (Wilson 2014; Gomez 2017).

### Governmentality and Biopower

Scholars have already begun to make the connection between how COVID-19 is managed in relation to a governmentality of capitalism (Ayala-Colqui 2020). This chapter seeks to continue this research agenda by asserting that racial capitalism has been allowed to run rampant as a result of the United States' governmentality of economy first. "Governmentality" is a term coined by Michel Foucault to describe the way formal and informal modes of governance operate on individuals. Governmental methods become a reigning ideology that obscures other governance priorities. Governmentality is able to operate through two types of what is known as biopower: biopower and disciplinary power. Biopolitics is used to describe the political regulations that govern human bodies (Taylor 2014). Disciplinary power is the way in which individuals govern each other in relation to established, often hegemonic, norms. It is our contention that the governmentality operating in the United States is one that promotes racial capitalism—especially during the COVID-19 pandemic.

## Methodology

In order to analyze how the aforementioned dimensions have contributed to the racialization of deaths in the time of COVID-19, we adopted a mixed-methodological approach under the framework of sociological institutionalism.

*Theoretical Approach*

Sociological institutionalism is a framework used to study how institutions interact with cultural norms and values. It differs from other approaches that focus on institutions because it allows researchers to focus on a broader concept of "institutions," one that includes cultural and systemic conditions (Hall and Taylor 1996). Other institutionalism approaches rely solely on historical precedent or assume that a person has the capacity to engage in rational decision-making. Instead, sociological institutionalism allows us to understand the impact of institutional structures and history in relation to how it influences an individual's place in society. Finally, sociological institutionalism was selected for its distinctiveness regarding how decisions are made within organizations. Instead of asserting that policymakers and implementers are rational actors, it posits that decisions are made based on how well they fit in already established rules and values (Hall and Taylor 1996). In other words, path dependency is considered regarding how people make decisions under this framework.

*Demographic Focus*

Attention must be given to the ways in which Asians have been discriminated against and harassed during the COVID-19 pandemic (see Ong [2020] for research related to this). However, the scope of this particular study focuses on the disparities found in Black, Hispanic, and Indigenous populations as it relates to work and the risk of COVID-19. In many cases, reliable data regarding Indigenous populations is absent. We argue that this reveals a glaring issue with reliance on population data, as many people of color actively avoid efforts related to collecting census data due to fear of being surveilled by the government (Lerman and Weaver 2014).

*Data Collection Approach*

Secondary data: Data was collected from multiple secondary sources including the Bureau of Labor Statistics (BLS), the Centers for Disease Control (CDC), the Council of State Governments (CSG), the US Census Bureau (CB), the

Bureau of Economic Analysis from the Department of Commerce (BEA), the COVID-19 Tracking Project done by *The Atlantic* (TP) and the Urban Institute.

Past studies: The impact of path dependency from past emergencies and its subsequent reification of negative outcomes are the primary focus of this chapter. As such, past historical analyses of past emergencies in the United States were reviewed to develop a more critical understanding of poor outcomes for non-White individuals. Past studies that evaluated the impact of individual-level factors related to health inequities were also analyzed in order to gain a holistic understanding of how individual factors have been influenced by institutional arrangements.

News articles: In the interest of representing the most recent narratives that have emerged during the COVID-19 pandemic, news articles regarding inequities and abuses related to race were consulted to gain an understanding of the first wave of impacts of governmental policies and programs on individuals. Many of these articles are informed by preliminary data related to outcomes.

As the outcomes of the COVID-19 pandemic are still developing at the time of this publication, no intention is made here to establish empirical causal links between the three dimensions. Instead, we argue, data must be understood along with systemic and historical factors that influence the numbers. Therefore, the authors seek to use this publication to set an agenda for future research related to race, governance, and disparate health outcomes.

## Substantive Discussion

In this section, we present the three dimensions that have resulted in the racial disparities during COVID-19. The dimension of path dependence sets the current context for the second dimension that asserts negative outcomes of COVID-19 governance occurred because of a focus on economy first. Finally, the risks racial capitalism has placed on Black people and Hispanic people are covered.

## Dimension One: Path Dependence/Reification

It is important to trace how path dependence and subsequent reification have been perpetuated by the governance of past emergencies in the United States. In particular, we discuss how past practices related to the AIDS epidemic, smallpox epidemic, and Tuskegee experiments have further expedited the disparities within communities of color and subsequent distrust of public health efforts in the United States.

## Historical Antecedents to Today's Path Dependence

Research related to race and health disparities often includes a remark about how people who are non-White underutilize prevention programs by public health departments. For example, efforts in North Carolina to perform AIDS testing and awareness within the Black community backfired as many people did not feel comfortable interacting with the government (Inrig 2011). In addition, government officials were unable to get proper buy-in from established Black community groups. To this day, AIDS incidence continues to be racialized. For example, Black people disproportionately represented 26 percent of US cases during the onslaught of the AIDS pandemic despite occupying 12 percent of the US population—disproportionation that exists to this day as Black and Hispanic women continue to see higher rates of incidence (Sutton et al. 2009)

Rhetoric surrounding health outcomes often places the onus on individuals as being to blame for their health disparities. For example, the racial disparities during the H1N1 pandemic were partially blamed on the inability to social distance and preexisting health conditions (Quinn et al. 2011). The lack of effectiveness of government officials in properly reaching non-White individuals is clearly distinguishable once the historical experience of non-White people in the United States is studied alongside public health efforts. These experiences, we argue, have created a context rooted in repeated abuses and inequitable practices. As a result, the lack of trust and legitimacy of public organizations continues with each new emergency.

One of the most well-known examples of the government perpetuating health inequities is the smallpox epidemic. Typically, rhetoric surrounding Indigenous infection and dispossession has been a primary focus of how pandemics are mishandled and perpetuated. However, the Black experience with smallpox is worthy of attention. In 1895, Black people who had migrated to Mexico from Alabama returned to the United States upon contracting smallpox, seeking assistance from their government (McKiernan-González 2014). At the time, Black people were seen as lucrative sources of human labor to build railroads. As US public officials grappled with treating the pandemic, this group of Black people was quarantined without initial resources in what is now known as Camp Jenner, having been subjected to policies made by White males without consideration of other races.

Black people were also used as the first test subjects to be inoculated with potential vaccinations. In some cases, they were told they were immune, only to later die because they contracted smallpox due to failed vaccinations (McKiernan-González 2014). In this example, Black people were both viewed as expendable tests subjects and valuable human capital whose utility was to serve White railroad owners. The migrants were able to use their awareness of the human capital they could provide to demand safer conditions for themselves at Camp Jenner. Despite the deeply racialized history of how smallpox was handled, practitioners continue to use the smallpox epidemic as an archetype for how other health emergencies in the United States are managed (Cardillo 2014).

One of the most egregious examples of government perpetuation of health inequities among Black people is the Tuskegee Syphilis Study. Much like their experience with smallpox at Camp Jenner, Black people were chosen as a favorable group to test medical experiments and theories on. In particular, researchers were interested in studying how untreated syphilis manifests in humans. To do this, many Black men were not made aware that they had syphilis as the researchers lied to them about the scope of the study despite treatment being available (Alsan and Wanamaker 2018). As of 2020, it had only been forty-eight years since the study concluded, making it reasonably deducible that some test subjects are still alive.

The aforementioned racialization of past medical emergencies is perpetuated as policymakers and public health officials continue to treat non-White people as if their context is the same as more privileged individuals in society. This approach reifies the disparate racial outcomes as if they are unintended externalities instead of something that is happening by design. The lock-in effects of each event have fortified existing systemically racist structures while officials simultaneously treat the inequitable outcomes as an unpredictable natural occurrence.

## COVID-19 and History Repeating Itself

These historical antecedents of emergency governance set the current context for COVID-19. Many communities of color are understandably distrustful of public health efforts as a form of self-protection. Mistrust of government becomes compounded by the fact that communities of color are disproportionately surveilled and incarcerated by the US government (Lerman and Weaver 2014). This complicates efforts to engage in disease prevention as contact tracers across the country seek to mitigate the effects of the virus by relying on individuals to (1) disclose COVID-19 symptoms and identity in order to get tested and (2) provide government contractors a list of people they have associated with in the days leading up to exposure. Many people on probation are not allowed to interact with felons (United States Courts 2020), causing the potential for people to see avoidance of contact tracing as a means of avoiding incarceration.

## Dimension Two: Governance During COVID-19

The former section demonstrated the way decisions are made and carried out during emergencies can subjugate people of color and further fracture their relationship with the government. In addition, the way an emergency is framed will influence how policies are made. This section explores the impact of governance decisions and a governmentality of economy first on individuals in the United States.

### The Implications of a Work from Home Culture

Forty-one states declared some form of a "stay at home" order (Council of State Governments 2020). This effectively forced job operations to be done remotely, if possible. School operations in many states also transitioned to an online format—even if it were not possible for students and families to cope effectively with this. Thirty-two states made their rules regarding telehealth operations more flexible, intending to provide ease and efficiency in meeting with and diagnosing patients.

The impact of these orders on people of color becomes clear once issues related to the digital divide are considered. As will be demonstrated later in this chapter, many positions Black and Hispanic individuals occupy necessarily places them in contact with other human beings, already complicating the equity of a work-from-home culture.

A lack of access to stable Internet or computers for school affects Black and Hispanic families differently. This is because in many areas that are predominantly non-White, Internet access is shoddy at best (Watkins et al. 2018). This has been exemplified in the news as children flocked to fast food restaurant parking lots in order to use Wi-Fi to do schoolwork (Dvorak 2020). A lack of access to online education has made it a rational choice for parents of color to prefer the less safe in-person classes, especially if they work for an essential business and lack access to affordable childcare.

Telehealth access and operation have resulted in a safer way to deliver medical services. Former studies on telehealth use found that there are disparities across racial lines in who can access telehealth, finding that Black people often did not have the resources to use the service (Graetz et al. 2016). It is not unreasonable to expect that these disparities have continued throughout the COVID-19 pandemic.

Figure 8.2 demonstrates the emerging disparities across sixteen quality of life dimensions during the COVID-19 pandemic. Data was collected by the Household Pulse Survey from the US Census Bureau over the course of eleven weeks between April and July 2020. From this table, the racial disparities become clear.

Even though the majority of the country is White, White individuals ranked below the average overall when it comes to experiencing issues related to the pandemic (the exception is credit card spending to meet needs, where they are similar to the average). Meanwhile, Asians rank second in terms of their situation in confronting problems as they experience a below-average reality in seven categories. The only categories where Black people are below-average in experiencing particular issues are credit card spending and savings spending, which in reality could be a result of lack of access to both. As such, the struggles of Black people and Hispanic people are worse than the average American's experience.

**Figure 8.2** Impacts on a variety of measures by Race/Ethnicity

| Category | All Americans | Asian | Black | Hispanic | White |
|---|---|---|---|---|---|
| Class Cancellation | 42% | 37% | 49% | 46% | 39% |
| Credit Card / Loan Spending (to meet needs) | 33% | 33% | 20% | 26% | 24% |
| Employment Income Loss | 49% | 50% | 55% | 61% | 44% |
| Expected Employment Income Loss (next four weeks) | 34% | 39% | 43% | 49% | 28% |
| Food Insecurity | 10% | 7% | 21% | 17% | 7% |
| Health Insurance Coverage (% uninsured <65) | 13% | 9% | 16% | 23% | 13% |
| Last Month's Mortgage Payments (% not paid) | 12% | 14% | 24% | 18% | 10% |
| Last Month's Rent Payments (% not paid) | 19% | 12% | 29% | 23% | 14% |
| Mental Health (% with symptoms of depression/anxiety) | 36% | 31% | 40% | 42% | 34% |
| Public Health Insurance Coverage | 23% | 21% | 34% | 25% | 19% |
| Savings Spending (used savings or sold assets to meet needs) | 23% | 24% | 19% | 24% | 23% |
| Stimulus Payment Spending (used it to meet needs) | 22% | 27% | 26% | 27% | 19% |
| UI Benefit Spending (Unemployment Insurance to meet needs) | 13% | 18% | 16% | 16% | 12% |
| Upcoming Mortgage Payments (% no confidence they can) | 17% | 23% | 29% | 30% | 12% |
| Upcoming Rent Payments (% no confidence they can) | 33% | 30% | 45% | 46% | 23% |
| Use of Stimulus for Expenses (rather than saving) | 73% | 74% | 83% | 81% | 69% |

Source: Household Pulse Survey.

## Governmentality of Economics in the COVID-19 Era

It's no secret that economic prosperity has been a governing ethos in the United States. Emergencies usually are followed by great economic need as a result of the disruption they caused. In many cases, we argue, the economy is prioritized as a governmental method of emergency governance—and the COVID-19 pandemic is no exception.

Following the September 11 attacks, economic devastation riddled small business owners in the areas surrounding where the World Trade Center once stood. In an effort to rebuild, proprietors were offered the opportunity to receive small business loans. Acceptance was based on the conditions for any other non-emergency loan, further displacing vulnerable, often non-White, business owners due to their ineligibility (Graham 2001). Post–Hurricane Katrina recovery efforts became racialized as state policies made it easier to dispossess Black-owned homes by deeming them unsalvageable, allowing gentrification and wealth accumulation to run rampant (Gotham 2014).

Some of the most active governance we've seen in relation to the COVID-19 pandemic has to do with the promulgation of grant and loan assistance provided to small business owners. As of October 2020, the primary methods of distributing finances have been through the Payroll Protection Program (PPP) and Economic Injury Disaster Loans. To disburse these loans, the Small Business Administration (SBA) worked with financial institutions that were also given the discretion to make loan eligibility decisions. This effectively places private sector banks in charge of the delivery of public goods.

Regarding PPP, preliminary studies regarding fund disbursal demonstrate that minority-owned businesses were underrepresented in who obtained resources (Morse 2020). Loans related to economic injury are problematic in consideration of past racist practices. Bates and Robb (2016) discovered that minority business enterprises were less likely to receive bank loans, and when they did, the amount was less than White-owned businesses. Giving financial institutions the authority to make these decisions allows a lack of credence given to concepts of equitable distribution. In addition, this private-public partnership results in a lack of government accountability or structural change to end discriminatory practices. Banks that are in charge of disbursing these loans are also actively earning interest on these loans (Small Business

Administration 2020), further incentivizing discrimination based on their perceived ability to pay the loans back.

The governmentality of economics has also resulted in the reopening of businesses. As of October 2020, there were 302 executive orders related to reopening businesses/employment, whereas only two executive orders were related to anti-discrimination and two related directly to the allocation of personal protection equipment (PPE) (Council of State Governments 2020).

In the fall of 2020 retail and restaurant workers had returned to work in an attempt to revive a decaying economy. However, at the same time, a lack of unified federal support for safety measures has resulted in frontline workers being exposed to individuals who are not adhering to safety standards such as mask-wearing and social distancing—two conditions that made Black and Hispanic workers during the H1N1 pandemic more susceptible to catching the virus (Kumar et al. 2012). News reports have emerged stating that retail workers are at most risk of being physically assaulted by trying to enforce mask mandates (MacFarquhar 2020; Porterfield 2020). The issue has become so problematic that the CDC was prompted to release guidance to workers on how to limit the chances of violence with individuals who refuse to comply (Centers for Disease Control and Prevention 2020b). However, this guidance encourages avoiding conflict, further allowing maskless people to be in near proximity to retail and food service workers (Weixel 2020). As will be demonstrated later, this is problematic as Black people and Hispanic people disproportionately occupy these jobs.

## Dimension Three: Racialization of Work in COVID-19

By tracing how governance of disasters has resulted in continued disparate outcomes with each event, it is clear that structural and institutional arrangements influence how successful vulnerable groups will be in surviving the health and economic impacts of a disaster. We will use this section to discuss how the racial disparities of COVID-19 are exacerbated by the fact that people of color disproportionately occupy essential—and especially vulnerable—frontline jobs.

During the H1N1 pandemic, the link between workplace conditions and virus susceptibility became clearer. Kumar et al. (2012) explored factors related to employment that made Black people and Hispanic people more vulnerable to H1N1. In particular, the lack of ability to take paid sick leave, inability to social distance, and lack of PPE in the workplace demonstrably increased the likelihood of H1N1 incidence. It is no secret that some jobs are more hazardous than others. However, many jobs well-known for being high risk are also known as having high reward. For example, mining jobs, typically known for many risks related to physical risk, pay an average of $110,582 (Bureau of Economic Analysis 2020). White individuals are predominant in this job type. In the context of viral pandemics, and COVID-19 in particular, precarious jobs known for being low-skilled and low pay have become essential under the governmentality of capitalism. A look into the occupational segregation inherent in these jobs reveals the deep racialization of work that has only been exacerbated by COVID-19.

## Occupational Segregation

In general, the American workforce experiences occupational segregation based on race. Figure 8.3 presents data related to workforce demographics in the United States.

Figure 8.3 offers insight into a variety of information. We see the total employment in each occupational sector ranked by the relative distribution of the workforce. The final four columns represent the rank within each race and ethnic group in terms of their employment. Further analysis would take up too much space to cover each sector. As such, we narrowed our focus to the top three sources of employment of all four racial and ethnic categories.

As can be derived from Figure 8.3, education and health services is the most likely industry for all groups; however, we start to see segregative patterns emerge after that. Wholesale and retail trade is the second or third spot, but for Hispanic people, professional and business services are not in the top three. In fact, it is the fifth most likely sector of employment. Instead, Hispanic people are more likely to be employed in leisure and hospitality, which also ranks as the fourth-highest sector for Black people. In order to offer the most relevant insight, we decided to explore the top three sources of employment for each race and ethnic group. As such, our analysis explores job types within education and health services, wholesale and retail trade, professional and business services, and leisure and hospitality.

**Figure 8.3** Occupational Sector Employment with Rank for Race/Ethnicity

| SECTORS | Number Employed (x1000) | % Total Workforce | White | Black | Asian | Hispanic |
|---|---|---|---|---|---|---|
| Education and health services | 35,894 | 22.78% | 1 | 1 | 1 | 1 |
| Wholesale and retail trade | 19,742 | 12.53% | 2 | 2 | 3 | 2 |
| Professional and business services | 19,606 | 12.45% | 3 | 3 | 2 | 5 |
| Manufacturing | 15,741 | 9.99% | 4 | 6 | 4 | 6 |
| Leisure and hospitality | 14,643 | 9.29% | 5 | 4 | 5 | 3 |
| Construction | 11,373 | 7.22% | 6 | 10 | 11 | 4 |
| Financial activities | 10,765 | 6.83% | 7 | 8 | 6 | 9 |
| Transportation and utilities | 8,991 | 5.71% | 8 | 5 | 8 | 7 |
| Other services | 7,617 | 4.84% | 9 | 9 | 7 | 8 |
| Public administration | 7,225 | 4.59% | 10 | 7 | 9 | 10 |
| Information | 2,766 | 1.76% | 12 | 11 | 10 | 12 |
| Agriculture, forestry, fishing, and hunting | 2,425 | 1.54% | 11 | 12 | 12 | 11 |
| Mining, quarrying, and oil and gas extraction | 750 | 0.48% | 13 | 13 | 13 | 13 |

Source: BLS.

Figure 8.4 shows that not only do these four sectors account for the top three sources of employment for all four racial and ethnic categories but they also account for 57.1 percent of all employment, and each racial group has at least half of all its employment covered within these four sectors.

Figure 8.5 represents detailed information from each of these four sectors of employment. We can look at the relative distribution of White people and non-White people in the overall workforce in the specific sector and in specific subsectors of each sector. There is one caveat: we only included these subsectors if there was information from the BEA about salary as that is relevant for understanding precarious work.

**Figure 8.4** Top Sources of Employment by Race

| Industry | Number Employed | % Total Workforce | % White | % Black | % Asian | % Hispanic |
|---|---|---|---|---|---|---|
| Education and health services | 35,894 | 22.78% | 22.08% | 27.96% | 22.53% | 17.41% |
| Wholesale and retail trade | 19,742 | 12.53% | 12.68% | 11.91% | 11.04% | 12.84% |
| Professional and business services | 19,606 | 12.45% | 12.40% | 10.11% | 18.46% | 11.27% |
| Leisure and hospitality | 14,643 | 9.29% | 8.92% | 9.89% | 9.91% | 12.63% |
| Total | 89,885 | 57.05% | 56.08% | 59.87% | 61.94% | 54.15% |

Source: BLS.

Income segregation operates in tandem with occupational segregation. What is interesting when analyzing the table is that whenever the average income is lower, you often see disproportionate representation from non-White people, in particular Black people and Hispanic people. On the other hand, many of the jobs where White people are disproportionately represented often come with a much higher wage. Figure 8.6 presents the average income range for jobs in which races are overrepresented.

As Figure 8.6 illustrates, in sectors where particular race and ethnic groups are disproportionately represented compared to their overall presence in the workforce, this overrepresentation comes with a much higher range of incomes. For White people, while some of the sectors pay a lower average salary than the entire workforce, they begin at a much higher income. In fact, while Black people in some cases earn above the average income in the total workforce, this is never the case for Hispanic people in sectors where they are disproportionately represented. Asians continue to represent a unique non-White racial identity as they are marginalized, but in several cases are easier able to earn better incomes. For example, in the sector where they are disproportionately represented with 23.5 percent of them filling jobs in computer systems design and related services, it also comes with an average income of $129,966.

**Figure 8.5** Occupational and Income Segregation by Race in Top Sources of Employment

| Category | Workforce (x1000) | White | Black or African American | Asian | Hispanic or Latino | Average Income |
|---|---|---|---|---|---|---|
| Overall workforce | 157,538 | 77.7 | 12.3 | 6.5 | 17.6 | $66,778 |
| #1 Educational services | 14,193 | 80.5 | 11.1 | 5.7 | 12.3 | $50,040 |
| #1 Health care and social assistance | 21,701 | 72 | 17.7 | 6.9 | 14.2 | $57,719 |
| Hospitals | 7,425 | 71.9 | 16 | 8.9 | 10.8 | $70,784 |
| Nursing care facilities (skilled nursing facilities) | 1,663 | 64.4 | 27.6 | 4.3 | 12.6 | $38,009 |
| Residential care facilities, except skilled nursing facilities | 995 | 67.5 | 23.9 | 4.8 | 12.6 | $38,009 |
| Social assistance | 3,430 | 71 | 20.1 | 4.6 | 19.4 | $29,907 |
| #2 Wholesale and retail trade | 19,742 | 78.6 | 11.7 | 5.7 | 18.1 | |
| Wholesale trade | 3,525 | 82.9 | 9.1 | 5.3 | 17.2 | $84,161 |
| Retail trade | 16,217 | 77.6 | 12.3 | 5.7 | 18.3 | $39,457 |
| #3 Professional and business services | 19,606 | 77.4 | 10 | 9.6 | 16 | $105,907 |
| Legal services | 1,747 | 84.8 | 7.3 | 5.3 | 11.7 | $108,469 |
| Computer systems design and related services | 3,703 | 66.1 | 8.1 | 23.5 | 7.4 | $129,196 |
| Other professional, scientific, and technical services | 489 | 82.5 | 7.8 | 7.4 | 12.2 | $97,254 |
| Management of companies and enterprises | 200 | 87.7 | 7.3 | 2.1 | 15 | $137,088 |
| Other administrative and other support services | 364 | 80.7 | 12 | 4.5 | 20.8 | $46,507 |
| Waste management and remediation services | 528 | 78.7 | 14.6 | 2.9 | 21.9 | $65,711 |

**Figure 8.5** Occupational and Income Segregation by Race in Top Sources of Employment *(continued)*

| Category | Workforce (x1000) | White | Black or African American | Asian | Hispanic or Latino | Average Income |
|---|---|---|---|---|---|---|
| #4 Leisure and hospitality | 14,643 | 74.6 | 13.1 | 6.9 | 24 | |
| Arts, entertainment, and recreation | 3,444 | 79.6 | 10.5 | 4.2 | 14.2 | $52,956 |
| – Independent artists, performing arts, spectator sports, and related industries | 944 | 83.5 | 9.9 | 3.3 | 12.9 | $100,006 |
| – Other amusement, gambling, and recreation industries | 2,085 | 77.3 | 10.8 | 5 | 15.5 | $34,370 |
| Accommodation and food services | 11,200 | 73 | 13.9 | 7.7 | 27 | $31,679 |
| – Accommodation | 1,489 | 67.3 | 17.9 | 9 | 28.8 | $42,569 |
| – Food services and drinking places | 9,711 | 73.9 | 13.2 | 7.5 | 26.8 | $29,555 |

*Source:* BLS and BEA.

## Unionization

A review of statistics related to union representation and race delivers seemingly promising news: Black people are more likely to be in a union than any other racial demographic. Figure 8.7 with information from the Bureau of Labor Statistics (BLS 2019) demonstrates this.

Regarding the growth of unionized workers, 11.5 percent of White workers are represented by a union and experienced no change from 2018 to 2019. Asian and Hispanic people increased their representation by unions between 2018 and 2019; Asian people went from 9.5 percent to 10 percent and Hispanic people or Latino/a moved from 10.1 percent to 10.2 percent. Despite Black people occupying the most space in unionization, the amount of Black, unionized individuals went down from 13.8 percent in 2018 to 12.7 percent in 2019 (Bureau of Labor Statistics 2019).

**Figure 8.6** Range of Disproportionate Workforce Presence and Average Income by Race

| Race and Ethnic Group | Overall Workforce Presence | Range of Disproportionate Representation | Range of Average Income |
|---|---|---|---|
| White | 77.7% | 78.7%–87.7% | $46,507–$137,088 |
| Black | 12.3% | 13.2%–27.6% | $29,555–$70,784 |
| Asian | 6.5% | 6.9%–23.5% | $29,555–$129,966 |
| Hispanic | 17.6% | 18.3%–28.8% | $29,555–$65,711 |

Source: BLS and BEA.

**Figure 8.7** Union Representation by Race

| Demographic | Represented by Union | Change Since 2018 |
|---|---|---|
| White | 11.5% | 0% |
| Black | 12.7% | -1.1% |
| Hispanic | 10.2% | -0.1% |
| Asian | 10.0% | +0.5% |

Source: BLS.

At first glance, this seems as if it is a win for racial equity and job protections. However, a closer look reveals the disparity involved with unionization. One primary reason why we do not see unionization of White individuals has to do with the fact that high-level employees and decision-makers are often barred from being a member (Homer, personal communication, 2020). Figure 8.8 shows that White people are overrepresented in executive-level positions within the private sector. The public sector is not immune to this disparity either, as exemplified in Figure 8.9. This is problematic because a disproportionate amount of White people in decision-making positions increases the likelihood of reification based on hegemonic ideals related to path dependency, limiting the capacity for culturally responsive change as it relates to workers' rights.

**Figure 8.8** Representation Among Non-Unionized Jobs in Private Sector by Race

| Demographic | Executive/ Senior Level Officials & Managers | First/Mid Level Officials & Managers | Professionals | Total |
|---|---|---|---|---|
| White | 2.29% | 11.90% | 25.41% | 39.60% |
| Black | 0.35% | 4.69% | 11.75% | 16.80% |
| Hispanic | 0.47% | 5.49% | 9.95% | 15.91% |
| Asian | 1.48% | 10.90% | 42.20% | 54.58% |

Source: Equal Employment Opportunity Commission (EEOC)

**Figure 8.9** Representation Among Non-Unionized Jobs in State and Local Government by Race

|  | Officials/ Administrators | Professionals | Total |
|---|---|---|---|
| White | 8.72% | 64.06% | 72.78% |
| Black | 5.41% | 58.33% | 63.74% |
| Hispanic | 5.61% | 61.39% | 66.99% |
| Asian | 9.91% | 63.64% | 73.55% |

Source: EEOC.

## *Precarity and Risk During COVID-19*

A deeper look into job type per industry reveals how people of color are placed in positions of precarity and risk during the COVID-19 pandemic. Referring back to Figure 8.5, we see that Black people and Hispanic people are highly overrepresented in professions related to medical services, food service, and social assistance—all services that received "essential" designations during the COVID-19 pandemic.

What's concerning is the fact that within medical services, Black people are more likely to work in nursing facilities where they are necessarily placed in direct physical contact with vulnerable populations. In addition, Black people and Hispanic people disproportionately work with individuals who require social assistance, increasing the likelihood of being unable to engage in social distancing as many of these positions require face-to-face interaction with people who do not have the means to access Internet services.

Regarding food services, the importance of gig workers increased in prevalence as restaurant and grocery delivery became paramount to supporting individuals who were privileged enough to comply with stay-at-home orders. Many news stories emerged regarding how precarious this work had become, with companies such as Amazon and Instacart failing to provide appropriate personal protective equipment (PPE) to gig workers during the onslaught of the virus (Selyukh and Bond 2020). The risks associated with working as a delivery driver became so high that the Centers for Disease Control released guidance specifically related to mitigating the spread of COVID-19 (Centers for Disease Control and Prevention 2020c).

## Conclusion

In this chapter, we documented how historical antecedents of racialized inequality persist over time, including during the current COVID-19 pandemic. In particular, we have set forth evidence that there is income and occupational segregation across racial dimensions and that this segregation can explain, in part, the disparate outcomes during COVID-19. With this in mind, we offer the following recommendations as researchers and practitioners alike continue to grapple with this pandemic in the United States.

### *Recommendations*

#### Challenge Existing Structures via Interdisciplinary Research

The data sources used for this study came from historians, economists, public health scientists, political scientists, sociologists, and others. This establishes the importance of developing a holistic, interdisciplinary approach to contextualizing the problem of racist institutions and how it interacts with issues of public health emergencies. Authors such as Chowkwanyun and Reed (2020) have called for similar approaches to understanding the racial patterns associated with COVID-19. We believe that situating the experience of people of color within the systems they interact with daily can result in finding pathways to challenging existing structures in favor of institutional reform.

Directly related to this is a call to action for scholars and practitioners alike to actively work to dismantle naturalistic conceptions of inequities and race that may have become inherent in their field. This allows us to rethink paradigms of emergency governance and seek ways to focus on issues of justice and equity within communities of color when developing policies and programs related to mitigation. Equity-oriented approaches to pandemics can also account for the additional racial discrimination Asians are facing during this time (Ong 2020).

### Rethink the Power of People of Color

People of color have long demonstrated their resilience and human capacity despite continuous attempts to disenfranchise them within the American diaspora. As the COVID-19 pandemic wages on, so does the fight for racial justice as anti-racist demonstrations have become a staple in urban cities across the country. Instead of viewing people of color as possessing attributes that limit their access and ability to thrive, we must understand the institutionalized and reified ways in which they have been purposefully excluded in favor of capitalistic practices that rely on the disposability of some groups. Earlier, the success of Black laborers to demand better medical attention at Camp Jenner relied on their understanding of how essential they were to efficiently build railroads (McKiernan-González 2014). Similarly, unions can become a catalyst for demanding institutional change (Reed 2020).

## Final Thoughts

While this chapter has started the conversation, in order to effectively dismantle White supremacist institutional arrangements, careful attention must be placed on continuing to challenge hegemony in the academic and governance arenas while also developing ways to sustain intersectional approaches to pandemics and other emergencies in the United States.

## References

Alsan, Marcella, and Wanamaker, Marianne. "Tuskegee and the Health of Black Men." *The Quarterly Journal of Economics* 133, no. 1(2018), 407–455.

Ayala-Colqui, J. "Viropolitics and Capitalistic Governmentality: On the Management of the Early 21st Century Pandemic." *Desde El Sur* 12, no. 2 (2020): 377–395.

Bates, Timothy, and Robb, Alicia. (2016). "Impacts of Owner Race and Geographic Context on Access to Small-Business Financing." Economic Development Quarterly, 30(2), 159–170.

Benach, Joan, Alejandra Vives, Gemma Tarafa, Carlos Delclos, and Carles Muntaner. "What should we know about precarious employment and health in 2025? Framing the agenda for the next decade of research." *International journal of epidemiology* 45, no. 1 (2016): 232–238.

Brown, Wendy. *Undoing the Demos: Neoliberalism's Stealth Revolution*. Cambridge, MA: MIT Press, 2015.

Bureau of Economic Analysis (2020) "Table 6.6D. Wages and Salaries Per Full-Time Equivalent Employee by Industry." *Bureau of Economic Analysis*. Accessed October 30, 2020. https://apps.bea.gov/iTable/iTable.cfm?reqid=19&step=2#reqid=19&step=2&isuri=1&1921=survey.

Cardillo, Julian. "Learning from Past Epidemics: What Can Smallpox Tell Us About Ebola?" *BrandeisNow*, December 2, 20214, https://www.brandeis.edu/now/2014/december/willrich-ebola-qanda.html.

Centers for Disease Control. "COVID-19 Hospitalization and Death by Race/Ethnicity." Accessed October 30, 2020a. https://www.cdc.gov/coronavirus/2019-ncov/covid-data/investigations-discovery/hospitalization-death-by-race-ethnicity.html.

Centers for Disease Control. "Limiting Workplace Violence Associated with COVID-19." Accessed October 30, 2020b. https://www.cdc.gov/coronavirus/2019-ncov/community/organizations/business-employers/limit-workplace-violence.html.

Centers for Disease Control. "Food & Grocery Pick-up and Delivery Drivers." Accessed October 30, 2020c. https://www.cdc.gov/coronavirus/2019-ncov/community/organizations/food-grocery-drivers.html.

Chowkwanyun, Merlin, and Adolph L. Reed "Racial Health Disparities and COVID-19—Caution and Context." *New England Journal of Medicine*

383 (2020):201-203. https://www.nejm.org/doi/full/10.1056/NEJMp2012910.

Council of State Governments. "The (2020) COVID-19 Resources for State Leaders—Executive Orders." Accessed October 30, 2020. https://web.csg.org/covid19/executive-orders/.

COVID Tracking Project. "Racial Data Dashboard." Accessed October 30, 2020a. https://covidtracking.com/race/dashboard.

COVID Tracking Project. "The COVID Racial Data Tracker." Accessed October 30, 2020a. https://covidtracking.com/race.

Dvorak, Petula. "When 'Back to School' Means a Parking Lot and the Hunt for a Wifi Signal." *Washington Post*, August 27, 2020, https://www.washingtonpost.com/local/when-back-to-school-means-a-parking-lot-and-the-hunt-for-a-wifi-signal/2020/08/27/0f785d5a-e873-11ea-970a-64c73a1c2392_story.html.

Gale Encyclopedia of US Economic History. "Smallpox Devastates Indigenous Populations." Volume 3 (2015):1218–1219.

Gomez, Diana Torres. "Blackness and Motherhood." *Medium*, March 9, 2017, https://medium.com/applied-intersectionality/blackness-and-motherhood-de400c98a4e1.

Gomez, M. B. "Neoliberalization's Propagation of Health Inequity in Urban Rebuilding Processes: The Dependence on Context and Path." *International Journal of Health Services* 47, no. 4 (2017): 655–689.

Gotham, K. F. "Racialization and Rescaling: Post-Katrina Rebuilding and the Louisiana Road Home Program." *International Journal of Urban and Regional Research* 38, no. 3 (2014): 773–790.

Graetz, Ilana, Gordon, Nancy, Fung, Vick, Hamity, Courtnee, and Reed, Mary E. "The Digital Divide and Patient Portals: Internet Access Explained Differences in Patient Portal Use for Secure Messaging by Age, Race, and Income." *Medical Care* 54, no. 8 (2016): 772–779.

Graham, Leigh T. "Permanently Failing Organizations? Small Business Recovery After September 11, 2001." *Economic Development Quarterly* 21, no. 4 (2007): 299–314.

Hall, P. A., and Taylor, R. C. "Political Science and the Three Institutionalisms." *Political Studies* 1, no. 44 (1996): 936–957.

Harvey, David. *A Brief History of Neoliberalism*. Oxford: Oxford University Press, 2005.

Inrig, Stephen. *North Carolina and the Problem of AIDS*. Chapel Hill: University of North Carolina Press, 2011.

Kalleberg, Arne L. "Precarious Work, Insecure Workers: Employment Relations in Transition." *American Sociological Review* 74, no. 1 (2009): 1–22.

Kumar, Supriya, Sandra Crouse Quinn, Kevin H. Kim, Laura H. Daniel, and Vicki S. Freimuth. "The Impact of Workplace Policies and Other Social Factors on Self-Reported Influenza-Like Illness Incidence During the 2009 H1N1 Pandemic." *American Journal of Public Health* 102 (2013):134–140.

Lerman, A., and Weaver, V. "'I Better Stay Below the Radar'": Fear, Alienation and Withdrawal." In *Arresting Citizenship*, edited by A. Lerman, and V. Weaver, 199–230. Chicago: University of Chicago Press, 2014.

Locke, J. (1689). *Second Treatise of Government*. Project Gutenberg. https://www.gutenberg.org/ebooks/7370.

MacFarquhar, Neil. "Who's Enforcing Mask Rules? Often Retail Workers, and They're Getting Hurt." *New York Times*, May 15, 2020, https://www.nytimes.com/2020/05/15/us/coronavirus-masks-violence.html.

Mckiernan-González, J. *At the Nation's Edge. In Precarious Prescriptions*. Minnesota: University of Minnesota Press, 2014.

Morse, Brit. "The PPP Failed Minority-Led Businesses. 3 Ideas for What Could Work Instead." Inc., August 13, 2020, https://www.inc.com/brit-morse/minority-led-companies-black-owned-businesses-phase-4-paycheck-protection-program.html.

Ong, E. "We Need Equity-Oriented Solutions to COVID-19: Asians Facing Stigma, Discrimination, Fear During Pandemic." *The Nation's Health* 50, no. 3 (2020): 10.

Porterfield, Carlie. No-Mask Attacks: Nationwide, Employees Face Violence for Enforcing Mask Mandates. Retrieved from *Forbes*, August 15, 2020, https://www.forbes.com/sites/carlieporterfield/2020/08/15/no-mask-attacks-nationwide-employees-face-violence-for-enforcing-mask-mandates/#a1e85cd60d6c.

Quinn, Sandra Crouse, Kumar, Supriya, Freimuth, Vicki S, Musa, Donald, Casteneda-Angarita, Nestor, and Kidwell, Kelley. (2011). "Racial Disparities in Exposure, Susceptibility, and Access to Health Care in the US H1N1

Influenza Pandemic." *American Journal of Public Health* 101, no. 2 (February 2011): 285–293.

Reed, T. F. "Toward Freedom: The Case Against Race Reductionism." London: Verso, 2020.

Robinson, Cedric J, and Kelley, Robin D. G. *Black Marxism*. Chapel Hill: University of North Carolina Press, 2000.

Selyukh, Alina, and Shannon Bond. "Amazon, Instacart Grocery Delivery Workers Demand Coronavirus Protection and Pay." NPR, March 30, 2020, https://www.npr.org/2020/03/30/823767492/amazon-instacart-grocery-delivery-workers-strike-for-coronavirus-protection-and-.

Small Business Administration. "Economic Injury Disaster Loan." SBA.gov. Accessed October 30, 2020. https://www.sba.gov/funding-programs/loans/coronavirus-relief-options/economic-injury-disaster-loans.

Sutton, Madeline Y, et al. "A Review of the Centers for Disease Control and Prevention's Response to the HIV/AIDS Crisis Among Black people in the United States, 1981–2009." *American Journal of Public Health* 99 no. S2 (2009): S351–S359.

Taylor, Dianna. *Michel Foucault: Key Concepts*. Taylor & Francis Group, 2014.

Urban Institute. "Tracking COVID-19's Effects by Race and Ethnicity." Accessed October 30, 2020. https://www.urban.org/features/tracking-covid-19s-effects-race-and-ethnicity.

US Bureau of Labor Statistics. "Unions—2019." Accessed October 30, 2020. https://www.bls.gov/news.release/pdf/union2.pdf.

US Bureau of Labor Statistics. "Labor Force Statistics from the Current Population Survey." Accessed October 30, 2020. https://www.bls.gov/cps/cpsaat18.htm?fbclid=IwAR0-kw1npuKwmb-9aR3zpvLQIdDwa8qwFWaO1iO-VQ3xsxkPvNO_yyreYHSk.

US Census Bureau. "Measuring Household Experiences During the Coronavirus Pandemic." Accessed October 30, 2020. https://www.census.gov/data/experimental-data-products/household-pulse-survey.html.

US Courts. "Communicating/Interacting with Persons Engaged in Criminal Activity and Felons (Probation and Supervised Release Conditions)." Accessed October 30, 2020. https://www.uscourts.gov/services-forms/communicating-interacting-persons-engaged-criminal-activity-felons-probation-supervised-release-conditions.

US Equal Employment Opportunity Commission. 2018. "Employment Statistics for Minorities and Women." Accessed October 30, 2020. https://www.eeoc.gov/employment/employment-statistics.

Watkins, Craig, Andres Lombana-Bermudez, Alexander Cho, Vivian Shaw, Jacqueline Ryan Vickery, and Lauren Weinzimmer. *The Digital Edge*. Vol. 4. NYU Press, 2018.

Weixel, Nathaniel. "CDC Warns Against Arguing with Anti-Mask Customers." *TheHill*, August 25, 2020, https://thehill.com/policy/healthcare/513643-cdc-warns-employees-not-to-argue-with-anti-mask-customers.

Wilson, Geoff A. "Community Resilience: Path Dependency, Lock-in Effects and Transitional Ruptures." *Journal of Environmental Planning and Management* 57, no. 1: 1–26.

Young, Iris Marion. *Inclusion and Democracy*. Oxford: Oxford University Press, 2002.

CHAPTER 9

# INTRODUCING THE STRATEGIC HEALTH AND ECONOMIC EMERGENCY MANAGEMENT PLAN FOR VULNERABLE POPULATIONS

*How to Protect Black Health and Black Wealth in the US Amid the COVID-19 Pandemic and Beyond*[1]

*Lori Latrice Martin*

ASSET POVERTY IS DEFINED AS the lack of access to liquid assets for at least three months to weather unexpected health and/or economic challenges (Haveman and Wolff 2005). Many Americans are asset poor. However, Black people in the United States are more likely to be asset poor than other groups. The overrepresentation of Black people among the asset poor, I argue, explains, in whole or part, why Black people are particularly vulnerable to death as a result of COVID-19 and economic hardships. The present study will examine racial disparities in COVID-19-related deaths, and unemployment rates, for example. Data and information from relevant local, state, and national sources will be analyzed. I contend that what is needed to both address the current impact of COVID-19 and mitigate the negative effects of future pandemics on Black health and Black wealth is a comprehensive strategy. This comprehensive strategy should not only

---

1 An earlier version of the chapter was published in the following book by the author: *Racial Realism and the History of Black People in America*, 2022. Albany, New York: SUNY Press.

provide short-term assistance to individuals and businesses but also should include a long-term plan—the Strategic Health and Economic Emergency Management Plan for Vulnerable Populations—that simultaneously addresses enduring racial divides in public education, access to quality and affordable health care, and returns on investments into home and business ownership.

## Racial Wealth Inequality and Black Asset Poverty in America

It is no secret that a relatively small percentage of Americans possess the majority of the nation's wealth. The remaining 99 percent of Americans may own various types and levels of assets. White Americans are more likely to possess assets than Black people in America and do so at higher levels. Jenna Ross, a writer for Visual Capitalist, recently published an article highlighting racial differences on various assets. Ross (2020) found that while 73 percent of White families owned homes, only 45 percent of Black families owned homes. Ninety percent of White families owned a car as compared to 73 percent of Black families. About one-third of Black families reported having retirement accounts compared to 60 percent of White families. A relatively small percentage of American families reported having family-owned business equity, but the percentages for White families still exceeded the percentages for non-White families. Fifteen percent of White families had some family-owned business equity, while 7 percent of Black families had family-owned business equity. Finally, Ross (2020) reported that about one-third of Black families had publicly traded stock. Over 60 percent of White families owned publicly traded stocks.

The median net worth for White households was $171,000, and the median net worth for Black households was only $17,600 (Ross 2020). White and Black families with similar levels of education often have very different levels of wealth (Oliver and Shapiro 1996; 2019). The median wealth for Black heads of households with a bachelor's degree was, on average, $68,000. The median wealth of White heads of households with no bachelor's degree was nearly $100,000 (Ross 2020). Laura Sullivan and her colleagues at the

Institute on Assets and Social Policy at Brandeis University found that student loan debt is a contributing factor in the racial wealth gap. Over 25 percent of student loan borrowers defaulted on their loans within twenty years. For Black borrowers, about 50 percent defaulted on their student loans within twenty years (Sullivan et al. 2019). Additionally, Sullivan et al. (2019) showed that for Black student loan holders in their thirties, on average, "total wealth is $10,700 in the red compared to a close to breakeven for White people with student debt" (1). Moreover, Ross's (2020) research showed that White families had home equity of more than $215,000. Black families had less than half the home equity of White families ($94,400).

About 20 percent of Black families have zero or negative wealth compared to only 9 percent of White households (Ross 2020). Black people are overrepresented among the asset poor (Martin 2013). Asset poverty is defined as a household that lacks net worth to sustain income for ninety days above the federal income poverty level or net worth equal to a quarter of the annual income poverty level (Haveman and Wolff 2005; Leonard and Di 2014). The lack of liquid assets, for example, places households at long-term risks for economic difficulties resulting from unexpected events such as a medical problem that leads to a large debt or sudden job loss. It is hard for households to recover. The implications are far-reaching. Assets are associated with the overall economic well-being of individuals, families, and communities. Home equity, for example, may be used to finance a child's education. Inheritances may be used to assist the next generation with a down payment on their primary residence or provide start-up capital for beginning a business. Asset ownership is often associated with access to amenities that provide for better quality and life, which may also translate into better overall health outcomes.

Researchers have identified many factors that contribute to racial wealth inequality and Black asset poverty in America (Baradaran 2019; Caner and Wolff 2014; Fisher and Weber 2004; Herring and Henderson 2016; Keister 2000; Keister 2008; Kochihar and Cilluffo 2017; Martin 2009; Martin 2019; Saez and Zucman 2018; Thomas et al. 2020). Racial disparities in labor force participation and educational attainment are two commonly cited reasons for differences between Black and White people regarding the types and levels of assets owned (Traub et al. 2017). However, research has shown that increasing either does little to narrow the racial wealth gap or diminish Black asset poverty (Traub et al. 2017). Inheritance has been shown to affect racial wealth inequality and Black asset poverty (Oliver and Shapiro 2006). Black people are less likely to receive inheritances than White people, and when Black people receive inheritances, the amount is lower than the average amount White people receive (Oliver and Shapiro 2006). Discrimination in mortgage lending and predatory lending practices are also cited as determinants of wealth inequality and Black asset poverty (Ross et al. 2007). Scholarly research continuously shows that Black people are more likely to experience discrimination throughout the home-buying process and are more likely to be victimized by predatory lending practices (Martin 2013). Black people have less access to real estate markets that enhance their investments into a primary place of residency (Ross et al. 2007). On average, Black people have lower housing values than White homeowners (Thomas et al. 2017).

The overrepresentation of Black people among the asset poor makes them particularly vulnerable to personal problems and social issues. Prior to the pandemic, black people were far more likely than other groups not to have access to sufficient assets that would allow them to meet their basic needs for a period of at least three months. The recent COVID-19 pandemic and its impacts on the United States are illustrative of just how vulnerable and endangered Black people are, especially Black people who are both income and asset poor. Black people working in the secondary segment of the economy in jobs that are often insecure and lack access to adequate health care likely contributed to the overrepresentation of Black people who suddenly found themselves unemployed or essential workers who could not stay at home. For example, about one-third of all bus drivers and nearly one-fifth of food service workers and grocery store associates are Black (Ray 2020). By mid-April 2020, more than twenty million Americans were unemployed (Long 2020).

The challenges facing Black-owned businesses were also clear. Black businesses have historically played important and complex roles within the Black community (Howard 2019). While E. Franklin Frazier called the significance of Black business into question in his book *The Black Bourgeoisie*, other scholars have focused on how such things as the self-help tradition have benefited Black people with an entrepreneurial spirit (Butler 1995; Butler and Herring 1992; Rhodes and Butler 2010). At the same time, Black businesses face many challenges that hinder their success, including racial and gender discrimination (Pantin 2018; Henderson et al. 2015). While Black business owners are a small minority of the US economy, many were nonetheless left out of programs aimed at protecting such businesses due to a host of structural barriers (Cerullo and Gandel 2020). The impact of the exclusion of many Black businesses may be underestimated due to the lack of race-specific data on the subject (Kranhold and Zubak-Skees 2020). Black business owners' access to financial capital has historically been tenuous and working with such institutions to secure support from the government proved difficult. The most convincing argument of the vulnerability of Black people, including Black people with few or no assets, can be seen in the overrepresentation of Black people among COVID-19-related deaths. This was particularly the case in cities where Black people possess few assets.

## Black Deaths and COVID-19

A report from APM Research Lab includes data on COVID-19 deaths by race in America. The report found that Black people have experienced 18.5% of all deaths of known race, but represent about 12.4% of the population. The report also showed that for every 100,000 Americans (of their respective group), nearly 125 Black people have died from the coronavirus, the second-highest actual mortality rate of all groups, behind only Indigenous people. The rate for Indigenous people was about 130. Moreover, in 21 states and Washington, DC, over 1 in 1,000 Black people has died. Black people are 2.7 times more likely to have died than White people, when age is taken into account.

Many have written about the role of racial discrimination and racism during the COVID-19 pandemic (Perry et al. 2020). Rashawn Ray was among the scholars to take a deeper dive and focus on specific places where Black people were overrepresented among COVID-19 deaths. Ray (2020) also explored why Black people were dying at higher rates of COVID-19. Ray (2020) observed that in Illinois, Black people made up about 16 percent of the population, but were one-third of people diagnosed with COVID-19. In Chicago, 70 percent of the people who died of COVID-19 were Black. Ray (2020) observed that similar patterns were evidenced in states like New York and the Carolinas. In Louisiana, about 30 percent of the population identified as Black. Seventy percent of COVID-19 deaths in Louisiana were Black deaths.

Although some have argued that racial disparities in the prevalence of preexisting health conditions explain the overrepresentation of Black people among COVID-19 deaths, Ray (2020) contended that structural conditions that are related to preexisting conditions and health disparities were more to blame. Debates about whether culture (Lewis 1966) or structure matters more dominate many disciplines (Wilson 1978; 1987; 1991; 2010). However, Ray (2020) made several evidenced-based arguments to support the role of structural and economic barriers in his explanations. Ray (2020) pointed to the linkages between the racial composition of neighborhoods and health outcomes and the role that public policies played in creating under-resourced Black neighborhoods, such as the policy of redlining (Martin 2019). Redlining identified predominantly Black neighborhoods as hazardous and poor places for financial investment from mainstream lenders, including the federal government (Massey and Denton 1993). Black neighborhoods often have a higher population density than other neighborhoods, making physical distance to flatten the curve in their communities more challenging (Massey and Denton 1993). Access to testing (Kim et al. 2020), pharmacies, and health care professionals were issues prior to COVID-19, but were factors that nevertheless served as structural barriers that contributed to the overrepresentation of Black people among COVID-19 deaths (Ray 2020).

Environmental racism and the criminalization of Black men may also explain COVID-19 deaths among Black people in America. Black people across the United States have faced greater environmental threats than other groups. Ray (2020) cites the toxic water in Flint, Michigan, and the high levels of lead exposure in Black communities in Baltimore. Finally, Ray (2020) argued that wearing personal protective equipment (PPE) like masks is interpreted differently based upon race and gender, which may have served as a deterrent for some Black men, for example, to embrace wearing a mask prior to statewide mandates. Historically, the dominant narrative about Black men in America includes characterizations of the group as violent and a threat to White people and broader society (Fashing-Varner et al. 2014). Perhaps Black men were hesitant to wear masks because of their perceived criminality, and wearing a mask outside of broad statewide mandates may have been hazardous to their safety.

### Sacrificing Blackness and Emergency Management Plans

The lack of consideration for how pandemics disproportionately affects Black people is not surprising. Blackness has historically been sacrificed during good times and bad times for the benefit of others. There is a growing body of literature about the use of people in prison, where Black people are again overrepresented. Black people, especially Black men, are more incarcerated in America's prisons and jails than other racial and gender groups. While incarcerated people are considered vulnerable populations, incarcerated Black people are at even greater risk for exploitation and other forms of unequal treatment. This was evidenced in the past with the passage of laws that led to the incarceration of Black people for the purpose of fueling the very profitable convict leasing program (Martin 2019). In more contemporary times, Black incarcerated people are used as a source of cheap labor: inmates create office furniture through Corcraft in New York; participate in prison rodeos; and in Louisiana, California, Washington, and North Carolina, they also fight dangerous fires (Martin et al. 2014; Purdum 2020).

North Carolina is home to the Building, Rehabilitating, Instructing, Development, Growing, Employing (BRIDGE) program. A report by Ashley Nellis (2016) for the Sentencing Project also found that more than half of the state prison population in North Carolina was Black. The rate for White people was 221 per 100,000 and 951 per 100,000 for Black people. J. Carlee Purdum (2020) questioned whether the BRIDGE program served to rehabilitate or exploit participants. BRIDGE is essentially an incarcerated labor program. The target population was originally between the ages of eighteen to thirty-two. According to Purdum (2020), the program houses, trains, and dispatches incarcerated men to respond to wildfires, disasters, and emergencies in the state. The program started after one of North Carolina's most costly wildfires in April 1985 (Purdum 2020). The wildfires, which destroyed homes and land, were fought by twenty-five civilian firefighters and seventy-five untrained incarcerated men (Purdum 2020). Program participants are "paid" a maximum of $1 per day. Although the program began with less than twenty participants, by 2018, there were nearly two hundred participants with more than six hundred eligible for the program (Purdum 2020). Eligibility requirements include meeting the age requirements, no sexual offenses, and other security and conduct requirements (Purdum 2020). "To date, more than 5,000 inmates have gone through the program, working more than 2.8 million man-hours. This has saved North Carolina more than 36 million dollars in labor costs" (North Carolina Forest Service 2022). According to Purdum (2020), the program is not as successful as officials claim and offers very little in the way of benefits for the most incarcerated men, and an unscientific review of images online of program participants points to the inclusion of incarcerated Black men. Beyond the anecdotal evidence provided by such images, the sheer numbers of incarcerated Black men makes them vulnerable: incarcerated Black men and Black women are vulnerable due to other threats within the criminal justice system ranging from asset poverty upon reentry into their respective communities, the increased likelihood of separation from their children, and an increased likelihood of negative and/ or deadly encounters with law enforcement officials (Fashing-Varner et al. 2014; Martin 2011).

Judith Saunders and others have written more broadly about vulnerable populations, especially in the aftermath of Hurricane Katrina. Vulnerable groups may best be understood as social groups with few resources "and consequent high relative risk for morbidity and premature mortality, and reduced quality of life" from the perspective of those in the health care system (Saunders 2007, 31). The definition can of course be broadened to include other areas of society, particularly where Black people have relatively few resources and are at risk for literal and figurative deaths and chronic conditions that reduce their quality of life.

Saunders (2007) observed that the vulnerable population model offers a way of understanding the many problems people faced as a result of

Hurricane Katrina and the responses of health care professions in meeting the identified challenges. The model calls for considering vulnerable populations at risk due to a host of factors. These factors are often structural or part of systems that often offer benefits to some groups at the expense of other groups. Race is just but one important way in which groups have been divided in America. Valued material and nonmaterial items such as property, power, and prestige have not been distributed equally, with White people reaping a disproportionate amount of benefits and Black people bearing the brunt of the miseries. This has caused some scholars to declare subordination as the permanent status of Black people in America (Bell 1992). Historically, Saunders (2007) argued, the healthcare system, for example, "has placed the source of the blame of vulnerability within the individual. Placing core vulnerability within the individual can result in individual blame, while absolving society, government, and industry of responsibility for conditions that give rise to vulnerability" (30–31).

Eisenman and colleagues (2007) also wrote about vulnerable groups and the lessons learned from Hurricane Katrina. The research team wrote about Katrina migrants from New Orleans staying in Houston, Texas. After conducting a content analysis of the in-depth interviews conducted with mostly low-income Black respondents, the researchers found, among other things, that a lack of trust in authorities increased their vulnerability. The scholars further acknowledged barriers related to shelter and transportation, but concluded that "removing the obstacles of shelter and transportation will be insufficient to ensure safety in future disasters. Policies must additionally address the important influence of extended families and social networks through better community-based communication and preparation strategies" (Eisenman 2007, 9–10). In other words, Eisenman et al. (2007) highlighted how big and complex emergency management plans are especially when it comes to chronically vulnerable populations, such as Black people, who through a series of public policies and private practices have had limitations placed on their abilities to control their own destinies for generations. What is required is a holistic approach that centers race and racism, and unapologetically creates opportunities for Black people to thrive before, during, and after the health and economic disasters that will surely come.

## Introducing the Strategic Health and Economic Emergency Management Plan for Vulnerable Populations

Historically and in contemporary times, responses to emergencies have best reflected what some have called a reactive science. Among the key events in the history of emergency management planning was the 1736 formation of the Union Five Company, the passage of the Disaster Relief Act of 1950, and the establishment of the Federal Emergency Management Agency after 9/11. The National Response Framework provides general guidance for addressing emergency management matters that might arise. One guiding principle is the responsibility of all levels of government, corporations, nonprofit organizations, and individuals. The framework stresses the importance of federal, state, tribal, and local planning and the need for mutual support. Unity of effort is stressed. The importance of planning is stressed as well (Eisenman et al. 2007; McArdle 2014; Saunders 2017). Three key benefits are outlined. One of the benefits of planning is the ability to determine in advance what actions and policies are to be followed. Second, planning provides guidance for other preparedness activities. Finally, planning contributes to unity of effort. In short, "planning is a foundational element of both preparedness and response" (Homeland Security 2008, 71). The US Department of Homeland Security also identified criteria for successful planning: acceptability, adequacy, completeness, consistency, and standardization of products, feasibility, flexibility, and interoperability and collaboration. The hallmark of any emergency plan includes an emphasis on preparation, response, recovery, and mitigation.

The Strategic Health and Economic Emergency Management Plan for Vulnerable Populations, with an emphasis on one of the most vulnerable populations in America—Black people—introduced here builds upon the national response framework and calls for planning that centers the experiences of Black people. It requires looking at the data on health and economic disparities between Black people and White people as part of the preparedness. This will allow for an assessment of the magnitude of the challenges that might lie ahead for Black people and other race-based vulnerable populations. The evidence is all around us about the limited access to health care, the overrepresentation of Black people among the uninsured, unequal treatment by health care officials, and persistent racial disparities where income, education, wealth, and criminal justice are concerned (Du Bois 1975; 1903; 1995; Fasching-Varner et al. 2014; Frazier 1937; 1939; 1957; 1974; 1927; Fryer 2016; Gray and Finley 2015; Gupta-Kagan 2019; Hammonds and Reverby; Hetey and Eberhardt 2018; Hinton et al. 2018; Kamalu et al. 2010; Li 2016; Yearby 2018).

Armed with data on racial inequalities on both health and economic outcomes, federal, state, and local governments, along with private corporations, nonprofits, and affluent individuals, should support efforts to prevent the exacerbation of Black and White differences related to health and economics and respond in the aftermath. This will require a move away from popular universal programs or race-neutral policies and initiatives, which treat everyone the same. Vulnerable populations, in this case, many Black people, lag behind White people in the United States, most significantly where asset ownership is concerned, because of unfair public policies and private practices. Student loan forgiveness, assistance with down payments and closing costs for first-time Black homebuyers, grants for Black start-up businesses, and investments into traditional public schools in majority-minority communities along with defunding charter schools and other so-called school choice options are good places to begin.

Much like the period following the Great Recession of the mid- to late-2000s, the full extent of what was required to dig the nation out of the economic ditch it had fallen into was not known until after the housing bubble burst, among other events. Likewise, careful attention must be paid in the aftermath of an emergency to determine what additional recovery measures are needed. "Recovery" may not be the best word in the case of vulnerable populations like Black people in the United States because recovery implies making an individual and/or group whole again. While Black people have experienced their fair share of harm, they have yet to experience a period where they are treated as total persons or experience health and economic outcomes that equal or exceed that of White people in America. Nevertheless, any stimulus package aimed at assisting large and small businesses and ordinary citizens must reflect the historically disadvantaged starting point of Black businesses and Black citizens and offer different levels of support.

While many Americans appreciated the financial support that came from the federal government during the COVID-19 pandemic, $1,200 was simply not enough for those who were already struggling financially before businesses and schools began to close their doors. Unfortunately, Black people have been disproportionately found among the individuals, households, and communities that have been caught up in the midst of an economic pandemic for generations. Moreover, environmental hazards, the stress of being Black in America, limited access to preventative care, and distrust of medical personnel necessitate adequate resources to ensure that Black people have access to clean air, water, and trustworthy health care officials. Recovery as part of the strategic emergency management plan proposed here would include an immediate influx of resources to health-related matters immediately following an emergency.

Hazard mitigation plans often include the identification of the most likely hazards. Again, scholars have shown over and over the many ways Black people are negatively affected by both health and economic emergencies. Based on the information we have about a particular type of emergency, every effort should be made to identify the most likely hazard or outcome(s) for Black people. For example, for Black people with assets, their overall net worth declines more than the overall net worth of White people (Holland 2016). Black homeowners do not readily enjoy the same types of returns on their investments as White people (Thomas et al. 2018) and may miss out on tax savings for homeowners because their overall economic standing might dictate that they file using a standard deduction versus itemized deductions (Martin 2019). The time has long since passed for abandoning the belief that health and economic emergencies affect people regardless of race in the same way. There is no one-size-fits-all emergency management plan, especially when it comes to meeting the needs of groups that remain in a perpetual state of vulnerability due to their race, which is the case for Black people.

The National Response Framework includes a number of key scenario sets and related national planning scenarios. The scenario sets include explosive, nuclear, radiological, biological, chemical, and cyberattacks, along with natural disasters and pandemic influenza. It could be argued that persistent and enduring racial disparities in health and overall economic well-being should be added to the list and planning efforts and actions toward addressing the gaps must be ongoing. The Grand Canyon–like racial wealth gap, the sea of Black people drowning in asset poverty, and the storm of diminished health care and quality of life is a national emergency created by public policies and practices and made worse by health and economic emergencies experienced simultaneously by large segments of the dominant racial group in America.

The Strategic Health and Economic Emergency Management Plan for Vulnerable Populations will require adequate funding from all levels of government and private companies, reasonable timetables, and public support. While support for race-specific policies is hard to come by, the killing of George Floyd has ushered in an unprecedented sense of inter-racial cooperation unseen since the modern-day civil rights movement in America. If there were ever a time to test the proverbial waters, now is the time. This would help meet the acceptability criteria for successful planning. The nation owes Black Americans a debt that is hard to quantify and one that is long overdue.

Additionally, the proposed plan represents a complete and holistic approach to dealing with the disparate impact of health and economic emergencies on Black people and other racially vulnerable populations. It focuses on different levels of health and economic opportunities as well as different dimensions. Moreover, the proposed plan should be regarded as feasible given the country's resources, which are readily deployed during the time of war, for example, or during a health or economic crisis, such as COVID-19 and the Great Recession. It is feasible to distribute the nation's resources in ways that are not necessarily equal but are both equitable and just.

## Conclusion

In the age of the George Floyd uprising, it is imperative that America recognizes as some places have begun to do that racism is a public health crisis. Americans must let go of the idea that there can be racism without racists

(Bonilla-Silva 2013). It is not only a public health crisis, but it is also a public wealth crisis. These are not public health crises in that they could not be predicted or are best understood as anomalies. Instead, they both represent a crisis that is of a magnitude that affects Black people, specifically, but also the country as a whole. Whereas some have described the Black family as in a state of crisis (Moynihan 1965) or education in a state of crisis (Martin 2015), this language is best reserved for the most vulnerable among us; historically, Black people have involuntarily and yet with bravery and creativity worn that label. The time is now for a national plan to address ongoing racial disparities in health and wealth, but it is also time to prepare with race-specific strategies to mitigate the damage of an emergency and finally flatten the curve of suffering that has beset far too many Black people.

In this chapter, I have shown that Black people in the United States are more likely to be asset poor than other groups. I explained why Black people were particularly vulnerable to death as a result of COVID-19 and economic hardships. This included so-called essential workers as well as Black entrepreneurs. The present study included racial disparities in COVID-19-related deaths and unemployment rates, for examples. It was shown that what is needed is a comprehensive strategy to address the current impact of COVID-19 and mitigate the negative effects of future pandemics on Black health and Black wealth. I presented a comprehensive strategy that not only provides short-term assistance to individuals and businesses but also should include a long-term plan—the Strategic Health and Economic Emergency Management Plan for Vulnerable Populations—that simultaneously addresses enduring racial divides in public education including racial school segregation (Brown v. Board; Onwuachi-Willig 2019), access to quality and affordable health care, and returns on investments into home and business ownership. In honor of the memory of George Floyd and the other Black men, Black women, and Black children who died unnatural deaths at the hands of law enforcement officials or ordinary White citizens before him, and in honor of the ones who sadly will befall the same fate, now is the time to address the racism as a public health and wealth matter in a meaningful way: one that centers race and racism and is focused on equity, humanity, and justice.

## References

APM Research Lab Staff. December 10, 2020. "Color of Coronavirus: 2020 in Review." https://www.apmresearchlab.org/covid/deaths-by-race-december2020?rq=deaths%20per%20100%2C000.

Baradaran, Mehrsa. *The Color of Money: Black Banks and the Racial Wealth Gap.* Cambridge, MA: Harvard University Press, 2019.

Bell, Derrick. "Racial Realism." *Connecticut Law Review* 24, no. 2 (1992): 363–379.

Bonilla-Silva, Eduardo. *Racism without Racists: Color-Blind Racism and the Persistence of Racial Inequality in the United States.* Lanham, MD: Rowman and Littlefield, 2013.

*Brown v. Board of Education.*, 347 US 483 (1954).

Butler, John Sibley. "Race, Entrepreneurship, and the Inner City." *USA Today Magazine*, 1995, 123(2596): 26.

Butler, John Sibley, and Cedric Herring. "Ethnicity and Entrepreneurship in America: Toward an Explanation of Racial and Ethnic Group Variations in Self-Employment." *Sociological Perspectives* 34, no. 1 (1991): 79–95.

Caner, Asena and Edward N. Wolff. "Asset Poverty in the United States, 1984–99: Evidence from the Panel Study of Income Dynamics." *Review of Income & Wealth* 50, no. 4 (2004), 493–518.

Cerullo, Megan. and Stephen Gandel. "Many Small Businesses Say Paycheck Protection Program Is Deeply Flawed." *CBS News*, April 15, 2020.

Du Bois, W.E.B. *Souls of Black Folks.* McClurg & Co, 1903.

Du Bois, W.E.B. *Darkwater: Voices from Within the Veil.* San Diego, CA: Harcourt, Brace, 1975.

Du Bois, W.E.B. *The Philadelphia Negro.* Philadelphia: University of Pennsylvania Press, 1995.

Eisenman, David P, Kristina M. Cordasco, Steve Asch, Joya Golden, and Deborah Glik. "Disaster Planning and Risk Communication with Vulnerable Communities: Lessons from Hurricane Katrina." *American Journal of Public Health* 97 (2007): 109–115.

Fasching-Varner, Kenneth, Katrice Albert, Rema Reynolds., and Lori Latrice Martin, (Eds.) *Trayvon Martin, Race, and American Justice: Writing Wrong.* Rotterdam, NE: Senses Publishers, 2014.

Fasching-Varner, Kenneth, Roland Mitchell, Lori Latrice Martin, and Karen Benton-Haron. "Beyond School-to-Prison Pipeline and Toward an Educational and Penal Realism." *Equity & Excellence in Education* 47, no. 4 (2015): 410–429.

Fisher, Monica, and Bruce A. Weber. "Does Economic Vulnerability Depend on Place of Residence? Asset Poverty Across Metropolitan and Nonmetropolitan Areas." *Review of Regional Studies* 34, no. 2 (2004): 137–155.

Frazier, E. Franklin. "The Pathology of Racial Prejudice." *The Forum* 70 (1927): 856–862.

Frazier, E. Franklin. "Negro Harlem: An Ecological Study." *American Journal of Sociology* 43, no. 1 (1937): 72–88.

Frazier, E. Franklin. *The Negro Family in the United States*. Chicago: University of Chicago Press, 1939.

Frazier, E. Franklin. *Black Bourgeoisie*. New York: The Free Press, 1957.

Frazier, E. Franklin. *The Negro Church in America. Sourcebooks in Negro History*. New York: Schocken Books, 1974.

Fryer, Roland. "An Empirical Analysis of Racial Differences in Police Use of Force." *NBER Working Paper Series*, Working Paper 22399 (2016).

Gray, Biko Mandela, and Stephen C. Finley. "God Is a White Racist: Immanent Atheism as a Religious Response to Black Lives Matter and AntiBlack State-Sanctioned Violence." *Journal of Africana Religions* 3, no. 4 (2015): 443–453.

Gupta-Kagan, Josh. "Reevaluating School Searches Following School-to-Prison Pipeline Reforms." *Fordham Law Review* 87, no. 5 (2019): 1–46.

Hammonds, Evelynn, and Susan M. Reverby. "Toward a Historically Informed Analysis of Racial Health Disparities Since 1619." *American Journal of Public Health* 109, no. 10 (2019): 1348–1349.

Haveman, Robert, and Edward Wolff. "Who Are the Asset Poor?: Levels, Trends, and Composition for the US." In *Inclusion in the American Dream: Assets, Poverty and Public Policy*, edited by Michael. Sherraden, 1983–1998. New York: Oxford University Press, 2005.

Henderson, Loren, Cedric Herring, Hayward Derrick Horton, and Melvin Thomas. "Credit Where Credit is Due? Race, Gender, and Discrimination in the Credit Scores of Business Startups." *Review of Black Political Economy* 42, no. 4 (2015): 459–479.

Herring, Cedric, and Loren Henderson. "Wealth Inequality in Black and White." *Social Problems* 8 (2016): 4–17.

Hetey, Rebecca C, and Jennifer L. Eberhardt. (2018). The Numbers Don't Speak for Themselves: Racial Disparities and the Persistence of Inequality in the Criminal Justice System. *Current Directions in Psychological Science* 27(3), 183–87.

Hinton, Elizabeth, LeShae Henderson, and Cindy Reed. *An Unjust Burden: The Disparate Treatment of Black Americans in the Criminal Justice System*. New York: Vera Institute of Justice, 2018.

Holland, Joshua. "The Average Black Family Would Need 228 Years to Build the Wealth of a White Family Today." *The Nation*, August 8, 2016, https://www.thenation.com/article/archive/the-average-Black-family-would-need-228-years-to-build-the-wealth-of-a-White-family-today/.

"How Distance Learning Illuminates Disparities Among Students and Teachers." *PBS News Hour*, June 23, 2020, https://www.pbs.org/newshour/show/how-distance-learning-illuminates-disparities-among-students-and-teachers.

Howard, Tiffany. "The State of Black Entrepreneurship in America: Evaluating the Relationship Between Immigration and Minority Business Ownership." Washington, DC: Congressional Black Caucus Foundation, 2019.

Jones, Janelle. "The Racial Wealth Gap: How African Americans Have Been Short-Changed Out of Materials to Build Wealth." *Working Economics* (blog), *Economic Policy Institute*, February 13, 2017. https://www.epi.org/blog/the-racial-wealth-gap-how-african-americans-have-been-shortchanged-out-of-the-materials-to-build-wealth/.

Kamalu, Ngozi, Margery Coulson-Clark, and Nkechi M. Kamalu. "Racial Disparities in Sentencing: Implications for the Criminal Justice System and the African American Community." *African Journal of Criminology & Justice Studies* 4, no. 1 (2010): 1–33.

Karjanen, David J. *The Servant Class City: Urban Revitalization versus the Working Poor in San Diego*. Minneapolis: University of Minnesota Press, 2016.

Keister, Lisa A. Conservative Protestants and Wealth: How Religion Perpetuates Asset Poverty. *American Journal of Sociology* 113, no. 5 (2008): 1237–1271.

Keister, Lisa A. *Wealth inequality in America*. Cambridge, MA: Harvard University Press, 2000.

Kim, Soo R., Matthew Vann, Laura Bronner, and Grace Manthey. (2020). "Want a COVID-19 Test? It's Much Easier to Get in Wealthier, Whiter Neighborhoods." *FiveThirtyEight*, July 22, 2020, https://fivethirtyeight.com/features/white-neighborhoods-have-more-access-to-covid-19-testing-sites/.

Kochihar, Rakesh, and Anthony Cilluffo. "How Wealth Inequality Has Changed in the US Since the Great Recession by Race, Ethnicity and Income." *Pew Research Center*, November 1, 2017, https://www.pewresearch.org/fact-tank/2017/11/01/how-wealth-inequality-has-changed-in-the-u-s-since-the-great-recession-by-race-ethnicity-and-income/.

Kranhold, Kathryn, and Zubak-Skees, Chris. "Small Business Loan Data Includes Little About Race." *Center for Public Integrity*, July 6, 2020. https://publicintegrity.org/health/coronavirus-and-inequality/small-business-loan-data-includes-little-on-owners-race-paycheck-protection-program/.

Leonard, Tammy, and Wenhua Di. "Is Household Wealth Sustainable? An Examination of Asset Poverty Reentry After an Exit." *J Fam Econ Iss* 35 (2014): 131–144.

Lewis, Oscar. "The Culture of Poverty." *Scientific American* 215, no. 4 (1966): 19–25.

Li, Bethany. "Now is the Time!: Challenging Resegregation and Displacement in the Age of Hypergentrification." *Fordham Law Review* 85, no. 3 (2016): 1189–1242.

Long, Heather. "US Now Has 22 Million Unemployed, Wiping Out a Decade of Job Gains." *Washington Post*, April 16, 2020, https://www.washingtonpost.com/business/2020/04/16/unemployment-claims-coronavirus/.

Martin, Lori Latrice. "Black Asset Owners: Does Ethnicity Matter?" *Social Science Research* 38 (2009): 312–323.

Martin, Lori Latrice. "Debt to Society: Asset Poverty and Prisoner Reentry." *Review of the Black Political Economy* 38, no. 2 (2011): 131–143.

Martin, Lori Latrice. *Black Asset Poverty and the Enduring Racial Divide*. Boulder, CO: FirstForumPress, 2013.

Martin, Lori Latrice, Kenneth Fasching-Varner, Molly Quinn, M., and Melinda Jackson. "Racism, Rodeos, and the Misery Industries of Louisiana." *Journal of Pan African Studies* 7, no. 6 (2014): 60–83.

Martin, Lori Latrice. *Big Box Schools: Race, Education, and the Danger of the Wal-Martization of Public Schools in America*. Lanham, MD: Lexington Books, 2015.

Martin, Lori Latrice. "Race, Wealth, and Homesteading Revisited: How Public Policies Destroy(ed) Black Wealth." In *How Public Policy Impacts Racial Inequality*, edited by Joshua Grimm and Jaime Loke, 140–165. Baton Rouge, LA: LSU Press, 2019.

Martin, Lori Latrice. 2022. *Racial Realism and the History of Black People in America*. Lanham, MD: Lexington Books.

Massey, Douglas S., and Nancy A. Denton. *American Apartheid: Segregation and the Making of the Underclass*. Cambridge, MA: Harvard University Press.

McArdle, Andrea. "Storm Surges, Disaster Planning, and Vulnerable Populations at the Urban Periphery: Imagining a Resilient New York After Superstorm Sandy." *Idaho Law Review* 50, no. 2 (2014): 19–47.

Moynihan, Daniel Patrick. "The Negro Family: The Case for National Action." Washington, DC: Office of Planning and Research, 1965.

Neillis, Ashley. "The Color of Justice: Racial and Ethnic Disparity in State Prisons. The Sentencing Project." *The Sentencing Project*, October 13, 2021, https://www.sentencingproject.org/publications/color-of-justice-racial-and-ethnic-disparity-in-state-prisons/.

North Carolina Forest Service. 2022. "Young Offenders Forest Conservation Program." https://www.ncforestservice.gov/fire_control/bridge.htm.

Oliver, Melvin L., and Thomas M. Shapiro. *Black Wealth/White Wealth: A New Perspective on Racial Inequality*. New York: Routledge, 2006.

Oliver, Melvin L., and Thomas M. Shapiro. "Disrupting the Racial Wealth Gap." *Context* 18 (2019): 16–21.

Omi, Michael and Howard Winant. *Racial Formation in the United States: From the 1960s to the 1990s*. New York: Routledge, 2006.

Onwuachi-Willig, Angela. "Reconceptualizing the Harms of Discrimination: How *Brown v. Board of Education* Helped to Further White Supremacy." *Virginia Law Review* 105, no. 2 (2019): 343–369.

Pantin, Lynnise E. "The Wealth Gap and the Racial Disparities in the Startup Ecosystem." *Saint Louis University Law Journal* 62, no.2 (2018): 419–460.

Perry, Andre, David Harsbarger, and Carl Romer. "Mapping Racial Inequity Amid COVID-19 Underscores Policy Discriminations Against Black Americans." *Brookings*, April 16, 2020, https://www.brookings.edu/blog/the-avenue/2020/04/16/mapping-racial-inequity-amid-the-spread-of-covid-19/.

Purdum, J. Carlee. "Rehabilitation or Exploitation? Incarcerated Fire Fighters in North Carolina." *Carolina Planning Journal* 45 (2020): 72–79.

Ray, Rashawn. "Why Are Black People Dying at Higher Rates from COVID-19?" *Brookings*, April 9, 2020, https://www.brookings.edu/blog/fixgov/2020/04/09/why-are-Black people-dying-at-higher-rates-from-covid-19/.

Rhodes, Colbert, and John Sibley Butler. "Organizational Membership and Business Success: The Importance of Networking and Moving Beyond Homophily." *Challenge*, 16, no. 1 (2010): 33–48.

Ross, Jenna. "The Racial Wealth Gap: Asset Type Held by Race." *Visual Capitalist*, June 12, 2020, https://www.visualcapitalist.com/racial-wealth-gap/.

Ross, Stephen, Margery Turner, Erin Godfrey, and Robin. Smith. "Mortgage Lending in Chicago and Los Angeles: A Paired Testing Study of the Pre-Application Process." *Journal of Urban Economics* 63, no. 3 (2007): 902–919.

Saez, Emmanuel and Gabriel Zucman. "Wealth Inequality in the United States Since 1913: Evidence from Capitalized Income Tax Data." *The Quarterly Journal of Economics* 131, no. 2 (2018): 519–578.

Saunders, Judith M. "Vulnerable Populations in an American Red Cross Shelter After Hurricane Katrina." *Perspectives in Psychiatric Care* 43, no. 1 (2007): 30–37.

Sullivan, Laura, Tatjana Meschede, Thomas Shapiro, and Fernanda Escobar. "Stalling Dreams: How Student Debt is Disrupting Life Chances and Widening the Racial Wealth Gap." *Institute on Assets and Social Policy. Brandeis University*, September 2019, https://heller.brandeis.edu/iasp/pdfs/racial-wealth-equity/racial-wealth-gap/stallingdreams-how-student-debt-is-disrupting-lifechances.pdf.

Thomas, Melvin, Cedric Herring, Hayward Derrick Horton, Moshe Semyonov, Loren Henderson, and Patrick Mason. "Race and the Accumulation of Wealth: Racial Differences in Net Worth Over the Life Course, 1989–2009." *Social Problems* 67, no. 1 (2020): 20–39.

Thomas, Melvin, Richard Moye, Loren Henderson, and Hayward Derrick Horton. "Separate and Unequal: The Impact of Socioeconomic Status, Segregation, and the Great Recession on Racial Disparities in Housing Values." *Sociology of Race & Ethnicity* 4, no.2 (2018): 229–244.

Traub, Amy, Laura Sullivan, Tatjana Meschede, and Thomas Shapiro. "The Asset Value of Whiteness: Understanding the Racial Wealth Gap." *Demos*, February 6, 2017, https://www.demos.org/research/asset-value-Whiteness-understanding-racial-wealth-gap.

US Department of Homeland Security. "National Response Framework," January 2008, https://www.fema.gov/pdf/emergency/nrf/nrf-core.pdf.

Wilson, William Julius. *The Declining Significance of Race*. Chicago: University of Chicago Press, 1978.

Wilson, William Julius. *The Truly Disadvantaged*. Chicago: University of Chicago Press, 1987.

Wilson, William Julius. "Studying Inner-City Social Dislocations: The Challenge of Public Agenda Research: 1990 Presidential Address." *American Sociological Review* 56 (1991): 1–14.

Wilson, William Julius. "Why Both Culture and Structure Matter in a Holistic Analysis of Inner-City Poverty." *The Annals of the Academy of Political and Social Science* 629 (2010): 200–219.

Yearby, Ruqaijah. "Racial Disparities in Health Status and Access to Healthcare: The Continuation of Inequality in the United States Due to Structural Racism." *American Journal of Economics and Sociology* 77 (2018): 1114–115.

CHAPTER 10

## THE VALUE OF INCARCERATED BLACK LIVES DURING THE COVID-19 PANDEMIC

*An Exploration of Healthcare Disparities of Incarcerated and Formerly Incarcerated Populations*

*Britany J. Gatewood*

*Ebony Russ*

*Yanesia Norris*

*A. Cayce*

THE COVID-19 PANDEMIC HAS DISPROPORTIONATE rates of infection within the Black community. In majority-Black counties and neighborhoods, infection rates are three times higher than majority-White counties, and the death rate, almost six times higher (Thebault et al. 2020). Historical inequalities have led to the disproportional spread of COVID-19 in the Black community. Black people are more likely than any other racial group to suffer preexisting health conditions (i.e., heart disease and diabetes); economic hardship; lack of access to quality healthcare; and overrepresentation in the criminal justice system due to a historical legacy of sociopolitical inequities (Gould and Wilson 2020). All of these factors have been shown to exacerbate the rate of infection and death from COVID-19.

However, there is little data about a high-risk population within the Black community—the incarcerated and formerly incarcerated. Majority-Black neighborhoods have a disproportionate number of people that have been touched by the criminal justice system. Numerous studies have shown that Black, impoverished people have been targeted by the criminal justice system, leading to disproportionate representation within carceral institutions (Alexander 2012; Butler 2010; Taylor 2016). Mass incarceration, which refers to the sharp increase of incarcerated persons and the expansion of the prison system, stems from labor and economic demands in the larger American society (Alexander 2012; Butler 2010; Taylor 2016). Although Black Americans only represent 12 percent of the US population, they make up 33 percent of the prison population (Gramlich 2020). In comparison, White people make up 63 percent of the population and only 30 percent of the prison population (Gramlich 2020). America's poorest neighborhoods and communities with the greatest number of non-White residents are more likely to interact with the criminal justice system and to see deadly police encounters (Feldman et al. 2019).

The collateral consequences of mass incarceration on the Black community now include the ramifications of COVID-19. High rates of incarceration in the Black community have led to intensified policing, the criminalization of residents, reduced economic opportunities, strained social relationships, and decreased health outcomes (Lopez-Aguado 2016; Mallik-Kane et al. 2018). The additional public health consequences of COVID-19 must be considered since 40 percent of the nearly 2.3 million incarcerated people are Black (Sawyer and Wagner 2020). More than 95 percent of incarcerated people are released back to the communities where they reside (Hughes and Wilson 2020). Therefore, their time in a carceral institution during a pandemic will have public health consequences for their community post-release.

In this chapter, the authors will explore the historical inequalities suffered by the Black community in social services, public health, and mass incarceration. Furthermore, the lives of those incarcerated and formerly incarcerated, before and during the global pandemic, will be explored. This will be shown through historical and current policies and procedures within the Department of Justice, Bureau of Prisons, and the Centers for Disease Control and Prevention. In addition, A. Cayce will share his experiences of incarceration.

Incarcerated for over twenty years within the Michigan Department of Corrections (MDOC), A. Cayce's firsthand accounts provide insight into historical health inequities and the present-day response to the pandemic.

### Race, Class, and Health Disparities Overview

Decades of scholarship show that the United States has a unique history of racial and class relations. All social institutions within the US contribute to and reproduce discriminatory policies, procedures, and rhetoric toward Black and poor people (Williams 2003). In turn, Black Americans have the highest percentage of adults in the U.S. living below the federal poverty level, the highest rate of unemployment, and median wealth of less than a third of White families (McIntosh et al. 2020; Semega et al. 2020). Socioeconomic status and race influence the quality of healthcare one receives. In correlation to their lower socioeconomic status, Black people tend to have access to substandard healthcare resources. Twelve percent of African Americans under the age of sixty-five do not have health coverage, in comparison to 8 percent of White Americans (Oser et al. 2016). In addition, most states that did not expand Medicaid with the 2020 Affordable Care Act (ACA), which gave more people opportunities to get health insurance, are located in the South, where the highest concentration of Black Americans live (Artiga et al. 2020). Statistically, Black people have a higher mortality rate from complications of preventable, treatable, and curable illnesses than White people (Office of Minority Health 2017). Racial biases of healthcare providers contribute to higher rates of morbidity and mortality among Black patients (Greenwood et al. 2020; Zestcott et al. 2016). Politics and practices inadequately address the needs of Black people and poor people in America and have created disparities in life outcomes.

The social determinants of health (SDH)—working conditions, employment, education, housing and food security, age, gender, race, living conditions, personal relationships, families, and one's communities, experience—all affect one's health, arguably even more than the healthcare system (Mikkonen and Raphael 2010; US Department of Health and Human Services 2020). According to the World Health Organization, the SDH are important markers of inequalities in health because

> The poor health of the poor ... is caused by the unequal distribution of power, income, goods, and services, globally and nationally, the consequent unfairness in the immediate, visible circumstances of people's lives—their access to healthcare, schools, and education, their conditions of work and leisure, their homes, communities, towns, or cities—and their chances of leading a flourishing life (2008, 1).

Black communities are not afforded the much-needed resources due to the systemic barriers that prevent their ability to thrive.

Those that enter into the criminal justice system from under-resourced neighborhoods and communities already are at a deficit in health outcomes. Incarcerated persons have higher rates of HIV, AIDS, hepatitis, tuberculosis, sickle cell, high blood pressure, diabetes, asthma, and sexually transmitted infections than the general US population (Dolan et al. 2016; Ndeffo-Mbah et al. 2018; Niveau 2005; Oser et al. 2016; Schnittker and John 2007; Wagner and Widra 2020). Moreover, Black inmates are at higher risk for preexisting conditions prior to entering a facility (Nowotny et al. 2017). Incarcerated Black people have the highest rate of mortality while in jail, mostly due to heart conditions (Carson and Cowhig 2020). Although incarceration exacerbates their conditions, their lives prior to detention, mostly in poor areas, influence their health status. Once released, the high rates of chronic health conditions, substance use disorders, mental illness, and infectious diseases leave with them (Federal Interagency Reentry Council, 2016). This causes high rates of mortality, recidivism, spread of diseases, and deteriorating health, which in turn affect their limited community resources. This cycle creates a public health crisis not only for those within the criminal justice system but also for those within Black communities too.

## Healthcare in Carceral Institutions

Historically, carceral institutions have high rates of infectious diseases and poor health outcomes for those with preexisting conditions (Dolan et al. 2016; Massoglia 2008; Ndeffo-Mbah et al. 2018; Schnittker and John 2007). The rates of chronic illnesses and infectious diseases remain four to seventeen times higher in correctional facilities (Dumont et al. 2012). Cancer and heart, liver, and respiratory diseases are the major causes of death in prisons (Carson and Cowhig 2020b). Scholarship shows poor healthcare services and living conditions in facilities promote the rapid spread of disease and illness. Overcrowding, poor hygiene among inmates, unsanitized and shared medical equipment, high turnover in jails, lack of health education, and lack of medical care staff contribute to poor healthcare within these institutions (Centers for Disease Control and Prevention 2020a; Ndeffo-Mbah et al. 2018; Owen 1998; Rebecca Project for Human Rights and National Women's Law Center 2010; Schnittker and John 2007). Most preexisting conditions prevalent in carceral facilities are among those known to increase the risk of severe illness when one contracts COVID-19 (Centers for Disease Control and Prevention 2020b).

Policies and practices within carceral institutions are known to discourage incarcerated persons from seeking medical help and/or prevent them from receiving proper medical care. Numerous court cases (i.e., *Estelle v. Gamble*, *West v. Atkins*, and *Weems v. United States*) have ruled that, under the Eighth Amendment, incarcerated persons have the right to be free from cruel and unusual punishment, which includes access to "adequate" medical care (Bondurant 2013). However, carceral institutions regularly create an environment where seeking medical care is discouraged. It is documented that there is a lack of properly trained medical staff, reuse of medical equipment and tools between patients, a lack of basic items for proper hygiene (i.e., soap and sanitary items for women), lag time between medical appointments, a lack of nutritious food, denial of care, and exposure to heat or cold within these facilities (Bondurant 2013; Gatewood 2020; Guo et al. 2019; US Department of Justice 2018; Wilper et al. 2009). Medical co-pays, lack of quality preventative and emergency care, and lack of oversight of grievances against medical staff dissuade inmates from seeking medical attention. Medical co-pays range from $2 to $5; however, incarcerated persons typically earn less than $1 a day (Wagner and Widra 2020). Incarcerated people typically avoid seeking medical care because they could not otherwise pay for other costly necessities on their menial wages. Susan Burton, who was incarcerated in numerous facilities, writes, "Suffering through minor things like a cold or the flu without any meds seemed, to me, a far better option than subjecting myself to the crapshoot they called a medical system" (2017, 87). Inmates often avoided going to the doctor because the medical co-pay was automatically deducted from your account, even if there was not enough money to pay (Burton and Lynn 2017). Incarcerated persons often avoid medical care because of the debt they incur for poor quality healthcare. Discouragement of medical attention and lack of medical care further put this vulnerable population in danger.

## My Experiences of Prison Medical Care, by A. Cayce

The following is a testimony from A. Cayce, an inmate in the Michigan Department of Corrections. He will speak about his medical care experiences while he has been incarcerated.

> *The MDOC (Michigan Department of Corrections) has a standing policy to give minimal care for inmates in order to save money. I have personally read medical reports coming from the head of the health department for the MDOC to take inmates off of pain meds even though they were on chronic care. Also, not to send any inmate to the hospital unless it was a dire emergency. I have watched inmates get stabbed multiple times and sit for thirty mins before they were taken to the hospital. Today, I just watched an inmate fall off the nursing cart on their way to health care.*
>
> *This has left inmates with broken bones, severe sprains, and torn ACLs and MCLs to be administered with Motrin and an ACE bandage. Even though inmates must pay the $5.00 co-pay, the normal response to a visit is, "Take a Motrin, drink water, exercise, stop exercising, don't smoke [cigarettes have been gone for years], and stretch." I have endured a torn hamstring and received some wet paper towels as a cold compress, and a handful of Advil. The over-the-counter medicines, you have to buy through the commissary [general store inside a facility where inmates can buy things], which means you have to have money to buy them. If you have an associate's degree, you get paid $3 a day, which was decreased from the $3.62 a day it used to be. If you do not have a degree, you get paid $1.17, which used to be $1.77 per day. Although you are not paid much, you have to pay for the over-the-counter medicines from your pay or if your family puts money on your account.*

Cayce reiterates much of what has been known about medical care within carceral institutions. Incarcerated persons do not receive the care that they need, even in times of emergency. By providing inadequate medical care, illness is exacerbated, and inmates are discouraged from seeking the care they need. From medical co-pays to discouraging policies to limited medical care, the status of healthcare within carceral institutions is dire.

## Healthcare of Formerly Incarcerated Individuals

Returning citizens face troubling circumstances once they are back in the community because many leave prison with little to no access to money, transportation, healthcare, housing, or social support. It is estimated that 68 percent of released inmates recidivate within three years, 79 percent within six years, and 83 percent within nine years (Alper et al. 2018). These stark numbers are due to the lack of resources afforded to the formerly incarcerated. Post-release resources for formerly incarcerated individuals vary from state to state and from year to year. Each state has its own reentry programs and allocated funding, while each institution has different community partnerships, if any. Resources available to those reentering the community are in constant flux as reentry community organizations gain and lose funding, as policies are being restructured, and as social safety nets are being taken away from the public as a whole.

Supplemental Security Insurance payments, Medicaid, Social Security payments, and Social Security Disability Insurance are terminated during periods of incarceration (Justice in Aging 2020). Therefore, when released, the formerly incarcerated have to apply for Medicaid benefits, when often they are not given the resources to be successful at applying (Justice in Aging 2020). Upon reentry into the community, many formerly incarcerated individuals experience challenges accessing healthcare. As a means to combat challenges accessing healthcare, returning citizens look to emergency rooms, halfway houses, support groups, and relapse prevention programs for healthcare support (Mallik-Kane et al. 2018). The expansion of Medicaid under the Affordable Care Act by thirty-seven states has helped to give this population access to healthcare (Lantsman and Osler 2020). However, healthcare stigma, lack of employment, and logistical barriers remain, and support varies from state to state (Mallik-Kane et al. 2018).

The majority of those released from prison have a mental illness diagnosis, chronic physical illness, and/or a history of substance misuse (Mallik-Kane et al. 2018). Continuity of care is an important priority in preventing the risk of drug-related relapse, reoffending, and even death (Mallik-Kane et al. 2018; Federal Interagency Reentry Council 2016). Due to the lack of services and care, overdose is the leading cause of death for formerly incarcerated individuals, which often occurs within two weeks of release (Federal Interagency Reentry Council 2016). Various agencies and community-based organizations are committed to expanding access to affordable healthcare to decrease mortality and recidivism (Federal Interagency Reentry Council 2016). However, not all who are released have access to these services and organizations. Strategies to ease the healthcare challenges and needs associated with reentry include:

- Encouraging connections between public health, human services, and corrections officials at the community level
- Improving accessibility of state-by-state information and resources on health care
- Supporting state Medicaid-housing technical assistance
- Increasing quality and access to health care coverage and continuity of care for the justice-involved population
- Promoting health technology to improve continuity of care
- Encouraging connections to health care coverage and services prior to release
- Creating tools and clarifying available sources of public assistance for corrections agencies to improve access to health care upon reentry
- Increasing research to track the effects of linking the criminal justice population to health care coverage and services
- Funding research to understand the impact access to health care can have on recidivism
- Improving access to medication-assisted treatment as a reentry strategy

- Facilitating access to identification, drivers' licenses, and sources of financial support
- Providing training and technical assistance to states on health care coverage options
- Expanding access to trauma-informed care (Mallik-Kane et al. 2018; Federal Interagency Reentry Council 2016)

The current challenges of reentry healthcare parallel those that exist within prison walls. Understanding reentry healthcare challenges can provide public health officials, medical professionals, and researchers with insight into prisoners' health and healthcare within carceral institutions.

## COVID-19 and Healthcare in Carceral Institutions

It is difficult to understand the true number of COVID-19 cases within carceral institutions. Research shows that the COVID-19 infection rate is higher among incarcerated people than in the general population and the numbers will continue to rise (Budryk 2020). Many public health advocates have connected the number of cases to the inability to properly quarantine inmates, lack of testing, lack of soap, medical mask shortages, poor social distancing, high prevalence of chronic and infectious diseases, and overall unsanitary conditions (Barr 2020; Budryk 2020; Cipriano 2020; Friedersdorf 2020; Justice Policy Institute 2020; Park et al. 2020). The Centers for Disease Control and Prevention (CDC) has recognized that carceral institutions have specific challenges in controlling the spread of COVID-19 among inmates, staff, and the recently released because of extant policies and practices (Centers for Disease Control and Prevention 2020a). According to Williams et al. (2020), carceral institutions cannot control the spread of COVID-19 because of the following:

1. Testing and screening for COVID-19 infections and contact tracing in jails and prisons are absolutely critical; however, it is not always possible or properly done.
2. Correctional facilities lack the medical supplies needed to treat people who get seriously ill from COVID-19 infection.

3. CDC guidelines are not tailored to correctional settings.
4. Social distancing is uniquely challenging due to the close nature of confinement.
5. The infirmaries and clinical spaces in jails and prisons are not built to contain the spread of the virus.
6. Correctional healthcare systems are typically understaffed.
7. Security often overrules health in prisons, making the doctor-patient relationship tense or non-existent.
8. Jail and prisons are not actually closed environments because of staff and volunteers entering and leaving.

Because of these conditions, there are "446 more positive COVID-19 cases per 100,000 people in correctional facilities than in the general US Population" (Black Public Defender Association & Center for Justice Research 2020). According to the *New York Times*, as of September 15, 2020, fifteen of the largest COVID clusters of cases in the United States are in jails and prisons (*New York Times* 2020). As of September 8, 2020, the Marshall Project reported that 121,217 people in prison have tested positive and 1,017 have died from the virus (Marshall Project 2020). Jails and prisons conducting mass testing are finding that the rapid spread of COVID-19 is hard to control.

Policies and practices in carceral institutions have changed due to the COVID-19 pandemic. As of June 1, 2020, all states (except Nevada) have suspended all co-pays for medical treatment for COVID-19-related illnesses (Wagner and Widra 2020). Eleven states have taken this further and suspended all co-pays for all medical treatments, and twelve states do not charge co-pays for incarcerated people (Wagner and Widra 2020). To prevent the spread, most carceral institutions have suspended visitations, and encourage video and phone calls, however, very few have decreased the high costs of video and phone calls (Wagner and Widra 2020). The Centers for Disease Control have set preventative protocols for correctional and detention facilities including: medical isolation/quarantine for confirmed cases, good hygiene practices, vigilant symptom screening, increased medical staff, wearing cloth face coverings and other PPE, social distancing, decreased admissions, and increased sanitation of facilities (Centers for Disease Control and Prevention 2020a). The Federal Bureau of Prisons' (BOP) policy follows the CDC's guidelines and additionally creates task forces to respond to the crisis (Federal Bureau of Prisons 2020). However, due to historic policies and practices, many of these guidelines are unable to be met by these facilities (Knopf 2020).

Face masks, which are critical to stopping the spread of the virus, are only required for staff in twenty states and only required for incarcerated people in fourteen states (Widra and Herring 2020). Numerous reports (Scott 2020; Toohey 2020) have been written about the lack of hand sanitizer, social distancing guidelines, PPE, and proper medical treatment during this pandemic. In the case of *Valentine v. Collier*, inmates in the Wallace Pack Unit, a geriatric state prison in Grimes County, Texas, claimed that the prison did not take the necessary precautions against COVID-19 in the facility (*Valentine v. Collier* 2020). This included inadequate cleaning of the facility, lack of alcohol-based sanitizer, and limited masks and gloves (*Valentine v. Collier* 2020). In response to the BOP's failure to enforce these policies, several senators introduced the COVID-19 in Corrections Data Transparency Act, which would require "Federal Bureau of Prisons (BOP), the United States Marshals Service, and state governments to collect and publicly report detailed data about the Coronavirus Disease 2019 (COVID-19) in federal, state, and local correctional facilities" (Warren 2020). Although this bill requires reporting, it does not require action to support the health of those imprisoned.

## My Experiences During COVID-19 by A. Cayce

The following is a testimony from A. Cayce, an inmate in the Michigan Department of Corrections. He will speak to his facility's response to the COVID-19 pandemic.

> *With the COVID-19, all healthcare callouts and medical pickups have been put on hold unless it is an emergency. They [medical staff] want to help us, but they are restricted by administration. The administration has the final say in what they can or cannot do, even though they are not the medical experts. JPay [the communication services] have given us one free stamp [paid vouchers to send*

*emails] and two five-minute free phone calls a week. If we are quarantined or on lockdown, we lose those privileges and have to wait until the next week.*

*We have been split where only one-half of the unit can enter the dayrooms [the recreational units], and anyone not wearing their masks will receive misconducts. We have been given three masks that are made of old clothes used for people being discharged from prison. We are only given masks when one of the three needs replacing because it is too tattered or worn. We are expected to wash these masks every day, but we are not given anything to wash them with. Inmates walk around with their masks off or under their noses and officers will tell them to put them back on, but as soon as they leave, they take them off.*

*Shakedowns have been done to inmates without gloves on many occasions and the food service is a mess. The officers are not really strictly enforcing the rules. Most inmates don't care about the virus. In the cafeteria, we are supposed to sit only two to a table, but we don't follow the rules. There are whole groups sitting at the tables and the officers do not stop them. All of our programming and college courses have not stopped. Now they have advanced students teaching the classes instead of the teachers coming in. They are still getting paid, but the inmates are doing all the work. They are trying to make things as virtual as possible.*

*The officers are the ones that bring COVID into the prisons. They do not tell us when an officer contracts COVID. One day, they just disappear and then come back a couple weeks later. They are the ones that are free to go in and out of the prison and have interactions with the public. We are just stuck in here. We have had no transports come into our facility since COVID, but they are beginning to bring other inmates in. They take our temperature each time we go, once a day, and they give us one assessment to fill out in August that includes asking if we had contact with someone with COVID, which we would not know.*

Cayce's experience is not limited to his facility. Countless news articles, op-eds, blogs, and social media posts have exposed the crisis that is within carceral institutions. Facilities do not have the capacity to comply with CDC and BOP guidelines due to historical policies and practices. This has put those incarcerated in danger of contracting COVID-19, in addition to the other infectious diseases prevalent within facilities.

## COVID-19 and Healthcare of Formerly Incarcerated Individuals

Reentry resources are necessary for returning citizens under normal operations, but have become critical for a chance of survival during the COVID-19 pandemic. Release without support can be lethal for returning citizens and Black communities because they do not have a continuation of care or resources to help them thrive. The COVID-19 pandemic has brought national attention to the call for depopulating prisons and jails (New York City Board of Corrections 2020; Bail Project 2020; We Got Us Now 2020; Williams et al. 2020). Some governors, sheriffs, and judges have moved toward compassionate release and other forms of decarceration only after public pressure, threats of litigation, and recognition that COVID-19-related infections and deaths are largely preventable (ACLU 2020; Scannell 2020). Decarceration is critical for managing the spread of COVID-19 within the prison walls, but it must be supported by proper reentry planning (Abraham et al. 2020). Formally incarcerated individuals are at high risk of contracting COVID-19 within institutions and upon release. Outside of the inadequate healthcare they receive while incarcerated, many do not have healthcare coverage after release. In the time of a global pandemic, without Medicare expansion to ensure they have healthcare access after release, it can be a death sentence for the population (Justice in Aging 2020). Some states have released pre-trial detainees that are charged with nonviolent offenses, but in some cases, those released have tested positive (Lantsman and Osler 2020).

Social determinants of health research has shown that transportation, healthcare resources, housing, and employment are needed for a citizen to thrive. During the pandemic, formerly incarcerated people without resources could create worse conditions for the Black communities they return to (Sawyer and Wagner 2020). With strained and depleted resources, impoverished communities are now tasked with helping those who re-enter them. Community-based organizations have been financially strained during this pandemic and have seen an increase in patrons and those seeking assistance. Those released are sent to halfway houses and reentry facilities; however, these facilities are unable to keep up with demand because of COVID-19 capacity restrictions and limited provisions for adequate healthcare and PPE

(Daniel and Sawyer 2020; Mallik-Kane et al. 2018). Because these carceral institutions are within poor communities, it increases the infection rate in these areas, particularly if COVID-19 was contracted prior to release. Those that stay with family and friends and not in a reentry facility have additional concerns. Members of the household may not have the resources to support due to financial strains, or they may fear contracting the virus because of the prior incarceration of one among them. Unless former prisoners re-enter under community supervision, researchers cannot accurately assess the extent of COVID-19 ramifications for the formerly incarcerated population. Once they are released from carceral institutions, they are rarely tracked unless the courts mandate supervision. Therefore, there are countless individuals we cannot account for and who cannot receive the resources they need to survive.

Employment, which was hard to obtain prior to the pandemic, has become nearly impossible for most. As of September 2020, unemployment rates increased in the majority of sectors, and low-wage jobs that this population typically acquires have disappeared (Bertram 2020; US Bureau of Labor Statistics 2020). According to the Internal Revenue Service, those citizens who were or are incarcerated were denied stimulus packages from the CARES Act (Raher 2020). Those that were incarcerated during the disbursement of the stimulus and now are recently released were also denied this relief. As of September 2020, there is an ongoing lawsuit against the US Department of the Treasury to render the same stimulus relief to these populations (Lieff, Cabraser, Heimann, and Bernstein 2020).

## Policy Recommendations

COVID-19 has exacerbated the deterioration of conditions in carceral institutions. Action needs to occur to ensure the health and safety not just of incarcerated persons but also their communities at large. Various organizations have published policy recommendations for carceral institutions that are similar to those released prior to the pandemic. This shows that systemic issues in these institutions did not begin with the global pandemic. Policies include:

1. Decreasing the number of incarcerated persons by releasing elderly (fifty and up) people, those with chronic illness, and nonviolent and low-level offenders (New York City Board of Corrections 2020; Bail Project 2020; We Got Us Now 2020; Williams et al. 2020).
2. Providing food, housing, employment, and other safety net program assistance to people released from carceral institutions, which includes services that connect clients to services (Black Public Defender Association and Center for Justice Research 2020; Johnson and Beletsky 2020).
3. Providing better quality of healthcare while incarcerated and after release (Black Public Defender Association and Center for Justice Research 2020; Johnson and Beletsky 2020).
4. Adequate PPE, hygiene products, increased testing and screening, and increased sanitation protocol of facilities (Bail Project 2020; We Got Us Now 2020).
5. Cancelation of all incarceration-related debts and fines and release those detained for fines or administrative reasons (New York City Board of Corrections 2020).
6. Ensuring communication with family members and loved ones is free (We Got Us Now 2020; Williams et al. 2020).
7. Ensure that COVID-19 programs or stimulus payments are also given to those with criminal records (Black Public Defender Association and Center for Justice Research 2020).

These recommendations, if implemented, will not only slow the spread of COVID-19 in carceral institutions but will also create more humane conditions beyond the pandemic.

## Conclusion

COVID-19 has devastated Black communities that were already under-resourced and plagued by institutional racism and classism. The collateral consequences of the criminal justice system have only deprecated these communities further. Public health ramifications stemming from historical inequalities have been exacerbated by the global pandemic. Mass incarceration, a system that encompasses incarcerated and formerly incarcerated persons, has failed to provide adequate healthcare prior to and during the COVID-19 outbreak. Inadequate healthcare systems for inmates and, later, limited health insurance for those released, create a dangerous health crisis for their hometowns. Although guidelines and recommendations have been set by the CDC and the BOP, carceral institutions are not in compliance. Precedence and existing policies have made it impossible for institutions to contain the spread of the virus. Without major changes in carceral institutions and reentry programs, Black communities will continue to be devastated by mass incarceration. COVID-19 has displayed even more the deep, historical inequalities embedded in US social institutions. As we face this global pandemic, the needs of the most marginalized must be met, and we must show that the lives of the incarcerated and formerly incarcerated matter.

## References

Abraham, Leola A., Timothy C. Brown, and Shaun A. Thomas. "How COVID-19's Disruption of the US Correctional System Provides an Opportunity for Decarceration." *American Journal of Criminal Justice* 45, no. 4 (2020): 780–792. https://doi.org/10.1007/s12103-020-09537-1.

ACLU. "Decarceration and Crime During COVID-19." *ACLU.org*, July 27, 2020, https://www.aclu.org/news/smart-justice/decarceration-and-crime-during-covid-19/.

Alexander, Michelle. *The New Jim Crow: Mass Incarceration in the Age of Colorblindness*. New York: The New Press, 2012.

Alper, Mariel, Matthew R. Durose, and Joshua Markman. (2018). *2018 Update on Prisoner Recidivism: A 9-Year Follow-up Period (2005–2014)*. Bureau of Justice Statistics, Washington, DC.

Artiga, Samantha, Kendal Orgera, and Anthony Damico. (2020, March 5). "Changes in Health Coverage by Race and Ethnicity Since the ACA, 2010–2018." *Kff.org*, March 5, 2020, https://www.kff.org/racial-equity-and-health-policy/issue-brief/changes-in-health-coverage-by-race-and-ethnicity-since-the-aca-2010-2018/.

Bail Project. (2020). "The Bail Project Urges Jail Releases Amid Coronavirus Spread" September 20, 2020, https://bailproject.org/covid-19.

Barr, Luke. "Despite Coronavirus Warnings, Federal Bureau of Prisons Still Transporting Inmates." *ABC News*, March 23, 2020, https://abcnews.go.com/Health/warnings-bureau-prisons-transporting-inmates-sources/story?id=69747416.

Bertram, Wanda. "Returning from Prison and Jail Is Hard During Normal Times—It's Even More Difficult During COVID-19." *Prison Policy Initiative*, September 2, 2020, https://www.prisonpolicy.org/blog/2020/09/02/covidreentry/.

Black Public Defender Association, and Center for Justice Research. (2020). "Save Black Lives: A Call for Racially-Responsive Strategies and Resources for the Black Community During the COVID-19 Pandemic." Black Public Defender Association, and Center for Justice Research, Washington, D.C. http://blackdefender.org/policy-saveblacklives/.

Bondurant, Brittany. "The Privatization of Prisons and Prisoner Healthcare: Addressing the Extent of Prisoners." *New England Journal on Civil and Criminal Confinement* 39, no. 2 (2013): 407–426.

Budryk, Zack. "70 Percent of Federal Inmates Tested for Coronavirus Have COVID-19." *The Hill*, April 30, 2020, https://thehill.com/policy/healthcare/495423-7-in-10-federal-prisoners-tested-for-coronavirus-have-positive-results.

Burton, Susan, and Lynn, Cari. *Becoming Ms. Burton: From Prison to Recovery to Leading the Fight for Incarcerated Women*. New York: The New Press, 2017.

Butler, Paul. "One Hundred Years of Race and Crime." *Journal of Criminal Law & Criminology* 100, no. 3 (2010): 1043–1060.

Carson, E. Ann, and Mary P. Cowhig. (2020a). *Mortality in Local Jails, 2000-2016-Statistical Tables*. U.S. Department of Justice, Washington, D.C. October 14, 2020, https://bjs.ojp.gov/content/pub/pdf/mlj0016st.pdf.

Carson, E. Ann, and Mary P. Cowhig. (2020b). *Mortality in State and Federal Prisons, 2001–2016*. U.S. Department of Justice, Washington, D.C. October 14, 2020, https://bjs.ojp.gov/content/pub/pdf/msfp0116st.pdf.

Centers for Disease Control and Prevention. (2020a, January 8). "FastStats—Health of Black or African American Population," January 8, 2020, https://www.cdc.gov/nchs/fastats/Black-health.htm.

Centers for Disease Control and Prevention. "Guidance on Management of Coronavirus Disease 2019 (COVID-19) in Correctional and Detention Facilities." July 22, 2020b, https://www.cdc.gov/coronavirus/2019-ncov/community/correction-detention/guidance-correctional-detention.html.

Centers for Disease Control and Prevention. (2020c, August 14). "Certain Medical Conditions and Risk for Severe COVID-19 Illness." August 14, 2020c, https://www.cdc.gov/coronavirus/2019-ncov/need-extra-precautions/people-with-medical-conditions.html?CDC_AA_refVal=https%3A%2F%2Fwww.cdc.gov%2Fcoronavirus%2F2019-ncov%2Fneed-extra-precautions%2Fgroups-at-higher-risk.html.

Centers for Disease Control and Prevention. "FastStats—Health of White Population.," January 8, 2020, https://www.cdc.gov/nchs/fastats/White-health.htm.

Cipriano, Andrea. "COVID-19 No Excuse for Ignoring Rights of the Incarcerated." *The Crime Report*, July 2, 2020, https://thecrimereport.org/2020/07/02/covid-19-no-excuse-for-ignoring-rights-of-the-incarcerated-paper/.

Commission on Social Determinants of Health. Accessed on October 30, 2020. *Closing the Gap in a Generation: Health Equity through Action on the Social Determinants of Health*. World Health Organization. October 30, 2020. https://www.who.int/publications/i/item/WHO-IER-CSDH-08.1.

Daniel, Roxanne, and Wendy Sawyer. "What You Should Know About Halfway Houses." Prison Policy Initiative, September 3, 2020, https://www.prisonpolicy.org/blog/2020/09/03/halfway/.

Dolan, Kate, Andrea L. Wirtz, Babak Moazen, Martial Ndeffo-mbah, Alison Galvani, Stuart A. Kinner, Ryan Courtney, Martin McKee, Joseph J. Amon, Lisa Maher, Margaret Hellard, Chris Beyrer, and Fredrick L. Altice. "Global Burden of HIV, Viral Hepatitis, and Tuberculosis in Prisoners and Detainees." *Lancet*, 388, no.10049 (2016): 1089–1102. https://doi.org/10.1016/S0140-6736(16)30466-4.

Dumont, Dora M., Brad Brockmann, Samuel Dickman, Nicole Alexander, and Josiah D. Rich. "Public Health and the Epidemic of Incarceration." *Annual Review of Public Health* 33 (2012): 325–339. https://doi.org/10.1146/annurev-publhealth-031811-124614.

Federal Bureau of Prisons. (2020). "BOP's COVID-19 Overview." October 21, 2020, https://www.bop.gov/coronavirus/overview.jsp#bop_covid-19_response.

Federal Interagency Reentry Council. "A Record of Progress and Roadmap for the Future." Washington, DC: Federal Interagency Council, 2016. https://nationalreentryresourcecenter.org/publications/the-federal-interagency-reentry-council-a-record-of-progress-and-a-roadmap-for-the-future/.

Feldman, Justin M., Sofia Gruskin, Brent A. Coull, and Nancy Krieger. (2019). "Police-related Deaths and Neighborhood Economic and Racial/Ethnic Polarization, United States, 2015–2016." *American Journal of Public Health* 109, no. 3 (2019): 458–464. https://doi.org/10.2105/AJPH.2018.304851.

Friedersdorf, C. "Can't We at Least Give Prisoners Soap?" *Atlantic*, April 1, 2020, https://www.theatlantic.com/ideas/archive/2020/04/make-soap-free-prisons/609202/.

Gatewood, Britany J. (2020). *Opposition Behind Bars: Incarcerated Black Working-Class Women and the Tradition of Resistance in the United States, 1970–2011*. Dissertation, Howard University, Washington, D.C.

Gould, Elise, and Valerie Wilson. "Black Workers Face Two of the Most Lethal Preexisting Conditions for Coronavirus—Racism and Economic Inequality." *Economic Policy Institute*, June 2020, https://www.epi.org/publication/Black-workers-covid/.

Gramlich, John. "Black Imprisonment Rate in the US Has Fallen by a Third Since 2006." *Pew Research*, May 6, 2020, https://www.pewresearch.org/fact-tank/2020/05/06/share-of-Black-White-hispanic-americans-in-prison-2018-vs-2006/.

Greenwood, Brad N., Rachel R. Hardeman, Laura Huang, and Aaron Sojourner. "Physician-Patient Racial Concordance and Disparities in Birthing Mortality for Newborns." *Proceedings of the National Academy of Sciences* 117, no. 35 (2020): 21194. https://doi.org/10.1073/pnas.1913405117.

Guo, Wilson, Ryan Cronk, Elissa Scherer, Rachel Oommen, John Brogan, Mohamed Sarr, and Jamie Bartram. "A Systematic Scoping Review of Environmental Health Conditions in Penal Institutions." *International Journal of Hygiene and Environmental Health* 222 (2019): 790–803. https://doi.org/10.1016/j.ijheh.2019.05.001.

Hughes, Timothy, and Doris James Wilson. "Reentry Trends in the US: Highlights." *Bureau of Justice Statistics*, October 2, 2020, https://www.bjs.gov/content/reentry/reentry.cfm.

Johnson, Paula. "Inner Lives: Voices of African American Women in Prison." New York: New York University Press, 2003.

Johnson, Sterling, and Leo Beletsky. "Helping People Transition from Incarceration to Society During a Pandemic." 2020, https://www.dataforprogress.org/memos/challenges-of-reentry-during-coronavirus.

Justice in Aging. *Medicare and People Leaving Incarceration: A Primer for California Advocates During the Pandemic*. Washington, DC: Justice in Aging, 2020. https://justiceinaging.org/wp-content/uploads/2020/08/Medicare-and-People-Leaving-Incarceration.pdf.

Knopf, Taylor. "COVID-19 Strains Fractured Prison Healthcare." *North Carolina Health News*, July 2, 2020, https://www.northcarolinahealthnews.org/2020/07/02/covid-19-puts-pressure-on-already-fractured-prison-health-system/.

Lantsman, Jacqueline, and Mark Osler. "How Can We Protect the Health of Justice-Involved Populations During the COVID-19 Pandemic? Decarceration and Timely Access to Medicaid Are Essential." *Health Affairs*, April 2020, https://www.healthaffairs.org/do/10.1377/hblog20200418.296283/full/.

Lieff Cabraser Heimann and Bernstein. (2020). "CARES Act Relief for Incarcerated People." October 1, 2020, https://www.lieffcabraser.com/cares-act-relief/.

Lopez-Aguado, Patrick. "The Collateral Consequences of Prisonization: Racial Sorting, Carceral Identity, and Community Criminalization." *Sociology Compass* 10, no. 1(2016): 12–23. https://doi.org/10.1111/soc4.12342.

Mallik-Kane, Kamala, Ellen Paddock, and Jesse Jannetta. (2018). *Health Care After Incarceration: How Do Formerly Incarcerated Men Choose Where and When to Access Physical and Behavioral Health Services?* October 30, 2020, https://www.urban.org/sites/default/files/publication/96386/health_care_after_incarceration.pdf.

Marshall Project. "A State-by-State Look at Coronavirus in Prisons." *Marshall Project*, September 11, 2020, https://www.themarshallproject. org/2020/05/01/a-state-by-state-look-at-coronavirus-in-prisons.

Massoglia, Michael. "Incarceration as Exposure: The Prison, Infectious Disease, and Other Stress-Related Illnesses." *Journal of Health and Social Behavior* 49, no. 1 (2008): 56–71.

McIntosh, Kriston, Emily Moss, Ryan Nunn, and Jay Shambaugh. "Examining the Black-White Wealth Gap." *Brookings*, February 27, 2020, https://www.

brookings.edu/blog/up-front/2020/02/27/examining-the-Black-White-wealth-gap/.

Mikkonen, Juha, and Dennis Raphael. (2010). "Social Determinants of Health: The Canadian Facts." October 6, 2020, http://listserv.paho.org/Archives/equidad.html.

Ndeffo-Mbah, Martial L., Vivian S. Vigliotti, Laura A. Skrip, Kate Dolan, and Alison P. Galvani. "Dynamic Models of Infectious Disease Transmission in Prisons and the General Population." *Epidemiologic Reviews* 40: 40–57 (2018). https://doi.org/10.1093/epirev/mxx014.

New York City Board of Corrections. (2020). "New York City Board of Correction Calls for City to Begin Releasing People from Jail as Part of Public Health Response to COVID-19." New York, October 21, 2020, https://www1.nyc.gov/assets/boc/downloads/pdf/News/2020.03.17%20-%20Board%20of%20Correction%20Statement%20re%20Release.pdf.

*New York Times*. "COVID in the US: Latest Map and Case Count" *New York Times*, September 14, 2020, https://www.nytimes.com/interactive/2020/us/coronavirus-us-cases.html#clusters.

Niveau, G. "Prevention of Infectious Disease Transmission in Correctional Settings: A Review." *Public Health* 120 (2005): 33–41. https://doi.org/10.1016/j.puhe.2005.03.017.

Nowotny, Kathryn M., Richard G. Rogers, and Jason D. Boardman. "Racial Disparities in Health Conditions Among Prisoners Compared with the General Population." *SSM—Population Health* 3 (2017): 487–496. https://doi.org/10.1016/j.ssmph.2017.05.011.

Office of Minority Health. "African American Death Rate Drops 25 Percent," May 2, 2017, https://www.minorityhealth.hhs.gov/omh/Content.aspx?ID=188&lvl=2&lvlid=8.

Oser, Carrie B., Amanda M. Bunting, Erin Pullen, and Danelle Stevens-Watkins. (2016). "African American Female Offender's Use of Alternative and Traditional Health Services After Re-Entry: Examining the Behavioral Model for Vulnerable Populations HHS Public Access." *J Health Care Poor Underserved* 27, no. 2A (2016): 120–148. https://doi.org/10.1353/hpu.2016.0052.

Owen, Barbara. *In the Mix: Struggle and Survival in a Women's Prison*. Albany: State University of New York Press, 1998.

Park, Katie, Tom Meagher, and Weihua Li. "Tracking the Spread of Coronavirus in Prisons." The Marshall Project, April 24, 2020, https://www.themarshallproject.org/2020/04/24/tracking-the-spread-of-coronavirus-in-prisons.

Raher, Stephen. "Since You Asked: Should Incarcerated People Be Receiving Stimulus Payments?" *Prison Policy Initiative*, May 18, 2020, https://www.prisonpolicy.org/blog/2020/05/18/checks/.

Rebecca Project for Human Rights, and National Women's Law Center. (October 2010). "Mothers Behind Bars: A State-by-State Report Card and Analysis of Federal Policies on Conditions of Confinement for Pregnant and Parenting Women and the Effect on Their Children." https://nwlc.org/wp-content/uploads/2015/08/mothersbehindbars2010.pdf.

Sawyer, Wendy, and Peter Wagner. "Mass Incarceration: The Whole Pie 2020." *Prison Policy Initiative*, March 2020, https://www.prisonpolicy.org/reports/pie2020.html.

Scannell, Kara. "Some Inmates Freed Because of Coronavirus Are 'Scared to Leave.'" *CNN*, April 4, 2020, https://www.cnn.com/2020/04/04/politics/freed-inmates-challenges-coronavirus/index.html.

Schnittker, Jason, and Andrea John. "Enduring Stigma: The Long-Term Effects of Incarceration on Health." *Journal of Health and Social Behavior* 48, no. 2 (2007): 115–130.

Scott, Michele. "During the Pandemic, a Prison Funeral for Our Angel." *The Marshall Project*, August 13, 2020, https://www.themarshallproject.org/2020/08/13/during-the-pandemic-a-prison-funeral-for-our-angel.

Semega, Jessica, Melissa Kollar, Emily A. Shrider, and John F. Creamer. (2020). *Income and Poverty in the United States: 2019*. United States Census Bureau, Washington, D.C. https://www.census.gov/content/dam/Census/library/publications/2020/demo/p60-270.pdf.

Taylor, Keeanga-Yamahtta. *From #BlackLivesMatter to Black Liberation*. Chicago: Haymarket Books, 2016.

Thebault, Reis, Andrew Ba Tran, and Vanessa Williams. "African Americans Are at Higher Risk of Death from Coronavirus." *Washington Post*, April 7, 2020, https://www.washingtonpost.com/nation/2020/04/07coronavirus-is-infecting-killing-Black-americans-an-alarmingly-high-rate-post-analysis-shows/?arc404=true.

Toohey, Grace. "Commissioner Regina Hill's Brother Dies of COVID-19 from Florida Prison" *Orlando Sentinel*, August 17, 2020, https://www.orlandosentinel.com/coronavirus/os-ne-coronavirus-orange-commissioner-regina-hill-brother-died-prison-20200817-ci7v7hpddvhevantrfh34z54ra-story.html.

United States District Court for the Southern District of Texas, Houston Division. 2020. *Valentine v. Collier.* https://casetext.com/case/valentine-v-collier-2.

US Bureau of Labor Statistics. "Supplemental Data Measuring the Effects of The Coronavirus (COVID-19) Pandemic on the Labor Market." *BLS.gov*, October 2, 2020, https://www.bls.gov/cps/effects-of-the-coronavirus-covid-19-pandemic.htm#.

US Department of Health and Human Services. (2020). "Social Determinants of Health." October 2, 2020, https://health.gov/healthypeople/objectives-and-data/social-determinants-health.

US Department of Justice. (2018). "Review of the Federal Bureau of Prisons' Management of Its Female Inmate Population (September 2018)." https://oig.justice.gov/reports/2018/e1805.pdf.

Wagner, Peter, and Emily Widra. "Five Ways the Criminal Justice System Could Slow the Pandemic." *The Prison Policy Initiative*, May 27, 2020, https://www.prisonpolicy.org/blog/2020/03/27/slowpandemic/.

Warren, Elizabeth. "COVID-19 in Corrections Data Transparency Act." August 6, 2020, https://www.warren.senate.gov/imo/media/doc/COVID-19%20in%20Correction%20Data%20Transparency%20Act%20Summary%20-%20FINAL%208.6.20%20(updated).pdf.

We Got Us Now. (2020). *Who We Are.* https://www.wegotusnow.org/who-we-are.

Widra, Emily, and Tiana Herring. (2020). "Half of States Fail to Require Mask Use by Correctional Staff." September 14, 2020, https://www.prisonpolicy.org/blog/2020/08/14/masks-in-prisons/.

Williams, Brie A., Cyrus Ahalt, David Cloud, Dallas Augustine, Leah Rorvig, and David Sears. (2020, March 26). "Correctional Facilities in the Shadow Of COVID-19: Unique Challenges and Proposed Solutions." https://www.healthaffairs.org/do/10.1377/hblog20200324.784502/full/.

Williams, Linda Faye. *The Constraint of Race: Legacies of White Skin Privilege in America.* University Park: Pennsylvania State University Press, 2003.

Wilper, Andrew P., Steffie Woolhandler, J. Wesley Boyd, Karen E. Lasser, Danny McCormick, David H. Bor, and David U. Himmelstein. "The Health and Health Care of US prisoners: Results of a Nationwide Survey." *American Journal of Public Health* 99, no. 4 (2009): 666–672). https://doi.org/10.2105/AJPH.2008.144279.

Zestcott, Colin A., Irene v. Blair, and Jeff Stone. "Examining the Presence, Consequences, and Reduction of Implicit Bias in Health Care: A Narrative Review." In *Group Processes and Intergroup Relations* 19, no. 4 (2016): 528–542. https://doi.org/10.1177/1368430216642029.

CHAPTER 11

# THE IMPACT OF COVID-19 ON AFRICAN AMERICANS EMPLOYED IN THE SERVICE SECTOR

*Anita Fernander*

*Lovoria Williams*

WHILE IT HAS BEEN DIFFICULT TO provide an exact accounting of how the novel SARS-CoV-2 (severe acute respiratory syndrome coronavirus 2, hereafter referred to as COVID-19) has affected racial/ethnic populations differentially, from the time COVID-19 took hold in the United States, it became evident that communities of color were disproportionately affected. For example, although African Americans represent 13.4 percent and Whites 61 percent of the US population, as of October 28, 2020, the number of COVID-19 cases (for which only 52 percent of the data was available by race/ethnicity) among African Americans was 16.6 percent compared to 46.9 percent among Whites. The number of reported deaths (for which 81 percent of the data was available by race/ethnicity) among African Americans was 20.2 percent compared to 54.1 percent for Whites (Centers for Disease Control and Prevention 2020a). Inconsistencies regarding how states and counties record and provide data by race/ethnicity exist. However, in almost every state where racial data is available, reports indicate that African Americans have higher rates of COVID-19 exposure, infection, hospitalizations, and death (COVID Tracking Project n.d.). A study by the Commonwealth Fund indicated that counties with relatively high proportions of African American populations face higher morbidity and mortality, and a higher rate of COVID-19 disease progression compared to counties with lower proportions of African Americans (Zephyrin et al. 2020). The 681 high-concentration African American counties included in the Commonwealth Fund investigation accounted for only one-third of the US population, but alarmingly accounted for 53 percent of COVID-19 cases and 63 percent of COVID-19 related deaths nationwide.

Despite inconsistencies in data collection and reporting, it is certain that African Americans (along with other racial/ethnic marginalized populations) are disproportionately affected by COVID-19 when compared to their White counterparts (CDC 2020b). History reveals that during public health crises severe illness and death rates are higher for African Americans (e.g., Fothergill, Maestas, and Darlington 1999; Rivera and Miller 2007). For example, during influenza pandemics in the United States from 1950 to 2005, African American mortality from pneumonia and influenza remained consistently higher than other racial/ethnic minority populations (Hutchins et al. 2009). In fact, the only year on record where African Americans did not have higher rates of morbidity and mortality due to influenza was 1918 (Gamble 2010). The lower morbidity and mortality may be attributed to the fact that during the period around 1918 there were large efforts on the part of African Americans to establish their own hospitals and healthcare institutions. Nevertheless, there is a common refrain known among many African American communities: "When White America gets a cold, Black America gets pneumonia." In the case of COVID-19, the refrain might be, "When White America gets the flu, Black America dies." This refrain reveals the fundamental reality of persistent structural and systemic inequalities that have existed in the United States for centuries that lead to health inequities among African Americans.

It is clear that individuals with preexisting chronic health and social conditions are more susceptible to COVID-19-related morbidity and mortality. In fact, the 2009 study published by Hutchins and colleagues predicted that "racial/ethnic minority populations would have less capacity to implement essential pandemic interventions and to tolerate a pandemic because of broad disparities in underlying health status and social factors." While it may be expedient to point to genetic differences, individual behaviors, or other racialized myths as the cause of preexisting chronic health conditions and/or COVID-19 susceptibility among African Americans, it must be emphasized that these preexisting chronic conditions are not accounted for by inherent biological predisposition due to race but are in large part due to structural and systemic preexisting conditions often referred to as the political and social determinants of health. Political determinants of health involve the systematic processes of structuring relationships, distributing resources, and administering power that determine the social determinants of health (Dawes, 2020). Social determinants of health (SDOH) are conditions in the environments where individuals are born, live, learn, work, play, worship, and age that include factors like economic stability, neighborhood and physical environment, educational opportunities, employment, community and social contexts, and the health care system that accounts for up to 80 percent of health risks and outcomes (Magnan 2017).

For African Americans, an additional SDOH is racial discrimination. Centuries of injustices based on structural and institutional racism embedded within the SDOH have created pre-pandemic social conditions whose combined effects create a complex interplay of circumstances of inequality that result in higher rates of chronic illnesses within the African American population that has made African Americans susceptible to COVID-19 morbidity and mortality. Since arriving as enslaved people on US soil, African Americans have had the worst health care, health status, and health outcome of any other racial group in the United States. Like a magnifying glass, COVID-19 has exposed and expanded existing inequities and inequalities among African Americans.

## The Impact of COVID-19 on Employment

Socioeconomic status (SES) is a fundamental health risk factor. The financial impact of COVID-19 has been documented to have created one of the most inequitable economic recessions in US history. According to a *Washington Post* article dated August 13, 2020, the economic recession caused by COVID-19 affected the wealthy the least and those at the bottom of the economic scale the most (Long 2020). A Pew Research Center study found only 27 percent of African Americans reported having rainy day funds, compared to 53 percent of Whites. Eighteen percent of African Americans were more likely to say their finances had been hurt due to COVID-19 compared to 8 percent of Whites (Parker, Horowitz, and Brown 2020). While low socioeconomic status (SES) is considered a fundamental cause of health, it is important to note that health disparities are greatest among middle- and upper-class African Americans when compared with middle- and upper-class Whites (Braboy-Jackson and Cummings 2011; Colen, Krueger, and Boettner 2018). This apparent paradox is counterintuitive to the established SES-health gradient.

A key variable that influences economic stability is employment status. Because of social-distancing mandates and guidelines instituted by various municipalities, consumers staying home to avoid infection, employers closing down for safety reasons, loss of demand because of income uncertainty, and supply chain issues, COVID-19 has differentially affected employment and severely affected jobs reflective of the service industry as well as other low-wage jobs—restaurants, hotels, entertainment venues, and other hospitality jobs—where a disproportionate number of racial/ethnic minorities work (Dalton 2020). In fact, the *Washington Post* recently noted that nine of the ten hardest-hit industries due to COVID-19 are service-related (Long, Van Dam, Fowers, and Shapiro 2020). Individuals employed in these occupations are less likely to have employee-paid insurance, work from home or from remote locations, or socially distance on the job like many higher wage, white-collar workers.

Gould and Wilson (2020) posit that African Americans face two of the most lethal preexisting conditions for COVID-19—racism and economic inequality. The following discussion illustrates how the SDOH of employment is a factor affecting economic stability and health status among African Americans and how structural racism in occupational and employment status has created an environment that has contributed to COVID-19 susceptibility and illustrates how structural racism creates health inequities in this population.

## How Structural Racism Impacts Employment Status among African Americans

*Occupational Status*

There exists a history of structural racism in employment by race—otherwise referred to as "occupational segregation"—in the United States that can be traced to the period immediately following slavery. During that period, African Americans were expected to work as service providers as housekeepers, caretakers, drivers, delivery workers, etc. Due to inequalities in education, residence, job search and referral networks, and persistent discriminatory hiring practices, African Americans remain overrepresented in these service-related jobs. Nearly 25 percent of African Americans are employed in service industry jobs compared to 16 percent of Whites (US Bureau of Labor Statistics 2020). For example, African Americans are disproportionately represented in employment in grocery, convenience, and drug stores (14.2 percent); public transit (26.0 percent); trucking, warehouse, and postal service (18.2 percent); health care (17.5 percent); and childcare and social services (19.3 percent). African American families earn seventy cents for every dollar earned by White families, highlighting racial inequalities in wage and salary (Farrell et al. 2020; Jones, Schmitt and Wilson 2018). In addition, African Americans with similar educational levels as their White counterparts make less for the same jobs and are less likely to receive employment benefits such as paid sick leave, healthcare insurance, or paid child leave than Whites (Maxwell and Solomon 2020). African Americans are overrepresented in nine of the ten lowest-wage jobs considered high-contact essential services (i.e., psychiatric aids, orderlies, nursing assistants, cooks and restaurant workers, pharmacy aids and technicians, food prep supervisors and servers, childcare workers, medical assistants, and funeral attendants; Fitzhugh et al. 2020). Furthermore, African Americans are overrepresented in frontline healthcare occupations—representing a third of nursing assistants, orderlies, and psychiatric aids—and in the areas of childcare and social services (19.3 percent of workers; Fitzhugh et al. 2020; Rho, Brown, and Fremstad 2020). It is also notable that only 20 percent of African Americans are able to work from home, compared with 30 percent of White workers (US Bureau of Labor Statistics 2019). The Bureau of Labor Statistics found that individuals employed in management, business, financial operations, professional, and related occupations are more likely to telework (44–58 percent of all workers) while relatively few (5–7 percent) individuals employed in service occupations telework (US Bureau of Labor Statistics 2020).

## COVID-19's Impact on the Occupational Status of African Americans

Occupational segregation as a form of structural racism has amplified the health and economic impact of the COVID-19 pandemic among African Americans. African Americans are more likely to be disproportionately represented in the service industry as essential workers that have been especially hard hit by COVID-19. A study conducted by the Kaiser Family Foundation found that African American adults were more likely than their White counterparts to indicate they were worried about contracting the virus at work (Hamel, Lopes, Munana, Artiga, and Brodie 2020). This concern has been validated by local and national news reports daily highlighting the plight of public transit workers, grocery store workers, and health care assistants being exposed to, becoming infected, and dying from COVID-19. Furthermore, service-related industries are more likely to come in contact with the public and risk exposure to COVID-19 as they are unable to shelter in place, practice physical distancing, or work from home. Therefore, it is not surprising that given the disproportionate representation of African American workers in essential service-related occupations that COVID-19-related illness, hospitalizations, and death are disparately high among African Americans.

## Unemployment Status

The issue many African Americans have historically been faced with is "last hired, first fired." In any given year, African Americans are twice as likely to be unemployed than their White counterparts (Buffie and Rawlins 2017). Furthermore, at every educational level, African Americans have higher unemployment rates compared to their White counterparts; African

Americans with college degrees have unemployment rates similar to that of Whites with high school diplomas, and African Americans with a college degree are more likely to be underemployed than their White counterparts (Williams and Wilson 2019).

## COVID-19's Impact on Unemployment among African Americans

According to the US Department of Labor, the unemployment rate during COVID-19 has been the highest since 1975. Between the months of February and April 2020, 10 percent of Americans between the ages of twenty to fifty-four lost their jobs; unemployment insurance claims spiked to over thirty million (Bureau of Labor Statistics 2020; Bernstein and Jones 2020). Furthermore, individuals employed in service occupations were among the most likely to become unemployed due to the pandemic (33 percent of workers in personal care and 24 percent of workers in food preparation).

Job losses from the pandemic have disproportionately affected African Americans in the service industry (US Bureau of Labor Statistics 2020) that play a role in shaping health and have affected COVID-19 incidence in this population. As expected, recent reports have noted that, due to COVID-19, 39 percent of jobs held by African American workers were vulnerable to reductions in hours or pay, temporary furloughs, or permanent layoffs (Fitzhugh et al. 2020). Recent studies found that during the period of the pandemic from February to June 2020, half of African Americans had job loss rates more than 50 percent higher than the job loss of Whites (Saenz and Sparks 2020). Furthermore, half of African Americans (compared to 42 percent of Whites) indicated someone in their household had lost a job or had their income reduced as a result of the pandemic, and one-third (compared to 17 percent of Whites) indicated that it had a major impact on their ability to afford basic needs like housing, utilities, and food (Hamel, Lopes, Munana, Artiga, and Brodie 2020; Parker, Horowitz, and Brown 2020). As businesses began reopening during the summer of 2020, the unemployment rate for Whites fell to 7.3 percent while for Black workers it remained high at 13.0 percent (Williams 2020). Furthermore, consistent with historical research that documents White workers being hired first following a recession, Whites have recovered more than half their jobs lost between April and February; African Americans have recovered just over a third of employment lost in the pandemic (Bureau of Labor Statistics 2020).

The implications of the occupational losses and health risks among African Americans due to working in service-related industries are substantial and bleed into other aspects of the SDOH including, for example, food and housing insecurity. Prolonged joblessness has led to mortgage defaults and failure to pay rents (Engelhardt and Eriksen 2020). Furthermore, the economic impact of job loss has led to food insecurity (Bauer 2020). Such housing and food insecurity will likely lead to further health disparities within the African American population, exacerbating an already vicious and virulent cycle.

## Recommendations

Because an individual's health is significantly determined by social factors, and the existence of health disparities is due to structural and systemic factors that impact the SDOH, it follows that a social justice approach for addressing health disparities is undertaken, not only in pandemic crises but also in times of normality when crises are not as apparent. While necessary, short-term cyclical interventions (like stimulus checks, nutritional support, housing, and childcare) to address COVID-19 disparities will not provide the structural and systemic changes warranted to address the extensive history of structural racial inequities in the labor market. The following recommendations are offered as initial starting points for federal, state, and local governments to frame long-term, sustainable, upstream policy and intervention approaches toward reducing the economic and social disparities resulting from occupational segregation that have the potential to contribute to the elimination of social and health inequities experienced by African Americans.

- Consider structural issues affecting African Americans in fiscal policy development: for example, when addressing inflation rates, the Federal Reserve should consider not only the overall unemployment rate but the African American rate as well (Bernstein and Jones 2020).

- Mandate the collection of accurate and consistent data related to the social determinants of health: To accurately understand how communities are affected by disease and illness, it is important that federal, state, and local governments collect and report accurate data in an organized, professional, and scientific manner. Such data will provide monitoring and tracking information as well as vital information on targeting interventions for health-disparate populations and allocating clinical and fiscal resources appropriately.
- Mandate universal healthcare access: investing in and ensuring that all individuals have universal access to healthcare is necessary for human and community well-being.
- Mandate universal basic income: for those who lose their jobs or who are unable to work, a basic universal income will allow families to access food and shelter to support their families and contribute to the economic health of their communities.
- Establish a reparations program: The legacy of stolen wealth and health, segregation, and redlining has yet to be addressed in this country. A reparation program that targets the racial wealth gap for African American descendants of slavery is necessary to provide vital aid and sustainability within African American communities. Such a program should focus on directing funds not just to individuals but also to African American–owned businesses and historically Black colleges and universities that create viable and sustainable job opportunities (including addressing the under-representation of racial/ethnic minorities in the health care professions workforce) for African Americans.
- Address the rights of the incarcerated and formerly incarcerated: Racial biases in the criminal justice system are widely acknowledged. Given that such biases exist, it is important to remove reentry barriers for the formerly incarcerated. Criminal background checks that are required to obtain employment places individuals in situations where they are not economically resourced, which can exacerbate preexisting health conditions and/or create disease and illness. In addition, it is important to reduce the use of money bail for nonviolent crimes. Many individuals remain in jail and prisons prior to being convicted,

- Promote and support cross-sector collaboration: Health care organizations have significant political power at both local and federal levels. On the local level, health care leaders can collaborate with social service organizations to advocate for paid sick leave, eviction and utility shut-off moratoriums, and economic support. On the federal level, health care advocates can push for expanded unemployment insurance, economic support, and protections for incarcerated people.

## Conclusion

The COVID-19 pandemic has affected all of society and it is evident that it has placed a glaring magnifying glass on historical and contemporary systemic and structural dynamics that determine occupational and employment status. These persistent systemic factors have had devastating economic, social, and health impacts on African Americans, especially as they continue to experience high levels of unemployment and slow rates of job recovery. Due to the COVID-19 pandemic, employment-related economic gains made following the Great Recession over the last decade were lost. The unemployment rate nearly tripled due to COVID-19, with African Americans employed in the hardest-hit employment sector—the service industry—disproportionately affected.

The recommendations suggested in this chapter are critical as economists have suggested that many of the service-related industries that racial/ethnic minorities are disproportionately employed in may not return to pre-pandemic levels for several years, with restaurants and entertainment venues going out of business, the hospitality and travel industries significantly affected due to employees adapting to working from home and videoconferencing, and hesitancy of people to engage in and/or afford leisure travel. Such outcomes are likely to widen the social, economic, and wealth gaps experienced by African Americans. Federal, state, and local policy makers must acknowledge these disparities and intervene aggressively to address occupational segregation and the subsequent impact it has on the health of its citizens.

## References

Bauer, Lauren. "The COVID-19 Crisis Has Already Left Too Many Children Hungry in America." *Brookings*, May 6, 2020, https://www.brookings.edu/blog/up-front/2020/05/06/the-covid-19-crisis-has-already-left-too-many-children-hungry-in-america/.

Bernstein, Jared, and Janelle Jones. (2020). "The Impact of COVID19 Recession on the Jobs and Incomes of Persons of Color." *Policy Futures* (blog), *Center on Budget and Policy Priorities*, June 2, 2020, https://www.cbpp.org/research/full-employment/the-impact-of-the-covid19-recession-on-the-jobs-and-incomes-of-persons-of.

Board of Governors of the Federal Reserve System. "Federal Open Market Committee, September 15–16 Meeting Statement." September 16, 2020, https://www.federalreserve.gov/monetarypolicy/fomcpresconf20200916.htm.

Braboy-Jackson, Pamela., and Jason Cummings. "Health Disparities and the Black Middle Class: Overview, Empirical Findings, and Research Agenda." In *Handbook of the Sociology of Health, Illness, and Healing: A Blueprint for the 21$^{st}$ Century*, edited by Bernice A. Pescosolido, Jack K. Martin, Jane D. McLeod, and Anne Rogers, 383–410. New York: Springer, 2011.

Buffie, Nicolas., and Sarah Rawlins. "The Different Experiences of Lack Unemployment and White Unemployment." *Center for Economic and Policy Research*, March 30, 2017, https://www.cepr.net/the-different-experiences-of-black-unemployment-and-white-unemployment/.

Bureau of Labor Statistics. (2020). "The Employment Situation—September 2020. (USDL-20-1838)." https://www.bls.gov/news.release/empsit.nr0.htm.

Centers for Disease Control and Prevention. "Demographic Trends of COVID-19 Cases and Deaths in the US Reported to CDC." CDC COVID Data Tracker, 2020a, https://covid.cdc.gov/covid-data-tracker/?cdc_aa_refval=https%3a%2f%2fwww.cdc.gov%2fcoronavirus%2f2019-ncov%2fcases-updates%2fcases-in-us.html#demographics. Accessed June 20, 2020.

Centers for Disease Control and Prevention. "COVID-19 Hospitalization and Death by Race/Ethnicity. Cases, Data and Surveillance." 2020b. https://www.cdc.gov/coronavirus/2019-ncov/covid-data/investigations-discovery/hospitalization-death-by-race-ethnicity.html. Accessed June 20, 2020.

Colen, Cynthia, Patrick Krueger, and Bethany Boettner. "Do Rising Tides Lift All Boats? Racial Disparities in Health Across the Lifecourse

Among Middle-Class African Americans and Whites." *Social Science and Medicine—Population Health* 6 (2018): 125–135. https://doi.org/10.1016/j.ssmph.2018.07.004.

COVID Tracking Project. "Racial Data Dashboard." *Atlantic Monthly Group*. Accessed October 28, 2020. https://covidtracking.com/race/dashboard.

Dalton, Michael. "Geographic Impact of COVID-19 in BLS Surveys by Industry." Monthly Labor Review. *Bureau of Labor Statistics*, August 2020, https://www.bls.gov/opub/mlr/2020/article/geographic-impact-of-covid-19-in-bls-surveys-by-industry.htm.

Dawes, Daniel. (2020). The Political Determinants of Health. Johns Hopkins University Press: Baltimore, Maryland.

Engelhardt, Gary, and Michael Eriksen. (2020). "Housing-Related Financial Distress During the Pandemic." September 20, 2020, *SSRN*, https://ssrn.com/abstract=3694767.

Farrell, Dianne, Fiona Greig, Chris Wheat, Max Liebeskind, Peter Ganong, Damon Jones, and Pascal Noel. "Racial Gaps in Financial Outcomes: Big Data Evidence." *JP Morgan Chase & Co. Institute*, April 2020, https://institute.jpmorganchase.com/institute/research/household-income-spending/report-racial-gaps-in-financial-outcomes.

Fitzhugh, Earl, Aria Florant, J.P. Julien, Nick Noel, Duwain Pinder, Shelley Stewart, Jason Wright, and Samuel Yamoah. "COVID-19: Investing in Black Lives and Livelihoods." *Mckinsey & Company Report*, July 8, 2020, https://www.mckinsey.com/featured-insights/mckinsey-live/webinars/investing-in-black-lives-and-livelihoods-what-stakeholders-can-do.

Fothergill, Alice, Maestas, E.G., and Darlington, J.D. "Race, Ethnicity and Disasters in the United States: A Review of the Literature." *Disasters* 23 (1999): 156–173.

Gamble, Vanessa. "'There Wasn't a Lot of Comforts in Those Days:' African Americans, Public Health, and the 1918 Influenza Epidemic." *Public Health Reports* 125, no. 3 (2010), 114–122.

Gould, Elise, and Valeri Wilson. "Black Workers Face Two of the Most Lethal Preexisting Conditions for Coronavirus—Racism and Economic Inequality." Washington, DC: Economic Policy Institute, 2020. https://www.epi.org/publication/black-workers-covid/.

Hamel, Liz., Lunna Lopes, Cailey, Muñana, Samantha Artiga, and Mollyann Brodie. *Race, Health, and COVID-19: The Views and Experiences of Black Americans*. San Francisco, CA: Kaiser Family Foundation, 2020. http://files.kff.org/attachment/report-race-health- and-covid-19-the-views-and-experiences-of-black-americans.pdf.

Hutchins, Sonja, Kevin Fiscella, Robert Levine, Danielle Ompad, and Marian Mcdonald. "Protection of Racial/Ethnic Minority Populations During an Influenza Pandemic." Am J Public Health 99, no. S2 (2009): S261-S270. https://www.ncbi.nlm.nih.gov/pmc/articles/PMC4504373/.

Jones, Janelle, John Schmitt, and Valerie Wilson. *Fifty Years After the Kerner Commission*. Washington DC: Economic Policy Institute, 2018. https://www.epi.org/142084.

Long, Heather. "The Recession Is Over for the Rich, But the Working Class Is Far from Recovered." *Washington Post*, August 13, 2020, https://www.washingtonpost.com/road-to-recovery/2020/08/13/recession-is-over-rich-working-class-is-far-recovered/.

Long, Heather, Andrew Van Dam, Alyssa Fowers, and Leslie Shapiro. "The COVID-19 Recession Is the Most Unequal in Modern US History." *Washington Post*, September 30, 2020, https://www.washingtonpost.com/graphics/2020/business/coronavirus-recession-equality/.

Magnan, Sanne. *Social Determinants of Health 101 for Health Care: Five Plus Five*. Washington, DC: National Academy of Medicine, 2017. https://nam.edu/social-determinants-of-health-101-for-health-care-five-plus-five/.

Maxwell, Connor and Danyelle Solomon. *The Economic Fallout of the Coronavirus for People of Color*. Center for American Progress (blog), April 14, 2020, https://www.americanprogress.org/issues/race/news/2020/04/14/483125/economic-fallout-coronavirus-people-color/.

Parker, Kim, Juliana Horowitz, and Anna Brown. "About Half of Lower-Income Americans Report Household Job or Wage Loss Due to COVID-10." *Pew Research Center*, April 21, 2020, https://www.pewsocialtrends.org/2020/04/21/about-half-of-lower-income-americans-report-household-job-or-wage-loss-due-to-covid-19/.

Rho, Hye, Hayley Brown, and Shawn Fremstad. "A Basic Demographic Profile of Workers in Frontline Industries." *Center for Economic and Policy Research*, April 7, 2020, https://cepr.net/a-basic-demographic-profile-of-workers-in-frontline-industries/.

Rivera, Jason, and DeMond Miller. (2007). "Continually Neglected: Situating Natural Disasters in the African American Experience." *Journal of Black Studies* 37 (2007): 502–522. https://doi.org/10.1177/0021934706296190.

Saenz, Rogelio and Corey Sparks. (2020). "The Inequities of Job Loss and Recovery Amid the COVID-19 Pandemic (National Issue Brief #150)." *Carsey School of Public Policy at the Scholars Repository*: 412. https://scholars.unh.edu/carsey/412.

US Bureau of Labor Statistics. "Table 1. Workers Who Could Work at Home, Did Work at Home, and Were Paid for Work at Home, by Selected Characteristics, Averages for the Period 2017–2018." *Economic News Release*, September 24, 2019, https://www.bls.gov/news.release/flex2.t01.htm.

US Bureau of Labor Statistics. "Supplemental Data Measuring the Effects of the Coronavirus (COVID-19) Pandemic in the Labor Market." Labor Force Statistics of the Current Population Survey. https://www.bls.gov/cps/effects-of-the-coronavirus-covid-19-pandemic.htm. Accessed: June 20, 2020.

Williams, Jhacova. "Laid Off More, Hired Less: Black Workers in the COVID-19 Recession." *The Rand Blog, Rand Corporation*, September 29, 2020, https://www.rand.org/blog/2020/09/laid-off-more-hired-less-black-workers-in-the-covid.html.

Williams, Jhacova and Valerie Wilson. (2019). "Black Workers Endure Persistent Racial Disparities in Employment Outcomes." *Economic Policy Institute*, August 27, 2019, https://www.epi.org/publication/labor-day-2019-racial-disparities-in-employment/.

Zephyrin, Laurie, David Radley, Yaphet Getachew, Jesse Baumgartner, and Eric Schneider. "COVID-19 More Prevalent, Deadlier in US Counties with Higher Black Populations." *To the Point* (blog), *Commonwealth Fund*, April 23, 2020, https://www.commonwealthfund.org/blog/2020/covid-19-more-prevalent-deadlier-us-counties-higher-black-populations.

PART THREE

# Personal Experiences
## with
# COVID-19

CHAPTER 12

# RISKS, RELATIONSHIPS, AND 'RONA

*How Five Black Mothers Navigate the COVID-19 Pandemic*

*Sandra L. Barnes*

AS OF OCTOBER 5, 2020, there had been about 7.48 million cases of the coronavirus and about 210,000 deaths in the United States (Centers for Disease Control and Prevention, 2020). Largely due to inconsistent adherence to Personal Protective Equipment (PPE) protocols, the daily rates of new cases continue to fluctuate across states with thousands of new COVID-19 cases daily (Baker and Witherspoon 2020). Despite only representing 13 percent of the US population, Black people represent 25 percent of US deaths due to COVID-19 (COVID Tracking Project 2020). Moreover, Black people are overrepresented in COVID-19 cases in twenty-eight of forty states (Henderson, Horton, and Thomas 2020). Scholarship tends to focus on health disparities (Dorn, Cooney, and Sabin 2020; Haynes, Cooper, and Albert 2020; Laster Pirtle 2020; Yancy 2020). It would also be fruitful to examine how COVID-19 is influencing other aspects of Black life. This study considers the experiences of Black mothers and their families.

Black mothers play a seminal role in their families and the Black community (Barnes 2005; Billingsley 1992; Hill 1999; Mendenhall et al. 2013; Stack 1974; Staples 1986). How are they negotiating the pandemic? What are their thoughts about its effects on their children, families, romantic partners, and the Black community? Are other factors influencing their experiences and survival strategies during this same period? This study is informed by a Black feminist lens and in-depth interviews with a cadre of Black mothers ages forty to seventy-seven years old who live in COVID-19 hotspots. Empirical findings about the number of COVID-19 cases and deaths by race as well as bivariate and content analyses are used to assess how such mothers understand and are living during these dynamics. Also, several interviews over time illuminate possible changes in attitudes and behavior as the pandemic progresses. Findings from this mixed-methodological case study illustrate some of the effects of COVID-19 racial turmoil from the perspective of mothers in a multigenerational family.

## Strengths and Challenges of Black Mothers: A Summary

Historic and contemporary scholarship documents the indelible role of Black mothers in the ability of Black families to survive and thrive (Billingsley 1992; Hill 2003; Stack 1974; Staples 1986). Rather than an indictment against Black fathers, such literature illustrates varied capacities among Black mothers that enable their families to be more adaptive and resilient despite diverse challenges and systemic constraints. Although the Black family has often been defined in opposition to the White family, race scholars provide a culturally informed portrait that illumines matrifocal, rather than matriarchal, families where mothers take on valuable roles that are often welcomed by their Black male partners and/or husbands (Billingsley 1992; Hall and King 1982; Staples 1986). For example, Staples's definition provides a counternarrative for ethnocentric depictions such as the Moynihan Report (1965) and corroborates other research on constrained resources and social services, economic and political inequities, and the beneficence of kinship networks (Billingsley 1992; Davis and Davis 1986; Stack 1974; Willie 1993; Willie and Reddick 2010).

Dynamics such as mass incarceration, unemployment, and underemployment of Black men often require certain Black mothers to take on instrumental and expressive roles and tap into resources via extended families to sustain their immediate families (Jarrett 1994; Mendenhall et al. 2013; Staples 1986; Western and Wildeman 2009). Many Black single mothers also face the psychological role strain of providing for the family while earning lower wages than Black men and White women (Barnes 2005; Western and Wildeman 2009). As single-parent households become increasingly common in the United States (Wildeman and Western 2009; Mendenhall et al. 2013), beginning in the 1990s, social researchers championed a shift from pathology—and the unidirectional study of it—to capacity-building research on Black matrifocal families and informal kinship networks (Mendenhall et al. 2013). Cultural resiliency theorists focus on the assets of Black family life, often from an Afrocentric perspective that emphasizes relationships between mothers, children, and extended kin (Collins 2005; Hill 2003; Sarkisian and Gerstel 2004). While structural resiliency theorists take a similar stance on the importance of culture, they also illustrate strategies that different racial and ethnic groups use to navigate structural inequities (Billingsley 1992; Stack 1974; Sarkisian and Gerstel 2004). Rather than debate such dichotomies, a broad sweep of this literature documents that the roles, responsibilities, trials, and triumphs of Black mothers are central to the success of such families.

Capacity-based conceptualizations of the Black family are often characterized by role flexibility, where members of nuclear, extended, and kinship networks serve social roles as needed by the core family (Littlejohn-Blake and Darling 1993). However, other studies show structural and racial correlates between poverty and food insecurity for Black families with children, particularly those headed by women (McDonough et al. 2020; Milliment et al. 2018; Ribar and Hamrick 2003). Thus, the feminization and juvenilization of poverty mean that a disproportionate percentage of Black females and their children live in poverty (Barnes 2005; Mendenhall et al. 2013). Such mothers are more apt to face inconsistent alimony and/or child support, a lack of gainful employment, limited educational attainment as well as limited childcare, healthcare, and low-cost housing. Even the most self-efficacious Black mothers are more apt to be employed in pink collar occupations that provide low wages and limited or no health insurance (Barnes 2005; Edin and Lein 1996; Hays 2003; Jarrett 1994; Mendenhall et al. 2013). Yet, this research consistently illustrates that, despite their marital status, the well-being of children tends to be foremost to most Black mothers (Barnes 2005; Billingsley 1992; Hall and King 1982; Mendenhall et al. 2013; Staples 1986). The above summary illustrates intentionality and strides toward self-sufficiency among many Black mothers as they care for their families, in general, and children, in particular, as well as some of the economic and non-economic obstacles that can undermine their families. How will this literature bear out when compared to current experiences among Black mothers today?

This study examines how challenges associated with the current COVID-19 pandemic and other contemporary problems are understood, experienced, and navigated by a cadre of Black mothers.

## The Effects of COVID-19 on the Black Community: A Summary

This study is informed by literature on the COVID-19 pandemic and related disparities in the Black community. As a result of COVID-19, Black people are more apt to lose both their lives and their livelihoods (Boesler and Pickert 2020; CDC 2020a; McNicholas and Poydock 2020). Black people are dying from COVID-19 at three times the rate of White people (Pilkington 2020). Henderson et al. (2020, n.p.) summarize their examination of the pandemic's racial impact by state: "Black people were overrepresented in COVID-19 cases in 28 states, Latinos in 20 states, and Asians in 3 states. Tragically, in almost every state that reported racial data (n=24), Black people were much more likely than any other ethnic group to die from COVID-19 infections. . . . In contrast, White people were underrepresented in the number of cases and deaths."

These trends also illustrate how the pandemic highlights chronic, preexisting racial disparities in this country (Brooks 2020; Dorn et al. 2020; Haynes et al. 2020; Laster Pirtle 2020; Poteat et al. 2020; Raifman and Raifman 2020; Yancy 2020). Studies show that some of the principal causes for such disparities include: underlying health conditions shaped by racism; dire living conditions; risky job environments as essential workers; inadequate access to healthcare; and multiple intersecting social and health risk factors (CDC 2020, 2020a; Hardeman, Medina, and Boyd 2020). Laster Pirtle (2020) emphasizes structural forces such as racial capitalism embedded in society that exacerbate the pandemic among Black people:

> Racism and capitalism mutually construct harmful social conditions that fundamentally shape COVID-19 disease inequities because they (a) shape multiple diseases that interact with COVID-19 to influence poor health outcomes; (b) affect disease

outcomes through increasing multiple risk factors for poor, people of color, including racial residential segregation, homelessness, and medical bias; (c) shape access to flexible resources, such as medical knowledge and freedom, which can be used to minimize both risks and the consequences of disease; and (d) replicate historical patterns of inequities within pandemics, despite newer intervening mechanisms thought to ameliorate health consequences. (1)

Moreover, research by Yancy (2020) shows that for majority-Black counties in the United States, the COVID-19 infection and death rates are more than three- and six times higher, respectively, than in primarily White counties. In addition, being multiply marginalized means Black people who are poor, disabled, and/or female are even more vulnerable (American Psychological Association 2020; Laurencin and McClinton 2020). Hardeman et al. (2020, n.p.) summarize the persistent challenges and possible policy solutions:

> Black communities bear the physical burdens of centuries of injustice, toxic exposures, racism, and white supremacist violence . . . . Racism is productive . . . . Any solution to racial health inequities must be rooted in the material conditions in which those inequities thrive. Therefore, we must insist that for the health of the Black community and, in turn, the health of the nation, we address the social, economic, political, legal, educational, and health care systems that maintain structural racism. Because as the COVID-19 pandemic so expeditiously illustrated, all policy is health policy.

This section documents some of the common health disparities linked to COVID-19 and related dynamics that disproportionately affect Black people (Poteat et al. 2020). This study considers how a group of Black mothers is navigating this ecological context.

## Applying a Black Feminist Lens to Black Mothers' Experiences

Developed to acknowledge and chronicle the historic experiences of Black women, a Black feminist lens remains relevant to examine the lives of Black mothers today. Because this theoretical model considers how historically oppressed groups resist marginalizing conditions and participate in personal as well as collective activism, it is an appropriate tool to study how Black mothers navigate challenges such as the COVID-19 pandemic. Black feminism considers how Black women have been economically, socially, and politically disenfranchised; understand their realities; are agentic; create counternarratives for themselves and their families; and strive to improve individually and collectively (Choo and Ferree 2010; Collins 1990, 2005; Harris-Perry 2004, 2013; hooks 1999, 2015). This same paradigm is used to assess correlates between patriarchy, racism, anti-racism, violence against people of color, and political action (Crenshaw 1994). As Collins (2005, 37, 96) notes, "Racism and heterosexism also share a common set of practices that are designed to discipline the population into accepting the status quo." Thus, racial, economic, social, and health disparities linked to COVID-19 and social problems during this same period will be used to document whether and how racism and related challenges are influencing the lives of a group of Black mothers.

Illuming the array of ways Black mothers exist is also central to Black feminism. Collins suggests that "as mothers, othermothers, teachers and sisters, Black women were central to the retention and transformation of [an] Afrocentric worldview . . . within African American extended families and communities" (Collins 1990, 10–11). Tools and capacities linked to self-reliance, independence, and discernment are central to this continual process. Because Collins also recognizes that "the mother/daughter relationship is one fundamental relationship among Black women [and] African American women as sisters and friends affirm one another's humanity, specialness, and right to exist" (1990, 96–97), the current study will examine some of the ways these seminal relationships manifest during the current period of medical and social unrest. This same lens can be used to illustrate how Black motherhood can be biological and fictive in nature as women identify needs both internal and external to their immediate families, locate the requisite resources to respond, and help mediate challenges during the process (Gilkes 2001). In this study, it will be important to consider challenges, access to resources, and strategies across time exhibited by Black mothers during the pandemic.

According to Black feminism, as "outsiders-within," Black women cultivate unique forms of wisdom (i.e., subjugated knowledges) to define themselves in positive, empowering ways—even in the presence of negative controlling images designed to have the opposite impact (Choo and Ferree 2010; Collins 1990; Crenshaw 1994, 2017). Additionally, this discernment helps them negotiate societal, familial, and personal situations. But how will this theoretical lens hold up when considering how Black mothers navigate problems today? This project specifically considers how a cadre of Black mothers understand multiple challenges they and their families are facing, the subjugated knowledge they employ, and whether their views and survival strategies change as the pandemic progresses over time (Collins 1990; West 1993). Black feminism recognizes that "empowerment involves rejecting the dimensions of knowledge, whether personal, cultural, or institutional, that perpetuate objectification and dehumanization" (Collins 1990, 230). Thus, Black feminism is a valuable framework when examining Black mothers' current experiences to uncover challenges and responses; document their voices; acknowledge unique wisdom, knowledge, and everyday resistance; and intentionally assess linkages between their experiences and systemic forces.

## Capturing Voices

This project is part of a multigenerational case study about the effects of COVID-19 on a Black family: the Marshalls. The current analysis focuses on the five mothers in the thirteen-person family. Rather than a survey and/or larger sample, a case study design is purposefully used to perform an in-depth analysis of a specific Black family. Additionally, the unique experiences among the Black mothers merited a separate analysis. To gauge possible changes in experiences, views, and behavior over time, the study includes a longitudinal component. Mothers were interviewed at two points in time—at the beginning of the summer and three months later (late May 2020 and ninety days later, in late August 2020). This period was chosen because of several societal dynamics that took place (for example, the COVID-19 pandemic's increased and continued global presence, social activism around police brutality and racism during the summer, school openings in the fall, and growing political tensions). Generalizability is not the objective but is rather to examine mothers' sentiments and how they possibly change over time as they navigate challenges and daily living (Yin 2017).

The family consists of a matriarch (widow), her offspring (four daughters and a son), and their seven offspring (including two minors). Mothers' ages range from forty to seventy-eight years old (mean age of 56.4 years old). The family matriarch, Constance, has an associate's degree; her four daughters each have master's degrees. This specific Black family was selected because multiple generations exist; each family member resides in a pandemic hotspot (i.e., densely populated cities in New York, Indiana, Georgia, and Illinois with a disproportionate percentage of COVID-19 cases and deaths); their demographic profiles are varied in terms of age, occupation, education, and place of residence; and, as these results suggest, their views can broadly inform us about important ways the COVID-19 pandemic and related problems affect the Black family. The family was identified and recruited by community partners of the researcher. Individuals were not provided a monetary incentive for participation in this project.

Findings are based on qualitative and quantitative analyses. Statistics on the pandemic's effects in the United States on Black people and White people provide the ecological context for an examination of the virus's effects on this specific group of Black mothers over time. The qualitative phase is based on in-depth interviews with five mothers (n=5); a total of ten interviews were performed. Each mother was interviewed at two points in time based on the same questions to capture possible changes in their experiences as the pandemic progressed and other incidents that might affect them and their families occurred. Interviews lasted between thirty to ninety minutes and were audiotaped and transcribed by this researcher. As well as capturing individual and family demographics, a total of ten questions and probes were posed to gather data about: life before and during COVID-19; employment, religious, and family experiences; beliefs about COVID-19; and strategies to navigate the pandemic.

Content analysis was used to identify emergent themes and response patterns (Hsieh, Hsiu-Fang, and Shannon 2005; Krippendorf 1980; Neuendorf 2002). During this phase, interview data were systematically examined by hand using two primary processes: open coding, to categorize and label broad concepts, and axial coding, in which links between these concepts and possible themes were determined. Line-by-line coding was used to identify common language among Black mothers as well as to identify frequently used verbiage (for example, specific ways mothers describe their COVID-19 experiences). This step differs from the earlier stage because it focuses on longer phrases rather than individual concepts/words. This process was continued to identify and confirm the most common patterns in these phrases. Representative quotes were also identified during this phase. Validity and reliability aren't typical criteria for qualitative analyses. However, the multiple data analysis steps used here provide confidence in the regularly occurring concepts and themes.

The quantitative analysis was based on US data collected by race via the *Atlantic*'s Racial Data Tracker (RDT) on July 10, 2020, and was last updated at 1:28 p.m. that day (COVID Tracking Project 2020). Figure 12.1 compares percentages of infections and deaths for White people and Black people in states where the Marshalls reside. The RDT indicates when a percentage likely represents a racial/ethnic disparity. It flags a group's case or death proportion as suggestive of racial/ethnic disparity when it meets three criteria: (1) is at least 33 percent higher than the census percentage of the population; (2) remains elevated whether we include or exclude cases/deaths with unknown race/ethnicity; and (3) is based on at least thirty actual cases or deaths. Statistical findings, emergent themes, thick descriptions, and representative quotes are provided below (pseudonyms are used).

### Findings

*COVID-19 Statistics in Key States by Race*

Figure 12.1 provides a summary of COVID-19 cases and death in states where the mothers in this study reside and presents the ecological context for their experiences and subsequent narratives. In Georgia, Black people comprise

31 percent of the populace, but 38 percent of COVID-19 cases and 47 percent of COVID-19 deaths. Next, Black people make up 14 percent of the population in Illinois, but represent 22 percent of COVID-19 cases and 28 percent of COVID-19 deaths. Thus, Black people in Illinois experience almost twice as many cases and twice as many deaths compared to their population presence. In Indiana, Black people comprise 9 percent of the state population, but represent 16 percent of COVID-19 cases and 16 percent of COVID-19 deaths. This means that Black people in Indiana experience almost twice as many cases and deaths from COVID-19 compared to their population presence. In New York, Black people comprise 14 percent of the state's population, but 25 percent of COVID-19 deaths. Overall, in the states listed in Figure 12.1, Black people are contracting COVID-19 at disproportionately higher rates as compared to their population presence; these patterns likely reflect racial/ethnic disparities. What are the experiences among mothers in the Marshall family as residents in these hotspots? Moreover, are there broader implications for understanding experiences in the Black community?

## Black Mothers' Voices and Experiences Navigating Challenges

Mothers' narratives support the following four themes: (1) "I'm More Careful": Mothers Describe Challenges; (2) Relationships, Romance, and 'Rona; (3) "I Hate Zoom": Navigating Challenges in Real-Time; and (4) "They've Been Doing This for Years": Racial Unrest Amid the Pandemic. Themes vary based on the concepts and topics emphasized. The first theme documents mothers' views about the nature of the pandemic and how their sentiments change over time. The second theme considers whether and how their romantic relationships have been influenced by the pandemic. Theme 3 provides strategies used at the outset of COVID-19 and how these practices have been nuanced as the pandemic continues. Lastly, in Theme 4, mothers describe how the current racial unrest, police murders, and protests have exacerbated their pandemic experiences. Findings document whether and how sentiments about the same queries change from May 2020 (Time 1 or T1) to August 2020 (Time 2 or T2) as well as whether and how a Black feminist lens can help understand mothers' experiences.

**Figure 12.1** Selected States and the Percentage of Cases and Deaths Where Race/Ethnicity Is Reported

| State | Percent of Cases that Include Race/Ethnicity Data | Percent of Deaths that Include Race/Ethnicity Data | Race | Percent of State Population | Percent of Reported Cases | Percent of Reported Deaths |
|---|---|---|---|---|---|---|
| Georgia | 71% | 99% | Black/AA | 31% | 38% | 47%* |
| | | | White | 53% | 34% | 46% |
| Illinois | 77% | 96% | Black/AA | 14% | 22%* | 28%* |
| | | | White | 62% | 28% | 45% |
| Indiana | 77% | 86% | Black/AA | 9% | 16%* | 16%* |
| | | | White | 84% | 59% | 70% |
| New York | 0% | 89% | Black/AA | 14% | Not reported | 25%* |
| | | | White | 56% | Not reported | 34% |

Source: *The Atlantic*'s Racial Data Tracker (The COVID Tracking Project 2020).* This percentage likely represents a racial/ethnic disparity. The tracker flags a group's case or death proportion as suggestive of racial/ethnic disparity when it meets three criteria: (1) is at least 33 percent higher than the Census Percentage of Population; (2) remains elevated whether we include or exclude cases/deaths with unknown race/ethnicity; and (3) is based on at least thirty actual cases or deaths. AA=African American. Figures accessed at 1:28 p.m. on July 10, 2020.

### *Theme 1: "I'm More Careful": Mothers Describe Challenges*

Each of the five mothers describes their COVID-19 experiences and how the pandemic has affected their families over time. Indicative of a Black feminist lens, their sentiments are imbued with family concerns, survival strategies, and subjugated knowledges (Collins 1990, 2005; Harris-Perry 2004, 2013; hooks 1999, 2015). Constance is the seventy-seven-year-old family matriarch and mother of four daughters and one son. The retired service provider describes her initial experiences as the world began to realize the nature, scope, and dangers of the coronavirus:

> **T1**: I miss going to church and going to the doctor. I get up and fix my own breakfast, and most of the time, I cook dinner. I fold up my clothes. Then I basically look at TV. Sometimes I get bored and sometimes I don't . . . . Sometimes it can be depressing. The conditions in the world today . . . I was surprised by the number of people who have died, and that the government knew about this and swept it under the rug. It's just devastating.
>
> **T2:** I'm more careful about going out and I definitely am not going out to restaurants. It's just changed the way I think and act. When we do go out, we get carry out, but we don't even do that too often. It stopped us from traveling and we don't visit as much. I look after [Lauren's two youngest children] so that keeps me busy . . . . It's been hardest not being able to go to church, not going to the doctor, and you're almost afraid to go to the grocery store. It just affects your whole life . . . . According to the scientists, we're supposed to have another upswing in the fall. The only way it will get better is if they come up with a vaccine. Personally, I wouldn't want to be the first one to try that vaccine, but if they show it will work, like they did with polio, then things will get better.

Constance's use of concepts such as "depressing" and "devastating" at Time 1 as well as "afraid" at Time 2 illustrate her anxiousness and concerns about COVID-19 (CDC 2020; Resnick 2020). For her, regardless of the time period, the inability to address her spiritual and health needs is most dire. Moreover, specific descriptions of how she occupied her time in-house in May give way to increased trepidation in August (i.e., "affects your whole life") when discussing venturing outside. Likely informed by subjugated knowledge, at both time periods, Constance is suspicious of institutions (i.e., the government, science) and their responses to the virus (Hardeman et al. 2020; Laster Pirtle 2020). Also, she lives with her daughter Lauren in Indiana and takes great pride as the primary caretaker for her daughter's two youngest children as Collins (1990, 119–20) suggests, "grandmothers . . . act as othermothers by taking on childcare responsibilities . . . . Othermothers—women who assist bloodmothers by sharing mothering responsibilities—traditionally have been central to the institution of Black motherhood."

The following sentiments by Constance's daughter Lana, a fifty-three-year-old social worker who lives in Georgia with her young adult son, show how anxiousness about COVID-19 turned into anger (Blazer 2020; De La Garza 2020). Lana initially wonders whether contracting the virus is inevitable; a specific death exacerbates her fears and reflects the disproportionate toll the pandemic is taking on Black people (Henderson et al. 2020; Pilkington 2020; Poteat et al. 2020):

> **T1:** Every time I cough, I think I have corona. So, it affects your mental health because it makes you feel that you are susceptible. Because so many people are getting it and there are so many unknowns, then why would you *not* get it [emphasis is hers]. Just in terms of sadness and worry about who might have been exposed. One of my close friend's mothers died from corona . . . . It can lead to sadness because of so many things. If I get it, will I be one of the people who dies, or will I have mild symptoms? Will my family members get it? Will I be able to see them? . . . I'm more mindful of sanitizing certain areas when, in the past, we weren't as mindful about doorknobs and banisters. I have a son here who is a frontline worker, so his routine has changed because he removes his clothes when he enters the house and bathes. There are no visitors either, neighbors and friends who would have otherwise visited. So, unless it's an essential person, no one visits my home.

In the above quote at Time 1, Lana provides a litany of common early concerns about COVID-19 (Alleyne 2020; Gordon et al. 2020). She also describes her daily activities and how she endeavors to prepare and protect her son, Donald, an essential worker. Lana's ability to navigate such challenges as a single mother reflects West's (1993, 90) remark that "the social burden of bearing and usually nurturing Black children . . . breeds a spiritual strength of Black women unbeknownst to most Black men and nearly all other Americans" (1993, 90). Over time, Lana expresses disdain because of the lack of national focus and leadership to combat the virus:

> **T2:** I am surprised the pandemic has lasted this long and that Americans are stupid. They do not want to adhere to guidelines. They're selfish and ignorant people to think only of themselves and not caring about vulnerable people like the elderly, young children, and people with preexisting medical conditions . . . . My insurance company [name] is working on a vaccine . . . . I have a prediction. I know there will be people like myself that will take the vaccine, but there will be people that won't take the vaccine. Just like people who don't take flu vaccines. But I believe people like me who will take the vaccine will hopefully balance it out.

As the pandemic has progressed, Lana's feelings shift from fear to frustration. Her words above at Time 2 (i.e., stupid, selfish, and ignorant) point to inconsistent PPE (i.e., personal protective equipment, including social distancing) compliance followed by spikes in the number of COVID-19 deaths and cases in the United States and in her state of Georgia (Beckett 2020). As of October 18, 2020, cases continued to trend up in all but two states in the country, and "twenty-seven states saw spikes between 10 percent and 50 percent: Alabama, Arizona, Colorado, Georgia, Idaho, Illinois, Indiana, Iowa, Kansas, Massachusetts, Michigan, Minnesota, Mississippi, Nebraska, Nevada, New Jersey, New Mexico, North Dakota, Ohio, Rhode Island, South Carolina, South Dakota, Texas, Washington, West Virginia, Wisconsin and Wyoming" (Holcombe 2020). Her mother's concerns, likely fueled by subjugated knowledge due to longer exposure to medical inequities, contrast Lana's anticipation of a vaccine (Laster Pirtle 2020; Poteat et al. 2020).

Next, forty-seven-year-old Lauren, an elementary school teacher with two daughters and a son who resides in Indiana, describes another side effect of the pandemic. Her mother Constance's recent heart attack and close quarters have heightened family tensions paralleling results from a 2019 University College of London study that "20 percent [of respondents] reported a worsening of relationships with other adults they lived with and 17 percent with children they lived with . . . , with 19 percent reporting a worsening of relations with children outside of the home, and 16 percent with parents or other relatives" (n.p.). Thus, COVID-19 undermines her family's quality of life, but its danger is not acknowledged by certain people in the United States (Beckett 2020; De La Garza 2020):

> **T1:** What continues to surprise me is how some people aren't taking COVID seriously . . . . We don't go as much, and it has shifted more responsibility on me. Mom did the grocery shopping and her own personal shopping. She hasn't been in a store since COVID started to keep her from being exposed. We have been more agitated because we are in a small space and we're together all the time. Before, me and the kids were gone all day and Mom had her alone time. Now it's in our face.
>
> **T2:** It has affected my kids' lives the greatest. Probably Claudia the most. She was getting tired of getting stuck inside. She would go stay at her father's house or with a girlfriend. With Donna, it didn't bother her as much. She made the best grades she's made all year. She was on the A honor roll. She wants to remain virtual in the fall because she got one-on-one support and she wasn't afraid to ask questions—you know that pressure being around other kids. I'm sure my job will do something hybrid, so I will still get to homeschool her in the fall.

Lauren's role as a mother means meeting decidedly differential needs of a son with special needs, a daughter entering adolescence, and another exiting this same developmental phase. As Collins (1990, 118, 133) notes, "the institution of Black motherhood consists of a series of constantly renegotiated relationships that African American women experience with one another, with Black children, with the larger African American community, and with the self . . . . Black motherhood can be rewarding, but it can also extract high personal costs." For Lauren, this means working with two ex-husbands who are inconsistently involved in their daughters' lives, providing support for an older daughter diagnosed with an anxiety disorder, and monitoring the learning needs of her youngest child. In doing so, Lauren emulates other Black mothers who "routinely encourage Black daughters to develop skills to confront oppressive conditions . . . and that education is a vehicle for advancement can also be ways of enhancing positive self-definitions and self-valuations in Black girls" (Collins 1990, 124). Moreover, at-home mentoring and support have helped improve both Lauren's youngest daughter's grades and her self-definition as a strong student (Collins 1990). Although they are adapting, helping her family navigate being sequestered is taking its toll on Lauren.

Lauren's oldest sister, a fifty-six-year-old marketing analyst, Lola, is the mother of three sons, two of whom live at home in Georgia. Although their social lives are limited, particularly Laurence's due to his girlfriend's health, Lola suggests the pandemic has resulted in a silver lining in the form of increased family time and work productivity:

> **T1:** I think my kids are enjoying it. We play board games and they go to the park too while also practicing social distancing. They seem to be adapting to it. They are taking online classes. I think they enjoy that. The difficulty is if they have company, it is only one person at a time. My son's girlfriend said she isn't coming for a while because he is around so many people at his job. She is concerned about COVID.

As time progresses, Lola describes educational issues (Binkley 2020; Lumpkin 2020) and Laurence's work challenges in a predominantly White space where customers refuse to comply with PPE guidelines (Blazer 2020; De La Garza 2020). Like most of the mothers here, the passage of time results in details about how they are navigating COVID-19:

> **T2:** They're both in college, but all of Levi's classes are online. We had to get a reduction in the termination fee for Laurence. We moved all his stuff to campus and then we had to move it out. They tried to charge us $2,000, but we got it down to $500. It didn't make sense to spend $4,000 to be on campus and then sit in his dorm because all his classes are online. We didn't find that out until we got there. . . . I know that Laurence is thinking about COVID at his job. He had a dream [last night] that someone was yelling in his face without a mask and he said that they were too close. For him to dream about it means it was on his mind. So that was kind of hurtful to know that as his mother. So, every day before he goes to work, I pray for him and cover him and his coworkers. I make sure they are taking their vitamin C and wearing their masks.

In addition to reconciling the value of online classes and campus living (Binkley 2020; Lumpkin 2020), Lola describes Laurence's deteriorating emotional state as an essential worker who faces controlling images daily linked to race and politics (Collins 1990; Harris-Perry 2004, 2013). Like other Generation Zs and Millennials, Laurence works to help sustain his family as he attempts to complete college despite an uncertain future (Rahim 2020; Van Dam 2020). Thus, Lola attempts to provide remedies to help her sons complete the daily routine but laments an inability to protect them from COVID-related trauma that is both physical and emotional ("Black Male Millennial: Unemployment and Mental Health" 2018; McNicholas and Poydock 2020; Resnick 2020).

This first theme differs from subsequent themes in its emphasis on the specific familial responses among the Marshalls and illustrates increasingly more dire concerns about the pandemic as time progresses accompanied by more detailed remedies. Moreover, as suggested by a Black feminist lens, the challenges facing the Marshall mothers and their children are correlated with the intersection of race, class, gender, and place in troubling ways (Collins 1990; Mendenhall 2013). Given these challenges, how are mothers reconciling other relationships?

## Theme 2: Relationships, Romance, and 'Rona

Fewer studies about the pandemic consider how Black romantic relationships are being affected. For example, according to a 2019 study by the University College of London (2020, n.p.), "18 percent of respondents reported a worsening of relationships with their spouse/partner.... Conversely, over a third of adults living with children reported improvements in their relationships, most commonly with their partner/spouse, neighbors, or other adults in their household." Long-distance interactions can strain close ties. Individuals who have been able to proactively and innovatively respond seem to be best prepared to ensure that such bonds are strengthened rather than broken (Ellison 2020; Hagberg 2020). Mothers here describe efforts to maintain romantic ties. For example, when fifty-six-year-old Lola's boyfriend's primary job as a frontline cook was furloughed, he became part of the 40 percent of non-elderly Black adults who lost work or wages because of COVID-19 (Brown 2020). Lola and Ron didn't spend less time together, but his precarious economic situation meant that dates that require money were curtailed:

> **T1:** Our dating life has not changed because Ron still comes over and does yardwork . . . we just use social distancing. But sometimes I'm still kind of close to him. We still do stuff; we just don't go out to eat or to the movie. . . . He only comes inside on Saturday night for dinner . . . . He got laid off from his main job. He's getting unemployment. The numbers dwindled since they were only doing pick-up orders. So, they told him they'd call him back when things started picking up. He has a second job at [name of Italian franchise].
>
> **T2:** We're [she and Ron] still spending time together. I haven't been cooking because he has been laid off. He's been bringing me breakfast, lunch, and dinner sometimes. He comes, drops the food off, and leaves.

Lola admits that they do not consistently engage in social distancing. Because Lola cannot confirm to what extent Ron uses PPE at home or at his part-time job as an essential worker, she may be inadvertently placing herself and her sons at risk by being "still kind of close to him" (Brooks 2020; Dorn et al. 2020; Haynes et al. 2020; Raifman and Raifman 2020; Yancy 2020). Moreover, Ron's job loss means he now exchanges certain in-kind services (i.e., free meals and yard work) to compensate for his inability to provide traditional dates. This pattern informs Collins's (2005) comment that "those African Americans who try to build their love relationships on the foundation of traditional gender ideology reserved for White people often find that the economic, political, and social opportunities denied to Black people limit their chances of success" (258–259).

In contrast, her younger sister's dating constraints are linked to PPE rather than finances. Fifty-three old Lana notes:

> **T1:** We cannot have date night. We used to do a lot of social activities—house parties. Going away for the weekend has been curtailed. But we've caught up on a lot of TV shows, a lot of Tyler Perry shows, so we've connected in other ways. . . . I didn't go to church anyway, so it did not affect it at all. However, I watch more spiritual shows online and more church services, but I don't miss going to the actual facility. But Tom's church does a lot of fun summer activities that I will miss.

Per the above quote, Lana and her fiancé, Tom, a retired accountant, reduce their busy social schedule at the outset of the pandemic. Travel and social events at his church and fraternity are temporarily supplanted by in-house movies, game nights, and virtual church services. And like her sister Lola, Lana cannot confirm that her fiancé practices social distancing when he's away from her. They are muddling through, but she pines for their past social schedule.

> **T2:** Social interactions are still the hardest. And I'm a social person. Also, personally, we have been active in terms of parties, eating out, and seeing friends on a regular basis. So, we have not been able to do these fun activities the way we used to. For example, we used to go to the [name of fraternity gala] each year. It was postponed and now it was canceled. One friend pretty much stays inside. He says he's afraid of the virus. I tell people that they don't have to justify or explain how they feel if they don't feel comfortable. This virus is affecting people differently.

It is common for mothers to provide more details at Time 2 as they reflect upon living in the pandemic over time. They specifically and vividly describe how COVID-19 is influencing their lives. Although Lana expresses frustrations at the myriad canceled events, she is adapting. Moreover, she is empathetic with individuals who are navigating the pandemic in diverse ways (Ellison 2020; Hagberg 2020).

Joy, over a decade younger than her siblings, uses social media to compensate for the social isolation the pandemic causes. A forty-year-old program director at a youth transition facility, Joy is more reluctant to interact with many people given Indiana's proportionately higher number of COVID-19 deaths and cases (Holcombe 2020). At Time 1, Joy suggests that platforms such as Facebook and Messenger are alternatives, albeit limited, to physical contact (Dimock 2019).

> **T1:** I do get lonely. I can't hang out with my friends. We text more. We try to schedule Zoom, but we communicate via Facebook and Messenger a lot. I see my partner, but she's the only one I allow myself to hang out with. Coming to my job helps because I can interact with the girls and that's enough for me.
>
> **T2:** I personally know of several people that have been affected by it . . . young people. I believe we should take it very seriously. But I also think this is a very good time to sit still and reflect on how fast life can get and how we overlook the really important things.

As an essential worker, Joy diligently uses PPE (McNicholas and Poydock 2020). A parent to a daughter, Joy is also fortified by her role as fictive kin for the young single mothers under her purview and periodic interactions with her partner (i.e., "enough for me"). The young girls at work serve as extended family and constitute Joy's "community othermother relationships . . . in response to the needs of their own children and of those in their communities" (Collins 1990, 131). Because her young charges are sequestered in their full-service facility, Joy's potential exposure to COVID-19 at work seems minimal. Yet, Joy's loneliness and sense of isolation are apparent, and her partner's social distancing practices are unclear (Resnick 2020). However, her advice on patience (i.e., "sit still . . .") represents subjugated knowledge as she ponders what is important in life (Collins 1990).

According to Theme 2, the mothers are initially reticent about social interactions at Time 1. Heightened anxieties and fears of the unknown are common. However, over time, the desire to spend time with their romantic partners and engage in "normal" activities from their past means cautiously venturing out. Remarks also suggest that Constance's four daughters are relaxing using PPE with their romantic partners despite otherwise strict adherence. Yet they can't confirm whether their partners are using PPE in their own circles. The implications for romance and risk are informed by the CDC's updated definition of close contact as "someone who was within six feet of an infected individual for a total of fifteen minutes or more over a twenty-four-hour period" (Sun 2020, n.p.). Applying a Black feminist lens to PPE adherence suggests that most mothers here "accept the rules but point to the virtual impossibility of following them" (Collins 2005, 249) and, in doing so, may be indirectly exposing themselves and their families to COVID-19 (Alleyne 2020; Gordon et al. 2020).

## Theme 3: "I Hate Zoom": Navigating Real-Time Challenges

According to a report by the College of London (2020), "a quarter of people have reported their relationships with colleagues and coworkers have worsened over lockdown, and a fifth have said their friendships outside of their household have also got worse" (n.p.). Four of the Marshall mothers are the primary breadwinners in their family; Constance's monthly retirement check and daily, free childcare for Lauren's children are also crucial to her daughter's financial stability (Collins 1990). Thus, they continue to work despite the pandemic. Theme 3 describes how the pandemic is affecting employment and daily experiences. Forty-year-old Joy's job has sequestered the youth under her purview. Her initial preoccupation with PPE is replaced by feelings of loneliness as the pandemic is prolonged:

> **T1:** I'm considered an essential worker, so I still have to go to work. So when I return, I Lysol spray my most touched items—doorknobs, remote control, even my phone. I work at a twenty-four-hour residential group home for teens and their babies. The girls have not been allowed outside other than walks with staff since the middle of March. They complete all their schooling online . . . . We also have food donated from restaurants so that staff can do more sanitizing and not have to cook meals. It is extremely hard.
>
> **T2:** I go to work four days a week and see Jenny. Normally, Monday through Thursday, I am by myself, but I also drive to see my mother. That can get lonely. I play with my dog. I am not a big TV person. I enjoy coloring. I have some coloring books and I really enjoy cooking, so I try to cook every day. And I attend lots of Zoom meetings . . . I hate Zoom . . . . Adjusting to the PPE has been hard. Having to wear a face mask. Dry skin from bleach water. Just the PPE of it. I now have face masks that are made for me.

In her latter quote, Joy reflects on how her established routine and daily activities have been altered due to COVID-19, as she attempts to proactively stave off depression (McNicholas and Poydock 2020; Resnick 2020). Anxiety is the most common mental disorder affecting Joy and about forty million other adults in the United States (ADAA 2020); video conferences can exacerbate such anxieties (Anderson 2020). Like many users, Joy considers platforms like Zoom necessary evils that facilitate work interactions, but increase fatigue

(Dimock 2019; Pickrell 2020). Such sites appear to be part of the present-day survival strategies of the mothers here (Collins 1990). Social distancing has resulted in a bevy of intersecting problems for social worker Lana:

> **T1:** We provide services to children and families, like home visits and needs assessments. Another layer is potential child abuse and neglect. When children were in schools, we could put eyes on them, but now we can't. Some of my parents suffer from depression and other mental health issues. It's very hard to monitor what they are doing.... I meet with families weekly by teleconference, but it's not the same. We have a large district. We have very affluent families and very poor ones. Some families do not have computers to use Zoom. So, I decided to use the same platform to be equitable.
>
> **T2:** It's been so hard because I like to see my clients and their children. Studies show that neglect and abuse numbers have gone down, but that's because now we can't see the kids. In the past, the kids were coming to school and we could physically see bruises or if they were malnourished, if their clothes were too small or dirty or signs of emotional abuse. The numbers have decreased because we can't monitor them because we can't see them. Also, I can't go into family homes to uplift families and see how things are going.

Lana details educational and related challenges that are going unchecked and the inability to proactively support youth. Based on subjugated knowledges about the effects of inequality, she intentionally offers equitable online services despite the inequities among her clients due to race, class, family structure, and their intersections because, as Crenshaw notes, "intersectionality [is] a prism to bring to light dynamics within discrimination . . . to make room 'for more advocacy and remedial practices' to create a more egalitarian system" (as quoted in Coaston 2019). Also, Lana's stance parallels Collins's (1990, 132) assessment that "motherhood—whether bloodmother, othermother, or community othermother—can be invoked by African American women as a symbol of power . . . not only from actions as mothers in Black family networks but from contributions as community othermothers." Thus, similar concerns and protective measures that Lana employs for her own son are provided for the children she serves at work.

COVID-19 has undermined employment, particularly for women and people of color (Boesler and Pickert 2020; Brown 2020; McNicholas and Poydock 2020). As a teacher, Lauren had to quickly transition to online teaching during spring 2020:

> **T1:** Thankfully, I'm still getting paid. We ended the school year virtually. In one way, it was easier because you didn't have to go into work every day. But it was also sad because we have eighty-six fifth graders and I had less than thirty who were regularly working on their virtual education. They didn't have devices to access the online learning activities. So, my job became calling students every day to make sure they were okay. I have a few students that I took food because their parents weren't working. It became more social work than teaching. . . . We gave out work packets and they were supposed to get free summer bridge books through Amazon, but the district set a cap at four hundred kids. Well, we have five hundred kids, just at our school. So many of our kids didn't get anything. You could track their progress using email, calls, or text messages, so you know they weren't learning.

Just as a disproportionate percentage of people of color have lost their jobs, been furloughed, or experienced lower wages due to the pandemic, reports show that from February to May 2020, "11.5 million women lost their jobs compared with 9 million men—underlining how women are more vulnerable to sudden losses of income" (Holpuch 2020, n.p.). Lauren is grateful to still have a job, but describes increased challenges working in a poor urban city (i.e., the digital divide, food insecurity, limited books and school supplies, and increased student absences) that require her to take on a social support role beyond teaching. Lauren questions whether many of her students are learning. The situation became more dire when school reopened in fall 2020:

> **T2:** The start of school was a disaster. The district didn't have masks or a plan to socially distance kids. They gave the kids one mask and a tiny bottle of hand sanitizer—and that was it. Then when we went online, we found out that the city was not wired with fiber optics so the Internet would go down—until we got hot spots, but it is still inconsistent. We had to figure out a way to get consistent food to children now that we are online. My church is a drop-off facility . . . . I am constantly stressed out. I know the kids aren't learning online the way they used to, but would it be better to go to school and catch corona? The adults are clueless, and the children are suffering for it.

Lauren describes disparate school conditions, poor preparation, underfunded schools, and inadequate technology. Going to school also meant poor youth are guaranteed two nutritious meals per day (McDonough et al. 2020; Milliment et al. 2020; Ribar and Hamrick 2003). The pandemic requires makeshift responses Lauren knows are inadequate and will ultimately mean negative educational, health, and mental outcomes for many youth long after COVID-19 has been contained (Dorn et al. 2020; Laster Pirtle 2020; Poteat et al. 2020; McDonough et al. 2020; Raifman and Raifman 2020; Resnick 2020; Yancy 2020).

*Theme 4: "They've Been Doing This for Years":*
*Racial Unrest Amid the Pandemic*

The fourth theme reflects a marked difference from the prior ones based on the increased emphasis on racial unrest during the pandemic. Mothers discuss the history of racism in the United States, resistance strategies for redress, and push back against controlling images (Collins 1990, 2005). Although forty-seven-year-old Lauren and her fifty-three-year-old sister, Lana, specifically mention the murders of Black men and subsequent protests at Time 1, over time, the increased protests and racial conflict begin to compete for the attention of the pandemic in each mother's minds and lives. Lauren remarks:

> **T1:** Physically, I've gained at least ten pounds because there's nothing to do all day but worry, so I snack. I noticed that my anxiety is higher. So, I've limited my social media and news intake because my nerves were just on edge. It started with the pandemic, and you just add on George Floyd. I just have to limit it.

It appears that the mothers here are preoccupied with adjusting to the pandemic at Time 1. Lauren's heightened anxiety negatively affects her physically (i.e., weight gain) and mentally (i.e., increased anxiety). She specifically points to both the pandemic and George Floyd's murder as the sources of this distress (Ellison 2020; Wedell et al. 2020) and practical efforts to curtail their effects on her. By Time 2, she describes a history of racial abuse in the United States and remedies, "White people have been killing us for centuries. We are just more aware of it now because of social media. It's gone too far, and they aren't going to stop until we stop them . . . . These police need to be fired." Theme 4 emphasizes the history of killing Black people with impunity of which society is now more aware due to social media (Gruenberg 2020; Moore 2013; Pilkington 2020; Wells-Barnett 2014). Mothers are clear about appropriate redress. Similarly, seventy-seven-year-old Constance reflects on the historic and systemic nature of brutality against Black people:

> **T1:** That's been going on for years. It just wasn't brought out in the public. We have been mistreated and killed, but now it's gotten out of hand. These police need to be fired or retrained, but you can't train some of them because they got that hate in them. They are just shooting people down.

Constance's comment about increased, unchecked violence against Black people is corroborated by a longitudinal study reported in the *Washington Post* that although African Americans "account for less than 13 percent of the US population, but are killed by police at more than twice the rate of White Americans" ("Fatal Force" 2020, n.p.). In the history of Black female resistance, Constance succinctly explains why (i.e., "They got hate in them") and how the situation should be addressed (i.e., retraining and/or termination) (Collin 1990, 2005). Like other mothers at Time 2, Constance declares, "There has just been injustice all the time ever since they brought us over as slaves. But somebody has to do something." Her remark supports existing literature on racism (Blumer 1958; Feagin 2008; Hardeman et al. 2020) that warrants action. Next, Lola provides a religious framework and religious and pragmatic remedies:

> **T1:** It grieves my heart that these things are happening, but this is not the first time. It's been going on a long time in our history. I'm happy about the people who are protesting peacefully. I'm just praying that we be the change that we want to see and that people in positions of power will not look away but will do their part as they see the peaceful protests to bring awareness to what is happening. So that they will see *all of us* [emphasis is hers] protesting. But we still must teach our young men and Black people in general that whatever the police say, keep your hands up and avoid confrontation.

Lola describes the effects of unrest on her (i.e., "grieves my heart"), but seems somewhat more confident than her sisters that, as Black people and their allies engage in peaceful protests, persons in power will effect change. Yet, her advice reflects the prudence and protective nature Black feminist literature suggests Black mothers must exhibit (Choo and Ferree 2010; Collins 1990, 2005; Harris-Perry 2004, 2013). Yet by Time 2, Lola's optimism is nuanced:

> **T2:** They need to keep working to get these police officers out of the force or retrained so that everyone is treating everyone like a person.... Like that guy that was shot seven times in the back. I know they [police] have some type of silent code. Those things have really grieved me, and I really didn't expect that during this pandemic.... I try to be the change that I want to see. I'm telling people to get out and vote and research these people we are putting in office to see what they stand for.

A seminal response noted in Black feminism, Lola continues to encourage Black people to be change agents for themselves and the Black community (Choo and Ferree 2010; Coaston 2019; Collins 1990; Crenshaw 1994, 2017). Her comment also includes more detailed, proactive ways Black people can be more agentic (i.e., vote, increased expectations of elected officials) as well as structural changes (i.e., remove bad police). She also references the negative, compounded effects of the pandemic and protesting taking place simultaneously. Moreover, Jacob Blake being shot seven times by police on August 23, 2020, in Kenosha, Wisconsin, seems to result in Lola's more somber tone and increased suspicions of police. As the mother of three sons, Lola's tempered hopes parallel Collins's (1990, 136–137) findings that "despite the obstacles and costs, motherhood remains a symbol of hope for many of even the poorest Black women ... her children offer hope." Additionally, fifty-three-year-old Lana offers multiple insights during her first interview:

> **T1:** I have a lot to say because this is about my current babies—my baby [her son, Donald] and other baby [her fiancé's grandson, Samson] and the world they will grow up in. Our society has become more dangerous, especially for younger citizens [Donald's] age. I'm just concerned as a parent in these times of racial unrest—all these hyped racial issues and hyped racial crimes. As a parent, it's disconcerting. I always give him extra reminders to be safe on his job, not to engage people at work around race issues.

> For example, at [Save-Mart], some people want to make the mask issue a race issue, especially at his location. So, I tell him not to engage people for his safety. And I try to instill positive mental health in him. In terms of my grandson, he is very young. I wonder what the world will be like in ten years when he's at school, as a teenager, in college, and what he may be exposed to in terms of racial disparities.

Lana's concerns and survival strategies above parallel Collins's (1990, 135) observations about Black motherhood: "Protecting Black children remains a primary concern of African American mothers because Black children are at risk." She describes generational concerns about her son's and grandson's safety and futures given the present-day racial unrest ("Black Male Millennial: Unemployment and Mental Health" 2018; McNicholas and Poydock 2020; Resnick 2020), blames politicians for fueling racial tensions and violence, and purposefully helps her son forge a positive self-definition (Collins 1990, 2005). Despite socializing her son to avoid negative racial encounters at his predominately White workplace as well as corresponding racist controlling images, Lana considers society to be largely dangerous for Black youth (Collins 1990, 2005; Harris-Perry 2004, 2013; hooks 1999, 2015). At Time 2, like Black feminists, she suggests that failure to inform Black youth about historic and present-day racism means failing to prepare them to navigate society:

> **T2:** A lot of this younger population have not been exposed to the racial issues like we were growing up. They were kind of oblivious to the racial issues we, our parents, and grandparents experienced and so now these things are coming to horrific light. They are being exposed to it and it's a rude awakening. My son used to think, "That was in the past and things are better now." And it is not. So now, they are seeing a lot.

Like her sisters and mother, Lana seems skeptical about structural reform and a future devoid of racial dangers for Black youth. Beyond physical concerns, Lana laments the mental trauma she suggests Black youth face as they reconcile the differences between the idealized post-racial age they believed existed and the present-day reality of racism (Feagin 2008; Hardeman et al. 2020).

According to the Marshall mothers in this fourth theme, the negative outcomes associated with the COVID-19 pandemic have only been exacerbated by increasing racial tensions. Despite providing their children with coping mechanisms, their concerns parallel reports of disproportionate police violence against the very youth they are endeavoring to rear and protect; "the rate of fatal police shootings among Black Americans was much higher than that for any other ethnicity, standing at 32 fatal shootings per million of the population" (Statista Research Department 2020). Yet, the mothers seem to hold on to some vestige of hope for their children as they protect, provide for, and affirm them (Collins 1990).

## Discussion and Conclusion

This study followed five Black mothers in the Marshall family over a ninety-day period to examine how they and their families navigated the COVID-19 pandemic. Four of them have been married; most raised their children alone for considerable periods of time and initially struggled as single mothers (Western and Wildeman 2009; Mendenhall et al. 2013). Their comments and experiences support the continued centrality of Black mothers in Black families and the Black community during challenging periods like the current pandemic (Barnes 2005; Billingsley 1992; Hill 1999; Mendenhall et al. 2013; Stack 1974; Staples 1986). Four themes emerged that focused on the challenges and strategies they employed, efforts to maintain romantic ties, workplace problems and remedies, and views about racial redress. Views were thoughtful, candid, and often sobering—and indicative of many of the traits, trials, testimonies, and triumphs documented in Black feminism. Mothers discussed survival strategies, controlling images linked to race and politics, their resulting subjugating knowledges, as well as proactive attempts to ensure that their children foster positive self-definitions despite the onslaught against Black bodies (Choo and Ferree 2010; Coaston 2019; Collins 1990; Crenshaw 1994, 2017). These findings illustrate the robustness of a Black feminist lens in examining and documenting the contemporary experiences of Black mothers and the physical and mental toll with which they contend (Mendenhall et al. 2013).

Findings here also suggest that the Marshall mothers are adaptive and resilient as they help their children navigate the pandemic. They expressed concerns and anxieties during their initial interviews that were informed by more detailed strategies and thoughts about COVID-19 during their second interview. For several mothers, concerns about contracting the virus as residents in hotspots compounded over time (CDC 2020, 2020a). Yet, close proximity to romantic partners with unconfirmed PPE practices may put the mothers and their families at risk. And social unrest around police brutality and racism exacerbated pandemic-related anxieties (Resnick 2020). It was common for mothers to recognize how race, gender, class, and place made them and their children disproportionately vulnerable to both the virus and racial violence (Dorn et al. 2020; Haynes et al. 2020; Laster Pirtle 2020; Poteat et al. 2020; Yancy 2020).

As expected, mothers with young sons were particularly concerned about growing racial tensions; several mothers suggested that current tensions reflect a history of racial oppression that goes unchecked and thus continues to rear its ugly head (Blumer 1958; Collins 1990; Feagin 2008; Hardeman et al. 2020; West 1993). Their solutions included microlevel, practical remedies (i.e., police terminations and reform, protests, and voting), microlevel redress (i.e., combating systemic racism), and existential change (i.e., addressing hate against Black people). Given that their concerns increased over the study window, it will be important to reexamine their experiences and thoughts at the next three-month wave. In the absence of a vaccine, will their anxieties increase, or will they have developed more adaptive attitudes and strategies? Additional studies based on larger samples will be fruitful. The current analysis was not designed for generalizability but rather to gather and document the rich narratives of a cadre of Black mothers to get a glimpse of their lives across time, and in doing so, document the unique voices of this invaluable segment of the Black community.

## References

Alleyne, Kenneth R. "Opinion: How COVID-19 Is a Perfect Storm for Black Americans." *Washington Post*, April 26, 2020, https://www.washingtonpost.com/opinions/2020/04/26/we-must-address-social-determinants-affecting-black-community-defeat-covid-19/.

American Psychological Association. "How COVID-19 Impacts People with Disabilities." *APA.org*, https://www.apa.org/topics/covid-19/research-disabilities.

Anderson, Katy. "Have You Experienced Video Conference Anxiety? Here Are 4 Ways to Cope." *Single Care*, August 25, 2020, https://www.singlecare.com/blog/zoom-anxiety/.

Anxiety and Depression Association of America (ADAA). "Facts and Statistics." Accessed October 20, 2020. https://adaa.org/about-adaa/press-room/facts-statistics.

Baker, Sam, and Andrew Witherspoon. "Coronavirus Cases Increase in 17 States." *Axios*, September 17, 2020. https://www.axios.com/coronavirus-map-new-cases-infections-united-states-6aee486c-d136-47c7-a865-052f90426316.html.

Barnes, Sandra. *The Cost of Being Poor: A Comparative Study of Life in Poor Urban Neighborhoods in Gary, Indiana*. New York: State University Press of New York, 2005.

Beckett, Lois. "Armed Protesters Demonstrate against COVID-19 Lockdown at Michigan Capitol." *Guardian*, April 30, 2020. https://www.theguardian.com/us-news/2020/apr/30/michigan-protests-coronavirus-lockdown-armed-capitol.

Billingsley, Andrew. *Climbing Jacob's Ladder: The Enduring Legacy of African-American Families*. New York: A Touchstone Book, 1992.

Binkley, Collin. 2020. "Unimpressed by Online Classes, College Students Seek Refunds." *APNews*, May 3, 2020, https://apnews.com/f18a0a48925a19586e4d810f6e88eff3).

"Black Male Millennial: Unemployment and Mental Health." *American Psychological Association*, August 2018, https://www.apa.org/advocacy/health-disparities/black-male-unemployment.pdf.

Blazer, Deborah. "COVID-19: How Much Protection Do Face Masks Offer?" *NewsNetwork*, May 19, 2020, https://newsnetwork.mayoclinic.org/discussion/covid-19-how-much-protection-do-face-masks-offer/.

Blumer, Herbert. "Race Prejudice as a Sense of Group Position." *Pacific Sociological Review* 1 (1958): 3–7.

Boesler, Matthew and Reade Pickert. "Salaries Get Chopped for Many Americans Who Manage to Keep Jobs." *Bloomberg*, May 27, 2020, https://www.bloomberg.com/news/articles/2020-05-27/salaries-get-chopped-for-many-americans-who-manage-to-keep-jobs.

Brooks, Rodney. "African Americans Struggle with Disproportionate COVID Death Toll." National Geographic, April 24, 2020, https://www.nationalgeographic.com/history/2020/04/coronavirus-disproportionately-impacts-african-americans/.

Brown, Steven. "How COVID-19 Is Affecting Black and Latino Families' Employment and Financial Well-Being." *Urban Institute*, May 6, 2020, https://www.urban.org/urban-wire/how-covid-19-affecting-black-and-latino-families-employment-and-financial-well-being.

CDC. "Coronavirus Disease 2019 (COVID-19)." *Centers for Disease Control and Prevention*. Accessed September 18, 2020. https://covid.cdc.gov/covid-data-tracker/?CDC_AA_refVal=https%3A%2F%2Fwww.cdc.gov%2Fcoronavirus%2F2019-ncov%2Fcases-updates%2Fus-cases-deaths.html#cases_totalcases.

CDC. "Social Distancing." *Centers for Disease Control and Prevention*. Accessed May 27, 2020. https://www.cdc.gov/coronavirus/2019-ncov/prevent-getting-sick/social-distancing.html.

Choo, Hae Yeon, and Myra Marx Ferree. "Practicing Intersectionality in Sociological Research: A Critical Analysis of Inclusions, Interactions, and Institutions in the Study of Inequalities." *Sociological Theory* 28, no. 2(2010): 129–149.

Coaston, Jane. "The Intersectionality Wars." *Vox*, May 28, 2019, https://www.vox.com/the-highlight/2019/5/20/18542843/intersectionality-conservatism-law-race-gender-discrimination.

Collins, Patricia Hill. *Black Sexual Politics: African Americans, Gender, and the New Racism*. New York: Routledge, 2005.

Collins, Patricia Hill. *Black Feminist Thought: Knowledge, Consciousness, and the Politics of Empowerment*. New York: Routledge Classics, 1990.

COVID Tracking Project. 2020. "Racial Data Dashboard." *COVID Tracking Project*. Accessed May 22, 2020. https://covidtracking.com/race/dashboard.

Crenshaw, Kimberlee. "Kimberlé Crenshaw on Intersectionality, More Than Two Decades Later." *News from Columbia Law*, June 8, 2017, https://www.law.columbia.edu/pt-br/news/2017/06/kimberle-crenshaw-intersectionality.

Crenshaw, Kimberlé. "Mapping the Margins: Intersectionality, Identity Politics, and Violence Against Women of Color." In *The Public Nature of Private Violence*, edited by Martha Fineman and Rixanne Mykitiuk, 93–118. New York: Routledge Press, 1994.

Davis, Angela, and Fania Davis. "The Black Family and the Crisis of Capitalism." *The Black Scholar* 17, no. 5 (1986): 33–40.

De La Garza, Alejandro. "'We All Worry About It.' Grocery Workers Fear Confrontations with Shoppers Over Mask Rules." *Time*, May 26, 2020, https://time.com/5841124/grocery-workers-masks/.

Dimock, Michael. "Defining Generations: Where Millennials End and Generation Z Begins." *Pew Research*, January 17, 20119, https://www.pewresearch.org/fact-tank/2019/01/17/where-millennials-end-and-generation-z-begins/.

Dorn, Aaron van, Rebecca E. Cooney, and Miriam L. Sabin. "COVID-19 Exacerbating Inequalities in the US" *Lancet* 395, no. 10232 (2020): 1243–1244.

Ellison, Katherine. "Stress from the Pandemic Can Destroy Relationships with Friends—Even Families." *Washington Post*, October 8, 2020, https://www.washingtonpost.com/health/stress-from-the-pandemic-can-destroy-relationships-with-friends--even-families/2020/08/07/d95216f4-d665-11ea-aff6-220dd3a14741_story.html.

Feagin, Joe. "The Continuing Significance of Race: Anti-Black Discrimination in Public Places." In *Social Stratification: Class, Race, and Gender in Sociological Perspective*, edited by David Grusky, 703–708. Boulder, CO: Westview Press, 2008.

Gilkes, Cheryl Townsend. *If It Wasn't for the Women*. Maryknoll, NY: Orbis Books, 2001.

Gordon, Colin et al. 2020. "COVID-19 and the Color Line." *Boston Review*. Retrieved May 18, 2020 (http://bostonreview.net/race/colin-gordon-walter-johnson-jason-q-purnell-jamala-rogers-covid-19-and-color-line).

Gruenberg, Mark. "Trump's Message to White Supremacists: It's OK to Gun Down Protesters." *People's World*, August 27, 2020, https://peoplesworld.org/article/trumps-message-to-white-supremacists-its-ok-to-gun-down-protesters/.

Hagberd, Eva. "The Pandemic Has Remade Friendships." *Atlantic*, September 22, 2020, https://www.theatlantic.com/family/archive/2020/09/pandemic-improved-friendship/616398/.

Hall, Ethel H. and Gloria C. King. "Working with the Strengths of Black Families." *Child Welfare*, no. LXI (1982): 536–544.

Hardeman, Rachel, Eduardo M. Medina, and Rhea W. Boyd. "Stolen Breaths." *New England Journal of Medicine* (June 10, 2020): 83: 197–199 (doi: 10.1056/NEJMp2021072).

Harris-Perry, Melissa. *Sister Citizen: Shame, Stereotypes, and Black Women in America*. New Haven, Connecticut: Yale University Press, 2013.

Harris-Perry, Melissa. *Barbershops, Bibles, and BET: Everyday Talk and Black Political Thought*. Princeton, NJ: Princeton University Press, 2004.

Haynes, Norrisa, Lisa A. Cooper, and Michelle A. Albert. "At the Heart of the Matter: Unmasking and Addressing COVID-19's Toll on Diverse Populations." *Circulation* (2020). 142: 105–07. https://doi.org/10.1161/circulationaha.120.048126.

Henderson, Loren, Hayward Derrick Horton, and Melvin Thomas. "Linking Higher Black Mortality Rates from COVID-19 to Racism and Racial Inequality." *ASA Footnotes* 48, no. 3 (May/June 2020).

Hill, Robert. *The Strengths of Black Families*. Lanham, Maryland: University Press of America, 2003.

Holcombe, Madeline. "As Coronavirus Surges Across the US, Only 2 States Are Trending in the Right Direction." *CNN*, October 18, 2020, https://www.cnn.com/2020/10/18/health/us-coronavirus-sunday/index.html.

Holpuch, Amanda. "The 'Shecession': Why Economic Crisis Is Affecting Women More Than Men." *The Guardian*, August 4, 2020, https://www.theguardian.com/business/2020/aug/04/shecession-coronavirus-pandemic-economic-fallout-women?CMP=oth_b-aplnews_d-1.

hooks, bell. *Ain't I a Woman: Black Women and Feminism*. New York: Routledge, 2015.

hooks, bell. *Talking Back: Thinking Feminist, Thinking Black*. New York: South End Press, 1999.

Hsieh, Hsiu-Fang, and Sarah E. Shannon. "Three Approaches to Qualitative Content Analysis." *Qualitative Health Research* 15, no. 9 (2005): 1277–1288.

Jarrett, Robin. "Living Poor: Family Life among Single Parent, African-American Women." *Social Problems* 41, no. 1(1994): 30–49.

Johnson, Walter, Jason Q. Purnell, Colin Gordon, and Jamala Rogers "COVID-19 and the Color Line." *Boston Review*, May 1, 2020, http://bostonreview.net/race/colin-gordon-walter-johnson-jason-q-purnell-jamala-rogers-covid-19-and-color-line.

Krippendorf, Klaus. *Content Analysis: An Introduction to its Methodology*. Beverly Hills, CA: Sage Publications, 1980.

Laster Pirtle, Whitney N. "Racial Capitalism: A Fundamental Cause of Novel Coronavirus Pandemic Inequities in the United States." *Health Education & Behavior* 47, no. 4 (2020): 504–8.

Laurencin, Cato T., and Aneesah McClinton. "The COVID-19 Pandemic: A Call to Action to Identify and Address Racial and Ethnic Disparities." *Journal of Racial and Ethnic Health Disparities* 7, no. 3 (2020): 398–402.

Littlejohn-Blake, Sheila M., and Carol Anderson Darling. "Understanding the Strengths of African American Families." *Journal of Black Studies* 23, no. 4 (1993): 460–471.

Lumpkin, Lauren. "Parent Sues George Washington University Over Tuition, Says Online Classes Not as Valuable." *Washington Post*, May 4, 2020. https://www.washingtonpost.com/local/education/parent-sues-george-washington-university-over-tuition-says-online-classes-not-as-valuable/2020/05/04/76a62d1e-8e4a-11ea-a0bc-4e9ad4866d21_story.html.

McDonough, Ian K., Roy Manan, and Punarjit Roychowdhury. 2020. "Exploring the Dynamics of Racial Food Security Gaps in the United States." *Review of Economics of the Household* 18 (2019): 387–412.

McNicholas, Celine, and Margaret Poydock. "Who Are Essential Workers?: A Comprehensive Look at Their Wages, Demographics, and Unionization Rates." *Economic Policy Institute*, May 19, 2020, https://www.epi.org/blog/who-are-essential-workers-a-comprehensive-look-at-their-wages-demographics-and-unionization-rates/.

Mendenhall, Ruby, Phillip J. Bowman, and Libin Zhang. "Single Black Mothers' Role Strain and Adaptation across the Life Course." *Journal of African American Studies* 17, no. 1 (2013): 74–98.

Millimet, Daniel, Ian K. McDonough, and Thomas Fomby. "Financial Capability and Food Security in Extremely Vulnerable Households." *American Journal of Agricultural Economics*, May 25, 2018, https://doi.org/10.1093/ajae/aay029.

Moore, A. "8 Successful and Aspiring Black Communities Destroyed by White Neighbors." *Atlanta Black Star*, December 4, 2013, https://atlantablackstar.com/2013/12/04/8-successful-aspiring-black-communities-destroyed-white-neighbors/.

Moynihan, Patrick D. 1965. *The Negro Family: The Case for National Action*. Washington, DC: Office of Policy Planning and Research, United States Department of Labor, 1965.

Neuendorf, Kimberly A. *The Content Analysis Guidebook*. Thousand Oaks, CA: Sage, 2002.

Pickrell, John. "'Zoom Fatigue' Is Real, and It's Causing a New Kind of Anxiety Amid Coronavirus Isolation." *Nature Index*, May 22, 2020, https://www.natureindex.com/news-blog/zoom-fatigue-stress-anxiety-video-conferencing-researchers-coronavirus-pandemic-covid.

Pilkington, Ed. "'It is Serious and Intense'": White Supremacist Domestic Terror Threat Looms Large in US" *Guardian*, October 19, 2020, https://www.theguardian.com/us-news/2020/oct/19/white-supremacist-domestic-terror-threat-looms-large-in-us?CMP=oth_b-aplnews_d-1.

Pilkington, Ed. "Black Americans Dying of COVID-19 at Three Times the Rate of White People." *Guardian*, May 20, 2020, http://www.theguardian.com/world/2020/may/20/black-americans-death-rate-covid-19-coronavirus.

Poteat, Tonia, Greg Millett, LaRon E. Nelson, and Chris Beyrer. "Understanding COVID-19 Risks and Vulnerabilities among Black Communities in America: The Lethal Force of Syndemics." *Annals of Epidemiology* (2020). https://doi.org/ 10.1016/j.annepidem.2020.05.004.

Rahim, Zamira. "Why Gen Z Will Be Hit the Hardest by the Financial Fallout from Coronavirus." *CNN Business* May 13, 2020, https://www.cnn.com/2020/05/13/business/coronavirus-generation-z-jobs-intl-gbr/index.html.

Raifman, Matthew, and Julia Raifman. "Disparities in the Population at Risk of Severe Illness From COVID-19 by Race/Ethnicity and Income." *American Journal of Preventive Medicine* (2020): 1–3.

Resnick, Brian. "A Third of Americans Report Anxiety or Depression Symptoms During the Pandemic." *Vox*, May 29, 2020, https://www.vox.com/science-and-health/2020/5/29/21274495/pandemic-cdc-mental-health.

Ribar, David C. and Karen Hamrick. 2003. "Dynamics of Poverty and Food Sufficiency." *USDA Economic Research Service U.S. Department of Agriculture.* June 16, 2022, https://www.ers.usda.gov/publications/pub-details/?pubid=46766.

Sarkisian, Natalia, and Naomi Gerstel. 2004. "Kin Support Among Black people and White people: Race and Family Organization." *American Sociological Review* 69, no. 6: 812–837.

Stack, Carol. *All Our Kin: Strategies for Survival in a Black Community.* New York: Harper & Row, 1974.

Staples, Robert. "The Political Economy of Black Family Life." *The Black Scholar* 17, no. 5 (1986): 2–11.

Statista Research Department. "Number of People Shot to Death by the Police in the United States from 2017 to 2020, by Race." *Statista*, October 5, 2020, https://www.statista.com/statistics/585152/people-shot-to-death-by-us-police-by-race/.

Sun, Lena. "CDC Expands Definition of Who is a 'Close Contact' of an Individual with COVID-19." *Washington Post*, October 21, 2020, https://www.washingtonpost.com/health/2020/10/21/coronavirus-close-contact-cdc/.

University College of London. "Friendships and Relationships Worsen During COVID-19 Lockdown." *Medical Xpress*, July 19, 2020, https://medicalxpress.com/news/2020-07-friendships-relationships-worsen-covid-lockdown.html.

Van Dam, Andrew. "Millennials Are the Unluckiest Generation in US History." *Washington Post* (May 27). Retrieved June 2, 2020 (Washingtonpost.com).

Wedell, Katie, Cara Kelly, Camille McManus, and Christine Fernando. "George Floyd Is Not Alone. 'I Can't Breathe' Uttered by Dozens in Fatal Police Holds Across US" *USA Today*, June 13, 2020, https://www.usatoday.com/in-depth/news/investigations/2020/06/13/george-floyd-not-alone-dozens-said-cant-breathe-police-holds/3137373001/.

*Washington Post.* 2020. "Fatal Force." June 16, 2022, https://www.washingtonpost.com/graphics/investigations/police-shootings-database/.

Wells-Barnett, Ida B. *On Lynchings.* Mineola, New York: Dover Books, 2014.

West, Cornell. *Race Matters.* Boston: Beacon Press, 1993.

Western, Bruce and Christopher Wildeman. 2009. "The Black Family and Mass Incarceration."

*The ANNALS of the American Academy of Political and Social Science* 621: 221–42.

Willie, Charles V. "Social Theory and Social Policy Derived from the Black Family Experience." *Journal of Black Studies* 23, no. 4 (1993): 451–459.

Willie, Charles V., and Richard J. Reddick. *A New Look at Black Families*. New York: Rowman and Littlefield Publishers, 2010.

Yin, Robert. *Case Study Research and Applications: Design and Methods* (6th Edition). Thousand Oaks, CA: Sage Publications, 2017.

Yancy, Clyde W. "COVID-19 and African Americans." *JAMA* 323, no. 19 (2020): 1891–1892. https://doi.org/10.1001/jama.2020.6548.

CHAPTER 13

## "SISTER SPACE"
### Clinical Insights from a Black Women's Virtual Support Group During COVID-19

*Haley L. Sparks*

THIS CHAPTER OFFERS AN OVERVIEW of and set of reflections for those conducting virtual support groups for Black women during the COVID-19 global pandemic and moving forward. During this time, Black women are coping with racial, interpersonal, intergenerational, interinstitutional, national, and global factors at once. I present the "Sister Space" virtual therapy program that I developed during the COVID-19 pandemic and hope that this model might offer a lasting blueprint for the care of Black women in a world shaped by ongoing racial injustice and a global pandemic. As a Black woman, a clinician, and a scholar, I offer my insights on how to support Black women in the age of COVID-19 in the midst of the increased visibility of racism and isolation. While the COVID-19 pandemic will eventually be contained, its effects, such as a more remotely connected world, will remain. This chapter offers an avenue to connect Black women in this emerging new world in addition to highlighting the contributions of person-centered, clinically informed psychological research.

The week before this support group started, footage of George Floyd, a Black man in Minneapolis, being murdered by a White policeman circulated the globe. This harrowing injustice, in addition to news of the murders of countless other Black people, such as Breonna Taylor and Ahmaud Arbery, contributed to nationwide protests in summer 2020 against systemic racism and police brutality. As an uprising for racial justice began to build around us, it also began to settle in for many that the effects of COVID-19 were not going away within a matter of weeks, months, or perhaps even years.

An almost immediate impact of COVID-19 was the transition to more remote and virtual options for daily life, including telehealth and teletherapy. As a result of social distancing, isolation also became a pressing concern for many in the age of COVID-19, potentially highlighting the growing need for virtual means of connection and solace such as virtual support groups. In response to various stressors and isolation associated with COVID-19, Black women specifically reported needs for strategies to feel less alone, such as participating in supportive groups of other Black women. While in-person support groups for Black women have been identified as meaningful avenues of support in past years, the age of COVID-19 has highlighted a clear need for more clinically informed research on virtual support groups for Black women as we move forward in a post-COVID-19 and increasingly virtual world.

Virtual support groups have been investigated for caregivers broadly and White individuals, but not yet for Black women specifically. Sister Space was designed to play a key role in Black women feeling more connected and less alone. In response to a virus that is affecting Black families and communities at disproportionate rates, it is crucial to create supportive telecare environments centering their needs. Historically, Black women have identified a variety of contexts in the United States that they do not feel have been created with them in mind (Henry 2017; Jordan-Zachary 2013). During times of COVID-19, it is paramount to investigate factors relating to mental health that are not often associated with Black women (e.g., emotional vulnerability; emotionality) in a context (i.e., a virtual support group) that is both somewhat anonymous and expressly centers them and their care. This study serves as an investigation of how Black women are experiencing the age of COVID-19, their experiences in a virtual support group, and how individuals can effectively facilitate virtual support groups for Black women.

In-person group therapy centering the needs and concerns of Black women has been recommended as a viable and beneficial therapeutic intervention option (Jones and Pritchett-Johnson 2018; Jones and Warner 2011). Support groups are useful in fostering connectedness when Black women may feel alone or isolated, developing women's social networks beyond that of their current environments, enhancing women's understanding of their intersecting identities, and empowering women through mutual sharing that may lead to support of their specific experiences (Short and Williams 2014). While in-person groups have been identified as useful tools for the support of Black women, little research exists investigating remote options for Black women's mental healthcare.

This is a particularly notable gap in social science and clinical literature regarding telecare in relation to COVID-19, as there has been some research indicating that COVID-19 disproportionately affects Black individuals in the United States (Shah, Sachdeva, and Dodiuk-Gad, 2020). Although the true scale of the COVID-19 racial disparity is unknown due to insufficient racial data reporting, Black Americans have been reported to be three times as likely to contract COVID-19 than their White counterparts in some areas of the United States (Yancy 2020). Black Americans are more likely to live in densely populated neighborhoods, limiting social distancing options, have less equitable healthcare access, and have lower rates of COVID-19 testing (Shah, Sachdeva, and Dodiuk-Gad 2020). Additionally, many Black Americans do not have access to privileges such as furlough from work, which might provide necessary reprieve from various life stressors during a global pandemic (Yancy 2020). Consequently, Black people's physical and mental health, families, and communities as a whole are being negatively affected during this time (Shah, Sachdeva, and Dodiuk-Gad 2020; Yancy 2020). Access to telehealthcare without risking continued exposure to COVID-19 outside the home might be particularly beneficial to Black Americans.

In her 2015 theoretical framework, "The Strong Black Woman Collective," Davis found that Black women, particularly within a context of a group of other Black women, may struggle with vulnerability, emotional intimacy, and emotionality as a result of pressures to appear strong. The Strong Black Woman (SBW) schema (Abrams et al. 2014) has been identified as a key aspect of womanhood for many Black women (Nelson, Caremil, and Adeoye 2016). It is characterized by the pervasive beliefs that Black women must assume multiple identities of breadwinners and nurturers, all independently of familial or social support (Abrams et al. 2014). Other aspects of the schema include defending oneself, depending solely on oneself, and caring for others, all while maintaining a strong facade (Watson and Hunter 2016). The SBW schema is directly associated with decreased perceived emotional support and increased psychological distress (Watson-Singleton 2017), and it has been found to increase Black women's susceptibility to depressive symptoms associated with stress (Donovan and West 2015). Internalization of the SBW schema may aptly be associated with decreased well-being, as social support has been found to be associated with well-being, particularly when self-help coping is low among Black women (Linnaberry, Stuhlmacher, and Towler 2014).

In times of COVID-19 and social distancing, the SBW schema might play important roles in the mental health of Black women (e.g., not feeling like they can be vulnerable), feelings of loneliness and isolation (e.g., only depending on oneself), and how Black women attempt to care for and remain strong for their families and other loved ones (Watson and Hunter 2016). In the face of ongoing and hyper-visualized racism in Trump's America and disproportionate loss due to COVID-19, Black women might feel an even more pressing need to be strong. During the age of COVID-19, the SBW schema might be more acute among Black women as they attempt to care for their children at home from school, for loved ones losing jobs, and for their communities ravaged by a pandemic all while appearing strong.

In-person support groups and group therapy have been identified as viable and beneficial therapeutic options for Black women, even amid the influence of the SBW schema (Jones and Pritchett-Johnson 2018). These groups have been found to be useful in fostering connectedness when women may feel alone or isolated as well as developing women's social networks beyond that of their current environments (Jones 2009). In times of COVID-19, Black women may feel particularly isolated and alone due to social distancing measures and increasingly visible systemic racism. In the midst of COVID-19, it might be particularly important for Black women to be able to network beyond their current environments, since they may be completely or partially isolated due to social distancing. Additionally, Black women during this time might be contending with how to support Black men in their lives and larger communities as police brutality becomes more and more visible, how to provide care and at-home learning to children while balancing school and work responsibilities, and how to address glaring issues of diversity, equity, and inclusion in their various institutions (e.g., school departments) as administrations increasingly look to individuals of marginalized groups to provide (often free) DEI consultation.

In response to the evolving COVID-19 pandemic, a multitude of outpatient healthcare practices transitioned to virtual care (Mehrotra et al. 2020). Virtual or online support groups have been identified as spaces that offer a certain anonymity due to lack of in-person contact (Andalibi, Haimson, De Choudhury, and Forte 2016). In these semi-anonymous spaces, group members may feel freer to be open and vulnerable with one another due to a certain level of comfort knowing their identities may remain somewhat unknown (Chung 2013). The anonymity that virtual support groups offer may be particularly beneficial for those who might feel they cannot be vulnerable in in-person groups. Judge, Yarry, Looman, and Bass (2013) identify educational skills, effective communication, remaining active, and recognizing emotions and behaviors as key factors to effective online support group facilitation skills. Although these recommendations were not based on virtual support group work with Black women, specifically, I use these skills, in addition to my own insights from previous groups, in the structuring and facilitation in Sister Space, the group centered in this chapter.

## Background: The Support Group

The sample for this study was nine self-identified Black graduate student women between the ages of twenty-two and thirty-one (mean age, twenty-eight years old). Participants were recruited via word-of-mouth, virtual flyers, and social media in the state of Michigan. This project consisted of an eight-week virtual support group that met on a weekly basis on Google Hangouts. Google Hangouts was chosen because it is HIPAA compliant and served as a confidential means for the group to congregate online. I facilitated this group along with another Black woman co-facilitator. This co-facilitator and I both have our limited licenses in social work and practice individual and group therapy. She and I were familiar with the dynamics of co-facilitating support groups with one another and have a good rapport.

Individuals who reached out during recruitment participated in a fifteen-minute prescreening phone call with me during which the woman was evaluated for her group readiness. For example, at the time of the group screening, it might have appeared that one woman might have benefited from more individualized mental health care rather than being in a group setting. Additionally, as I recruited participants and had a better feel for the group members, I assessed potential group cohesion (e.g., considering if person A, person B, and person C seemed like they would remain respectful of each other's perspectives and take up appropriate amounts of space). During group screenings, I encouraged help-seeking, validated the woman's potential concerns, and addressed any misinformation about therapy or the proposed study as a whole. These prescreening phone calls also served as a way for me to get to know and connect with group members for the first time. This step was crucial in helping group members feel more at ease, having spoken to one of the facilitators before the group sessions began.

This specific support group hosted in summer 2020, entitled "Sister Space," used the "Whole Black Women" (WBW) support group format. Although the group format was originally intended for in-person care, my co-facilitator and I were familiar with the group format and had already seen it successfully translated to an online forum in response to COVID-19 and social distancing measures in the area for a previous group. Although this previous virtual group did not officially provide data for this current project, its group members have informally reported feeling that the WBW support group format is a meaningful source of virtual support during COVID-19, and they hope to continue the group indefinitely.

Sister Space consisted of eight ninety-minute semi-structured, process-oriented group sessions. The general format of the support group each week was check in, theme presentation, interpersonal reflection and response, individual sharing, and check out. Each week, one group member shared a theme of her choosing for the week. For example, one week was "love," and the leading group member asked other members to share what love looked like for them. Group members reflected on the theme and the group processed responses and reflections together. The first group session's format also had an additional group expectations conversation and the naming and description of the SBW schema. The group expectations conversation in a lot of ways introduced members to each other, the facilitators, and the culture of the group. In this conversation, facilitators reminded group members that what was shared in the space would stay in the space (with some legal exceptions). Facilitators additionally shared what they hoped to get out of the group (e.g., a sense of fulfillment after feeling seen by other Black women). Facilitators then invited group members to share what they hoped to get out of the group ("I hope to build up my community of Black women in Michigan for grad school."). Finally, facilitators invited group members to share what they expected or what they did not expect within the space of the group (e.g., Can group members cuss? Do I have to say something specific if I feel like I need to leave my computer for a second? Are we all expected to be sitting upright, not in bed? Can my child sit in on a session with me? Can I be in my pajamas?). This conversation started to help form the culture of the group. Additionally, it provided some insights into considerations for virtual support groups specifically (e.g., dress code; location of group members when they attend group; expectations surrounding lateness).

In the first full group session, I named and defined the SBW schema (i.e., "The Strong Black Woman schema is a set of societal pressures that compels Black women to present an image of strength, suppress their emotions, resist vulnerability, and help others, even at their own expense."). In previous work with Black women in a support group, my colleague and I found that an explicit naming and description of the SBW schema empowered Black women to explore their vulnerability and connect with others in an affirming and validating environment (Jones and Sparks n.d.). Naming and defining the SBW schema may be particularly important in times of COVID-19 and beyond since Black women might feel particularly pressured to be strong for their families and friends in the face of a global pandemic, increasingly visible systemic and violent racism, and physical and emotional isolation due to social distancing.

## Data Collection and Analysis

### Individual Interviews

I administered individual (verbal) pre-, midpoint-t, and post-assessments to better understand participants' experiences with being vulnerable, connecting with others, isolation, and virtual group work. These assessments were thirty-minute individual interviews the week before the support group, after four weeks of group meetings, and the week after the group's conclusion (after all eight weeks). I completed three interviews with each participant. These interviews gave me a better understanding of key issues for participants, in addition to their experience with support groups (i.e., Have you ever participated in a support group before? Was it in person? Virtual? Can you tell me a bit about your experience with it?). These assessments allowed for the investigation of participants' experiences with emotional vulnerability, emotional intimacy, and feedback on the virtual group, specifically group expectations and culture, facilitation decisions, and intragroup dynamics at various points during the Sister Space project. All assessments were administered and recorded in Google Hangouts.

## Group Data Collection

Both visual and audible recordings were necessary during group sessions since indicators of vulnerability or connection might either be audible and/or visual. I needed to both see and hear group members' participation to have a better understanding of being vulnerable (e.g., Is a group member nodding vigorously?), feelings of connection (e.g., a participant snapping in response to a fellow group member's reflection, but her audio is on mute, so I would only be able to see it), and dynamics in virtual groups overall (e.g., group members may often be on mute to limit audible distractions, but they may be indicating support to other group members in visual ways, such as head nods or in the Google Hangouts "chat" function). Group members signed an informed consent form prior to participation agreeing to be filmed, and I solicited participants' verbal consent before recording each session. Group members indicated that my asking for consent to record before each session contributed to their feeling respected and cared for throughout the Sister Space project.

## Facilitation Decisions

Throughout this project, I aimed to develop a set of best practices for facilitators to consider and contemplate group processes. This included self-reflection, debriefing with peers, and consultation with trusted advisers.

Immediately following each session (whether that be group or individual interviews), I wrote progress notes as well as journal entries in a personal assessment log. Progress notes helped me keep track of what happened in that session, how participants were engaging with the theme and each other that day, and how the session progressed overall. As time went along, I had better insight into the participants' personalities, so my notes became more refined and distinct to what I knew about each woman. For example, in one of my progress note entries, I observed that a woman who for the first three sessions of the group was more reserved in her group contributions became much more engaged when we spoke about mental health struggles. When addressing a subject that is often seen as taboo in the Black community (e.g., mental illness; previous suicidality), this particular group member reported feeling validated that other women also struggled with their mental health in the past. This validation allowed her to engage more with her fellow group members about a subject that she previously felt alone with.

A personal assessment log in general allows facilitators to intentionally self-monitor (e.g., what made me sad; what made me frustrated; what made me concerned) since facilitation can erroneously center on group members' experiences only. As I conducted the group work, it became apparent to me that it is a near impossibility to extract the facilitator(s) experience and feelings from the group. Consistent with the caretaking role of the SBW schema, some of the Black women participating in Sister Space were acutely aware of my feelings and wanted to care for them. In an individual interview, one participant noted to me, "I also know that you are a Black woman with her own feelings too. We're all going through it, and I want to hold space for you too." I was asked if I was "okay" countless times. Group members encouraged me to say more about how I was doing in check in and check out. When conducting groups for Black women, Black women facilitators may have trouble distancing themselves from group processes both because they are Black women themselves and because group members might encourage facilitators to participate more in attempts to care for them. In the discussion, I will elaborate on how attempting to be a removed facilitator could have deleterious effects.

After each group session, I would also meet with my co-facilitator to debrief. Having a co-facilitator doing virtual support group work is beneficial for a number of reasons that I will elucidate further in the discussion. As we debriefed, my co-facilitator and I would discuss how the processing of that week's theme went, if any group member(s) seemed "off," if we should follow up with them, and dynamics we picked up on. As I took more of a lead in facilitation, my co-facilitator was able to take more of an observatory role of intragroup dynamics. Subsequently, these sessions allowed for us to share things we observed that the other missed and deliberate on any assumptions or experiences we had. These debriefing sessions were recorded so they might inform my facilitation choices and recommendations moving forward.

Each week of Sister Space, I also had weekly two-hour consultations with a clinical supervisor with over thirty years of clinical experience, including group work with various populations. Clinical supervision has been found to be an important component of therapy in order for clinicians to consider therapeutic approaches and techniques for specific cases, ethical concerns, and cultural competency (Aponte and Ingram 2018). At the time of Sister Space in 2020, I had worked with this supervisor for two years, and we have established an open and dynamic rapport that allows me to present challenging cases and complicated ethical concerns and for her to provide useful suggestions, thoughtful considerations, and forthright feedback (e.g., how I might handle a situation with an upset group member). I found that each of these forms of reflection proved crucial to the further facilitation and implementation of Sister Space in addition to the project as a whole.

## Discussion

While Sister Space was created, implemented, and further refined during the age of COVID-19, my findings and facilitation decisions for this group can serve as recommendations for ongoing infrastructure for the support of Black women moving forward in an increasingly remote world. As I conducted prescreening and pre-group interviews for Sister Space, many participants spoke of wanting "new ways to connect with people [they didn't] see, but hope[d] [were] out there." That is, they were looking for ways to meet and share space with other Black women because those connections felt somewhat sparse in their current social contexts. Although these individual prescreening and pre-group interviews were conducted during the first few weeks of social distancing measures in the United States, Black women were already feeling isolated. That is, COVID-19 did not introduce Black women to feelings of isolation. Black women on various university campuses were not seeing women who looked like them or could seemingly affirm their experiences before the pandemic hit the United States in vast numbers. In one case, a participant specifically reported, "[Feeling isolated] is actually nothing new to me." In this case, the participant was not indicating that her life was continuing in its satisfactory way, but rather this sense of being alone was not foreign to her as a Black woman in graduate school and in this country.

For many around the world, the beginning half of 2020 centered COVID-19 and the resulting feelings of isolation due to social distancing measures. As I interviewed Black women in the United States and reflected on my time as a clinician working with Black women, I understood that conducting a virtual support group during and post-COVID-19 cannot center feelings of isolation from a pandemic. Black women's isolation has stemmed from centuries of exclusion in this country. In fact, some women in Sister Space resented the implication that isolation was new for so many populations in the United States. One participant remarked, "I'm looking around and asking, 'Is this new for you guys? You're just now getting a taste?' This pandemic is just a further reminder." This participant was reminded that other populations might be feeling acute isolation for the first time in the age of COVID-19 while isolation was intricately engrained in her experience as a Black woman, independently of a pandemic. Consequently, facilitation of virtual support groups for Black women during and after COVID-19 needs to acknowledge years of isolation before the pandemic began. Facilitation of this Sister Space group had to validate Black women's feelings of anger as they looked around and once again realized that feelings of isolation were somehow new for many in the United States. In a world where Black women are often not allowed to be angry, it might be particularly important to offer an environment where Black women's anger is not only seen but also accepted and held. As a facilitator, I intentionally held space for Black women's anger, in addition to their notions of isolation being widened and deepened, not significantly emerging for the first time with the burgeoning pandemic.

Additionally, facilitators working with Black women during the age of COVID-19 and beyond must hold space for a variance of experiences between women. While some women might not feel a novelty surrounding isolation in any aspect of their lives, some might be experiencing some new levels of isolation. One participant remarked, "I'm the only Black woman in my department, so being alone in that is nothing new. But it's starting to get to me at home." This woman's roommate decided to move home with her parents during the early months of 2020, and the physical solitude was a new form of isolation for this woman. Just as there can be a variance in experiences with isolation between Black women, there can be a variance in kinds of isolation within one person. In their academic departments, workplaces, and larger university settings, most Black women reported a pervasive loneliness. However, there might be some areas (e.g., home life) where solitude might appear in new ways. It is crucial for facilitators and researchers working with Black women to avoid the assumption and implication that their experiences are the same. Furthermore, it is important to avoid implying that one experience is superior to another. Facilitators must model to group members the value of multiple truths and experiences at one time. The modeling of multiple truths can be done using not just group members' experiences but facilitator experiences as well.

As a Black woman, researcher, and clinician, it may be beneficial to remember that my experiences can be helpful contributions to group work being done with other Black women. In a space where group members expressly sought a place to connect where others may have "an intimate understanding of why I may be doing what I am doing without explanation," I cannot act removed and as if their experiences are simply an enigmatic phenomenon. I cannot act as a distant researcher solely attempting to collect data. I cannot further contribute to Black women feeling misunderstood and isolated in their experiences. One participant plainly demonstrated her frustrations: "I'm just so tired of calmly explaining myself and being looked at like I'm crazy." Both facilitators and researchers hoping to uplift Black women must resist the conventional guideline to remain somewhat distant and detached in their work. We cannot take the "outside looking in" approach to research when working with a population that already feels excluded and misunderstood in this country. Rather, empathy and indicating a level of personal understanding might ground and validate Black women in their various social contexts.

As Sister Space progressed, I increasingly saw the benefits of having multiple Black women facilitators doing this more personalized and immersive work. Some benefits were apparent when I designed this project, including the decision to include the specific co-facilitator that I chose. As previously mentioned, my co-facilitator and I had worked with multiple groups prior to Sister Space. Our rapport and comfort with each other helped to make other group members feel comfortable in the virtual space of the group. We made jokes with one another to ease discomfort and were familiar enough with one another to read each other's body language through our computer screens. Because I was taking more of a lead in the facilitation, my co-facilitator could take notes and more intricately observe nonverbal dynamics as I took more of an active role in engaging with participants verbally. Additionally, my co-facilitator and I have different strengths that we use in conjunction with one another. For example, my co-facilitator was more adept at using the chat function during Sister Space meetings (e.g., typing "Welcome" to a latecomer and explaining the theme to her without disrupting the verbal conversations; noticing when someone wrote a question or included a comment in the chat). While I focused more on verbal cues and gave verbal affirmations, my co-facilitator helped the women who preferred to participate more in the chat feel seen and included.

Some benefits of co-facilitation became more apparent as we (and the pandemic) progressed. A few hours before our third Sister Space session, I learned that a family member of mine had contracted COVID-19. As a Black person in the United States, this experience was certainly not unique to me nor was the pressure to continue on as I felt like my family and the world were being ravaged by the pandemic. I myself was feeling the pressure of the SBW schema to carry on and be strong for my group members. However, at the beginning of that session, I asked my co-facilitator to take the lead for the day. Having a co-facilitator be able to be the more active facilitator as I continued to process COVID-19 reaching my family was immensely valuable. Modeling needing my co-facilitator's help further humanized me as a Black woman facilitator. Additionally, publicly asking for help actively defied the SBW schema and some original notions of what strength had to be.

In response to my admitting to needing help, one group member reflected in her individual midpoint interview, "Being transparent about whatever you're going through. Whatever you're feeling, that is strength. Being able to share with others and get support for that. That is strength." Another participant noted, "I realized, 'You will have those moments where you feel like you cannot get to the top, and those don't make you weak.'" The demonstration of asking for help by a facilitator in a group setting can help Black women further engage their preconceived notions of strength and their previous understanding of what makes a person "weak."

The rejection of the idea of what is "weak" is particularly important in times of COVID-19 and beyond. People around the world have been found to be struggling with psychological and emotional fatigue during the COVID-19 pandemic (Fofana et al. 2020; Morgul et al. 2020). This fatigue leads to burnout and significant decline in mental health and productivity in many areas of life (e.g., work) (Fofana et al. 2020). Consequently, as one participant shared, "[getting] to the top" might be more strenuous than ever. As time progresses, there might be a temptation to expect people's productivity and output to return to that which was before the pandemic, despite the pandemic persisting. One participant lamented in the group, "Now that it's been a few months [with COVID-19], you know, my adviser is giving me deadlines and just expecting me to go back to a normal workday." However, the extended nature of the pandemic, in conjunction with little information on when the pandemic might be contained, might further contribute to burnout. People's output will likely continue to dwindle over time, not rebound simply because an arbitrary amount of time has passed.

Facilitators working with Black women who might be operating with the SBW schema must remind them that it is not "weak" to fall short of a goal, particularly when facing immense stressors during the age of COVID-19. Black women have not failed to be strong simply because they need help in the midst of a global pandemic and hyper-visible racism and police brutality. This reality might be particularly difficult to remember if the co-facilitator(s) is a Black woman who might be informed by the SBW schema herself. As facilitators conducting support groups for Black women during COVID-19, we must redefine and reimagine both strength and weakness to match the innumerable stressors Black women face in our homes, communities, and the world around us.

Throughout building and implementing Sister Space, I designed opportunities for reflection at a number of levels. These levels were on an individual level and an interpersonal level with peers and trusted advisers. These forms of reflection or supervision are crucial to implementing virtual support group work with Black women for a number of reasons. Virtual support group work can be isolating. In many of my individual consultations, participants specifically noticed the potential difference in experiences if the group were in person. One participant noted, "In person, I might be able to stay after the group and give a hug or say 'Hey, I've had that [experience] too; Let's connect.' There's not as much space to connect on a one-on-one level in the virtual space." When feeling isolated, it is crucial for facilitators to have outside feedback in addition to intentional self-reflection. Debriefing and external feedback can help facilitators feel less isolated in their own work during COVID-19 in addition to considering perspectives they might be overlooking. For example, while my co-facilitator and I are both Black women, we come from different backgrounds. During our debriefing following a week where "pleasure" was the theme, my co-facilitator and I realized we had different experiences with the concept, one laden with intergenerational shame and silence and one more notably carefree. Fortuitously, the following week's theme was intergenerational patterns and trauma. With the previous week's debrief in mind, I asked participants if intergenerational patterns and pleasure were connected for them. Similar to my co-facilitator and my discrepancy in understandings of pleasure, group members diverged in their experiences with pleasure and intergenerational patterns. Allowing myself to be informed by debriefing with my peer, in addition to group members, led to a richer discussion than if I had simply relied on my own experiences and conceptualizations.

In clinical environments, the concept known as the "person of the therapist" is integral to working with others. The person of the therapist is a concept that both acknowledges the potential benefit of what the therapist may personally bring to the therapeutic relationship between themselves and the client and requires a facilitator to recognize who they are and what they bring of their personal selves, good and bad, to their therapeutic (i.e., group) work (Aponte and Kissil 2017). This requires that a facilitator work to gain insight into themself and consistently strive to address their biases, assumptions, perceptions, and sensitivities when working with clients. This concept may be useful to researchers in their analyses of qualitative data. The person of the therapist applied in scholarly inquiry requires that researchers remain aware of their potential assumptions and biases and attempt to challenge them in pursuit of a more thorough and accurate understanding of a phenomenon. In Sister Space, I remained actively aware of my own personal contributions and reactions to interactions with participants with my detailed personal assessment journal. In this journal, I recorded my personal feelings, judgments, concerns, biases, assumptions, and reactions to my research with the group (e.g., potential assumptions about women in academic departments different from my own).

In my personal assessment log, I observed a certain level of discomfort coming up for me as Sister Space participants, still consistent with the SBW schema, insisted on caring for me. One participant offered, "I hope you're okay. Conducting research and working with people can be a challenge. I pray that you are okay. I want to hold space for you." As I reflected on my discomfort with participants attempting to hold space for my care, I understood a certain level of identification with the SBW schema within myself. Not only was my discomfort with being cared for in part attached to my internalization of the SBW schema but perhaps my desire to investigate the care of Black women through support groups was also tied to certain aspects of the SBW schema as well. Just as I feel invested in caring for other Black women through my clinical work and research, my participants felt invested in caring for me. However, as the SBW schema includes a drive to care for others, there is often an innate discomfort in allowing oneself to be cared for. In the researcher role, the desire to not allow participants to express concern for my well-being was even stronger. I initially felt a stronger need to hide my need for care from the Sister Space members in my attempts to remain professional and true to my role as a researcher (and a strong Black woman). However, as participants' calls for me to share more in the group and allow myself to be supported became louder, I understood that my distance was affecting the work. In a project that was investigating connections between Black women in a virtual world and attempting to break down some of the limitations of the SBW schema, how could I continue to uphold a level of strong detachment? How could I not share any of my life or any need for care as a Black woman when I was asking the women of Sister Space to do the exact opposite? The investigation of the SBW schema within myself and how it might be hindering my work helped me to redefine how I chose to show up as a facilitator and a researcher. I allowed myself to more fully integrate into the group, sharing more of myself, to contribute to deepened levels of connection, more intimate levels of sharing among group members, and a better understanding of myself.

During a supervision consultation, a trusted adviser noted, "No one group is the same." At the time of this chapter, I had conducted five support groups with Black women, two of them virtually. I have found this observation to be entirely true. While the group members are certainly different, the ongoings and outcomes of groups can be different as well. I can use the same group format and receive entirely different results. As researchers, we view ourselves as experts. Clinicians, however, are taught that they are never the experts, and that they can use the same formula (e.g., the "Whole Black Women" support group format) and observe vastly differing outcomes. With clinical training, we understand that the participant is the expert in their own lives. As a clinical researcher, conducting investigations on support groups, I can use my experiences to recommend resisting the idea of expertise when conducting virtual support groups for Black women. While we can be familiar, well-versed, and even have the experience of the populations or phenomena we are uplifting, as researchers, I suggest we always approach from a place of the student, rather than the teacher. Facilitating support groups for Black women is about engaging curiosity in their experiences and the nuances of their positions, rather than asserting that facilitators and scholars have all the answers. If we allow ourselves to fully immerse our whole beings into the work, in addition to curiously engaging with our participants, we might emerge with richer understandings, more empathetic insights, and more relevant scholarship.

## Conclusion

We as researchers might truly benefit from taking the risk to more fully and personally immerse ourselves in the work. We must take the risk for our participants, our audiences, and ourselves. This risk might result in a more nuanced understanding of participant experiences, in addition to our own experiences as researchers. As we enter into an increasingly remote world, largely due to the COVID-19 pandemic, we must find new ways to connect. Virtual support groups offer a viable avenue of social connection for Black women in a world that already isolated them in many ways. When Black women already often feel misunderstood, it is not enough to simply observe them and report back. We must challenge ourselves as facilitators in these virtual groups to show up as ourselves, not just as someone there to analyze them. COVID-19 is a clear call to challenge ourselves to more fully connect with people, even in the midst of a global pandemic or various societal pressures, such as the SBW schema. As the world will continue to transform due to the COVID-19 global pandemic, so must social science research.

Self-reflective qualitative work and clinical training can allow us an opportunity to deepen research. We can engage with participants in a way that makes them feel more valued, validated, and included, which might be particularly meaningful for Black women during the global COVID-19 crisis and beyond. Approaching qualitative investigations primarily with a level of curiosity, reflexivity, and humility—rather than assumed expertise—might result in lessened isolation for participants and a greater understanding for facilitators. With a group where isolation is "nothing new" and a time when the Black community is facing significant stressors from a number of origins, it is our responsibility to connect with and better serve Black women. While COVID-19 will eventually be contained, the pursuit of more thoughtful research, more informed clinical training, and the upliftment of Black women must continue.

### References

Abrams, Jasmine, Morgan Maxwell, Michell Pope, and Faye Belgrave. "Carrying the World with the Grace Of A Lady and the Grit of A Warrior: Deepening Our Understanding of the 'Strong Black Woman' Schema." *Psychology of Women Quarterly* 38, no. 4 (2014): 503–518.

Andalibi, Nazanin, Oliver Haimson, Munmun De Choudhury, and Andrea Forte. "Understanding Social Media Disclosures of Sexual Abuse Through the Lenses of Support Seeking and Anonymity." In *Proceedings of the 2016 CHI Conference on Human Factors in Computing Systems* 1, no. 1(2016): 3906–3918.

Aponte, Harry and Mary Ingram. (2018). "Person of the Therapist Supervision: Reflections of A Therapist and Supervisor on Empathic-Identification and Differentiation." *Journal of Family Psychotherapy* 29(1): 43–57.

Aponte, Harry and Karne Kissil. "The Person of the Therapist Training Model." In *Encyclopedia of Couple and Family Therapy*, edited by Jay Lebow, Anthony Chambers, and Douglas Beunlin, 1–8. New York City: Springer International Publishing AG, 2017.

Chung, Jae Eun. "Social Interaction in Online Support Groups: Preference for Online Social Interaction Over Offline Social Interaction." *Computers In Human Behavior* 29, no. 4 (2013): 1408–1414.

Davis, Shardé. "The 'Strong Black Woman Collective': A Developing Theoretical Framework for Understanding Collective Communication Practices of Black Women." *Women's Studies in Communication* 38, no. 1 (2015): 20–35.

Donovan, Roxanne and Lindsey West. "Stress and Mental Health: Moderating Role of the Strong Black Woman Stereotype." *Journal of Black Psychology* 41, no. 4 (2015): 384–396.

Fofana, Nina, Faiza Latif, Summaira Sarfraz, Muhammad Bashir, and Bushra Komal. "Fear and Agony of the Pandemic Leading to Stress and Mental Illness: An Emerging Crisis In the Novel Coronavirus (COVID-19) Outbreak." *Psychiatry Research* 291, no. 1 (2020): 113230.

Henry, Millsom. "Ivory Towers and Ebony Women: The Experiences of Black Women in Higher Education." In *Changing the Subject* 1, no. 1 (2017): 42–57. Milton Park, Oxfordshire: Taylor and Francis, 2017.

Jones, Lani. "Claiming Your Connections: A Psychosocial Group Intervention Study of Black College Women." *Social Work Research* 33, no. 1 (2009): 159–171.

Jones, Lani and Lynn Warner. "Evaluating Culturally Responsive Group Work with Black Women." *Research on Social Work Practice* 21, no. 6 (2011): 737–746.

Jones, Martinque and Brandi Pritchett-Johnson. "Invincible Black Women": Group Therapy for Black College Women." *The Journal for Specialists in Group Work* 43, no. 4 (2018): 349–375.

Jordan-Zachery, Julia. "Now You See Me, Now You Don't: My Political Fight Against the Invisibility/Erasure of Black Women in Intersectionality Research." *Politics, Groups, and Identities* 1, no. 1 (2013): 101–109.

Judge, Katherine, Sarah Yarry, Wendy Looman, and David Bass. "Improved Strain and Psychosocial Outcomes for Caregivers of Individuals with Dementia: Findings from Project ANSWERS." *Gerontologist* 53, no. 2 (2013): 280–292.

Linnabery, Eileen, Alice Stuhlmacher, and Annette Towler. "From Whence Cometh Their Strength: Social Support, Coping, and Well-Being of Black Women Professionals." *Cultural Diversity and Ethnic Minority Psychology* 20, no. 4 (2014): 541–549.

Mehrotra, Ateev, Kristin Ray, Diane Brockmeyer, Michael Barnett, and Jessica Anne Bender. "Rapidly Converting to 'Virtual Practices': Outpatient Care in the Era of Covid-19." *NEJM Catalyst Innovations in Care Delivery* 1, no. 2 (2020): 1–5.

Morgul, Ebru, Abdulbari Bener, Muhammed Atak, Salih Akyel, Selman Aktaş, Dinesh Bhugra, Antonio Ventriglio, and Timothy Jordan. "COVID-19 Pandemic and Psychological Fatigue in Turkey." *International Journal of Social Psychiatry* 67, no. 2 (2020): 128–135.

Nelson, Tamara, Esteban Cardemil, and Camille Adeoye. "Rethinking Strength: Black Women's Perceptions of the 'Strong Black Woman' Role." *Psychology of Women Quarterly* 40, no. 4 (2016): 551–563.

Shah, Monica, Muskaan Sachdeva, and Roni Dodiuk-Gad. "COVID-19 and Racial Disparities." *Journal of The American Academy of Dermatology* 83, no. 1 (2020): E35.

Short, Ellen and Wendy Williams. "From the Inside Out: Group Work with Women of Color." *The Journal for Specialists in Group Work* 39, no. 1 (2014): 71–91.

Watson, Natalie and Carla Hunter. "I Had to Be Strong" Tensions in the Strong Black Woman Schema." *Journal of Black Psychology* 42, no. 5 (2016): 424–452.

Watson-Singleton, Natalie. "Strong Black Woman Schema and Psychological Distress: The Mediating Role of Perceived Emotional Support." *Journal of Black Psychology* 43, no. 8 (2017): 778–788.

Yancy, Clyde. "COVID-19 and African Americans." *Jama* 323, no. 19 (2020): 1891–1892.

# CHAPTER 14

# BLACK LIVES MATTER
# #SAYTHEIRNAMES

*Tiffany Grant*

> *Perfect storm: a critical or disastrous situation created by a powerful concurrence of events*
>
> —Merriam-Webster

IN MAY 2020, AS THE WORLD collectively experienced the devastating reality of the COVID-19 pandemic, the world was simultaneously stunned as a video of another case of police brutality emerged in the United States. On May 25, 2020, while arresting George Floyd, an unarmed, forty-six-year-old Black male, for allegedly attempting to pass a counterfeit $20 bill as payment, a White police officer placed his knee on the neck of Mr. Floyd for over eight minutes (Oppel Jr. and Barker 2020). Although Floyd was heard saying "I can't breathe" over twenty times, and officers called for immediate medical assistance for Floyd, the knee remained in place, and none of the officers present gave medical aid. After nearly seven minutes, Floyd became unresponsive and motionless, and even after another officer found no pulse, the knee remained on the neck of George Floyd for more than two more minutes (Hill et al. 2020; Oppel Jr. and Barker 2020). Mr. Floyd was eventually taken by ambulance to a nearby hospital, where he was pronounced dead. His death was ruled a homicide (Hill et al. 2020), sparking worldwide outrage and protests. His murder, while shocking, was not surprising to Black people in the United States, who experience racial inequities and death at the hands of the White majority so often that the Black Lives Matter Foundation was created as a reminder that Black lives are not negligible. The Black Lives Matter Foundation seeks to affirm the humanity, contributions, and standing of Black people in a country that has historically deemed Black people as inferior.

The Black Lives Matter Foundation was founded in 2013 after the arrest, trial, and acquittal of George Zimmerman for the murder of Trayvon Martin, an unarmed Black teenager (Lebron 2017). In the moments immediately before his death, Trayvon was carrying a bag of Skittles and some juice from a recent purchase and was conversing with a friend on his cell phone. Zimmer called a non-emergency police line to report that Martin looked suspicious and was told by the dispatcher not to follow Martin. Zimmerman ignored this advice, and moments later, Martin was dead (Blow 2012). Zimmerman was acquitted under Florida's Stand Your Ground Law, which granted him the right to use lethal force against Martin in self-defense (Alvarez and Buckley 2013). Martin's death resulted in nationwide outrage and gave birth to the Black Lives Matter movement (Lebron 2017). Black Lives Matter desires to inculcate the idea that Black skin is neither inherently a weapon to be feared nor a signal to dehumanize individuals who bear it. The concept that Black people are valued less than their White counterparts dates back more than four hundred years ago when Africans were brought to the United States to work as enslaved people. Although enslaved people were granted freedom over 150 years ago, and laws have been instituted to prevent race-based discrimination, there is multi-institutional pervasive oppression of individuals of color that facilitates the systemic and structural racism that has explicitly and implicitly served to disempower and demoralize them.

Institutional oppression establishes systems that are favorable to a preferred group while simultaneously instituting barriers for members of the non-preferred group. Historically, Black people and individuals of color have been denied similar access to the economic, social, and political power enjoyed by the White majority in the United States. Laws and practices are made accordingly, allowing the oppression to occur in a continuum. Black people have been so adversely affected by these norms that racial disparities have resulted in the inability to achieve equity with White America. Lavalley has put forth that nearly every aspect of American society has been affected by racial identity and racism, and these structures are "imbued in every economic, social, political, scientific, judicial, healthcare, and religious system in the nation" (Lavalley and Johnson 2020). Data from 2013 in the Survey of Consumer Finances revealed that White people's median net worth was $143,000 while the median net worth for Black people was $8,935 (Herring and Henderson 2016). This racial wealth gap ($134,065) more than doubles when the mean net worth for both Black people and White people is taken into account (Herring and Henderson 2016) and a racial wealth gap remains consistent across all income groups except the bottom 20 percent, where the median net worth is effectively $0 (McIntosh et al. 2020).

The racial wealth gap results from decades of racial inequities and a shortage of wealth-accumulation opportunities for people of color. Historically, White people have received favor in lending and ownership, allowing them to purchase homes and establish businesses while simultaneously acquiring wealth. Despite laws that were to protect against discrimination, Black people were systematically denied these same opportunities through redlining, which prevented the acquisition of mortgages, loans, insurance, and other services that would have allowed the opportunity to build wealth (Herring and Henderson 2016; Keister 2000; Kirp et al. 1995; Lipsitz 2006). Consistent with lack of wealth, unemployment and poverty rates among Black people and other people of color are more than double that of White people, and significant disparities exist in educational attainment and health (Singh et al. 2017). Consequently, many people of color live in low-income areas and experience little opportunity for economic advancement, and many of them will continue to remain subject to the social norms that promote inequities based on race.

"Racism has created a set of dynamic, interdependent, components or subsystems that reinforce each other, creating and sustaining reciprocal causality of racial inequities across various sectors of society" (Williams et al. 2019). Racism helps establish social norms that manifest in stereotypes and prejudice toward people of color and enforces the differential treatment they experience throughout multiple systems and institutions (Williams et al. 2019). It can be seen in the justice system through racial profiling and excessive sentencing of Black people compared to White people convicted of similar crimes. According to the *Washington Post* database Fatal Force, Black people and Hispanics are killed at disproportionately higher rates than White people, and Black people are killed at twice the rate of White people (*Washington Post* 2016). These killings occur in all fifty states and primarily involve Black males (*Washington Post* 2016). A 2016 report indicated that Black people are incarcerated at five times that of White people, and in twelve states, Black people constitute more than 50 percent of the prison population (Nellis 2016). This is underscored by the fact that Black people make up only 13 percent of the United States population. These disparities are manifestations of discriminatory practices that are pervasive and affect the everyday lives of Black people in America.

In addition to inequities in the justice and financial systems, Black people and other people of color experience inequities in the healthcare system that can have significant adverse effects on their quality of life and mortality rates. Knowledge of the social determinants of health is important to comprehend how these disparities are established and their influence on individuals and communities. "Social determinants of health are conditions in the social environment in which people are born, live, learn, work, and play that affect a wide range of health, functioning, and quality of life outcomes and risks" (Singh et al. 2017). It has already been stated that Black people experience higher poverty rates and lower educational attainment and live in low-income, disadvantaged neighborhoods. Poverty is correlated with chronic illnesses such as heart disease, diabetes, and obesity, and these illnesses are associated with poorer health outcomes and increased risk of mortality (Noonan et al. 2016; Singh et al. 2017). Chronic exposure to discriminatory acts is a significant driver of stress, which can lead to the same chronic illnesses associated with poverty (Goosby et al. 2018). Additionally, poverty and discrimination result in limited access to adequate housing, and low-income areas often lack access to healthy food and healthcare services, leading to poor eating habits and contributing to the cycle of chronic illness (Singh et al. 2017). This lack of access severely limits the ability to achieve health equity that is on par with White people and enables the health disparities prevalent in communities of color. Black people experience health disparities at alarmingly high rates compared to their White counterparts, and treatment inequities play a critical role in the establishment and retention of these health disparities in the Black population.

Studies have suggested that patients of color receive differential treatment during their interactions with healthcare providers (Miller and Peck 2019; Mitchell and Perry 2020; Peck and Denney 2012; Ross et al. 2012), and this treatment was often correlated with poorer health outcomes. The 2018 National Healthcare Quality and Disparities Report indicated that Black people, Native Americans, Alaskan Natives, and Hawaiian and Pacific Islanders received worse care in 40 percent of the quality measures that were assessed in the study (Health and Services 2019), and Hispanic people received worse care in 35 percent of the quality measures assessed (Health and Services 2019). A systematic review evaluating implicit racial/ethnic bias among healthcare professionals found that thirteen of the fifteen studies concluded that healthcare professionals were more likely to associate Black people with negative words than White people (Hall et al. 2015). This same study found that implicit bias was significantly correlated with patient-provider interactions, treatment decisions, and health outcomes (Hall et al. 2015). Patients of color are more likely to experience microaggressions during interactions with their physician (Miller and Peck 2019), causing damage to the relationship between patient and provider and contributing to health disparities (Blair et al. 2013). One study found that primary care clinicians showed "substantial implicit bias" against both Latinos and African Americans (Blair et al. 2013), and others have shown that this bias is often associated with the clinician communicating with a harsher tone and allowing less time for patient questions (Cooper et al. 2012). When their symptoms are overlooked and perspectives discredited, Black patients attribute this to discrimination (Cuevas et al. 2016). Taken together with decreased access to healthcare, differential access to quality health care contributes to poorer health and health outcomes in people of color. Thus, it is not surprising that health disparities are more frequently observed in communities of color, and this is only underscored by the fact that people of color are disproportionately burdened by higher rates of morbidity and premature mortality as well (Frieden et al. 2019). Consequently, Black people have a lower life expectancy, and there are marked racial/ethnic and socioeconomic disparities in overall mortality and mortality from leading causes of death (Singh et al. 2017).

## Enter COVID-19

The outbreak of the COVID-19 that occurred in Wuhan, China, in 2019 rapidly made its way across the globe in 2020. The first documented case of COVID-19 in the United States occurred in Washington State in January 2020 (Holshue et al. 2020). At the time of this writing (January 2021), the United States now reports over twenty-five million cases of the virus, which has led to an unprecedented 421,000 COVID-19 deaths (Smith et al. 2020). Horton has posited that COVID-19 is not a pandemic but rather a "syndemic," where "two categories of disease are interacting with specific populations" (Horton 2020). The combination of COVID-19 and an array of non-communicable diseases cluster on a background of social and economic disparity exacerbates the adverse effects of each separate disease (Horton 2020), creating a synergistic epidemic. These non-communicable diseases include asthma, diabetes, and hypertension, which disproportionately affect Black people and other people of color, lead to more severe disease, and increase the mortality rates of affected individuals (Worland 2020). Racial inequities in education, employment, financial status, and housing have direct implications for this impact. Lower socioeconomic status is associated with discriminatory practices and directly impacts health status (Yaya et al. 2020). Poor individuals are more likely to have low health literacy, preventing them from understanding basic health information and making them more vulnerable (McNeely et al. 2020). The legacy of discrimination faced by Black people has placed many in low-income neighborhoods that are often replete with pollution and lack nutritious food options, facilitating the development of diseases like asthma and diabetes and contributing to obesity (Worland 2020). Black people and people of color are also more prone to occupational exposure to COVID-19 as they are often employed at jobs where they are deemed essential workers and are likely to take public transportation to these jobs (McNeely et al. 2020; Shamus 2020). The health disparities induced by racial inequities in concert with COVID-19 have synergistically increased deaths in Black communities at rates that neither could accomplish alone and that are disproportionately higher than any other ethnicity.

No one is immune to COVID-19, as it does not discriminate based on race. "And yet, from the very beginning of the pandemic, the virus has exposed and targeted all of the disparities that come along with being Black in America" (Peck 2020). From the beginning, COVID-19 has infected and killed Black people at alarmingly high rates. In states like Illinois, Black people constituted 37 percent and 45 percent of confirmed cases and deaths, respectively, but are only 16 percent of the state population (Yaya et al. 2020). Similar trends can be found in other states, and overall, 30 percent of COVID-19 infections occur in Black people, who only comprise 13 percent of the United States population (Thakur et al. 2020; Yaya et al. 2020).

Health disparities plaguing communities of color contribute to these high rates, as does healthcare workers' implicit bias. Despite having apparent symptoms of COVID-19, Black people have routinely been denied testing and/or treatment for COVID-19 and have been forced to die at home (Eligon 2020; Grubbs 2020; Mitropoulos and Moseley 2020; Peck 2020; Shamus 2020; Yaya et al. 2020). In many of these cases, multiple members of the same family have died within days to weeks of each other (Peck 2020; Shamus 2020). For example, nine-year-old Kimora Lynum presented with a 103-degree temperature, but was sent home without being tested (Grubbs 2020). Kimora was her mother's only child, and at the time of her death, the youngest to die from COVID-19 in Florida. Twenty-three-year-old Deshaun Taylor died after being diagnosed with COVID-19 and pneumonia. Despite being diabetic and therefore at high risk for severe disease, he was sent home twice rather than admitted for treatment (Grubbs 2020). The implicit bias of healthcare workers against Black people has a direct impact on the death rates that Black people are experiencing from COVID-19. Similar to the knee of a police officer on the neck of George Floyd, Vanessa Grubbs has described the actions of the healthcare system in response to Black people with COVID-19 as a "chokehold to Black people" that directly contributes to the demise of Black people at disproportionate rates (Grubbs 2020).

## Chris's Story

Christopher (Chris) Joffrion was born in Louisiana on June 17, 1977, the third child of four and the second son of his African American parents. I was the fourth child, the second daughter, and Chris's baby sister by seventeen months. On my last birthday, I officially became older than my older brother. At forty-two-years old, Chris took his last breath in this world on April 6, 2020. His cause of death: COVID-19.

We grew up together in our stable middle-class family, and both of our parents worked to provide a home and affirm each of us in their way. In junior high and high school, Chris was on the debate team. He was a prolific talker and a master debater who had the trophies and awards to prove it. His ability to converse with anyone regarding most anything was one of his most endearing qualities throughout his life. Chris went to college, and though he finished much of his degree work, he left before meeting his degree's full requirements. However, during this time, he met Pamela (Pam) Johnson, the woman he would eventually marry and spend the rest of his life with. They married on January 1, 2005.

During their life together, Pam and Chris worked hard to establish a comfortable living for themselves and eventually their son, Gabriel (Gabe) was born in June 2006. Pam described Chris as her "friend and comforter." She said that he treated her like a queen and was teaching Gabe to be a prince. Chris was known for his frequent Facebook posts indicating that he was having dinner "with his beloved family." Chis enjoyed cooking with Gabe and would often share images of the food they had prepared together. He understood the importance of his presence in his son's life and made it no secret to Gabe that his father loved him. Birthdays and holidays were significant events in their home, and each person was made to feel special on these very days. Chris was a huge fan of the New Orleans Saints and the Chicago Cubs, and one of his most cherished gifts was a Cubs jersey gifted to him by Pam. Together Chris, Pam, and Gabe were an independent unit, filled with love, joy, and hope for their future.

Chris had a larger-than-life personality, and a laugh that some might say was funnier than any joke you may have ever heard. His laugh, smile, jovial personality, and his remarkable ability to find humor in most things were some of the things that most remember him for. Chris's figure loomed large. He was tall. He was also obese. To those that knew him, they knew him as amiable. To strangers, however, his presence was undoubtedly intimidating. As his size grew, along with the increase came the medical conditions associated with it. Over the years, one by one, he was also diagnosed with hypertension, obstructive sleep apnea, and diabetes. He also had asthma. These conditions were well-controlled with medication, dietary changes, and nightly use of a continuous positive airway pressure machine. Chris and Pam had recently purchased new vehicles for themselves and were making plans to move out of their apartment into their first home as a family during the summer of 2021. COVID-19 had more sinister plans for Chris and those of us who loved him.

Chris worked from home, and therefore as COVID-19 stay-at-home orders were issued for his home state of Louisiana, he was unaffected. Pam recalls that he started feeling cold-like symptoms on Monday, March 30, 2020, and she urged Chris to call his doctor to report his symptoms. Chris reached his doctor's office and spoke to a nurse who encouraged him to take over-the-counter cold medicine and stay home. There was no concern since, at that point, he had not run a fever. By Thursday, he had developed a prominent cough and congestion. At that point, Chris went to a Quick Care Urgent Care Center, which is associated with a major healthcare network in their area. It was there that Chris was tested for strep throat, the flu, and COVID-19. The strep throat and flu tests came back negative. However, he was told that he had pneumonia and possibly COVID-19. He was sent home with antibiotics, a breathing treatment, and cough medicine. Despite having diabetes, asthma, and hypertension, which were positively correlated with more severe disease in patients with COVID-19, there was no recommendation for a hospital admission. The results of the COVID-19 test that he took would take up to five days. Despite his symptoms, diagnosis of pneumonia, and health history, there was no urgency for him to receive a rapid COVID-19 test or for him to be admitted to the hospital. We are well aware that either a hospital admission or a rapid test may have altered the care he received from that point forward. With no other recourse, Chris went back home, where he quarantined alone inside the bedroom he shared with Pam and immediately started taking the medications he had been prescribed.

During this time, Pam noted that he was sleeping a lot and barely eating. An avid water drinker, he was barely ingesting fluids. When he was awake, Chris would speak to Gabe through the door, while other times, they would text and play games over the phone. Pam spent much of those days at the door doing her best to provide what was needed. She urged Chris to go back to the doctor, but he insisted that nothing would be done until the test came back. She learned this to be the case, as she called his doctor several times. Each time, she only spoke to a nurse, who simply recommended that he continue to stay home and take the medications as prescribed. It was also during this time that Chris began running low-grade fevers. During the evening of April 3, our older sister reached out to Chris because he had been uncharacteristically quiet, absent from our family chats and from their personal chats. The two of them corresponded through text messages. She asked him if he was sick, and he responded, "I'll tell y'all when I know. Just keep praying." His response was alarming, and then she asked him outright if he had the virus. Again, he responded that he was not sure and did not want to say anything until he knew with certainty. After she pressed him more, he said, "I have pneumonia, and they suspect I have coronavirus." Knowing then that Chris's chronic health issues put him at high risk for more severe COVID-19, she was admittedly afraid for his life. However, Chris did not want our parents or his siblings (which included me and our oldest brother) to know what he was facing until he was confident of the diagnosis. He wanted to spare us the worry, but he had no way of knowing that in less than seventy-two hours, he would be gone.

Our sister shared with me screenshots of the messages that she and Chris had shared. Realizing that news reports indicated how rapidly the virus progressed, I felt that our parents *needed* to know. So, in the early morning hours of April 4, I called our parents and told them. Our parents spoke to Chris that afternoon, and our mother was encouraged because "he sounded like himself." I texted him Saturday evening to inquire how he was feeling, and he replied that he was okay, but tired. I bombarded him with questions, as is my usual. I encouraged him to stay hydrated. However, he indicated that his appetite had been suppressed, and he was tired. It is an odd thing to sense the extreme fatigue he was experiencing even through text, but I did. I imagined that he was struggling to keep up the conversation, so I asked him if I could call him the next day (Sunday) to hear his voice. His reply to me was: "It's fine, Tiffany." We never spoke on Sunday. I never heard his voice again, and those were the last words my brother ever said to me. My last words to him were: "Take care, Chris," and on Sunday, "Just saying hi and I love you." While I am encouraged that these were my last words to him, I have no idea if he ever saw them.

On Monday, April 6, Pam said that he got up feeling somewhat normal and was laughing and joking with Gabe. By lunchtime, Pam described him as being "foggy," and she attributed this to low blood sugar. She attempted to check it, but was unable to get a reading. She gave him some orange juice, and he seemed better. However, he declined rapidly later that afternoon, exhibiting a complete lack of lucidity along with periods of confusion. As she spoke to him, he told her to be quiet because he was "with a customer." She said he was looking around her as if she was blocking some imaginary screen he was using to assist the customer. Extremely distressed by this change in behavior, Pam knew he needed immediate medical attention. She called her sister, who lived just a couple of minutes away, and asked her to pick up Gabe. She then called 911. She asked them to do a health check on her husband, who had been tested for COVID-19 and awaiting results. She told them that he had diabetes, high blood pressure, and was acting confused. They arrived just as her sister was departing with Gabe.

She said the EMTs arrived dressed in hazmat suits. They tried to get a blood sugar reading, but similar to Pam; they were unable to get a reading. However, when they assessed his oxygen saturation, Pam indicated that they were overcome with a sense of urgency. The EMTs helped him up, and he walked down their hallway in what Pam described as an "unsteady bounce." When he made it to the end of the hall, he fell. The EMTs got him on a stretcher, and Pam followed in time to see his eyes roll back and his arms go limp. Pam said her entire body went numb from the image. Pam noted that the ambulance remained in place for a while with Chris inside before pulling off. This made that feeling worse. Pam went back inside, made the necessary phone calls to family, and then called the hospital. She was told that he coded on the way to the hospital and that she needed to get to the hospital. To this day, Pam is triggered by flashing lights and sirens and has no memory of her trip to the hospital.

When she got to the hospital, she was expecting to be taken back to see him, but instead was sent to another room. Pam recognized the room as the same room where she was told of the death of another family member, and in an instant, she knew what the news would be. The doctor came in and said to her that Chris had died before making it to the hospital. Yet, in the time between his arrival to the hospital and Pam's arrival there, they had already tested Chris for COVID-19 using a rapid test. The same test that they refused to give him on Thursday when it could have made a difference in the outcome. The rapid test was positive. Chris was dead, and nothing at all could reverse the outcome. They preferred to use a rapid test postmortem to place a cause of death on a death certificate, but when he was alive, and medical intervention could have saved his life, one was refused. Chris died on Monday, April 6, 2020, and the results of the test that he had taken the previous Thursday came back on April 9. The same nurse who insisted that Chris should not return for another assessment but that he should continue to stay home and take the medications as prescribed relayed the news to Pam. Our family will never know if Chris had advocated heavily for hospital admission when he went in on Thursday if he would still be here. Unfortunately, that decision was left solely in the hands of the medical professionals who had seemingly dismissed his suffering as inconsequential. What is painfully clear is that Chris did not have a fighting chance at home without any kind of medical intervention. On April 6, 2020, the map of my family was irreparably altered, and our hearts were irrevocably broken.

Our family is grateful that Chris spent his last moments surrounded by love and not in a hospital alone or with a stranger. It is somewhat of a consolation among a litany of complaints and "what ifs" that we will have to contend with. Pam was given only three days to plan his funeral. Chris had a life insurance policy that provided the financial means for his funeral and that has continued to provide for his family since his death. Knowing that Chris was not one to enjoy dressing up in a suit and tie, Pam decided to bury him in his beloved, never worn, Cubs jersey.

## The Aftermath and Conclusions

COVID-19 unleashed a storm that has ravaged the country and decimated communities of color across the United States. Implicit and explicit biases targeted against people of color have placed them at a severe disadvantage in the fight against COVID-19. The staggering death rate of people of color from COVID-19 has magnified the vulnerability caused by the health disparities that plague people of color and that are perpetuated by the biases of the structural systems that make up the foundation of the United States. In the wake of these deaths, families are left devastated by physical and economic losses. Many families undoubtedly have lost sources of income that have plunged them into a financial hole that will be difficult to overcome. For the poor, many social determinants of health are expected to worsen due to COVID-19 and its aftermath (Shah et al. 2020). Many of these, like employment, housing, food, education, and healthcare, are already significant issues for the poor.

While very personal to me and the rest of our family, Chris's story is not unique. It is a story that has been repeated many times over in Black families across the United States. It is a very painful reminder of the injustices people of color have faced for centuries in this country and will continue to face if allowed to continue. People of color are disproportionately harmed by mass incarceration, police brutality, poverty, and clinician bias against them. Ample evidence exists to establish the relationship between race, racism, and health status. Black people and people of color disproportionately succumb to premature death due to health disparities and access to quality healthcare. George Floyd's death in the backdrop of COVID-19 has raised significant awareness of these inequities. Consequently, the American Medical Association, the American Academy of Pediatrics, and the American College of Emergency Physicians have all declared racism a public health crisis, as did several states (Grubbs 2020). However, health equity cannot be achieved until we have achieved racial equity, and in this regard, the United States has miles to go.

The very harsh reality in terms of COVID-19 outcomes is that the greatest comorbidity for infected individuals is a darker skin tone. As the number of COVID-19 deaths continues to climb, so too does the grief and impact of these lives lost. In the case of systemic racism, there are many victims, and every victim of a crime deserves to be called by name. Just as we are encouraged to say the names of Trayvon Martin, George Floyd, Ahmaud Arbery, Breonna Taylor, and the many others who died because of racial biases against Black people, so too should we be encouraged to remember and honor the many thousands of lives lost to COVID-19 for the same reasons. For each number, there is a name. For each name, there was a family who loved them. Each of their lives mattered, and it should be criminal to think otherwise. Racial equity should demand it.

## References

Alvarez, Lizette, and Cara Buckley. "Zimmerman Is Acquitted in Trayvon Martin Killing." *New York Times*, July 13, 2013.

Blair, Irene V., Havranek, Edward P., Price, David W., Hanratty, Rebecca, Fairclough, Diane L., Farley, Tillman., Hirsh, Holen. K., and Steiner, John. F. (2013). "Assessment of Biases Against Latinos and African Americans Among Primary Care Providers and Community Members." *American Journal of Public Health* 103, no. 1 (2013): 92–98. https://doi.org/10.2105/ajph.2012.300812.

Blair, Irene V., Steiner, John F., Fairclough, Diane L., Hanratty, Rebecca., Price, David W., Hirsh, Holen K., Wright, Leslie A., Bronsert, Michael, Karimkhani, Elhum, and Magid, David. J., and Havranek, Edward P. (2013). Clinicians' Implicit Ethnic/Racial Bias and Perceptions of Care Among Black and Latino Patients. *The Annals of Family Medicine* 11, no. 1: 43–52.

Blow, Charles. "The Curious Case of Trayvon Martin." *The New York Times*, March 16, 2012.

Cooper, Lisa A., Roter, Debra L., Carson, Kathryn A., Beach, Mary Catherine, Sabin, Janice A., Greenwald, Anthony G., and Inui, Thomas S. "The Associations of Clinicians' Implicit Attitudes About Race with Medical Visit Communication and Patient Ratings of Interpersonal Care." *American Journal of Public Health* 102, no. 5 (2012): 979–987.

Cuevas, Adolfo G., O'Brien, Kerth, and Saha, Somnath. "African American Experiences in Healthcare: 'I Always Feel Like I'm Getting Skipped Over.'" *Health Psychology* 35, no. 9 (2016): 987.

Eligon, John "Black Doctor Dies of COVID-19 After Complaining of Racist Treatment." *New York Times*, December 23, 2020.

Frieden, Thomas, Jaffe, Harold W., Moolenaar, Ronald L., Leahy, Maureen A., Martinroe, Julia, C, and Spriggs, Stephen R. (2019). "Centers for Disease Control and Prevention. Health Disparities and Inequalities Report—United States, 2013." MMWR 2013;62 (Suppl 3).

Goosby, Bridget J., Cheadle, Jacob E., and Mitchell, Colter "Stress-Related Biosocial Mechanisms of Discrimination and African American Health Inequities." *Annual Review of Sociology* 44 (2018): 319–340.

Grubbs, Vanessa. "The Health Care System Has the Black Community in a Choke Hold." *CHCF* (blog) *California Healthcare Foundation*, August 4, 2020, http://www.chcf.org/blog/health-care-system-has-black-community-choke-hold/.

Hall, William J., Chapman, Mimi V., Lee, Kent M., Merino, Yesenia M., Thomas, Tainayah W., Payne, B. K., Eng, Eugenia, Day, Steven H., and Coyne-Beasley, Tamera "Implicit Racial/Ethnic Bias Among Health Care Professionals and Its Influence on Health Care Outcomes: A Systematic Review." *American Journal of Public Health* 105, no. 12 (2015): E60–E76.

Department of Health and Human Services. "2018 National Healthcare Quality and Disparities Report." https://www.ahrq.gov/research/findings/nhqrdr/nhqdr18/index.html.

Herring, Cedric, and Henderson, Loren "Wealth Inequality in Black and White: Cultural and Structural Sources of the Racial Wealth Gap." *Race and Social Problems* 8, no. 1 (2016): 4–17.

Hill, Evan, Ainara Tiefenthäler, Christiaan Triebert, Drew Jordan, Haley Willis, and Robin Stein. "How George Floyd was killed in police custody." *New York Times*. May 31, 2020.

Holshue, Michelle L., Debolt, Chas, Lindquist, Scott, Lofy, Kathy. H., Wiesman, John, Bruce, Hollianne, Spitters, Christopher., Ericson, Keith, Wilkerson, Sara, Tural, Ahmet, Diaz, George, and Cohn, Amanda. "First Case of 2019 Novel Coronavirus in the United States." *New England Journal of Medicine* 382. (2020) 929–936.

Horton, Richard "Offline: COVID-19 Is Not a Pandemic." *Lancet* 396, no. 10255(2020): 874.

Keister, Lisa A. "Race and Wealth Inequality: The Impact of Racial Differences in Asset Ownership on the Distribution of Household Wealth." *Social Science Research* 29, no.4 (2000): 477–502.

Kirp, David L., Dwyer, John P., and Rosenthal, Larry A. *Our Town: Race, Housing, and the Soul of Suburbia*. New Brunswick, NJ: Rutgers University Press, 1995.

Lavalley, Ryan, and Johnson, Khalilah R. (2020). "Occupation, Injustice, and Anti-Black Racism in the United States of America." *Journal of Occupational Science*, 1–13.

Lebron, Christopher J. *The Making of Black Lives Matter: A Brief History of An Idea*. Oxford: Oxford University Press, 2017.

Lipsitz, George. *The Possessive Investment in Whiteness: How White People Profit from Identity Politics*. Philadelphia: Temple University Press, 2006.

McIntosh, Kristen, Moss, Emily, Nunn, Ryan, and Shambaugh, Jay "Examining the Black-White Wealth Gap." Washington, DC: Brooking Institute, 2020.

McNeely, Connie L., Schintler, Laurie. A., and Stabile, Bonnie. (2020). "Social Determinants and COVID-19 Disparities: Differential Pandemic Effects and Dynamics." *World Medical and Health Policy* 12, no. 3: 206–217.

Miller, Leslie R., and Peck, B. M. "A Prospective Examination of Racial Microaggressions in the Medical Encounter." *Journal of Racial and Ethnic Health Disparities* 7, no. 3 (2019): 519–527.

Mitchell, Jamie A., and Perry, Ramona. "Disparities in Patient-Centered Communication for Black and Latino Men in the US: Cross-Sectional Results from the 2010 Health and Retirement Study." *Plos One* 15, no. 9 (2020): E0238356.

Mitropoulos, Arielle, and Moseley, Mariya "Beloved Brooklyn Teacher, 30, Dies of Coronavirus After She Was Twice Denied A COVID-19 Test." *ABC News*, April 28, 2020. https://abcnews.go.com/Health/beloved-brooklyn-teacher-30-dies-coronavirus-denied-covid/story?id=70376445.

Nellis, Ashley. *The Color of Justice: Racial and Ethnic Disparity in State Prisons*. Washington, DC: Sentencing Project, 2016.

Noonan, Allan S., Velasco-Mondragon, Hector E., and Wagner, Fernando A. (2016). "Improving the Health of African Americans in the USA: An Overdue Opportunity for Social Justice." *Public Health Reviews* 37, no. 1 (2016): 1–20.

Oppel Jr., Richard A., and Barker, Kim "New Transcripts Detail Last Moments for George Floyd." *New York Times*, July 8, 2020, https://www.nytimes.com/2020/07/08/us/george-floyd-body-camera-transcripts.html.

Peck, B. M., and Denney, Meridith. "Disparities in the Conduct of the Medical Encounter: The Effects of Physician and Patient Race and Gender." *Sage Open* 2, no. 3 (2012). https://doi.org/10.1177%2F2158244012459193.

Peck, Patrice. "The Virus Is Showing Black People What They Knew All Along." *Atlantic*, December 22, 2020, https://www.theatlantic.com/health/archive/2020/12/pandemic-black-death-toll-racism/617460/.

Ross, Paula T., Lypson, Monica L., and Kumagai, Arno K. "Using Illness Narratives to Explore African American Perspectives of Racial Discrimination in Health Care." *Journal of Black Studies* 43, no. 5 (2012): 520–544.

Shah, Gulzar H., Shankar, Padmini, Schwind, Jessica S., and Sittaramane, Vinoth "The Detrimental Impact of the COVID-19 Crisis on Health Equity and Social Determinants of Health." *Journal of Public Health Management and Practice* 26, no. 4 (2020): 317–319.

Shamus, Kristen. J. "Family Ravaged by Coronavirus Begged for Tests, Hospital Care but Was Repeatedly Denied." *USA Today*. April 20, 2020. https://www.freep.com/story/news/local/michigan/wayne/2020/04/19/coronavirus-racial-disparity-denied-tests-hospitalization/2981800001/.

Singh, Gopal K., Daus, Gem P., Allender, Michelle, Ramey, Christine T., Martin, Elijah K., Perry, Chrisp, De Los Reyes, Andrew A., and Vedamuthu, Ivy P. "Social Determinants of Health in the United States: Addressing Major Health Inequality Trends for the Nation, 1935–2016." *International Journal of MCH and AIDS* 6, no. 2 (2017): 139.

Smith, M., Yourish, K., Almukhtar, S., Collins, K., Ivory, D., and Mccann, A. "Coronavirus in the US: Latest Map and Case Count." *New York Times*. January 2021.

Thakur, Neeta, Lovinsky-Desir, Stephanie, Bime, Christian, Wisnivesky, Juan P., and Celedón, Juan C. "The Structural and Social Determinants of the Racial/Ethnic Disparities in the US COVID-19 Pandemic. What's Our Role?" *American Journal of Respiratory and Critical Care Medicine* 202, no. 7(2020): 943–949.

*Washington Post*. (2016). "Fatal Force." *Washington Post*. https://www.washingtonpost.com/graphics/investigations/police-shootings-database/.

Williams, David R., Lawrence, Jourdyn A., and Davis, Brigette A. "Racism and Health: Evidence and Needed Research." *Annual Review of Public Health* 40 (2019): 105–125.

Worland, Justin. (2020). "America's Long Overdue Awakening to Systemic Racism." June 11, 2020 *Time*. https://time.com/5851855/systemic-racism-america/.

Yaya, Sanni, Yeboah, Helena, Charles, Carlo H., Otu, Akaninyene, and Labonte, Ronald (2020). "Ethnic and Racial Disparities in COVID-19-Related Deaths: Counting the Trees, Hiding the Forest." *BMJ Global Health* 5, no. 6: E002913.

CHAPTER 15

## CONCLUSION: THE PATH FORWARD

*Loren Henderson*

*Melvin Thomas*

*Hayward Derrick Horton*

THIS VOLUME EXAMINES HOW IMPACTFUL, unequal, and far-reaching the COVID-19 pandemic is. It reveals the various ways systemic racism, and the inequality it perpetuates, provides the material and ideological context that shaped the differences in exposure and vulnerability to the deadly virus. It has also shown the disparate experience of economic hardship caused by the lockdowns and layoffs. COVID-19 deepened and exposed long-standing racial, class, and gender disparities in health, education, housing, employment, and wealth. From the founding of the United States until now, African American, Latino, Native American, and Asian people have not been given the same opportunities and rewards given to those of European descent. On every measure of material well-being, there are large disparities between White people and people of color. White people have higher median incomes, education, lower unemployment, higher status occupations, lower poverty rates, better housing, greater wealth, longer life expectancies, and lower mortality rates than African Americans, Latinos, and Native Americans. The racial disparities in COVID-19 infections and deaths are linked to these racial inequalities. Racial and ethnic groups in the United States find themselves in different socioeconomic conditions that influence their vulnerability to COVID-19.

Several chapters in this collection demonstrate how central public policies are to sustaining or dismantling barriers that provide protection from contracting COVID-19. They argue that those who benefit from

White supremacy are committed to maintaining their perceived duly earned privileges, despite the innumerable cost to those in vulnerable populations or more ironically to themselves. The authors in this collection show how racist and classist policies not only harm those at the margins but also those in the highest rungs of society. For example, many political leaders pushed for discriminatory and illogical policies and practices in healthcare (e.g., refusing to require masks, firing or silencing public health workers) during the pandemic. And in spite of their outright denial or intentional downplaying of the seriousness of COVID-19, former President Trump and high-ranking officials were either hospitalized or lost their lives to COVID-19. These instances of exposure and loss of life seemed to do little to move the intractable ideologies held by these leaders who continued to fight against social justice policies on every hand.

The authors in this volume provide clear examples of the ways in which systemic racism operates at the state, institutional, and individual levels and converge to create the predictable racial and ethnic disparities we continue to observe under the COVID-19 pandemic. For example, they show how racist responses in data collection practices have created an underreporting of cases and death by race. This clear omission of race-based data collection was only rectified by public demands from those researchers, scholars, journalists, and social justice activists who knew full well that these omissions were rooted in a history of medical mistreatment and exclusion of racial minorities (Washington 2006). Scholars knew to shine the spotlight on existing inequalities that would grow from the pressures of the pandemic. Scholars, knowing what to look for (e.g., racist practices in healthcare, housing, and employment) as the COVID-19 pandemic unfolded, forced the world to reckon with the continued systemic racism plaguing Black people and other minorities in America. White supremacy, systemic gendered racism, and class inequalities helped to generate multifaceted, interlocking, group-based conflicts that appear to be insurmountable social problems. We understand how these structures operate to create the many inequalities we see under the COVID-19 pandemic.

It is important here to emphasize what racism is and how it affects all of us. Racism is an organized social system in a society. It affects all of our institutions and organizations including federal and state governments and our criminal justice, educational, economic, and health care systems. The result is that all our institutions routinely provide material advantages for White people and material disadvantages for African Americans, Latinos, and Native Americans. Systemic racism exists when power and resources are routinely unequally distributed to the benefit of one racial group and to the detriment of other racial groups, resulting in a racially stratified society.

Racist ideologies rationalize and justify the position of White people at the top of the hierarchy and non-White people beneath them. Ideological racism is a defense of White privilege and power according to Wellman (1993). It is "culturally sanctioned beliefs, which, regardless of intentions involved, defend the advantages White people have because of the subordinated position of racial minorities" (Wellman 1993, 4). The racist ideology that defends White power and privilege may be traditional (e.g., the idea that Blacks are genetically inferior) or new forms of White supremacy that emphasizes the cultural superiority of White people (e.g., Black people just need to work harder). These views have been referred to as symbolic racism, laissez-faire racism, or cultural racism. These new forms are often not recognized as racism, but ideologically, they work the same way as the traditional forms. They provide an explanation for why White people are at the top of the racial hierarchy and why they should be there. Individual prejudice and racial hatred are serious problems for people of color. However, the racial hierarchy can continue without those as long there are pervasive and culturally accepted beliefs that justify it. As Wellman (1993, 4) states, "It is necessary to broaden the definition of racism beyond prejudice to include sentiments that in their consequence, if not in their intent, support the racial status quo." Kwame Ture and Charles Hamilton (1992) introduced the term "institutional racism" to account for both attitudes and practices that led to racist outcomes through unquestioned bureaucratic procedures. They treated individual and institutional racism as comparable to the distinction between overt and covert racism. While individual racism could be seen and heard, institutional racism was a more subtle process that could not be reduced to the acts of individuals. They made it clear that White people collectively benefit from the process, even if individual White people did not wish to discriminate.

## So, Where Do We Go from Here?

At this point, we want to provide both hope and strategies for those who are interested in real social change that alleviates suffering and puts us on a path forward to ending systemic racism, which is the root cause of the racial disparities in the impact of COVID-19. In fact, because racial disparities in COVID-19 infections and deaths clearly map along with other racial disparities in such things as income, wealth, poverty, etc., we can expect future pandemics and traumas to follow the same pattern. Social crises always hit disadvantaged racial and ethnic groups much harder. For example, although the Great Recession created economic hardships for millions in the United States, its impact varied dramatically by race. Between 2005 and 2009, White people lost 16 percent of their net worth. During that same period, African Americans lost more than half of their net worth (53 percent) and Latinos lost two-thirds of their net worth (66 percent). African Americans and Latinos experienced much greater job losses and foreclosures also (Pew Research Center, Social and Demographic Trends 2011). Therefore, effective solutions must address inequalities in all social institutions, and not just those that are healthcare-related.

We must remove all institutional policies and practices that reinforce the racial hierarchy. Discriminatory practices in employment, housing, education, and business investments, for example, must be stopped and replaced with practices that create opportunities for those who had previously been locked out. African American communities historically have been impoverished and White communities have been enriched by discriminatory federal policies such as redlining and FHA lending policies as well as discriminatory real estate practices such as restrictive covenants, blockbusting, and a lack of capital investments in minority communities and schools. Although these policies and practices are illegal today, their impact continues to shape our urban environments and make African American and Latino communities more vulnerable to future pandemics and social crises. Reversing this situation will require a massive redirecting of public and private resources that will create economic development leading to job-, educational-, and wealth-creating opportunities.

There are several changes to our healthcare system that could make a significant impact. The most obvious one is universal health care. Unlike most other Western industrialized nations, health care in the United States is an expensive commodity that only those who have the financial means can purchase. Even those with health insurance often struggle with deductibles, co-pays, doctor's fees, and other charges. African Americans and Latinos are less likely to be able to afford quality health care than White people. Universal health care would remove the financial obstacles to quality health care and thereby make minority and other disadvantaged communities be able to deal with COVID-19 and future pandemics.

Another important change could significantly improve the health care delivery in African American and Latino communities—increasing the number of African Americans and Latinos in the medical fields, especially as doctors. This could potentially help with the hesitancy some have in dealing with the medical profession. It could also help reduce the unequal treatment minorities receive in hospitals and doctor's offices.

## What Can We Do as Individuals?: Be an Antiracist

As Angela Davis stated: "In a racist society, it is not enough to be non-racist. We must be anti-racist." According to Anneliese Singh, "the term 'antiracist' refers to people who are actively seeking not only to raise their consciousness about race and racism but also to take action when they see racial power inequities in everyday life." Being a non-racist is not enough to be an effective agent of social change (Kendi 2019). In fact, in the context of a racist society, being a non-racist is effectively a "passive racist" as Beverly Tatum's (2015) analogy illustrates:

> I sometimes visualize the ongoing cycle of racism as a moving walkway at the airport. Active racist behavior is equivalent to walking fast on the conveyor belt. The person engaged in active racist behavior has identified with the ideology of White supremacy and is moving with it. Passive racist behavior is equivalent to standing still on the walkway. No overt effort is being made, but the conveyor belt moves the bystanders along to the

> same destination as those who are actively walking. Some of the bystanders may feel the motion of the conveyor belt, see the active racists ahead of them, and choose to turn around, unwilling to go in the same destination as the White supremacists. But unless they are walking actively in the opposite direction at a speed faster than the conveyor belt—unless they are actively antiracist—they will find themselves carried along with the others. (21)

Although the problems associated with systemic racism seem insurmountable and institutions change slowly, we all can commit to being antiracists. This means we reject the ideologies that rationalize and justify racial inequality and challenge the racial inequities we see around us every day. We may not individually be able to change the world, but we certainly can work to change the part of the world we currently occupy.

## References

Braithwaite, Ronald L., Sandra E. Taylor, and Henrie M. Treadwell, Eds. *Health Issues in The Black Community*. New York: John Wiley & Sons, 2009.

Kendi, Ibram X. *How to Be an Antiracist*. New York: One World, 2019.

Pew Research Center, Social and Demographic Trends. *Wealth Gaps Rise to Record Highs Between Whites, Blacks, Hispanics.* Tuesday, July 26, 2011.

Tatum, Beverly. "What Is Racism Anyway?" Understanding the Basics of Racism and Prejudice. In *Getting Real About Race: Hoodies, Mascots, Model Minorities, and Other Conversations*, edited by Stephanie M. McClure, and Cherise A. Harris, 15–24. Los Angeles: Sage Publications, 2015.

Ture, Kwame, and Charles V. Hamilton. *Black Power: The Politics of Liberation in America*. New York: Vintage, 1992.

Washington, Harriet. *Medical Apartheid: The Dark History of Medical Experimentation on Black Americans from Colonial Times to the Present*. New York: Doubleday Books, 2006.

Wellman, David. *Portraits of White Racism*. Berkeley: University of California Press, 1993.

# EPILOGUE

## THE PANDEMIC CONTINUES

AS THE COVID-19 PANDEMIC BEGAN to ravage the United States, the coauthors of this volume grew deeply concerned about the impact of COVID-19 on communities of color and those who we felt were most likely to bear the brunt of the worst impacts of the pandemic. This edited volume will apply to several audiences, including social theorists, public policymakers, health professionals, and graduate students, so we'll explain why we choose to include an epilogue. The epilogue will address some unanswered questions that some readers may have after reading this book. The epilogue will discuss why we felt the need to push for the rapid call of papers for this volume in June 2020. It will also seek to address two lingering questions that you as readers may have such as: (1) why are the chapters in this volume providing inconsistent data and news accounts on the topic of COVID-19? and (2) where is the discussion about vaccines?

To address these questions, we will situate how difficult it was for sociologists during the first few months of the pandemic to document the rapid pace of transmission of the virus and the multilayered consequences from March 2020 to September 2020. In this epilogue, we will address how rapidly the science about COVID-19 and the reported cases of COVID-19 were changing during the call for chapters in this volume (June 2020–September 2020). In addition, we seek to update some key developments that have occurred after the submissions for publication of the chapters included in this volume.

We note that our intellectual intuition during the first few months of the pandemic prompted us to reach out to leading scholars to gather academic theorizing and publicly available data on this novel virus. Our years of training as sociologists allowed us to wade through and see past the collective public fear, paralysis, and bewilderment that COVID-19 was causing in March 2020 to chart a path forward based on the wisdom described in Harriet Washington's book *Medical Apartheid*: "A Nigerian proverb . . . 'Don't let the lion tell the giraffe's story'" (2006, 8). This African proverb is a key principle of Black sociology that warns us to recognize what history has already taught us: if we don't document the story (our story), the narrative will be shaped by others who may not care to tell our story in ways that reflect our lived experiences. More importantly, we sought to provide a scholarly treatment of the early days during the COVID-19 pandemic affecting the United States to enshrine within the historical record for the expressed purposes of allowing scholars and laypersons alike to use this book as a historical reference to understand the rapidly evolving nature of the COVID-19 pandemic.

In March 2020, SARS-CoV-2, a virus that most people had never heard of, became all anyone was talking about. Given its transmissibility and morbidity rates, the virus warranted its newfound public health attention (Effenberger 2020). Initially, public health officials and politicians were often inconsistent and generally all over the place with their recommendations and descriptions of the virus. As we now know, on February 10, 2020, there was a downplaying of the seriousness of SARS-CoV-2 to the American people by the federal government. The former president Donald Trump told the American public, "Looks like by April, you know in theory when it gets a little warmer, it miraculously goes away."

On February 7, 2020, the former President Trump had told Bob Woodward in a private interview that he had been informed by his advisers that, "It's also more deadly than even your strenuous flu . . . . This is deadly stuff." On March 19, he went on to tell Woodward, "I wanted to always play it down. . . . I still like playing it down, because I don't want to create a panic" (Gregorian 2020). Although this deliberate deception impacted the entire United States population, it did not affect all Americans equally. Americans with lower levels of education and who were supporters of the President were more likely to believe the virus was a hoax (Ugarte, Cumberland, Flores, and Young 2021); in addition, they were also more likely to ignore mask mandates, one of the most effective tools against transmission. In conjunction with inconsistent scientific reports and disinformation about the virus, the lies spread by former President Trump resulted in tens of thousands of Americans making deadly choices concerning social distancing and masking and ultimately being exposed to the deadly virus. Given that the scientific community knew that the virus could stay suspended in the air in droplets for hours, that individuals could be asymptomatic for days, and that wearing N95 masks was a viable way to prevent the transmission of the virus, it seemed nonsensical that President Trump would vow not to require universal masking, link not wearing a mask to personal freedom (BBC 2020a), and go directly against the suggestions of the WHO to require universal masking in public places (BBC 2020b.)

In April 2020, the American Sociological Association called for articles by leading scholars on COVID-19 (Henderson et al 2020). In that issue, we published "Sociologists Link Higher Black Mortality Rates from COVID-19 to Racism and Racial Inequality." As scholars studying racial and gender health inequity, we began pouring through the literature looking for clues about the virus, how likely it was to spread, and more importantly, how to help those in minority communities who historically have been the most likely to suffer the most deleterious consequences of any pandemic. It rapidly became evident that the racial data on COVID-19 cases and mortality were scattered or not reported at all federal, state, or local levels. We began following the data on the CDC website, the Johns Hopkins Resource Center website, local state health departments, and in the news. It was a rapidly changing and highly inefficient way to collect, analyze, and compare racial disparities on COVID-19. At this point, social justice activists, public health officials, journalists, researchers, and congresspersons began demanding race-based data collection on cases and mortality related to COVID-19. We understood the role of systemic racism in maintaining inequality, and we were skeptical that the absence of racial data was an innocent omission. There had been a call to examine and reduce health disparities in the United States since January 2000, when the Department of Health and Human Services launched Healthy People 2010, a comprehensive, nationwide health promotion and disease prevention agenda. This plan set the stage for examining the social determinants of health that lead to inequality. Following the call in Healthy People 2010 to work toward reducing health inequality, we began to track the rising COVID-19 cases and mortality rates. We were increasingly troubled by the lack of data on people of color. In addition, we were concerned with racial and gender health inequality. Along with other scholar-activists, we began to call for the transparent and intentional tracking of racial and ethnic data collection at the state and federal levels.

From December 2019 through the time the chapters were submitted to this volume, the scientific and political data on COVID-19 were rapidly evolving. Nevertheless, we felt it was essential to put forth the best theory and research on race and the COVID-19 pandemic.

Throughout this book, the chapter authors present a disturbing picture of racial and gender disparities in COVID-19. They demonstrate how minorities already precariously situated within the social hierarchy came to experience some of the most devastating consequences from the beginning of the pandemic. As the daily rates of COVID-19 rose and fell from one state to another, as the virus moved across America, the chapter authors courageously constructed their chapters. It's critical that the readers of this volume note that the federal government was nefariously slow in tracking racial COVID-19 data. Scholars, journalists, and public health officials used the best data they could collect and analyze based on existing local and state-level data.

The lack of a centralized federal database, combined with the rapid transmission of the virus, made reporting consistent COVID-19 data nearly impossible. Despite the lack of reliable and consistent national data, many scholars turned to state-level data and the Johns Hopkins Pandemic Coronavirus Research Center dashboard to track daily cases, mortality, and testing. The Pandemic Coronavirus Research Center was developed as a rapid response "with a three-part mission: to spotlight systemic deficiencies in the collecting and reporting of pandemic data; to examine how those challenges hinder COVID-19 responses; and to explore possible solutions to improve public data" (Porterfield 2022).

It cannot be overstated how disheartening it was for scholars, and public health officials alike, to need such a center. The distrust and disappointment created by the federal response to the pandemic under the Trump administration were enormous. As our chapter authors worked tirelessly in the face of the real mortal threat known as COVID-19, their ability to report COVID-19 data was nothing short of herculean. Their chapters in this volume serve as a historical testament to the rapidly changing science and data on COVID-19.

## The COVID-19 Pandemic Since the Completion of These Chapters

An impressive scientific-technological feat was achieved during the writing of the final chapters submitted for this volume. Scientists, such as Kizzmekia Corbett, an African American woman viral immunologist at NIH, led a team to develop a coronavirus vaccine. Once scientists had released the genetic sequence of SARS-CoV-2, the race to create a vaccine commenced (Soh et al. 2021). The FDA approved three mRNA vaccines that effectively promoted an immune response to the virus: BNT162b2 by BioNTech/Pfizer, mRNA-1273 by Moderna, and the JNJ-78436735 by Janssen Pharmaceuticals Companies of Johnson & Johnson (Soh et al. 2021; CDC 2022). Although the mRNA vaccines for COVID-19 appeared by many to have been developed at lightning speed, the reality is the technology that made them mRNA COVID-19 vaccines had been in the works for decades.

With the development of these vaccines, hope was brought to the world. There was a general belief that the scientific community had beaten the virus and that we had finally turned a corner on the pandemic. Unfortunately, the rollout of the vaccine was relatively slow and chaotic in the US and nearly non-existent for those in developing countries. The development of the mRNA COVID-19 vaccines had undergone some of the highest scientific scrutiny of any vaccine ever created because of the global access to the data, governmental financial support, and collaboration of those in the medical and manufacturing community (Australian Department of Health 2022). Despite the extreme security and support from the FDA through emergency use, many Americans remained skeptical that the vaccines were efficacious and expressed extreme vaccine hesitancy. Vaccine hesitancy has been particularly acute for African Americans, who are less likely to be vaccinated than other racial/ethnic groups (Willis 2021). This hesitancy is understandable because of the legacy of the Tuskegee experiments and racism in healthcare that has given African Americans reason to be cautious. However, there is evidence that this may be changing. Pandamsee et al. (2022) found vaccine hesitancy declining among African Americans. They conclude:

> Using seven waves of nationally representative panel data collected between December 2020 and June 2021, this study found rapid reductions in COVID-19 vaccine hesitancy among Black individuals in the US. Although Black and White individuals entered the period of vaccine availability with a comparable willingness to get vaccinated, Black individuals overcame their hesitancy more quickly. A key factor associated with this pattern seems to be that Black individuals more rapidly came to believe that vaccines were necessary to protect themselves and their communities. (9)

This suggests that continuing the lower vaccination rates of African Americans may be due to factors other than vaccine hesitancy. Some of those factors may be the same ones that have resulted in the higher rates of hospitalizations and deaths from COVID-19 for African Americans discussed in the chapters of this volume. This is an important area for future research.

As the CDC and President Biden encouraged Americans to take the vaccine, the positivity rate for the delta variant, which was the dominant strain in the United States when the vaccines became available, was starting to decline. Those who were fully vaccinated were less likely to suffer severe disease or mortality than those who were not. By October 2021, we had some of the lowest positivity rates, hospitalizations, and mortality since early in the pandemic. Many Americans expressed feeling like life was going back to normal (i.e., traveling freely, eating in restaurants, attending public events, and children going to school in person). Unfortunately, a new, more transmissible variant (omicron) that could significantly evade the vaccine's immune response emerged on the global scene in November 2021 and quickly became the dominant variant in the United States and globally. The rapidly mutating coronavirus continues to bring new challenges to the worldwide community to contain and eradicate the virus (Soh et al. 2021).

## Where We Are Today

Although the omicron variant seemed to produce typically less severe symptoms than the delta variants, its greater transmissibility had resulted in significant hospitalizations and deaths. Even though the current vaccines are effective against it, this is true—the vaccine dramatically reduces severe outcomes. As of this writing, we are still grappling with some of the worst COVID-19 case counts since the beginning of the pandemic. This situation is fueled by a significant number of people who still refuse the vaccines when they are readily available and those in more impoverished countries who have no or limited access to the vaccines. Unfortunately, because so many are unable or unwilling to take the vaccines, the virus will continue to spread, making the emergence of new variants likely. This means that COVID-19 is an ongoing pandemic that will not go away anytime soon.

## References

Australian Department of Health. "Is It True? Were COVID-19 Vaccines Developed Too Quickly to Be Safe?" Accessed on January 29th, 2022. https://www.health.gov.au/initiatives-and-programs/covid-19-vaccines/is-it-true/is-it-true-were-covid-19-vaccines-developed-too-quickly-to-be-safe.

BBC. "Coronavirus: WHO Advises to Wear Masks in Public Areas," June 6, 2020a, https://www.bbc.com/news/health-52945210.

BBC. "Coronavirus: Donald Trump Vows Not to Order Americans to Wear Masks," July 18, 2020b, https://www.bbc.com/news/world-us-canada-53453468.

Centers for Disease Control and Prevention. "Different COVID-19 Vaccines." Accessed January 27, 2022. https://www.cdc.gov/coronavirus/2019-ncov/vaccines/different-vaccines.html#print.

Effenberger, Maria, Andreas Kronbichler, Jae Il Shin, Gert Mayer, Herbert Tilg, and Paul Perco. "Association of the COVID-19 Pandemic with Internet Search Volumes: A Google Trends Analysis." *International Journal of Infectious Diseases* 95 (2020): 192–197.

Gregorian, Dareh. The Washington Post. "Trump told Bob Woodward he knew in February that COVID-19 was 'deadly stuff' but wanted to 'play it down.'" https://www.nbcnews.com/politics/donald-trump/trump-told-bob-woodward-he-knew-february-covid-19-was-n1239658.

Henderson, Loren, Melvin Thomas, Hayward Derrick Horton. 2020. Linking Higher Black Mortality Rates from COVID-19 to Racism and Racial Inequality. ASAFootnotes. pg. 31.

Padamsee, Tasleem J., Robert M. Bond, Graham N. Dixon, Shelly R. Hovick, Kilhoe Na, Erik C. Nisbet, Duane T. Wegener, and R. Kelly Garrett 2021. "Changes in COVID-19 Vaccine Hesitancy Among Black and White Individuals In the US." *JAMA Netw Open* 5, no. 1. (2022): e2144470. https://doi.org/10.1001/jamanetworkopen.2021.44470.

Porterfield, Joshua E. "Johns Hopkins Coronavirus Resource Center," January 20, 2022, https://coronavirus.jhu.edu/pandemic-data-initiative/expert-insight/q-and-a-two-years-and-many-pandemic-data-challenges-later.

Soh, Sandrine M., Yeongjun Kim, Chanwoo Kim, Ui Soon Jang, and Hye-Ra Lee. "The Rapid Adaptation of Sars-Cov-2–Rise of the Variants: Transmission and Resistance." *Journal of Microbiology* 59, no. 9 (2021): 807–818.

Ugarte, Dominic A., Cumberland William G., Flores, Linda, and Young. Sean D. "Public Attitudes About COVID-19 in Response to President Trump's Social Media Posts." *JAMA Netw Open* 4, no. 2 (2021): e210101. https://doi.org/10.1001/jamanetworkopen.2021.0101.

Washington, Harriet. *Medical Apartheid: The Dark History of Medical Experimentation on Black Americans from Colonial Times to the Present.* New York: Doubleday, 2006.

Willis, De, Andersen, Ja, Bryant-Moore, K, et al. "COVID-19 Vaccine Hesitancy: Race/Ethnicity, Trust, and Fear." *Clin Transl Sci* 14 (2021): 2200–2207. https://doi.org/10.1111/cts.13077.

Zou, Huachun, Yuelong Shu, and Tiejian Feng. "How Shenzhen, China Avoided Widespread Community Transmission: A Potential Model for Successful Prevention and Control of Covid-19." *Infectious Diseases of Poverty* 9, no. 1 (2020): 1–4.

# CONTRIBUTOR BIOGRAPHIES

**Sandra L. Barnes**, PhD is the C.V. Starr Professor of Sociology and administrative Chair in the Dept. of Sociology at Brown University. Her articles have been published in numerous journals, including *Social Forces*, *Social Problems*, *Journal for the Scientific Study of Religion*, and *Journal of African American Studies*.

**Eduardo Bonilla-Silva,** PhD is the James B. Duke Distinguished Professor of Sociology at Duke University. He is known for his work on racial theory, color-blind racism, race and methodology, and race and emotions, and for his book *Racism Without Racists*.

At the time of the writing, **Matthew Boykin** was a graduate student at Boston University's School of Public Health working as a research assistant with Dr. Michael Siegel. He is currently working as a Biostatistician in North Carolina.

**Letisha Engracia Cardoso Brown**, PhD is an Assistant Professor in the Department of Sociology at the University of Cincinnati. She is a Black feminist scholar whose work primarily focuses on the lived experiences of Black women and girls in sports, media, and education.

**David L. Brunsma**, PhD is a Professor of Sociology in the Department of Sociology at Virginia Tech. He is a founding and former co-editor of *Sociology of Race and Ethnicity* and currently a founding co-editor of the book series of the same name with University of Georgia Press. He lives and loves in Blacksburg, VA.

**Arthur Cayce** is currently incarcerated within the Michigan Department of Corrections, where he ministers and is a mentor for those with mental health diagnoses. He is from Detroit, Michigan and holds a Bachelor's Degree from Calvin University.

**Isabella Critchfield-Jain** is an undergraduate at Boston University (Class of 2022) studying neuroscience and public health.

**Alana Dass** received a BS in Biology from Cornell University in 2020. Currently, Alana is pursuing a Masters of Public Health at New York University. Her areas of interest include policymaking to address systemic and institutional health inequities.

**David G. Embrick**, PhD is an Associate Professor with a joint position in Africana Studies and Sociology at the University of Connecticut, and is the Director of the Sustainable Global Cities Initiative at UConn Hartford.

**Anita F. Fernander**, PhD is the inaugural Chief Officer for Justice, Equity, Diversity & Inclusion and Professor and Interim Chair of the Department of Population Health and Social Sciences in the C.E. Schmidt College of Medicine, Florida Atlantic University.

**Dr. Britany J. Gatewood** is a Visiting Assistant Professor at George Washington University and she earned her PhD in Sociology from Howard University. Her research focuses on social movements within carceral institutions and the political practices of Black women and their children.

**Tiffany J. Grant**, PhD is Assistant Director for Research and Informatics and Co-leader of the University of Cincinnati Libraries Research & Data Services Unit. Her research interests include infectious diseases, microbiology, and the intersection of health disparities and health/racial equity.

**Inaash Islam**, PhD is an Assistant Professor of Sociology at Saint Michael's College. Her research interests include race, racism, Islamophobia, identity, and social media. Her current work examines how global Muslim racialization shapes western Muslim and non-Muslim perceptions of Muslim women.

**Joong Won Kim**, PhD is an instructional faculty member in the Department of Sociology at the University of Tennessee, Knoxville. His work can be found in academic peer-reviewed journals such as *Ethnic and Racial Studies, American Behavioral Scientist, and Sociological Inquiry*.

## CONTRIBUTOR BIOGRAPHIES

**Lori Latrice Martin**, PhD is Associate Dean in the College of Humanities and Social Sciences and Professor in the Department of African & African American Studies at Louisiana State University.

**Dr. Steve McGlamery**, an Illinois native, is an experienced college instructor and currently an Instructor of Sociology at the University of Tennessee, Knoxville. His areas of focus include racism, inequality, religion and qualitative methods. His dissertation is on Southern Baptists and race from 1970–1999.

**Jan-Martijn Meij**, PhD is an Assistant Professor of Sociology at Florida Gulf Coast University. His work focuses on social inequality and he is a co-editor for the book *Music Sociology: Examining the Role of Music in Social Life* (Routledge 2013).

**Yanesia Norris** is a graduate of Spelman College, where she majored in Political Science and Philosophy, and Howard University where she obtained her Master's in Sociology with a concentration in social inequality.

**Diane L. Odeh**, MPA is a Public Affairs and Policy doctoral student at Portland State University. Her research employs a critical theory lens on the governance of marginalized communities and their experience with policy and community engagement processes.

**Alicia Owens** is an undergraduate student at Georgetown University. Alicia worked on three research papers with Dr. Michael Siegel during her time at Natick High School. She is now planning to study cognitive science at the Georgetown College of Arts and Sciences.

**Ebony Russ**, PhD is a postdoctoral fellow at Harvard University and a Professor of Sociology at George Washington University. Russ's research interests include African American health disparities, cardiovascular diseases, race, juvenile justice, criminology, mental health education attainment, and mixed methodological research.

**Michael Siegel**, PhD is a Visiting Professor in the Department of Community Health Sciences at the Tufts University School of Medicine. His current research focuses on the relationship between structural racism and racial health inequities.

# CONTRIBUTOR BIOGRAPHIES

**Haley Lillian Sparks**, PhD, LLMSW is a psychologist, therapist, and lifelong learner. She currently serves as the director of Equity, Diversity and Inclusion in the External Affairs division at UCLA. Her work centers recognizing and uplifting the humanity of others.

**Johnny Eric Williams**, PhD is a professor in Sociology at Trinity College in Hartford, Connecticut. His research is in the area of science, systemic white racism, politics, and culture.

**Lovoria B. Williams**, PhD, APRN-BC, FAAN is an Associate Professor at the University of Kentucky and the Associate Director for Cancer Health Equity at the Markey Cancer Center, where she holds the endowed Research Professorship in Cancer Health Equity.

# ABOUT THE EDITORS

**Melvin E. Thomas**, PhD is an Associate Professor in the Department of Sociology and Anthropology at North Carolina State University. He earned a PhD in Sociology from Virginia Polytechnic Institute and State University and is a former president of the Association of Black Sociologists (ABS). His research focuses on racial and social class inequalities and how both impact the lives of minorities in the US. He has published extensively, including multiple articles in the top journals in sociology such as, the *American Sociological Review, American Journal of Sociology, Social Problems, Sociology of Race and Ethnicity, Sociological Quarterly, Sociological Inquiry, Sociological Forum, Sociological Spectrum*, and *City and Community*. He has recently co-edited *Color-Struck: How Race and Complexion Matter in the Color-Blind Era*. Professor Thomas has served on the ABS Executive and Publication committees. He is currently co-editor of ABS's journal, *Issues in Race and Society*.

**Loren Henderson**, PhD is an Associate Professor in the Department of Sociology, Anthropology, and Public Health at the University of Maryland Baltimore County. She takes a social psychological approach to researching issues in American higher education, with an interest in how the presence of others affects educational outcomes such as achievement, motivation, and social development. Her research examines the formation and evolution of the social networks of international students who attend US colleges and universities. She also researches how computer-mediated communication affects academic work and workplaces.

**Hayward Derrick Horton**, PhD is Professor of Sociology at the State University of New York at Albany's School of Public Health. He holds a PhD from the Pennsylvania State University and is a former president of the

## ABOUT THE EDITORS

Association of Black Sociologists (ABS). Professor Horton specializes, and has published extensively in, the areas of race and ethnicity, demography, entrepreneurship, and economic/community development. He introduced the first sociological model of Black community development—the Black Organizational Autonomy (BOA) Model. He also introduced a new paradigm into the field of demography—Critical Demography. He is the co-editor of ABS's journal, *Issues in Race and Society*, and has co-authored and co-edited several books including his latest two books, *Color-Struck: How Race and Complexion Matter in the Color-Blind Era* and *Race, Population Studies, and America's Public Schools*.

# Index

*Race, Ethnicity and the Covid-19 Pandemic*
Melvin E. Thomas, Loren M. Henderson, and Hayward Derrick Horton, eds.
*(pages in italics refer to tables; n refers to footnote)*

**A**
abstract liberalism, 45, 47, 52
Adams, Jerome, 55–56, 143
Affordable Care Act (ACA) (2020), 217, 220
Africa
   first case of coronavirus in, 4
   as testing ground for potential vaccine, 61
African Americans. *see* Blacks
age
   adjusted death rates, by race and ethnicity, U. S., *147n*
   *vs.* crude death rate racial/ethnic disparities, *91*, 94
   government collects COVID-19 data on, 132
   linear regression analysis on, *92–93*
   as most important predictor of COVID-19 mortality, 73
   state racism index adjusted for, *92*
agricultural products, 50
AIDS
   among incarcerated persons, 218
   impact upon Black community, 171–72
   prostitutes' exposure to, 61
Alaskan Natives, 29, 71, 129, 133, *167*, 319
Alcindor, Yamiche, 56
alimony, 257
Amanpour, Christiane, 117
Amazon
   on essential workers as heroes, 48
   failure to provide PPE, 49, 186
   free summer books from, 278
American Academy of Pediatrics, 327
American College of Emergency Physicians, 327
*American Community Survey 2019*, 79, 81, *82n*
American Medical Association, 327
American Public Media (APM) Research Lab, 73, 74–75, 94, 197
American Sociological Association, 335
"America Together" (Fox News), 60
Anarcha (slave woman), 111
Anderson, Elijah, 35
anxiety, 276
apartheid
   "American," 57
   medical, 18, 340
Apartheid (South Africa), 140, 151, 153–55
APM Research Lab, 197
Arbery, Ahmaud, 295, 327
*Are Prisons Obsolete?* (Davis), 110
Army Corps of Engineers, U. S., 115

# INDEX

Asian Americans
  Democrats on racist views expressed against, 27
  effect of COVID-19 upon, 170, 181, 258, 333
  hate crimes against, 31
  income potential, 175
  and union representation, 183
asset poverty
  among released prisoners, 200
  defined, 193, 195
  impact upon Blacks, 194–97, 205
Athabaskan language, 130
Atherwood, Serge, 76
*Atlantic, The*, 138n, 171
axial coding, 263

## B

bail, 247–48
Baker, Marissa G., 81
banks, 171–72
Barkley, Charles, 58
Bass, David, 299
Bates, Timothy, 177
Begin highway, 149
*Behavioral Risk Factor Surveillance System (BRFSS) 2019*, 84–85
Betsey (slave woman), 111
Bezos, Jeff, 53
Biden, Joe
  addresses disproportionate death rate of Blacks, 147
  on communicating COVID-19 pandemic rates, 55n
  encourages vaccination, 344
biologization of culture, 55
biopower and biopolitics, 169
Birx, Deborah, 55, 61
Black, Indigenous, and people of color (BIPOC), 18, 27, 28, 31
  *see also specific ethnic groups*

*Black Bourgeoisie, The* (Frazier), 196
Black Consciousness Movement, 140
Black feminism
  and Black Mothers' experience, 260–61, 265, 277
  and educating young about racism, 279
  encourages Blacks to be proactive, 282
  and personal-protection equipment (PPE), 275
  and police brutality, 281
Black Lives Matter
  hostility to, 26
  Martin's murder as foundation for, 316
  protests during summer 2020, 30
  public response to, 28
Black Lives Matter Foundation, 315–16
*Black Marxism* (Robinson), 141
*Black on Both Sides: A Racial History of Trans Identity* (Snorton), 111
Blacks
  COVID-19's effect on, 54, 197–99, 239–48, 258–59, 333
  effect of asset poverty on, 194–97, 205
  effect of Great Recession upon, 336
  effect of smallpox on, 172–73
  effect of wealth inequality on, 194–97
  employed in nursing facilities, *182*, 185–86
  households and lack of savings, 53
  households without vehicles, 52n
  as laborers on railroad, 181
  mass incarceration of Black men, 256

## INDEX

men killed at higher rates than Whites, 317–18
most likely to suffer from preexisting health conditions, 81, 96, 156, 215, 240–41, 258
need for more in medical field, 337
representation in service industries, 243–44
Trump on COVID-19's effect upon, 54, 143
unemployment rate, 7, 196, 244–45
and union representation, 183
vaccine hesitancy among, 343–44
Black Solidarity Statement with Palestine (2015), 148$n$
Black women
and Black feminism, 260–61
case studies of Black mothers, 261–85
effect of mass incarceration upon, 256
effect of unemployment and underemployment of Black men on, 256
role of, in families, 256–58
Blake, Jacob, 282
blockbusting, 336
Bonilla-Silva, Eduardo, 62$n$, 139
Boston University Center for Antiracist Research, 73
bounty rewards, 114
Brandeis University Institute on Assets and Social Policy, 195
Brunsma, D. L., 19, 20
Buckner, Kam, 31
Budweiser, 48
Buffett, Warren, 53
Building, Rehabilitating, Instructing, Development, Growing, Employing (BRIDGE), 199–200
Burden-Stelly, C. P., 140

burnout, 308
bus drivers, 50, 51, 196
businesses
Black vs. White family-owned, 194
challenges facing Black-owned, 196–97
grants for Black start-up, 203

## C

Camp Jenner, 181, 187
capital investments, lack of, in minority communities, 336
capitalism
government prioritizes economy first, 166
link with imperialism, 133
racial, 258–59
carceral institutions. *see* prisons
CARES Act, 117, 222
Carson, Ben, 55
Cassidy, Bill, 57–58
Cayce, A., 216–17, 220–21, 225–26
Census Bureau, U. S., 169, 170
census data, limitations of, 170
Centers for Disease Control and Prevention (CDC)
collects data on Native Americans, 131, 133
data collection for path dependency, 170–71
encourage vaccines, 344
and guidance for delivery workers, 186
on incarcerated and formerly incarcerated prisoners, 223
issues non-enforceable guidance, 59$n$
link between racial segregation and COVID-19, 8
mortality rate by race 2020, 147
National Center for Health Statistics, 78–79

# INDEX

Centers for Disease Control and Prevention (CDC) *(continued)*
  protocols for prisons and detention facilities, 224–25
  and racial disparities of COVID-19, 166
  on spacing for meat packers, 32
  website, 131, 341
Chambers, Brittany D., 80
chat function, 302, 307
checkpoints (to check for symptoms of COVID-19), 116
Cheyenne River Sioux Reservation, 116
childcare
  lack of affordable, 169
  paid leave, 243
child support, 257
China and Chinese
  anti-Chinese response to pandemic in U. S., 25
  Trump on the China virus", 28, 48
Chowkwanyun, Merlin, 186
clinical supervision, 304
CNN
  Amanpour's interview with Mottley, 117
  "The Color of COVID", 58
  and Sellers, 56*n*
coding, 263
Collins, Patricia Hill, 260, 282
colonialism
  effect upon Native Americans, 133
  and health disparities, 10, 133, 144
  intertwined with racial capitalism, 141, 142, 144, 155
color-blind ideology, 45
*"Color-Blind Racism in Pandemic Times"* (Bonilla-Silva), 62*n*
"The Color of COVID" (CNN show), 58

Commerce, U.S. Department of. Bureau of Economic Analysis, 171
Commonwealth Fund, 239–40
Commonwealth Vulnerability Index, 117
computers
  lack of Wi-Fi for, 175
  seeing body language on screens, 307
  systems design of, 181, *182*
Confederate flags, 29
Constitution, U. S., 129
construction workers, 50
contact tracing, 27, 174
convict leasing program, 199–200
Cooper, Amy ("Central Park Karen"), 26, 34
Cooper, Christian, 34
Cooper, Lisa, 138
co-pays for medical treatment, 219–21, 224, 337
Corbett, Kizzmekia, 337
Corcraft, 199
Coronavirus Task Force, 54
"Coronavirus: We're in This Together" (*USA Today* column), 60
correctional officers, 50
Cotton, J. Jason, 109, 117
Council of State Governments (CSG), 170
"COVID-19 Among American Indian and Alaska Native Persons (AI/ AN)-23 States, January 31-July 3, 2020" (CDC), 133
"COVID-19 Hospitalization and Death by Race/Ethnicity" (CDC website), 166
COVID-19 in Corrections Data Transparency Act, 225
COVID-19 pandemic

## INDEX

access to testing for, 198
age as predictor of mortality, 73
death statistics in states by race/ethnicity, 257–58, *259*
delta *vs.* omicron variant, 344–45
effect on Black mothers, 261–81
effect on employment, 241–46
effect upon food insecurity, 51–54
effect upon Native Americans, 54*n*, 125–33, 319, 333
effect upon romantic relationships, 272–75
federal response to Hurricane Katrina compared to, 35–36
first documented case in U. S., 3, 320
and healthcare for formerly incarcerated individuals, 221–22
and healthcare in prisons, 223–25
hospitalizations and death by race and ethnicity, 10, *11–12, 167*
impact of mass incarceration on, 216, 230
impact on Blacks, 54, 197–99, 239–48, 258–59, 333, 341
number of cumulative cases worldwide, *6, 9*
precarity and risk during, 185–86
quality of life dimensions during, 169, *170*
and racial inequality, 6–8, *8–9,* 10–13, *11*
statistics in states by race/ethnicity, 263–64, *265*
and structural racism, 71–99, 117
timeline, 3–5
vaccine development and access for, 27, 343–44
as white space, 17–37
COVID-19 Racial Data Tracker, 73, 94
COVID-19 Tracking Project *(The Atlantic),* 138*n,* 171
Crenshaw, Kimberlé., 277
criminal background checks, 247
criminal justice system reform, 247–48
Critical Race Theory (CRT), 127–29, 132–33
crude death rate, 73–75, 78, 79, 85, 88–89, *91,* 94
cultural racism, 14, 29, 45, 335
cultural resiliency, 257
culture wars, 27–28
Cuomo, Andrew, 45

### D

Dakota Access Pipeline, 115
dark proletariat, 140
data
   age and gender analysis, 132
   CDC analyzes for path dependency, 170–71
   census, 170
   collection and analysis for Sister Space, 301–4
   for Marshall family case study, 262–64, *265*
   and omission of race-based data, 328
   and person of the therapist in analyzing, 310
   reasons for inconsistent, 339–40
   from Survey of Consumer Finances, 317
Davis, Angela, 110, 337
Davis, Shardé, 297
death rates
   Black and COVID-19, 197–99
   in prisons, 219
   by race, *12*
*Decennial Census 2010,* 80

delivery workers, 49, 186
delta variant, 344–45
Democratic Party
  on Asian American racist views, 27
  Fox claims undermine Trump's reelection, 28
  as part of White guilt, 25
  on "welfare queens and dependency," 51
Dikos Ntsaaígíí-19
  COVID-19 in Athabaskan language, 130
Diné. *see* Navajo Nation
direct care workers, 32–33
  *see also* nurses and nursing; phlebotomists and phlebotomy
Disaster Relief Act (1950), 202
disciplinary power, 169
disinfectant, as potential cure for virus, 61
doctors
  increasing number of Black and Hispanic, 337
  suggest virus vaccine test in Africa, 61
  and swabbing for blood, 51
Doctors Without Borders, 117
dress codes, 301
drug overdose, 222
Du Bois, W. E. B., 140

**E**

Economic Injury Disaster Loans, 177
education
  Black *vs.* White, and unemployment status, 7, 244–45
  home equity to finance, 195
  racial disparities in, 195–96
Eighth Amendment, 219

Eisenman, David P., 201
employment
  effect of COVID-19 pandemic on, 241–46
  effect of structural racism upon, 243–45
  Federal Reserve and Black unemployment rate, 246
  for formerly incarcerated individuals, 222
  occupational and income segregation by race, *176–77*
  racial disparities in, 195–96
  as social determiner of health, 227
  sources of, by race, *175*
entertainment venues, 242
environment and racism, 198
*Essence*, 56n
essential workers
  in Gaza and West Bank, 149
  hazard pay for, 32, 49, 51, 57
  as heroes, 48–49, 128
  not able to telework, 129, 196
  racial composition of, 7–8, 126–27, 244, 320
  risky job environments for, 258
  wages of, 9
*Estelle v. Gamble*, 219
ethnicity
  death statistics by states, *259*
  disproportionate workforce presence by, *184*
  and hospitalizations and death rates, 10, *11–12*, 166, *167*
  occupational sector employment by, *174*
  quality of life dimensions impact upon, *170*
  unemployment rate by, *8*
Evans, Christin, 34–35
executive orders, 178

# INDEX

**F**

Facebook, 274, 322
face recognition systems, 27
factory workers, 59n
family-owned businesses, 194
Fanon, Frantz, 110
Fatal Force (database), 317
Fauci, Anthony, 54, 55, 56–57
Feagin, Joe, ix
Federal Drug Administration (FDA), 337
Federal Emergency Management Agency, 202
Federal Housing Administration (FHA), 336
federal minimum wage, 53
Federal Reserve System, 246
Feeding America (website), 51
felons, 174
feminist scholars
  on race and gender, 47
  *see also* Black feminism
firefighters, prisoners used as, 200
first-world nation, U. S. as, 131
Fitzpatrick Lisa, 60
Floyd, George, 26, 61, 205, 206, 280, 295, 315, 321, 327
folx (word used to signal inclusion of groups commonly marginalized), 141, 143–47, 152–53
food insecurity, 51–54, 240, 257
food service workers, 196
  *see also* restaurant servers
*Forbes*, 60
Ford, Chandra L., 80
Ford, T. N., 146
Foucault, Michel, 169
Four Corners Area, 129, 130
Fox News
  and "America Together" motto, 60
  claims pandemic hoax, 28
Frazier, E. Franklin, 196

**G**

Garbett, L., 149
Garcia, Marc, 81
Gates, Bill, 53
Gaza health system, 138
Gee, Gilbert C., 92
gender
  co-exists with class and race inequality, 48, 60–61, 111, 197, 271, 285, 333, 341–42
  feminist scholars on, 47
  government collects COVID-19 data by, 132
  incarceration rates by, 199
  as a social determinant of health, 217
  and use of PPE, 198–99
General Counsel, Office of. US Commission on Civil Rights, 116
Generation Zs, 271
*German Ideology, The* (Marx), 47
gig workers, 113, 151, 168, 186
Gini coefficient, 52–53
Goldstein, Joshua R., 76
"Good Job" (song), 51
Google, 56n
Google Hangouts, 299, 302
Gould, Elise, 242
Government Accountability Office (GAO)
  issues non-enforceable guidance, 59n
governmentality of economics, 169, 171–72
government and people's distrust of, 172, 174, 260
Gradient metrics, 28
Grant, Tiffany (as sister of Christopher Joffrion), 321–26
grant assistance, 177
Great Recession, 7, 203, 205, 248, 336

— 359 —

Greene, Marjorie Taylor, 128*n*
grocery store and delivery workers, 53, 186, 196
Groos, Maya, 80
Grubbs, Vanessa, 321
Guardian, 150

**H**
H1N1, 172. 178–79
Hacker, Andrew, 140
Hamilton, Charles, 335
hand sanitizer, 225
hantavirus, 129
Hardeman, Rachel, 36
Harris, Kamala, 35
hate crimes, 31
Hawaiians, 319
hazard pay, 32, 49, 51, 57
Health and Human Services, U. S. Department of, 132, 341
healthcare
 access to, 198
 cross-sector collaborations, 242
 and disparities by race, 54–59
 effect of colonialism upon, 10, 133, 144
 effect of financial charges in, 337
 effect of insurance coverage disparities upon, 84–85, 217
 for formerly incarcerated individuals, 221–23
 for Hispanics, 319
 inequities in Black *vs.* White, 196, 202, 318–19, 327
 lack of access to, for gig economy, 168
 medical co-pays, 219–21, 224, 337
 medical literature, 143, 144
 in Palestine, 148–51
 preexisting conditions, 81, 96, 156, 172, 198, 215, 240–41, 247, 258
 in prisons, 218–21
 privatized White *vs.* Black advantages of, 144
 as social determiner of health, 227
 universal, 247, 336–37
 and vulnerability of individual, 195
health conditions, preexisting
 Blacks most likely to suffer from, 81, 96, 156, 215, 240–41, 258
 criminal background checks, 247
 effect of prison upon, 218–21
 and H1N1 pandemic, 172
Healthy People 2010, 132, 341–42
Henderson, Armen, 31–32
Herrenvolk ideology, 25–28
Hispanics
 effect of COVID-19 upon, 258, 333
 effect of Great Recession upon, 336
 effect of H1N1 upon, 178–79
 employed in leisure and hospitality, 179
 and households without vehicles, 52*n*
 lack of quality healthcare for, 337
 men killed at higher rates than Whites, 317–18
 need for more in medical field, 337
 quality of healthcare received by, 319
 unemployment rate of, 51*n*
 and union representation, 183
 zero wealth of, 53
Homeland Security, U. S. Department of, 202
home ownership
 assistance with down payment and closing costs, 203
 Black *vs.* White, 194
 equity used to finance child's education, 195
Home Owners' Loan Corporation's (HOLC), 113
Horse, Aggie J. Yellow, 131

Horton, Hayward, 131
Horton, Richard, 320
hospitality industry, 179, 242
hospitalization rates by race/ethnicity, 11, *167*
Household Pulse Survey, 175
households
  effect of Hurricane Katrina upon, 177
  with formerly incarcerated individuals, 222
  multigenerational, 145
  single-parent becoming more common, 256
  and tax deductions for, 204
  without vehicles, 52*n*
housing
  housing bubble burst, 203
  housing insecurity, 246
  lending and ownership policies favorable to Whites, 317
  and predatory lending practices, 196
  as social determiner of health, 221
Huanan Seafood Wholesale Market, 3
Hudson, P. J., 140
Huffman, Stephen A., 29
Human Development Index (HDI), 119
Hurricane Katrina
  effect upon Black households, 177
  effect upon vulnerable populations, 200–201
  federal response to, 35
Hutchins, Sonja, 240
hydroxychloroquine, 61

I
ideological racism, 12, 335
immigrant detention centers, 141
implicit bias, 319, 321
incarceration rates, 80, *82*, 168
Indian Health Service, 129, 133

Indians. *see* Indigenous people and land; Native Americans
Indigenous people and land
  death rate from COVID-19, 197
  Locke on, 168
influenza pandemics
  1918, ix, 146, 240
  1950-2005, 240
inheritances, 195, 196
Instacart, 49, 180
institutional racism, 229, 241, 335
insurance, 82, 237
Internal Revenue Service, 228
International Monetary Fund, 150
Internet
  lack of access to, 169, 279
  and precarious employment, 180
isolation
  CDC guidelines for isolation in prisons, 224
  discussions of, in Sister Space, 301–2, 305–6, 312
  isolation index, 80
  social media to compensate for, 274
Israel, 139, 144, 148–51

J
Jabalia refugee camp, 148
Jackson, Ketanji Brown, 35
janitors, 8, *9*, 50, 51
JBS Beef Plant, 50
Jenny (Joy Marshall's friend), 276
Jim Crow racism *vs.* color-blind racism, 45
Joffrion, Christopher, 321–27
Johns Hopkins University of Medicine
  Bloomberg School of Public Health, 132
  Coronavirus Research Center (JHCRC), 18, 131, 137*n*, 152, 341, 342

# INDEX

Johnson, Gabriel, 322
Johnson, Pamela, 322–26
Johnson & Johnson. Janssen
    Pharmaceuticals, 343
Jones, Van, 59
Journal of Racial and Ethnic Health
    Disparities (2021), 99*n*
Judge, Katherine, 299
Justice, U. S. Department of, 216
Justice Statistics, Bureau of, 81

## K

Kaiser Family Foundation, 244
Kelly, Robin D. G., 156
Keys, Alicia, 51
kinship networks, 256, 257
Kraft-Heinz, 48

## L

Labor, U. S. Department of, 245
Labor Force Survey, 151
Labor Statistics, U. S. Bureau of
    data collection by, 170
    and marginally attached, 7
    on telework, by race, 243–44
    and union representation, by race, 183
laissez-faire racism, 14, 335
Latinos. *see* Hispanics
leisure industry, 179
life expectancy
    Black *vs.* White, 94, 146, 319
    and HDI, 119, 137*n*
linear regression analysis, 77, 78, 85, 92, *95*, *97*
    age-adjusted mortality rates Black *vs.* White, *92–93*
line-by-line coding, 263
Liu, Sze Yan, 80
lockdowns
    economic hardship caused by, 333
    effect upon personal relationships, 275
    meat-processing plants exempted from, 32
    in prison, 226
    state and local mandates for, 26, 29–30, 126
    in Wuhan, 3
Locke, John, 167–68
London, University College of, 263, 266, 269
Looman, Wendy, 299
Lucy (slave woman), 111
Lukachko, Alicia, 80
Lynum, Kimora, 321

## M

mail-in ballots, 116
Marshall, Claudia, 263
Marshall, Constance, 259–60, 262, 269–70, 274–75
Marshall, Donald, 267, 282–83
Marshall, Donna, 263
Marshall, Joy, 274–75, 276
Marshall, Lana, 261–62, 267–68, 271–72, 276–78
Marshall, Lauren, 260, 262–64, 270, 272, 274
Marshall, Laurence, 270–71
Marshall, Levi, 271
Marshall, Lola, 270–71, 272–73, 281–82
Marshall Project, 224
Marshals Service, U. S., 225
Martin, Lori Latrice, 193*n*
Martin, Trayvon, 316, 327
Marxism and Karl Marx
    essential ideology of, 47
    and racial capitalism, 168
    Robinson challenges notion of capitalism, 141

masks and mask mandates
  and Black men's resistance to,
    198–99
  N95 masks, 49, 341
  for prisons, 225
  public response to, 28–29
  as racial issue, 277
  and restaurant and retail workers, 178
  state mandates on, 29
  Trump administration downplays, 24
  Trump supporters ignore, 334–35
mass incarceration, 25, 224
  *see also* prisons
matrifocal *vs.* matriarchal families, 256
McConnell, Mitch, 128*n*
McWhorter, John, 56*n*
meat-processing workers and plants,
    32, 50, 51, 59*n*
Medicaid
  expansion under Affordable Care
    Act, 221
  for formerly incarcerated
    individuals, 221
  lack of expansion of, 217
  work requirements and spending
    caps, 57
*Medical Apartheid* (Washington), 340
medical literature
  bias in, 143, 144
  on relation of telecare and
    COVID-19, 297
Medicare
  expansion for formerly incarcerated
    individuals, 221
mental health
  as taboo topic in Black community,
    303
Merriam-Webster, 315
Messenger, 274
Michigan Department of Corrections
    (MDOC), 217, 220, 225–26

Millennials, 271
Mineo, Liz, 116, 117
mining jobs, 179
minority-owned businesses, 177
Moderna, 5, 337
Morales, Laurel, 117
mortgage defaults, 246
mortgage lending, 196
Mottley, Mia, 109, 117
Moynihan Report (1965), 256

**N**
N95 masks, 49, 341
National Healthcare Quality and
    Disparities Report (2018), 319
National Response Framework, 204
Native Americans
  CDC collects data on, 131, 133
  communities in the U. S., 114–17
  effect of 1918 influenza pandemic
    upon, 54*n*, 129
  effect of colonialism upon, 133
  effect of COVID-19 among, 54*n*,
    125–33, 319, 333
  effect of smallpox upon, 129, 168
  effect of systemic racism upon,
    133–34
  quality of healthcare received by, 335
naturalization, 45
Navajo Nation, 116–17, 125, 127,
    129–31
Nazi
  concept of "master race," 25–28
  signs with Nazi symbols, 29
NBC News, 128*n*
Nellis, Ashley, 199
neoliberalism, 165, 167–69
*New England Journal of Medicine*, 36
*New York Post, The*, 56*n*
*New York Times*, 224
Nicholls, Alicia, 109

# INDEX

9/11 attacks, 177, 202
1918 influenza pandemic, 54$n$
  Black vs. White mortality rates, 146, 240
  compared to COVID-19 pandemic, ix
  effect upon Native Americans, 54$n$, 129
Novak, Michael, 141
nurses and nursing
  Blacks employed in nursing facilities, *182*, 185–86
  Hispanics employed in nursing facilities, *182*, 185–86
  lack of protective gear for nurses, 49–50
  nurse aides, 32
  and swabbing for blood, 51

## O

Obamacare exchange, 57
Occupational Safety and Health Administration (OSHA)
  issues non-enforceable guidance, 59$n$
occupational segregation, 165, 166, 179–81, *180–83*, 186, 243, 244, 246, 248
Odoms-Young, Angela, 52
Offord, Catherine, 109
Oglala Sioux tribe, 116
Ohio Commission on Minority Health, 29
omicron variant, 344–45
online classes, 169, 271, 276
open coding, 263
Ortiz-Ospina, Esteban, 119

## P

Pacific Islanders, *12*, 71, 319
Palestine

COVID-19 in Palestinian territories, 140, 148–51
Palestinian Authority (PA), 150
racial capitalism in, 140, 148–51
Pandamsee, Tasleem J., 344
path dependency, 166
  historical antecedents to, 172–73
  as scapegoat for reification, 166, 168–69, 171–72
  and sociological institutionalism, 170
Payroll Protection Program (PPP), 177
PBS, 56
perfect storm defined, 315
personal assessment journal, 303, 310–11
personal-protection equipment (PPE)
  Amazon and Instacart fail to provide, 180
  and Black feminism, 275
  as deterrent for Black men, 198–99
  effect upon dating, 273, 275, 285
  and executive orders, 178
  inconsistent adherence to protocols, 255, 262, 264–65
  lack of, in prisons, 225
person of the therapist, 309–10
petrochemical industry, 146–47
Pew Research, 27
Pfizer/BioNTech, 60–61, 150, 337, 343
pharmacies, 198
phlebotomists and phlebotomy, 50–51
Pierre, J., 140
police brutality and racism, 79–80, 280–82, 284, 285
pollution, 57, 156, 320
poverty
  asset poverty, 193, 194–97, 200, 205
  in Black families headed by women, 257
  culture of poverty discourses, 55

federal poverty level, 217
link with chronic illnesses, 318
in Palestinian territories, 148
racial and ethnic disparities in, x, 6–8, 10, 18, 54n, 57, 80, *83*, 126, 317, 327, 333, 336
precarious work
defined, 168
and risk during COVID-19, 179–80
and salary, 180
precarity and risk, 166, 185–86
predatory lending practices, 196
Prison Policy Initiative, 33
prison rodeos, 199
prisons
AIDS and HIV in, 218
correctional officers, 50
COVID-19 in, 223–25
decarceration to combat COVID-19, 33, 147
healthcare for formerly incarcerated, 221–23, 227–28
healthcare system in, 218–21
medical co-pays in, 219–21, 224
not in compliance with CDC and BOP, 225, 230
policy recommendations for, 223, 228–29
prisoners used to make PPE equipment, 128
racial disparity in, 80–81, *82*, 85, *90*, 92, 199, 216, 318, 327
rights of incarcerated and formerly incarcerated, 247
*see also* Cayce, A.
Prisons, Federal Bureau of (BOP), 216, 225
probation, 168
progressive scholars, 47
progress notes, 303
prostitutes, 61

Providence Saint John's Health Center, 49–50
public transportation, 320
Purdum, J. Carlee, 199–200

Q
Quick Care Urgent Care Center, 323

R
race
death statistics by states, *259*
discrimination and social determinants of health (SDOH), 241
and disparities in healthcare, 54–59
and disparities in impact of COVID-19, 71–77, *75*, 166, *167*
disproportionate workforce presence, *184*
employment and education disparities in, 195–96
hospitalizations and death rate by, 10, *11–12*, 167
and non-unionized jobs, *185*
occupational and income segregation by, *176*
occupational sector employment, *174*
quality of life dimensions impact upon, *170*
top sources of employment by, *175*
union representation by, 183–84, *184*
wealth inequality and Black asset poverty, 194–97
racial capitalism
basis of, 141–42
emergence of, 140–41
as fundamental cause of public health issues, 18, 258–59
as global phenomenon for racial inequalities, 134

racial capitalism *(continued)*
   and health inequalities, 142–44
   intertwined with colonialism, 141, 142, 144, 145
   Israel/Palestine context, 140, 148–51
   and neoliberalism, 169
   path dependency scapegoat for reification, 168–69, 171–72
   and precarious work, 167–68
   Robinson on, 139, 140–42, 151, 168
   South African context, 140, 151–55
   in United States, 140, 144–48
Racial Data Tracker (RDT), 263
racial ideology, 47–48
racialization of work, 178–81, *182–85*, 183–86
racial profiling, 317
*Racial Realism and the History of Black People in America* (Martin), 193n
racism
   color-blind *vs.* Jim Crow, 45
   and COVID-19 pandemic, 6–8, *8–9*, 10–13, *11*, 333
   cultural, 14, 29, 45, 336
   defined, 334–35
   ideological, 12, 335
   institutional, 229, 241, 335
   laissez-faire, 14, 335
   minimization of, 45
   and police brutality, 280–82, 284, 285
   as a public health crisis, 327
   structural, 76–77, 79–81, 85, 93–94 243–245
   symbolic, 14, 335
   systemic, ix– xi, 12, 46, 58, 61–62, 127–34, 285, 295, 298, 327–28, 333–38
"Racism: Science and Tools for the Public Health Professional" (Ford), 80

railroads, 173, 187
Ray, Rashawn, 197–98
reactive science, 202
Reagan, Ronald, 167
Reber, S., 146
recidivism, 218, 221, 222
redlining, 113, 198, 317, 336
Reed, T. F., 186
Reeves, R. V., 146
refugee camps, 142
reification, 110, 166, 168–69, 171–72, 184
Remy, Jan Yves, 110
rent, *176*, 246
reparations program, 247
Republican Party
   inflames racial tensions, 27
   says pandemic exaggerated, 28
   on "welfare queen and dependency," 51
reservations
   displacing Indigenous groups into, 114
   structure of, 116
   *see also specific reservations*
restaurant workers
   Blacks overrepresented as, 243
   importance of, during stay-at-home orders, 186
   lack of safety measures for, 178
   low wages of, 53
restrictive covenants, 336
retail workers, 178, 179, *180–82*
retirement plans, 53, 194, 275
risk and precarity, 166, 185–86
Robb, Alicia, 177
Robinson, Cedric
   on medical researchers' bias, 143
   on racial capitalism, 139, 140–42, 151, 168
Ron (Lola Marshall's partner), 272–73

Roser, Max, 119
Ross, Jenna, 194–95

**S**
safety net, 10, 46, 53, 229
salary
  and precarious work, 180
  racial and ethnic disparities in, 181, 243
Samson (Lana's partner's grandson), 282
Sanders, Bernie, 53
SARS-CoV-2 virus, 109
Saunders, Judith, 200–201
Save-Mart, 277
savings
  as net worth, 10
  racial disparities in, 53, 145, 175 *176*, 242
schools
  lack of capital investments in, 203, 336
  lack of computers in, 169
  transition to online format in, 168
science
  changes in response to COVID-19 pandemic, 343–45
  distrust of, 266
  and racism in, 60–61, 80
  reactive, 202
*Scientist, The*, 109
Sellers, Bakari, 56*n*
Sentencing Project, The, 198
service industry
  African America occupations greater risk of contracting virus, 244
  effect of COVID-19 upon, 242–43
  percentage of Blacks in, 244
settler colonialism, 144, 155
shelter, barriers to, 201

sick leave, 49, 51, 145, 179, 243, 248
Sims, J. Marion, 111
Singh, Anneliese, 337
Sister Space
  background, 299–301
  data collection and analysis, 301–4
  and discussions of isolation, 301–2, 305–6, 312
  facilitator's personal assessment journal, 310–11
  multiple facilitators for, 307–8
  reasons for creating, 295–99
  and The Strong Black Woman (SBW) schema, 297–98, 300–301, 303, 307–8, 310–12
  uses "Whole Black Women" format, 300
slavery
  reparations for, 247
  structural racism stems from, 243
Small Business Administration (SBA), 177
small business loans, 177
smallpox
  and effect upon Blacks, 172–73
  effect upon Native Americans and Alaska Natives, 129, 168
Smithfield, 50
SNAP, 54*n*
Snorton, C. Riley, 111
social determinants of health (SDOH), 217–18, 221, 241–42, 246, 318
social distancing
  and dating, 272–73, 275
  and effect upon employment, 242
  for H1N1, 172
  inconsistent compliance with, 262
  lack of, in Gaza, 142
  lack of, in nursing facilities, 179–80
  in meat-packing plants, 32

social distancing *(continued)*
  in prisons, 225
  and restaurant servers, 178
  Trump administration downplays, 24
  violations to, 32
  youth frequently disregard, 145
social media
  and awareness of racism, 280
  to combat isolation, 274
  and recruitment for Sister Space, 299, 302
Social Security, 221
Social Security Disability Insurance, 221
socioeconomic status (SES), 241–42
sociological institutionalism, 170
"Sociologists Link Higher Black Mortality Rates from COVID-19 to Racism and Racial Inequality," 341
South Africa, 138, 140, 151–55
South African National Department of Health, 138$n$
South Dakota, 116
speculum (medical instrument), 111
Standing Rock Reservation, 115, 120
Stand Your Ground Law, 316
Staples, Robert, 256
State Health Departments, 131
state racism index, 78, 79–81, *82–83*, 85, 92–94, *95*, 98
  age-adjusted death rate Black *vs.* White, *92*
  and racial disparity incarceration rates, 83
  variables in model, *97*
states, COVID-19 statistics by, 262
stimulus checks, 246
stock ownership, 53, 194
"Stolen Breaths" (NEJofM article), 36

Strategic Health and Economic Emergency Management Plan for Vulnerable Populations, 194, 200–205
"Strong Black Woman Collective, The" (Davis), 297
The Strong Black Woman (SBW) schema, 297–98, 300–301, 303, 307–8, 310–12
structural racism
  as cause of racial health disparities, 127, 130, 132
  and COVID-19 mortality rates, 71–99, 117
  defined, 127
  effect upon health of minority populations, 57–58
  and food insecurity, 52
  impact upon employment status, 243–45
  increasing awareness of, 61
  minimization of, 29
  and multi-institutional oppression, 316
student loan debt
  contributing factor in racial wealth gap, 195
  forgiveness to address racial inequality, 197
subordination, 201
suicide
  rate, 137$n$
  as taboo topic in Black community, 303
Sullivan, Laura, 194–95
Supplemental Security Insurance, 221
supply chain issues, 242
Survey 160, 28
Survey of Consumer Finances, 317
symbolic racism, 14, 335
symptom tracking, 116

synergistic epidemic, 320
syphilis, 111–12, 173
systemic racism, 46, 127–32
   causes of, 12
   connection with COVID-19 pandemic, ix–xi, 58, 327–28, 333–38
   growing awareness of, 61–62, 295
   impact upon Black women, 285, 298
   impact upon Native Americans, 133–34

### T

Tan, Shin Bin, 80
Tatum, Beverly, 337
taxes
   Israel and Palestinians', 150
   savings for homeowners, 204
Taylor, Breonna, 34, 295, 327
Taylor, Deshaun, 321
telehealth, 168, 169, 296, 297
teletherapy, 296
   *see also* Sister Space
telework
   Black *vs.* White statistics, 243–44
   not possible for many people, 144–45, 244
   in South Africa, 151
   work from home culture, 168–69
temp work, 151
Thatcher, Margaret, 167
Thomas, Melvin, 131
Tom (Lana Marshall's partner), 273
"Toward the Sociogenic Principle: Fanon, Identity, the Puzzle of Conscious Experience, and What It Is Like to Be 'Black'" (Wynter), 112
transportation
   barriers to, 201
   as social determinant of health, 221

   and vehicle ownership, 52$n$, 194
Treasury, U. S. Department of, 228
treaty violations, 115
Trump, Donald and Trumpism
   on Blacks' mortality rate, 54
   blames Blacks for susceptibility to COVID-19, 143
   calls COVID-19 "the China virus," 28, 48
   downplays COVID-19 pandemic, 24, 28, 334, 340–42
   on inflaming racial hatred, 26–28, 30, 48, 298
   seeks to restrict voting rights of Indigenous groups, 115–16
Ture, Kwame, 335
Tuskegee Syphilis Study, 172, 173, 344
   "Tuskegee Study of Untreated Syphilis in the Negro Male," 111–12
*Two Nations: Black and White, Separate, Hostile, Unequal* (Hacker), 140
Tyson, 50

### U

unemployment
   of Blacks in service industry, 196, 242–46, 248
   Blacks *vs.* Whites, 7, 244–45
   COVID-19's impact on Black men, 241–46
   effect upon Black mothers, 256
   of Hispanics, 51$n$
   of U. S. 2020, 51
   in U. S by ethnicity, 8
unemployment insurance, 151, *176*, 245, 248
Union Five Company, 202
unions and unionization, 59$n$, 183–84, *184–85*, 187

# INDEX

United Nations Declaration on Rights of Indigenous Peoples, 115
United Nations Development Programme, 119
United States
  first documented case of COVID-19 pandemic, 3, 320
  first fatality from COVID-19, 4, 109
  as first-world nation, 11, 137, 137$n$
  racial capitalism in, 144–48
  racialized social systems in, 133
  social vulnerability index for, 112–13
  suicide rate of, 137$n$
universal basic income, 247
universal healthcare, 247. 336–37
Urban Institute, 171
*USA Today*, 60
US Climate Resilience Toolkit, 118, 119
USDA, 54$n$

## V

vaccinations and vaccine access
  Africa as testing ground for, 61
  for BIPOC, 27
  Blacks for smallpox, 173
  development, 343–44
  hesitancy, 134, 337–38, 339
  inequities in distribution of, 27, 99, 134
  lack of, for Palestinians, 150
  lack of access to, in impoverished countries, 345
  and Marshall family, 262
*Valentine v. Collier*, 225
vehicle ownership
  Black *vs.* White, 194
  households without, 52$n$
Viola, Michael, 35–36
virtual support groups. *see* Sister Space
Visual Capitalist, 194

voting, 282, 285
vulnerability index, 109–10, 117–21

## W

Wallace Pack Unit (prison), 225
Wallet Hub (blog), 80
*Wall Street Journal, The*, 56$n$
Walmart, 48
Washington, Harriet, 340
*Washington Post*, 241, 242, 281, 317
water, toxic, 198
Waters, Maxine, 56$n$
wealth
  defined, 10
  gap, by race, 317
  inequality and Black asset poverty, 194–97
  racial wealth inequality, *11*
*Weems v. United States*, 219
"welfare queen and welfare dependency," 51, 167
Wellman, David, 12–13, 335
*West v. Atkins*, 219
Whites
  age-adjusted mortality rates, *vs.* Black, *92–93*
  Democrats *vs.* Republicans, 25
  effect of 1918 influenza pandemic upon, 146, 240
  effect of Great Recession upon, 336
  family-owned businesses, 194
  healthcare available to, 196, 318–19, 327
  and home ownership, 194
  privilege and ideological racism, 12
  and student loan default, 195
  as teleworkers, 243–44
  and unemployment status, 7, 244–45
  and vehicle ownership, 52$n$, 194
White space, 17–18
  aesthetics of, 21–22, 28–30

## INDEX

cultures of, 19–20
establishing, 20–21, 23–25
ideological terrain of, 21, 25–28
as interaction order, 22
protecting of, 22–23, 33–35
and social distancing, 30–33
and White supremacy, 18–20, 23–24, 27, 36
White supremacy
new forms of, 335
public policy and, 133–34
roots of, 133–34
traditional vs. new, x, 13–14
and white space, 18–20, 23–24, 27, 36
"Whole Black Women" (WBW) support group format, 300
Wi-Fi, 175
wildfires, 199–200
Williams, David R., 57
Wilson, Valeri, 242

Woodward, Bob, 340
World Bank, 150
World Health Organization (WHO)
and COVID-19 pandemic timeline, 3–4
on social determinants of health (SDH), 217–18
on universal masking in public, 341
World Meters Coronavirus Update, 138$n$
World Trade Center, 177
*Wretched of the Earth, The* (Fanon), 110
Wynter, Sylvia, 112

### Y

Yarry, Sarah, 299
Yearby, Ruqaijah, 57

### Z

Zimmerman, George, 316
Zoom, 274, 275–77